Reactions to Milan Rai's previous book *War Plan Iraq*

'Most Iraqis, whether inside Iraq or in exile feel that the war on Iraq is immoral and illegal. *War Plan Iraq* proves that opposing the war does not mean supporting Saddam's regime. Opposing the war means supporting the Iraqi people.'
> Haifa Zangana, Iraqi writer in exile
> Member of Act Together: Women against sanctions and war on Iraq

'This book is thorough, irrefutable testimony to why there should be no war with the Iraqis.'
> John Pilger

'It is vitally important to get across to the British people that Trident is being aimed at what appears to be a non-nuclear country, and that there are nonviolent ways of dealing with Iraq's suspected weapons of mass destruction. *War Plan Iraq* is a valuable contribution to these efforts.'
> Carol Naughton,
> Chair of the British Campaign for Nuclear Disarmament (CND)

'This excellent book reveals the extent of the injustices perpetrated against the Iraqi people.'
> Alice Mahon MP

'This book is an excellent weapon for all those opposed to Bush's war. Compulsory reading for every centre-left politician.'
> Tariq Ali

'A remarkably thorough account, and required reading for anyone concerned about the risk of war.'
> Paul Rogers,
> Professor of Peace Studies, Bradford University

'A timely and important book.'
> Hilary Wainwright,
> *Red Pepper*

D1490942

Reactions to other publications by Milan Rai

Gene Genie: Making Choices About Genetic Engineering
The Text Of The Exhibition (Drava Papers, 2001)

'**Gene Genie's striking imagery and thoughtful analysis pose important questions and help to promote democratic decision-making about the release of genetically-engineered organisms.**'
>   Ben Savill, Research and Campaigns Officer,
>   National Federation of Women's Institutes

'**Gene Genie sets out the science behind genetic engineering in a simple and understandable way - a valuable tool.**'
>   Kathryn Tulip, Genetix Snowball

Tactical Trident: The Rifkind Doctrine and the Third World (Drava Papers, 1995)

'**As an example of how rich countries gamble with the security of their own people to maintain influence and control across the globe, this is vital reading**'.
>   Greg Kent, *Spur*, the World Development Movement magazine

'It is vital that public debate based on knowledge of reality of the British Bomb rather than vague generalities about "defence" and "deterrence" takes place. This pamphlet is an essential contribution to that debate.'
>   Janet Bloomfield,
>   Chair of the British Campaign for Nuclear Disarmament (CND)

'**An effective study of a core part of British defence policy which is all too easily ignored.**'
>   Paul Rogers, Professor of Peace Studies, Bradford University

'Excellent.'
>   Bob Aldridge, former Trident designer

Britain, Maastricht and the Bomb:
The Foreign and Security Policy Implications of the Treaty of European Union
(Drava Papers, 1993)

'**Of all the hours of debate on the Maastricht Treaty that dominated the British Parliament, and to a lesser extent other member states' Parliaments, few were spent on the crucial issues of the future foreign and defence policy of a "united" Western Europe. Milan Rai's thoroughly researched pamphlet lifts the lid of this exceptionally murky aspect of the Maastricht process.**'
>   Jeremy Corbyn MP (from the Preface)

Regime Unchanged

Regime Unchanged

Why the War on Iraq Changed Nothing

MILAN RAI

Pluto Press

London • Sterling, Virginia

First published 2003 by Pluto Press
345 Archway Road, London N6 5AA
and 22883 Quicksilver Drive, Sterling, VA 20166-2012, USA

www.plutobooks.com

British Library Cataloguing in Publication Data
A catalogue record for this book is available from the British Library

ISBN 0 7453 2200 X hardback
ISBN 0 7453 2199 2   paperback

Library of Congress Cataloging in Publication Data applied for

10 9 8 7 6 5 4 3 2 1

Typeset in Garamond by ARROW Publications.

Printed and bound in the European Union by
Antony Rowe Ltd, Chippenham and Eastbourne, England

Dedication

This book is dedicated to Ahmed al-Ani, and to all the bereaved children of Iraq, in the hope that they will see justice done.

Milan Rai,
1 July 2003

'You don't understand. Our policy is to get rid of Saddam, not his regime.'
   Richard Haass, director for Middle East Affairs
   on the US National Security Council, March 1991[1]

'The White House's biggest fear is that UN weapons inspectors will be allowed to go in.'
   Top US Senate foreign policy aide, May 2002[2]

'This is wrong. What are you Brits going to do, roll over like nice little doggies just because America says so?'
   Scott Ritter, former US Marine,
   former UN weapons inspector, July 2002[3]

CONTENTS

ACKNOWLEDGEMENTS

I would like to acknowledge over a decade of stimulating friendship and supportive joint activism within ARROW (Active Resistance to the Roots of War). I count myself very fortunate to have worked for over a decade alongside so many extraordinary people, including (at one time or another, or continuously) David Polden, Andrea Needham, Virginia Moffat, Cedric Knight, Susan Johns, Emily Johns, Richard Crump (the poet of the anti-sanctions movement), Chris Cole, Emily Apple and Noor Admani.

This book is also, in part, the product of the development of understanding during five years of work in the anti-sanctions campaigning group **voices in the wilderness uk**, with more brave and committed folk, including Emma Sangster, Joanne Macinnes, Salih Ibrahim, Les Gibbons, Gareth Evans, Richard Byrne and Glenn Bassett. A special tribute is due to Gabriel Carlyle, who as well as being a vital member of ARROW has since its inception been an indomitable joint co-ordinator and the real linchpin of **voices uk**.

Across the Atlantic, I'd also like to acknowledge the many inspirational people of **voices in the wilderness** in Chicago, including Danny Muller, Ceylon Mooney and the incomparable Kathy Kelly. The presence of the Iraq Peace Team in Baghdad before and during the war (a project initiated and supported by **voices us**) was a shard of humanity in a dreadful time.

I offer my apologies for the inconsistent transliteration of Arabic names in the pages that follow. I have tried to follow the sources except where they conflict.

Many thanks to Sam Hamill for permission to use an excerpt from his poem 'State of the Union 2003'.

Warm thanks to Cedric Knight for a crucial few days' assistance, and to Susan Johns for her customary perspicacity. Heartfelt thanks to Emily Johns, Arkady Johns, and Patrick Nicholson for all their tolerance and support during the production of this book. Without whom, nothing.

Meg and Joshua, you were part of the making of this book. Rest in peace.

MAP OF IRAQ

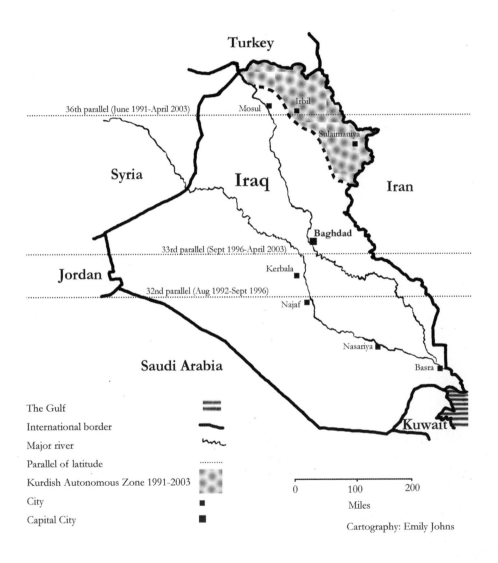

Turkey

36th parallel (June 1991-April 2003)

Mosul ■   Irbil ■

Sulaimaniya ■

Syria

Iraq

Iran

Baghdad ■

33rd parallel (Sept 1996-April 2003)

Kerbala ■

Jordan

32nd parallel (Aug 1992-Sept 1996)

Najaf ■

Nasariya ■

Basra ■

Saudi Arabia

Kuwait

The Gulf
International border
Major river
Parallel of latitude
Kurdish Autonomous Zone 1991-2003
City ■
Capital City ■

0   100   200

Miles

Cartography: Emily Johns

Echoing Voices

'I respect that a number of bereaved parents have stepped forward to support the conflict, but personally, I never thought that I could be so ashamed at the single-minded aggressiveness with which this Government invaded Iraq.

'The military is asking bereaved families to make suggestions for a memorial service—mine is simply that our Prime Minister and any other Members of Parliament with blood on their hands have the decency to stay away.

'I salute every person who continues to question this government's motives for going to war. We owe it to all those who have lost their lives to find out exactly what they were fighting for.'

Catherine Green, sister of Lieutenant Philip Green, who died in a helicopter crash in the early days of the war on Iraq, 1 July 2003.[1]

'At the end of this whole process, we need to go back over it, and ask why this has happened.'

Tony Blair at a joint press conference with President Bush, 27 March 2003.[2]

'In the aftermath of an invasion which is now recognised all over the world to have been conceived, born and carried out in mendacity, we have, it seems, only one obligation, and it is one which may one day even provide our shivering democracy with a useful antibiotic. It is to set out and nail the remaining lies which the belligerent are still trying to advance for their cover.'

David Hare, playwright, 23 June 2003.[3]

'No convincing evidence has been provided by Washington and London that Iraq possesses weapons of mass destruction, or that it poses a threat to its neighbours (let alone to the West), or that there is any operational connection between the Iraqi regime and al-Qa'eda.

'Thus far it has all been mere assertion, not worth a damn.'

Corelli Barnett, historian, 30 December 2002.[4]

'If they are saying it's about the fact they have biological weapons and might have nuclear weapons and that gives us the liberty to pre-empt and strike because we think they might hit us, then what prevents Pakistan from attacking India, what prevents India from attacking Pakistan, what prevents us from going into North Korea? I believe —though I may be wrong because I am no expert—that this war is about what most wars are about: hegemony, money, power and oil.'

Dustin Hoffman, actor, 5 February 2003.[5]

'As the son of Iraqi exiles myself, please allow me to correct the erroneous impression that most Iraqi exiles are longing for Bush and Blair to do the "honourable" thing and attack Iraq. Most of us are in fact deeply worried about the coming war and are praying that by some miracle it does not happen.

'I feel that those of us who do favour the stance taken by Britain and the US are being naive in their belief that military action will be the precursor to the implementation of "freedom and democracy" in our homeland. Given that in the past both these countries supported Saddam, glossed over his use of chemical weapons, and have presided over a sanctions policy that has lead to the deaths of well over half a million Iraqi children, why should I now believe Bush and Blair when they say they have the best interests of the Iraqi people at heart?'

Daoud Fakhri, London, 21 February 2003.[6]

'You say I am pro-war. This is incorrect. I have always said everything should be done to avoid war. I joined 36 other Iraqis in signing an appeal urging Saddam to relinquish power as the only way to avert war and spare the Iraqi people further suffering.'

Adnan Pachachi, exile, former Iraqi Foreign Minister, who the US tried to persuade to take a leading role in the post-war interim authority, 24 February 2003.[7]

'It is hard to find an Iraqi who has not suffered under Saddam; from executions to imprisonment, stories speak for themselves. Many are, however, sceptical of war or military strikes which could cost the lives of thousands of Iraqis. Add to this the uncertainty behind American intentions, and how the US let down the Iraqi people after the popular uprising in 1991.

'Tony Blair is not right to claim that four million Iraqis support war; the majority in fact strongly call for regime change. This could possibly be achieved through helping Iraqis topple Saddam or offering the dictator an "exile package" to rid Iraqis from his tyranny. Mr Blair and Mr Bush need to listen to Iraqis and not let them down again.'

Mohammed Al-Hilli, Iraqi exile in the UK, 25 February 2003.[8]

'I am from Baghdad and still have family and friends living in Iraq . . .

'Large numbers of Arabs are phoning or sending e-mail messages to say how pleased they feel that there are millions of people willing to march in support of the people of Iraq and Palestine. The West is no longer the enemy, just Bush, Blair and Israel. This will certainly reduce the threat of terrorism, unless a new war takes us back to a new level of hostility . . .

'No to Blair's war and no to his cruel sanctions. Let the people of Iraq live and they will liberate themselves from this dictator.'

Professor A. Almaini, Edinburgh, 25 February 2003.[9]

'The President of the United States represents a maximum of about 4 per cent of the world's population. He should surely accept that there are many others with a right to have their views taken into account when assessing the threat to the world.'
British Rear Admiral Ron Holley, 13 February 2003.[10]

'Even when Bush tries to reassure the world that he is no lone ranger, he can look like his own caricature. One senior Bush aide recalls President Bush telling Czech President Vaclav Havel in Prague last fall: **"I know some in Europe see me as a Texas cowboy with six-shooters at my side. But the truth is I prefer to work with a posse"**.'[11]

In a December 1999 debate among Republican presidential hopefuls, George W. Bush was asked what he would do if he discovered Saddam Hussein had weapons of mass destruction. Mr Bush replied, **'Take 'em out.'** The moderator, Jim Lehrer, followed up. Had Mr Bush said he would take Saddam Hussein out? **'Take out the weapons of mass destruction,'** Mr Bush replied.
In September 2000, Mr Bush's running mate Dick Cheney said the US was right not to have gone to Baghdad in 1991. The US should not act **'as though we were an imperialist power, willy-nilly moving into capitals in that part of the world, taking down governments.'** A Bush–Cheney administration would **'maintain our current posture vis-a-vis Iraq.'**[12]

'The government is runing itself exactly like the Sopranos. Are we going to try and talk to Saddam Hussein without jumping in and killing people first? I don't believe we're going to wait until the last resort to do it. That's what bothers me.'
George Clooney, actor.[13]

'Soon Iraqis will see the great compassion of the US and the world.'
President Bush, 25 March 2003.[14]

'War is painful, so painful for everyone. I cannot support it because it brings pain like this. It cannot be right.'
Dr Wael al-Shehaby, Umm Qasr hospital, 26 March 2003, after spending the morning struggling to save the life of a 24-year-old electrical engineer whose back had been ripped open by shrapnel from an American shell. The man's 27-year-old sister died instantly in the blast at their home near the port city of Umm Qasr.[14]

'I don't want it to turn into a war. I wouldn't like to see anyone hurt. I think the reality of war would shock people. I found it shocking in the Falklands—we had 23 killed in the South Atlantic, and around 250 in total.'
Sergeant-Major Chris O'Meara, 22 January 2003. Sergeant-Major O'Meara fought in the 1982 Falklands War as a teenager, in Britain's 3 Brigade Parachute Regiment.[16]

'Was the overthrow of Saddam Hussein worth all the violence and chaos in Mosul, Kirkuk and Baghdad? Was it worth the death of my 25-year-old translator, the only support of his widowed mother? She doesn't think so. At the moment I am finding it hard not to agree with her.

'I think if I really were absolutely honest, I don't like wars for a start. And I don't like the people who provoke wars. On the other hand, I am awfully glad to see the back of Saddam Hussein, who really was the nastiest dictator in modern times. I just feel that the better time to have got rid of him was in 1991, when his own people would have done it, and it is difficult to do it on behalf of other people.'

John Simpson, BBC World Affairs Editor, June 2003.[17] Mr Simpson was wounded on 6 April by US F-15 jets firing on US troops he was accompanying. His translator Kamaran Abdurazaq Muhamed and 13 other people were killed. Mr Simpson described the aftermath of the attack as a 'scene from hell.'

'My anti-Americanism has become almost uncontrollable. It has possessed me, like a disease . . . I now loathe the United States and what it has done to Iraq and the rest of the helpless world . . . I have tried to control my anti-Americanism, remembering the many Americans that I know and respect, but I can't keep it down any longer.

'I detest Disneyfication, I detest Coca-Cola, I detest burgers, I detest sentimental and violent Hollywoold films that tell lies about history. I detest American imperialism, American infantilism, and American triumphalism about victories it didn't even win [in Vietnam] . . . I hate feeling this hatred. I have to keep reminding myself that if Bush hadn't been (so narrowly) elected, we wouldn't be here, and none of this would have happened. There is another America.

'Long live the other America, and may this one pass away soon.'

Margaret Drabble, author, May 2003.[18]

The children have seen so much death
that death means nothing to them now.
They wait in line for bread.
They wait in line for water.
Their eyes are black moons reflecting emptiness.
We've seen them a thousand times.

Soon, the president will speak.
He will have something to say about bombs
and freedom and our way of life.
I will turn the TV off. I always do.
Because I can't bear to look
at the monuments in his eyes.

Sam Hamill, US poet (excerpt from 'State of the Union 2003').[19]

Reminded by a journalist in late January 2003 that President Bush goes to bed by 10pm, and sleeps like a baby, US Secretary of State Colin Powell replied,

'I sleep like a baby too—every two hours I wake up screaming.'[20]

'Tony Blair assures us he will account to God over his decision to slaughter innocent Iraqis. Which is bizarre logic. First I don't remember God voting at the last election or paying the taxes which foot the £3 billion war bill. Second, why didn't he listen to every major Christian leader on Earth (apart from a Texan evangelist) who said the war was wrong.

'And didn't we get into this whole war business in the first place after religious fanatics flew planes into the World Trade Centre because they were following the "will of God". On a global scale, how many people believe Blair's God is any better than Osama bin Laden's?'

Brian Reade, journalist, 8 May 2003.[21]

'To prosecute a war in the 21st century you have to have exhausted every other means at your disposal. That has clearly not yet happened. There has to be a clear and imminent danger to this country and to our allies. Realistically there isn't.

'You would perhaps expect my constituents in [the British Army garrison town of] Warminster to be a little bit more pro-conflict than the general population. In fact that is not the case. They have a clear appreciation of exactly what a war would mean and the kind of injuries that may be sustained. There is widespread concern, notably in my constituency among people with military experience, people who are currently serving and their families about exactly what a war might mean to them and their loved ones.'

Andrew Murrison, Conservative MP and former Royal Navy surgeon who served in the Gulf War of 1991, 27 February 2003.[22]

'We should avoid it because of the consequences of war. How many other terrorists will we recruit in the long standing battle against international terrorism, which is going to be far harder to win? And what will we have done to the stability of Saudi Arabia, Pakistan, Egypt?

'Next time a large bomb goes off in a western city, how far did this policy contribute to it? Next time an Arab or Muslim regime is toppled by a regime far more extreme, how far did this policy contribute to it?'

Kenneth Clarke, Conservative MP, former Chancellor of the Exchequer, 26 February 2003.[23]

'As the Prime Minister tries to rally the nation behind his policy towards Iraq, he continues to fail to produce any evidence of the existence of weapons of mass destruction. This inevitably leads to the suspicion that no such evidence exists.

'Even if the weapons do exist, where is the evidence of intent to use them? War is too important and unpleasant a business to be undertaken on the basis of a hunch, however good that hunch may be.'

British Vice-Admiral Sir James Jungius, 11 January 2003.[24]

'What if the West seeks to justify military action on pre-emptive grounds—arguing that military action is necessary even though we cannot provide strong evidence of a threat to the West's interests? Or what if we seek to justify military action on the ground that Saddam's regime is abhorrent and should be changed?

'These latter two arguments erode global stability.'

Andrew Tyrie, Conservative MP, *Axis of Instability* (March 2003).[25]

'Inspection is a better way of disarming than bombing. It has not been shown that there is any near-term threat from Iraq to Europe or beyond. War is always an uncertain venture, and may lead to a situation far worse than the one we have now.'

Sir Timothy Garden, Former Air Chief Marshal of the Royal Air Force, 21 January 2003.[26]

'If President Saddam Hussein has said the United Nations inspectors can come without condition, what right has he [President George W. Bush] to come in and say that offer is not genuine? On this question of Iraq they are absolutely wrong. It is the United Nations that must decide. We must condemn that very strongly. That's why I criticise most leaders all over the world for keeping quiet when one country wants to bully the whole world.'

Nelson Mandela, 18 September 2002.[27]

'When does compassion, when does morality, when does caring come in?

'Many of us are deeply saddened to see a great country such as the United States aided and abetted extraordinarily by Britain—[It is] mind-boggling . . . I'm shocked to see a powerful country use its power frequently, unilaterally. The United States says "you do this" to the world, "if you don't do it, we will do it"—that's sad.'

Archbishop Desmond Tutu, Nobel Peace Prize winner, 5 January 2003.[28]

'We may not approve of the regime in Iraq but that doesn't mean we see it as our responsibility to remove. Put simply, we do not want the 21st century to be a century of war.'

Tayyib Erdogan, de facto leader of Turkey, 21 February 2003.[29]

At the White House, officials said that just before President Bush addressed the nation on 19 March 2003, declaring the start of hostilities, he pumped his fist, winked, and said,

'I feel good.'[30]

INTRODUCTION
Tony Blair Wobbled

We Nearly Derailed The War On Iraq

PARTIAL DEFEAT, PARTIAL VICTORY

This book is designed to be read by anyone with an open mind who is willing to test official justifications for the war on Iraq against the available evidence. The results make for grim reading. A war supposedly waged for disarmament actually involved the deliberate destruction of the UN weapons inspection effort, just as it was about to launch a new and decisive period of investigation. A war supposedly for 'regime change' actually ended with the restoration of leading fascists to power, and the attempted re-nazification of Iraq.

This introduction, in contrast with the rest of the book, is written specifically for those millions of people around the world who opposed the war, for us to understand what power we actually wielded. Left-wing British playwright David Hare wrote a few months after the official end of the war, 'Those of us who opposed the war from the start have won the argument and lost all influence . . . we are left at the end of it all in the curious position of finding no satisfaction or purpose in our own rightness. The policies are not going to change. We are going to be ignored.'[1]

The truth is rather different, though it is not one that is transmitted through the mass media or recorded in the triumphalist instant history books. We were not ignored. The astonishing truth is that the combined efforts of anti-war movements around the world very nearly succeeded in detaching the British Government, and British military forces, from the US invasion of Iraq. This could have derailed the war.

As I pointed out in my earlier book *War Plan Iraq: Ten Reasons Against War On Iraq*, Tony Blair was the Achilles' heel of the US war effort. Politically indispensable, Mr Blair was a weak link—though not the weakest link—and he nearly broke.

In the summer of 2002, even right-wing political leaders in the US were warning of the need for international support for military action. Chuck Hagel, a Republican Senator from Nebraska, commented, 'I don't think it is in the best interests of this country ... or any of our allies for us to act unilaterally.'[2] Retired US Rear Admiral Stephen Baker, an operations officer in the Gulf War, remarked dryly, 'It is a good idea when leading a charge to occasionally stop and look behind to see whether anyone is following.' If such a check had been carried out in August 2002, Admiral Baker observed, George W. Bush would have found behind him 'some of his staff, a vaguely supportive Congress, a nervous Defense Department and the British Prime Minister, Tony Blair.' 'That's about it.'[3]

A major poll carried out in August 2002 by the Chicago Council on Foreign Relations and the German Marshall Fund found only 20 per cent of US citizens supported a unilateral invasion of Iraq. 65 per cent of US respondents believed that an invasion should be carried out only with UN authorisation and the support of allies. The report also noted that 'not much concern about Iraq emerges spontaneously when people are asked about big problems facing the country.' Iraq or Saddam Hussein were mentioned by a mere three per cent of respondents when asked to name the two or three biggest problems facing the United States. Only one per cent named Iraq when asked to identify the two or three biggest problems facing the country today.[4] In January 2003, a national poll on US attitudes to war on Iraq found 83 per cent support for going to war with Iraq if this was in concert with major US allies and with the full support of the United Nations Security Council. If the US went to war with just one or two of its major allies—without the support of the United Nations—this support fell to 47 per cent. If Washington acted alone, without the support of the UN, only 34 per cent of the US public would be supportive.[5] In March 2003, another poll found 77 per cent of people in the US saying 'we absolutely need' to have British support in the event of war in Iraq.[6]

Former US Ambassador to the UN, Richard Holbrooke observed, 'If there is one country in the world that might find a way to support us without a UN resolution, it would be the UK.'[7] A prescient remark. Anatol Lieven, analyst at the Carnegie Endowment for International Peace, suggested that 'Britain is at least as important as all the other European states put together. If Britain came out publicly and said it was against it, it would really shake them.'[8] Another quite prescient remark. Britain very nearly did have to come out publicly to withdraw its support for the war.

Britain was not only politically essential. Anthony Luttwak, member of the National Security Study Group of the US Department of Defense and a fellow of the Center for Strategic and International Studies, noted just days before the war began that the military importance of the British contribution to the invasion force had waxed and waned. At first, when US Defense Secretary Donald Rumsfeld intended to go in light and fast, Afghan-style, the British were significant. As the size of planned US deployments increased, however, the British contribution became less significant. However, when the Turkish Parliament refused to allow the US access to northern Iraq via Turkish territory, this stranded a significant proportion of the US invasion force on the wrong side of the

Suez Canal, and the British element once again grew in importance. In mid-March 2003, observed Mr Luttwak, with US and British forces 'Sandwiched together, with units under each other's command, Yanks and Brits are more closely integrated than they have been since the Second World War—and that is why a last-minute withdrawal by Mr Blair has become simply unthinkable.'[9]

WOBBLY TUESDAY

But the unthinkable was thought:

> By Tuesday [11 March 2003], there were serious worries in the White House that Mr Blair, its staunchest ally, might not survive the political crisis at home. Geoff Hoon, the Defence Secretary, tried to explain the problems to Donald Rumsfeld, the US defence secretary, in a telephone call which had meant to be devoted to the fine detail of the war plan.[10]

The *Sunday Telegraph*, the newspaper most closely linked to the British Armed Forces, went on to reveal that on Tuesday 11 March, 'Mr Hoon's department [the Ministry of Defence] was frantically preparing contingency plans to "disconnect" British troops entirely from the military invasion of Iraq, demoting their role to subsequent phases of the campaign and peacekeeping.'[11]

Having concluded his phone conversation with Mr Hoon, Mr Rumsfeld suggested publicly that US troops could go to war without the British if necessary. Asked, 'Would the United States go to war without Great Britain?' Mr Rumsfeld replied with breathtaking candour: 'This is a matter that most of the senior officials in the government discuss with the UK on a daily or every-other-day basis.' He added, 'what will ultimately be decided is unclear as to their role; that is to say, their role in the event that a decision is made to use force.' He hinted that the British might only have a 'role in a post-Saddam Hussein reconstruction process or stabilisation process.' '[U]ntil we know what the resolution is, we won't know the answer as to what their role will be and to the extent they're able to participate in the event the president decides to use force.'[12]

The follow-up question was predictable: 'We would consider going to war without our closest ally, then?' Mr Rumsfeld once against threw diplomacy to the winds: 'That is an issue that the president will be addressing in the days ahead, one would assume.'[13]

The *Daily Telegraph* reported that the US Defence Secretary had become 'deeply exasperated' by Mr Blair's insistence that a second resolution was necessary, and had lost all patience with the delays that the negotiations at the UN were causing. Mr Rumsfeld was said to have confided to a friend, 'I am learning to hate the British.'[14] Several sources within the Bush administration stated that the Rumsfeld comments were an attempt (successful as it turned out) to force the Prime Minister's hand.[15] From the British side of things, Mr Hoon's Cabinet colleagues apparently believed that he had 'over-reached' himself in stressing the Government's difficulties over the war: 'During the transatlantic telephone conversation on Tuesday, Mr Hoon stressed the political problems the Government was having both with MPs and the public. But according to one Whitehall source, he gave Mr Rumsfeld the impression that Britain would not play a front-line role.'[16] In the event, the MOD and the Pentagon both had to issue corrections and retractions, and Mr Blair had to give President Bush his personal assurance that British troops were ready to make a 'significant contribution' to any conflict.

THE CORE OF THE STORY

Whether the emphasis falls on Mr Hoon's maladroit diplomacy or on Mr Rumsfeld's bitterness at the British-inspired delays, the underlying reality was that the British Government was panicking. As the *Daily Telegraph* put it, ' "Wobbly Tuesday" was the lowest point of the crisis for Mr Blair.'[17]

The anti-war movements very nearly defeated the British Government. Only days away from the first missile launch and the first air raid, the British Government was shaken to the core, having to draw up hasty plans for withdrawing from the invasion. This withdrawal would have had an explosive political impact on the US war effort, with unpredictable consequences. It is certainly conceivable that Washington could have been forced to scale back or postpone the onslaught on Iraq.

On 'Wobbly Tuesday', the Blair Government was facing danger on a number of fronts. There was to be a vote on the war in Parliament on 18 March, which the Government might not win. There were two Cabinet ministers on the verge of resigning as a matter of principle over the issue. The Leader of the House of Commons, Robin Cook, did so. International Development Secretary Clare Short, whose resignation would have carried significantly more weight with backbench Labour MPs, did not. There were persistent rumours that the Attorney-General had given ambiguous or even negative legal advice to the Government. The overwhelming political problem was that the long-hoped-for second UN Resolution failed to arrive. The *Financial Times* described the failure of diplomacy—'if that is not too polite a word for the bullying and bribing in which both camps are indulging'—as a 'diplomatic train-wreck'.[18]

THE GLOBAL ANTI-WAR MOVEMENT

Why did the UN Security Council refuse to bow to US pressure and British pleading? In large measure because the Governments making up the membership of the Security Council were forced into opposition by the enormous anti-war movements in their own countries. Chile, for example, shaken by anti-American demonstrations, grew more hostile to war throughout February 2003, and began to act in concert with Mexico. One Chilean official observed acidly, 'We know very well in Latin America that if the Americans want a regime change, they can do it without resorting to bombing cities.'[19]

At one point, Mr Rumsfeld distinguished between 'old Europe', which was hostile to the war, and 'new Europe'—the countries of the former Soviet empire in Eastern Europe—who were more supportive. In truth, the real division was between those

Governments which served the will of the people on this issue—including Turkey, Germany, and France—and those Governments which set their course against the democratic will of their own populations—including Spain, Poland, Romania and Britain

In Spain, Prime Minister Jose Maria Aznar, the third man on the international stage beside George W. Bush and Tony Blair in the run-up to war, was confronted by 91 per cent opposition to the war, according to opinion polls from the Government's own official polling agency.[20] Over the preceding year, the proportion of Spanish people with a favourable view of the US had dropped from 50 per cent to 14 per cent.[21] Romania signed a pro-US letter siding with Washington and London at the end of January 2003,[22] but polls in Bucharest showed 87 per cent opposition to the deployment of 278 non-combat troops to the Gulf. Poland despatched 200 special forces soldiers to the region, despite 75 per cent public opposition to the war.[23] In Britain, one of the 'newest' of the new European countries, if modernity is measured in terms of slavishness, the polls swung here and there, but there was clear opposition before the war to military action without UN authorisation. In early February, an ICM poll for the BBC programme 'Iraq: Britain decides' found 45 per cent of people opposed to war either with or without a fresh UN mandate; 40 per cent supportive of military action only if it was authorised by the UN; and only 9 per cent approving of an invasion without a further mandate from the UN—the course that was eventually taken.[24] Throughout these countries there were massive demonstrations, culminating in the historic mobilizations of 15 February 2003.

In December 2002, the Pew Research Centre found that 83 per cent of Turks objected to their country being used as a launching pad for an invasion. Opposition to war ran at 71 per cent in Germany, 64 per cent in France and 79 per cent in Russia—and in all these 'old' countries foreign policy largely reflected this overwhelming tide of opinion.[25] This was of critical importance in triggering the diplomatic 'train wreck' at the Security Council which denied the US and UK any shred of international legitimacy.

Public opposition forced the Turkish Parliament to refuse to allow Washington the use of Turkish bases and a Turkish land corridor to invade northern Iraq. 'Given that 85 per cent of the Turkish people don't want a war, the party and government feel we must exhaust all peaceful solutions before reluctantly becoming involved in a war,' said Murat Mercan, deputy chair of the ruling Justice and Development Party (AKP) in January 2003.[26] It appears that the offer by the US of a $26 billion bribe in loans and grants actually deepened public hostility. By mid-February, opposition to an Iraqi war was nearer 95 per cent.[27]

The *Financial Times* suggests that the sheer scale of popular opposition to the war 'may have been the deciding factor'. Turkish parliamentarians were being rung on their mobile phones by angry constituents as the Government proposal was being debated.[28] It is an extraordinary indictment of British politics that despite the dependency of the Ankara on US power, the dominant role of the military in Turkish political life, and the prospect of a desperately-needed multi-billion dollar bribe, Turkish democracy expressed the wishes of the people better than did the mother of parliaments.

Paul Wolfowitz, US Deputy Defence Secretary, blamed the Turkish military for not forcing the elected politicians into line: 'Many of the institutions we think of as the traditional strong support in the [US–Turkish] alliance were not as forceful in leading in that direction—particularly the military. For whatever the reason, they did not play the strong leadership role on that issue that we would have expected.' After the war, the Turkish Ambassador to Washington worried, 'Can you punish Turkey for acting democratically? Our American friends should be proud this happened in an exercise of democracy.'[29] But it is obedience, not democracy, that is the transcendent value for the US.

Incidentally, when the Greek Ambassador told US President Lyndon Johnson that his country objected to US plans to partition the independent Republic of Cyprus between Greece and Turkey, the President responded,

> Fuck your parliament and your constitution. America is an elephant, Cyprus is a flea. Greece is a flea. If these two fellows continue itching the elephant, they may just get whacked by the elephant's trunk, whacked good . . .
>
> If your Prime Minister gives me talk about democracy, parliament and constitution, he, his parliament and his constitution may not last very long.

Furthermore, the President added, 'maybe Greece should rethink the value of a parliament which could not take the right decision.'[30] Democracy equals obedience. Incidentally, not long after President Johnson's remarks, the generals took over Greece.

THE THREAT OF RESIGNATION

The global anti-war movement denied Britain and the US their second UN Resolution. This put Tony Blair's war policy in danger, and his political career on a knife-edge. Mr Blair was prepared to risk all. In an interview with the *Sun* newspaper, Mr Blair said that he had told Whitehall officials to make preparations for his resignation in the days before the vote on war with Iraq on 18 March 2003. The Prime Minister also said he sat down with this three oldest children to discuss what would happen if he lost the vote, explaining that it was possible things would not go his way.[31] In his speech to the House of Commons on 18 March, before the critical vote on war, Mr Blair hinted that he might resign as Prime Minister if the vote went against him: to pull back from war at this point would be to 'put at hazard all that we hold dearest' and to have 'faltered'. Mr Blair said, 'I will not be party to such a course.'[32]

New Labour MP, Tom Harris, spoke up after a meeting of the Parliamentary Labour Party on Wednesday 12 March: 'I was equivocal about whether we should go to war without a second resolution, but I now think this has been turned into a vote of confidence in Tony Blair and if that's what it has been turned into, I'm completely unequivocal.'[33] As Matthew d'Ancona of the *Sunday Telegraph* points out, Mr Blair used to be regarded by his entire party 'as a sort of intergalactic megabeing who had descended into their midst and, by means which they did not fully understand, transformed a party of losers into an electoral juggernaut.'[34] This perception has suffered considerable damage, after of a string of political disasters, but continues to hold sway.

Curiously, the myth is entirely unfounded, as the head of the MORI opinion poll organisation explained in the aftermath of the 1997 New Labour landslide. Professor Robert Worcester's analysis of the polls showed that a Labour victory was a foregone conclusion after years of Conservative failure.[35] Veteran Labour MP Roy Hattersley, a former deputy leader of the party, made the following observation after reviewing Professor Worcester's analysis:

> So a crucial question still needs to be asked. Why did New Labour, so obsessed by the polls, not take notice of the one which showed that the Tories had already lost the election and that victory was possible without parroting so many Conservative policies and values? The answer stands the usual formula of political deception on its head. New Labour did not abandon socialism in order to win. Winning was the excuse for abandoning socialism.[36]

Despite his political dispensability, Mr Blair's resignation threat, conveyed privately and publicly, helped to curb the rebellion of the Parliamentary Labour Party, along with a series of distortions and deceptions, including a gross misrepresentation of the position of President Jacques Chirac. Contrary to the repeated and vehement accusations from the Government front bench, President Chirac did not rule out the use of force under any circumstances.[37] With this and other lies, a parliamentary majority was secured, Britain joined the invasion force, and the war finally went ahead.

THE OTHER POSSIBLE RUPTURE

There was another fault line in the US–UK relationship, derived from the fundamental political importance of the second UN Resolution to the British Government. US Secretary of State Colin Powell made it clear in late February that he did not expect this Resolution to set a 'timeline' for Iraq.[38] However, the concept of a deadline became a central issue in the tortuous British negotiations in the Security Council. Eventually, after weeks of uncertainty, the US was forced to accept the idea of a deadline—but limited this to a few days. The emerging consensus on the Security Council in the last few days before war, however, was a proposal that Baghdad should be given a further 30 days. This very nearly precipitated a breach between London and Washington as Mr Blair grasped for political straws.

> Looking back, French and British officials acknowledge a further irony. In the last few days before the resolution was withdrawn, Mr Blair was concerned that France might in the end agree to a plan that would impose a 30-day deadline for Iraq to comply with tough benchmarks. British officials believe that, at that late stage, Mr Blair would have been forced to accept the proposal. The US, they suspect, would have opposed it, splintering the small and fragile coalition. The French feared they might have to accept an equally difficult outcome.

If the British proposed a tough and serious deadline—of about 30 days—they might well have signed on.[39]

Britain would have compromised by lengthening the period of assessment. France would have compromised by accepting the inevitability of war after this period was over.

The pressure from the domestic anti-war movement in Britain, inside and outside the Labour Party, and the anti-war stance taken by Security Council members under pressure from their own populations, brought Washington and London to the brink of an extraordinary rupture over the second Resolution.

THE HUMAN CONSEQUENCES OF PROTEST

The anti-war movement did not only succeed in mounting an unprecedented global mobilization which managed to deny Washington and London a second UN Resolution. There were consequences on the ground also. Another major achievement of the global anti-war movement was to force the US and UK to moderate their attacks on Iraq, particularly, it seems, on the civilian infrastructure in Iraq. If the electricity sector had been systematically targeted, for example, as it was in 1991, and as it was in the Kosovo war, the consequences for the Iraqi people could have been devastating. The electricity system was vital to providing clean drinking water and preventing water-borne diseases. Unfortunately, looting and disorder after the war seem to have undone a lot of the restraint forced on the US military.

The war did come, despite enormous efforts by millions of people, in Britain, the United States, and in countries around the world. But the work of the anti-war movement may well have saved a considerable number of lives in Iraq. It also helped to lay the basis for a stronger movement better able to prevent the next war.

CHAPTER I
Argument Over

The War Was Wrong

NEVER HAVE SO MANY BEEN SO RIGHT

Leaning over, the soldier peeled off the Stars and Stripes which he had placed there moments before. He replaced it with the Iraqi flag, covering the face of the statue. Within minutes the figure of Saddam Hussein had tumbled to the ground, to be trampled by dozens of jubilant Iraqis. The war was symbolically over. The United States and Britain had won—without bloody urban warfare, without the use of chemical and biological weapons, without the deaths of hundreds of thousands of civilians, without months of struggling against Vietnam-style guerrilla warfare, without causing hundreds of thousands of refugees, without significant disruption to the world economy, and without an eruption of rioting throughout the Middle East. For British Prime Minister Tony Blair, the war had been won without inflicting immediately fatal damage to his leadership, and without tearing the Labour Party in half.

Nick Cohen, a left-liberal journalist for the left-liberal *Observer* newspaper in Britain, supported the war (as did his editors), and he revelled in its outcome: 'Has the left—by which I mean the left that opposes new Labour—begun to grasp the magnitude of its defeat?' When the politically committed make 'false prediction after false prediction', as both right- and left-wing opponents of the war did, according to Mr Cohen, 'they appear shameless or stupid': 'When they are proved wrong, Blair wins and deserves to win.'[1]

US Secretary of State Donald Rumsfeld, visiting US troops in Iraq, was asked whether he had received many apologetic calls from critics of the war. He replied gleefully, 'There were a lot of hand-wringers around, weren't there? You know, during World War II, Winston Churchill was talking about the Battle of Britain and he said, "Never have so many owed so much to so few". A humorist in Washington . . . sent me a note paraphrasing that [saying], "Never have so many been so wrong about so much."'[2]

Were the opponents of the war wrong? Should they have apologised?

No.

The anti-war argument did not rest on predictions about how costly or difficult the war would be. The anti-war argument rested on the overwhelming evidence that the intended war was illegal, immoral, unjustified, unpopular and anti-democratic.[3]

THE ANTI-WAR ARGUMENTS

The central anti-war argument was not that US and British soldiers would lose their lives in grinding urban warfare or prolonged guerrilla warfare, or that the civilian population would be butchered or driven into exile in their hundreds of thousands, or that British and US economic interests would be damaged by world recession or the Arab backlash against the war.

The central anti-war argument was that the war was wrong, not that it might be too costly. The war was not necessary as a method of dealing with Iraq's suspected weapons programmes. The weapons inspection process had barely begun—it had not been exhausted—by 17 March 2003.

Secondly, the war was an illegitimate war for US domination, not for Iraqi liberation. It was clear six months before it was launched that this was not a war for 'regime change', this was a war intended to achieve 'regime stabilisation' and only 'leadership change.'[4]

On these core issues, the global anti-war movement was right. On these central moral and legal issues, never before have so many been so right about so much of real and lasting significance. The massive demonstrations of 15 February 2003 were right. The war was a crime.

NON-MILITARY MEANS NOT EXHAUSTED

Keeping for the moment to the issue of necessity, the anti-war argument would not be affected by the discovery of weapons of mass destruction in Iraq—or 'programmes'. The anti-war argument was that non-military means of dealing with Iraq's alleged weapons of mass destruction had not been exhausted, were far from being exhausted, and in fact were barely beginning to get into their stride when the war was initiated, as we shall see.[5]

Dr Hans Blix, head of the UN weapons inspection agency UNMOVIC, said in March 2003 that with 'a proactive Iraqi attitude', it would take only months to verify sites and items, to analyse documents, and to interview relevant persons: 'It would not take years, nor weeks, but months.'[6] No evidence was ever produced that Iraq would develop either the capability or the intention to use weapons of mass destruction aggressively 'within months'. There was time, then, for inspections to run their course.

RISK ASSESSMENT

As Dr Glen Rangwala pointed out a year before the war took place, for there to be a real threat from Iraq, there had to be both a weapons capability and an aggressive intent to use it.[7] While confident statements were made concerning Iraq's non-conventional capabilities, little was said regarding Iraq's short-term or medium-term military intentions. British Vice-Admiral Sir James Jungius KBE observed in January 2003, 'Even if the weapons do exist, where is the evidence of intent to use them? War is too important and unpleasant a business to be undertaken on the basis of a hunch, however good that hunch may be.'[8] Former Tory Cabinet Minister Douglas Hogg expanded on this vital point:

> The real question is not whether he's got weapons of mass destruction, but rather whether—if he has got those weapons—he is a grave and imminent threat to the rest of us. There are lots of other countries in the world that do have weapons of mass destruction, or are likely to acquire them, but we don't necessarily conclude that they are a grave and imminent threat sufficient to justify war. So even if he had these things, unless he's a grave and imminent threat there isn't a moral basis for war, because the doctrine of self-defence isn't properly invoked.[9]

Ignoring these simple principles, British and US war leaders claimed confidently that weapons of mass destruction existed in Iraq, and that the mere existence of these weapons posed a threat so grave that military action could no longer be delayed. Britain's Parliament was assured in September 2002 that 'Saddam has continued to produce chemical and biological weapons, and that he has been able to extend the range of his ballistic missile programme. His military planning allows for some of the WMD to be ready within 45 minutes of an order to use them'. This had been 'established beyond doubt', according to British Prime Minister Tony Blair.[10]

US Secretary of State Colin Powell told the UN Security Council on 5 February 2003, 'Saddam Hussein and his regime are concealing their efforts to produce more weapons of mass destruction.' Mr Powell stressed the validity of his conclusions: 'My colleagues, every statement I make today is backed up by sources, solid sources. These are not assertions. What we are giving you are facts and conclusions based on solid intelligence.' Mr Powell said that even as the Security Council was debating Resolution 1441 in the autumn of 2002, 'we know from sources that a missile brigade outside Baghdad was dispersing rocket launchers and warheads containing biological warfare agent' to locations in western Iraq.[11]

PUBLISH THE EVIDENCE

At the time of writing, none of these claims has been substantiated by discoveries on the ground in Iraq. None of the other detailed claims made in official speeches and dossiers has been borne out by evidence on the ground. The British and US governments have entered a convoluted, looping and mutually contradictory series of explanations for the lack of finds. There is one simple step they could take to redeem themselves, however. It would be to publish the evidence that they kept secret before the war because of the danger to informants inside Iraq.

Colin Powell told the Security Council, in his long and detailed presentation on 5 February 2003, that some of the sources for his statement were 'people who have risked their lives to let the world know what Saddam Hussein is really up to'. Now that the regime in Iraq has crumbled, and no longer poses a threat to these informants, the United States and Britain should be able to publish the evidence on which they based their categorical statements of 'truth', and to produce for questioning the eyewitnesses whose 'evidence' helped to precipitate the deaths of thousands of people.

If the evidence is convincing, and the eyewitnesses are credible, then the US and UK can claim to have been honest themselves, and to have acted in good faith. This would not justify the war, because evidence of a weapons capability does not itself constitute evidence of an immediate threat, and because non-military means of disarming Iraq had not been exhausted when President Bush issued his ultimatum on 17 March 2003. But at least the US and British Governments could say that they had spoken the truth as far as it was available to them.

On the other hand, if, as is almost certainly the case, the 'evidence' provided by Iraqi informants is dubious and unconvincing, then the US and British Governments would stand convicted of dishonesty in a matter of life and death.

THE 'CHILDLIKE' FORGERY

So far, only one piece of 'intelligence' has been subjected to independent verification. In the British Government dossier on Iraq's weapons, published in September 2002, it was claimed that Iraq had attempted to acquire uranium from an African country. No date was given, no country was identified. The letters on which this claim was based were passed to the International Atomic Energy Agency, which pronounced them 'not authentic'.[12] US intelligence officials were less restrained. They described anonymously how 'secret documents' on Saddam Hussein's supposed attempt to purchase uranium were passed to the United States by the British intelligence agency MI6, and then submitted to the UN even though they contained 'laughable and childlike errors'. 'These are not the kind of forgeries that you would expect to fool a professional intelligence agency,' said one US official.[13] US sources told CNN that one of the documents was a letter discussing the uranium deal supposedly signed by the President of Niger, Tandja Mamadou. The sources described the signature as 'childlike' and said that it clearly was not President Mamadou's. Another letter, written on paper from a military government that had held power in the 1980s, bore the date of October 2000 and the signature of a man who by then had not been the foreign minister of Niger for 14 years, US intelligence sources said.[14]

Despite these 'childlike errors', the letters were endorsed as conclusive evidence by Prime Minister Blair, who included the following statement in his weapons dossier in September 2002: 'there is intelligence that Iraq has sought the supply of significant quantities of uranium from Africa.'[15] The 'laughable' forgery was also endorsed by President George W. Bush, who referred to the uranium-from-Africa claim in his State of the

Union address on 28 January 2003: 'The British government has learned that Saddam Hussein recently sought significant quantities of uranium from Africa'.[16]

In June 2003, amid a storm of condemnation over the misuse of intelligence, the British Government attempted to protect itself from criticism by claiming that they had another, independent source of information about Iraqi attempts to purchase uranium from Africa. British officials claimed that Britain had never been in possession of the forged documents passed to the IAEA by US officials.[17] This contradicted the accounts given by US intelligence officials, and by President Bush.

ACCIDENTAL ACCURACY

Honesty is judged by whether a person deals reasonably with the evidence available to them, or whether that evidence is twisted (or manufactured) to suit a particular purpose. Therefore it is possible that one or more of the claims made by Mr Blair and Mr Powell may be both accurate and dishonest. Only publication of the evidence that they possessed at the time of making their statements can establish whether they spoke honestly or dishonestly as they attempted to persuade sceptical populations to support the coming war.

JUDGING THE HIDDEN EVIDENCE

Finally, it should be pointed out that where the evidence for some claim is not publicly available, we can make some judgement by examining the trustworthiness of any accompanying claims that can be verified independently. The British Government's weapons dossier made a large number of unverifiable claims based on 'secret intelligence'. It also contained a few verifiable claims. If the claims which can be checked fall apart on inspection, the whole document must then be regarded as suspect and unreliable. The uranium-from-Africa story was tested independently. It fell apart in spectacular fashion.

Another story in the weapons dossier which could be checked was the British Government's account of the inspection process in Iraq. There is a section of the dossier entitled, 'History of UN Weapons Inspections.' It is said without qualification that, 'Iraq consistently refused to allow UNSCOM inspectors access to any of these eight Presidential sites.'[18] But it is a matter of record that Iraq permitted UNSCOM weapons inspectors access to all eight of the sites in question in 1998, first to allow a survey team to assess the size and scope of the sites (15-18 February 1998), and then for inspections. Tim Trevan, former UNSCOM inspector and now an advisor to the British Government, records the latter event in the chronology in his book, *Saddam's Secrets: The Hunt for Iraq's Hidden Weapons*: '4 April 1998, Access to the presidential sites is obtained.'[19]

If the British Government is so careless with facts which can be so easily checked, then it does not deserve to be trusted when it makes major claims that are not supported by evidence—and for which it refuses to reveal the evidence, despite the fact that the threat to Iraqi informants has now evaporated.

ASYMMETRICAL ARGUMENTS

The anti-war movement warned of possible consequences of a war against Iraq. Thankfully, many of those warnings did not come to pass. The accuracy or inaccuracy of those warnings have no impact on the core arguments against the war. As we shall see during the course of this book, the war *was* unnecessary. It was unjustified. It was immoral. It was illegal. It was anti-democratic. It was a war built on lies.

Whether or not weapons of mass destruction are found in Iraq, the simple fact remains that the non-military disarmament path of inspections remained open on 17 March 2003, when President Bush issued his ultimatum. Far from being exhausted, the path of inspections was about to open out into a broad road of disarmament, a development required by a UN Security Council Resolution, as we shall see.

On the other hand, the many categorical statements and detailed claims of British and US war leaders about Iraq's weapons of mass destruction—which were the central justification for the war—have, up to the time of writing, proven to be little more than empty words. This is a fatal blow to the central pro-war argument as presented by Prime Minister Tony Blair and President George W. Bush. It is not the opponents of the war who appear 'shameless and stupid'. It is not the critics of the war who should apologise for their misconduct.

And what of the argument that, regardless of the fate of Iraq's suspected weapons, the war was justified because it changed an appalling regime which did not deserve to exist on the face of the earth? This was the cruellest lie of them all, as we shall see. Victory for George W. Bush and Tony Blair brought not 'regime change', but the attempted re-nazification of Iraq.

CHAPTER II
'Regime Change'

A Prior Commitment

A PRIOR COMMITMENT

It could be argued that the countdown to war began on 11 September 2001. According to CBS News, Defence Secretary Donald Rumsfeld, still working in his office in the Pentagon as fire-fighters struggled with the effects of strike on the building, wrote a note that he wanted 'best info fast': 'Judge whether good enough hit SH at the same time. Not only UBL [Usama Bin Laden]. Go massive. Sweep it all up. Things related and not.'[1] At a Cabinet meeting the following day to discuss the US response to the terrorist atrocities—at a time when the source of the suicide attacks was quite unknown—Mr Rumsfeld asked President Bush and his senior advisers, 'Why shouldn't we go against Iraq, not just al-Qaeda?'[2] His proposal was postponed. However, at the end of the Presidential order to begin preparations for a war on Afghanistan, signed on 17 September 2001, a clause was attached directing the Pentagon to draw up military options for the invasion of Iraq.[3] The question of Iraq erupted into the public domain on 14 September, when Mr Rumsfeld's protégé and deputy at the Pentagon, Paul Wolfowitz, stated that the United States' new 'war on terrorism' would include 'ending states who sponsor terrorism', widely interpreted as a threat against Iraq.[4]

Alternatively, one could trace the origins of the war further back in time. Donald Rumsfeld and Paul Wolfowitz (the latter a member of the 1991 Bush Administration that waged war on Iraq) both had a long-standing prior commitment to resuming large-scale US military action against Iraq. They were both signatories to a letter to President Bill Clinton in January 1998 under the auspices of the 'Project for the New American Century' (PNAC), a lobby group dedicated to US 'global leadership'. The eighteen right-wing signatories to the letter were convinced that US policy toward Iraq was 'not succeeding', and that 'we may soon face a threat in the Middle East more serious than any we have known since the end of the Cold War'. They urged the President to adopt a 'new strategy' towards Iraq which should aim 'at the removal of Saddam Hussein's regime from power'.

This meant 'a willingness to undertake military action'. Removing Saddam Hussein and his regime from power needed to become 'the aim of American foreign policy', in order to 'protect our vital interests in the Gulf'. Other signatories to the letter included John Bolton, who became Under Secretary of State for arms control in the State Department under George W. Bush; Zalmay Khalilzad, who became the President's special envoy to the Iraqi opposition; and Richard Perle, who was the chair of the Pentagon's Defense Advisory Board under President Bush until he resigned on 27 March 2003.[5]

'LEADERSHIP CHANGE' THROUGH SANCTIONS

A commitment to removing Saddam Hussein from power was nothing new. US sanctions policy towards Iraq, under both President Clinton and his predecessor, President George Bush Sr, had been aimed at precisely this goal. Secretary of State Colin Powell conceded as much in February 2002: 'Sanctions and the pressure of sanctions are part of a strategy of regime change [along with] support for the opposition and reviewing additional options that might be available of a unilateral or multilateral nature.'[6] For reasons set out elsewhere, I believe that it is more appropriate to describe US policy as one of 'leadership change' rather than 'regime change'. However, for the moment, we will follow the conventional terminology.

UN Resolution 687, which re-imposed economic sanctions on Iraq after the 1991 war, stated that oil exports would remain under an embargo until Iraq had completed a verified disarmament process. President Bush Sr, however, widened the goal of the sanctions policy. The President said in April 1991, 'There will not be normalised relations with the US until Saddam Hussein is out of there. And we will continue economic sanctions.'[7] 'Bush Links End of Trading Ban to Hussein Exit', reported the *New York Times* on 21 May 1991. There was Anglo-American unity on this point, then as now. The British Ambassador to the United Nations, Sir David Hannay, stated during discussions on Resolution 687 in early 1991, 'My Government believes that it will in fact prove impossible for Iraq to rejoin the community of civilised nations while Saddam Hussein remains in power.'[8] Prime Minister John Major was more forthright: 'Britain will veto any UN resolution designed to weaken the sanctions regime we have set in place for so long as Saddam Hussein remains in power.'[9] The strategy was summed up by *New York Times* Diplomatic Correspondent Thomas Friedman in July 1991. Mr Friedman said that economic sanctions would continue until there was a military coup within Iraq which would create 'the best of all worlds': 'an iron-fisted Iraqi junta without Saddam Hussein', a return to the days when Saddam's 'iron fist . . . held Iraq together, much to the satisfaction of the American allies Turkey and Saudi Arabia.'[10]

THE HUMAN COST OF SANCTIONS

Comprehensive economic sanctions were not in fact successful in hastening the end of the Iraqi President, but they were successful in hastening the end of hundreds of thousands of Iraqi lives. In August 1999, UNICEF revealed that in the south/centre of Iraq—home to 85 per cent of the country's population—the death rate among children under five had more than doubled during the period of sanctions. The death rate rose from 56 deaths per 1000 live births (1984–1989) to 131 deaths per 1000 live births (1994–1999). Infant mortality—defined as the death of children in their first year—had increased from 47 to 108 deaths per 1000 live births within the same time frame. UNICEF Executive Director Carol Bellamy noted that there had been a substantial reduction in child mortality throughout Iraq during the 1980s (despite the Iran-Iraq war). If this had continued through the 1990s, she said, there would have been half a million fewer deaths of children under five in the country as a whole during the eight year period 1991 to 1998. 500,000 children died who would otherwise have lived.[11] While Ms Bellamy did not draw the obvious conclusion, it seems reasonable to deduce that most of these lives would not have been lost if Iraq had not been suffering the weight of UN economic sanctions, imposed at the behest of Washington and London.

LIBERATION: THE CLINTON WRIGGLE

It would be inaccurate to describe US policy towards Iraq under President Clinton as simply one of 'containment'. While they turned out to be embarrassing failures, there were several significant covert operations launched against Baghdad in 1995 and 1996. In the latter case, the US appears to have infiltrated CIA paramilitary officers into the attempted intrusive inspection of Republican Guard and Special Republican Guard facilities by UN weapons inspectors in June 1996, in order to contact élite Iraqi commanders in an ambitious multi-million-dollar coup attempt co-funded by Saudi Arabi, Britain and Kuwait. The noted Middle East commentator Dilip Hiro observes, 'Once the Iraqi regime had got over its alarm and shock, it stiffened its stance on UNSCOM inspections. It now perceived these exercises as part of communications channels for coordinating a coup to be staged after its attention had been diverted by US military strikes.'

Following this and other failures, Secretary of State Madeleine Albright attempted to increase the incentives for a coup within Iraq by signalling US willingness to drop economic sanctions in the event of a military take-over. Ms Albright stated in March 1997 that 'a change in Iraq's government could lead to a change in US policy': 'Should that occur, we would stand ready, in co-ordination with our allies and friends, to enter rapidly into a dialogue with a successor regime.' If the new Government co-operated with UN weapons inspectors, and if Iraq remained 'independent, unified, and free from undue external influence, for example from Iran', then 'the international community, including the United States, would look for ways to ease Iraq's reintegration.' Interestingly, a National Security Council official clarified that human rights and democracy were not conditions for Iraq's rehabilitation: even 'modest steps' would be acceptable.[12]

'Regime change' was thus encouraged by the Clinton Administration, especially after a Republican-dominated Congress passed the Iraq Liberation Act in late 1998 authorising the President to grant up to $97 million to arm and finance Iraqi opposition groups.

CLINTON'S CRUISE MISSILE DIPLOMACY

The Project for the New American Century signatories were not urging President Clinton to pursue an entirely new policy towards Iraq. They were urging him to drop his 'containment' policy and to pursue the existing goal of 'regime change' more explicitly and more forcefully. We should recall that President Clinton used considerable force against Iraq on two occasions. On 26 June 1993, the United States fired twenty-three Tomahawk cruise missiles at the headquarters of an Iraqi intelligence agency in Baghdad (three missiles missed their target, landed on neighbouring houses and killed civilians), on the bizarre grounds that the United States was entitled to defend itself against an alleged Iraqi conspiracy to carry out an attempt on the life of President George Bush Sr two months earlier.[13] In mid-December 1998, the United States and Britain launched a joint four-day bombing campaign against Iraq known as 'Operation Desert Fox', which involved firing 415 cruise missiles against Iraqi targets.[14] Neither of these military attacks was authorised by the United Nations Security Council, and neither of them was permitted by the United Nations Charter.

These were the most intense attacks carried out under Clinton, but there was also the continuous low-level warfare involved in maintaining the 'no-fly zones' over northern and southern Iraq. In April 1991, the United States and Britain ordered Iraq not to fly aircraft above the 36th parallel covering much of northern Iraq. In August 1992, a similar order was made for Iraqi airspace below the 32nd parallel. In September 1996, the southern no-fly zone was raised to the 33rd parallel, ensuring that most of Iraqi airspace was banned to both military and civilian flights by Iraqi aircraft. (France participated in patrolling the no-fly zones for many years, but ended its involvement after Operation Desert Fox in December 1998.[15]) During 1999, UN Humanitarian Coordinator Hans von Sponeck reported later, UN staff observed 28 US or UK air strikes in Iraq out of a total of 132 recorded incidents which reportedly lead to the deaths of 144 civilians, and injuries for 446 more.[16] While the US and UK claimed to be upholding UN Security Council Resolution 688, which called on the Ba'athist regime to cease its repression of the Iraqi people, that Resolution did not contain any provisions for enforcement, did not establish any 'no-fly' zones in Iraq, and did not authorise the use of military force.[17]

In brief, President Clinton was no stranger to the illegal use of force against Iraq, unauthorised by any UN Resolutions.

'REGIME CHANGE' BY ENCLAVE

President Clinton had, by the time of the PNAC letter in January 1998, developed a policy of 'containment plus regime change' towards Iraq.[18] The PNAC agenda, which became a serious influence on US foreign policy towards Iraq under President George W. Bush, involved a greater willingness to use military force on a larger scale. The shift in rhetoric from 'containment' to 'regime change' did not signal a move from 'legality' to 'illegality', or from 'multilateralism' to 'unilateralism'. President Clinton's policy towards Iraq was riddled with illegality. As for 'multilateralism', you could hardly find a clearer example of US unilateralism than Operation Desert Fox, launched as the UN Security Council sat down to consider Iraq's record of cooperation with UN weapons inspectors, and to decide on the appropriate action to take towards Baghdad.[19]

However, it would be wrong to suggest that the PNAC in 1998 was proposing the kind of full-scale invasion of Iraq that took place in the spring of 2003. Mr Wolfowitz, then dean of the Nitze School of Advanced International Studies of the Johns Hopkins University, made a very different proposal on behalf of the hawks in September 1998:

> Administration officials continue to claim that the only alternative to maintaining the unity of the UN Security Council is to send U.S. forces to Baghdad. That is wrong. As has been said repeatedly in letters and testimony to the President and the Congress by myself and other former defense officials, including two former secretaries of defense, and a former director of central intelligence, the key lies not in marching U.S. soldiers to Baghdad, but in helping the Iraqi people to liberate themselves from Saddam. . .
>
> The heart of such action would be to create a liberated zone in Southern Iraq comparable to what the United States and its partners did so successfully in the North in 1991.

Mr Wolfowitz remarked, 'This would be a formidable undertaking, and certainly not one which will work if we insist on maintaining the unity of the UN Security Council.'[20] In other words, it would require illegal intervention in Iraq.

The right-wing *Weekly Standard* commented, 'This is not a plan for victory on the cheap'. The liberated zone would have to be protected by the US military from the air 'and, if necessary, on the ground'. That would require 'beefing up our ground and air forces' in the Middle East. 'But unlike a one-shot cruise-missile strike, the Wolfowitz plan offer[ed] a chance for a lasting solution to the Iraqi crisis.'[21]

This 'enclave' proposal spawned variants and much debate among hawks.[22] It reached its final form in the plan put forward by the Iraqi National Congress (INC), the umbrella group for the Iraqi opposition, in late 2001. Drawing on advice from US Special Forces General Wayne Downing, the INC drew up an imaginative war plan for taking on Baghdad. Revised after 11 September, the plan called for:

- military training and arms for 5,000 Iraqi dissidents,
- an invasion of southern Iraq by this force (supported by thousands of US Special Forces troops and some mercenaries),
- the declaration by the US of a 'no-drive' zone in southern Iraq, banning the movement of Iraqi tanks and armoured vehicles, to protect the invasion force,
- support and participation from Iran,
- an uprising by Iraqi Shias in the south, and
- preparations for attack by Kurdish groups in the north of Iraq.

According to investigative journalist Seymour Hersh, 'If all went as planned, dissent would quickly break out inside the Iraqi military, and Saddam Hussein would be confronted with a dilemma: whether to send his elite forces south to engage the Americans or, for his own protection, keep all his forces nearby to guard against an invasion from the north.' The whole purpose of this strategy was to provoke a retaliation from Baghdad's heavy armour. A US adviser to the INC told Mr Hersh that success depended on tempting an Iraqi military response: 'if he doesn't come, you go home and say we failed.' On the other hand, if the Iraqi tanks did come, they would be destroyed by US air power. The fall-back position would be, if the tanks did not come, but the INC managed to capture Basra, then 'that's the end. You don't have to go to Baghdad. You tie up his oil and he'll collapse.' (The consequences for the humanitarian oil-for-food programme of ending the sale of oil for an extended period do not seem to have received a great deal of consideration.) The INC–Downing plan was then augmented and modified by a Pentagon planning group on the orders of Paul Wolfowitz, by then US Deputy Defence Secretary, and sent to the US Joint Chiefs of Staff (who tore it to pieces).[23]

While it is clear that there were differences between President Clinton's 'containment plus regime change' and the Paul Wolfowitz 'enclave' strategy, it would be wrong to conclude that there was a fundamental legal or political difference between the two approaches towards Iraq. Both involved the illegal and unilateral use of force, and both aimed to topple Saddam Hussein. It would also be wrong to misunderstand the January 1998 letter from the Project for the New American Century as a blueprint for the kind of war that eventually took place in March-April 2003. The PNAC signatories were committed to explicitly targeting Saddam Hussein, and they were prepared to engage the regime with considerable military forces, but they were not proposing a full-scale US invasion of Iraq. The Wolfowitz 'enclave' strategy of employing Iraqi exiles to do the main fighting was an attempted middle way between fostering coups and shooting cruise missiles at one end of the scale, and the half-million-strong invasion advocated by the Pentagon at the other end of the scale. (The whole range of options was illegal, it is worth bearing in mind.) Note that the Wolfowitz plan was not simply a propaganda device adopted in 1998 to cloak a hidden determination to launch a major invasion once in office. The plan was actively championed by Mr Wolfowitz after 11 September, when he sent it to the (extremely hostile) Joint Chiefs of Staff. The hawks believed in the exile invasion option, and they saw that as the road to 'regime change'. (The professional military, on the other hand, saw it as the road to a 'Bay of Goats', a national humiliation to compare with the failed invasion of Cuba using a similar strategy in 1963.[24])

The difference between the Clinton approach to Iraq and the Bush approach to Iraq can be summed up in a word. President Clinton's Undersecretary of State Thomas Pickering said in August 2000 regarding US policy towards Iraq, 'Our magic formula, in reality, is patience.'[25] In contrast, the 'magic formula' of the Administration of George W. Bush was to be 'impatience'.

CHAPTER III
First Strike

The February 2001 Bombing Of Baghdad

TRANSLATING COMMITMENT INTO ACTION

President Bush entered the White House determined to take decisive action against Saddam Hussein. David Frum, one of the President's speechwriters, met Mr Bush for his first briefing in mid-February 2001. Mr Bush made clear among other things his 'determination to dig Saddam Hussein out of power in Iraq.' Mr Frum later wrote, 'He spoke with a commanding self-assurance I had never seen in his public appearances, not even in the small-scale events I had attended over the previous three weeks.'[1]

It was not merely a matter of words. On 16 February 2001, US F-16 strike aircraft and British Tornado GR1 bombers hit targets around the Iraqi capital, Baghdad, beyond the boundaries of the 'no-fly' zones the US and Britain had declared over southern and northern Iraq. The US warplanes fired new satellite-guided AGM-130 missiles at five radar and command centres to the north, north-west and south of Baghdad. The RAF Tornados launched an unknown number of Paveway III 'bunker-busters' (designed to destroy heavily fortified installations) at the southern-most target, An Numaniyah control centre, the only target inside the southern no-fly zone.[2]

In his first public statement on the bombing, George W. Bush said, 'Saddam Hussein has got to understand that we expect him to conform to the agreement that he signed after he lost the 1991 Gulf war. We will enforce the no-fly zone, both south and north.'[3] Michael O'Hanlon, at the mainstream think-tank the Brookings Institution in Washington DC, described the President as seeming to 'merge different concepts in his head in a random and somewhat illogical way.' Mr O'Hanlon pointed out that the 3 March 1991 cease-fire agreement did not impose no-fly zones on Iraq. In fact, the agreement was actually quite notorious at the time for *lifting* the total no-fly zone over Iraq, and was widely criticised for this very reason. The US commander-in-chief of the 1991 war effort,

General Norman Schwartzkopf, had banned anything flying in Iraqi airspace. However, at the end of the 3 March meeting to negotiate the surrender, Iraqi generals pleaded to be allowed the use of helicopters. This was permitted.[4] In the days that followed, Iraqi helicopter gunships were used, under the eyes of US and UK pilots, against rebels in the civil war which had been encouraged by President Bush Sr. Pentagon spokesperson, Pete Williams, acknowledged that Iraq was using helicopters against the rebels, saying, 'Is our policy somewhat ambiguous? Yes.'[5] So if President Bush Jr expected Baghdad to live up to the agreement signed at the end of the war, he should have followed the policy of his father and allowed the helicopter gunships to fly freely, strafing rebels and civilians.

Kenneth Adelman, a hawk in the Cheney-Rumsfeld mould,[6] had told the *New Yorker* magazine some weeks earlier, 'Ideally, the first crisis [of the new Bush administration] would be something with Iraq. It would be a way to make the point that it's a new world.' The London *Guardian* commented, 'Sentiments like this raise the possibility that the Pentagon and the White House played more of a role in creating the conditions for [the US/UK air strikes of 16 February 2001] than they are letting on.'[7] The *Observer* noted two days after the bombing that after President Bush's inauguration on 20 January, US/UK attacks on Iraqi anti-aircraft targets were 'ramped up again', with nine attacks on Iraqi anti-aircraft targets in the southern no-fly zone before 16 February.[8] According to figures released by Downing Street, the frequency of US/UK attacks in the southern no-fly zone more than doubled from an average of 0.85 attacks per week in 2000 to 2.25 attacks per week in the first few weeks of Mr Bush's Presidency.[9]

It may be that the large-scale US/UK bombing of Iraq on 16 February 2001, President Bush's first major foreign policy action, was partly motivated by a desire to begin moving towards large-scale military intervention. If so, there were two notable responses from the rest of the world which foreshadowed later developments: an enormous wave of hostility from world opinion, and a combination of public solidarity and private reluctance from the British junior partner. To take only one example of international outrage, Egyptian President Hosni Mubarak said, 'The air raids have just complicated the situation and killed innocent people. . . I don't believe Saddam is a threat to the world. Iraq is not a superpower, and it doesn't have sophisticated transcontinental missiles.'[10] The London *Guardian* said simply, 'This American president is dangerous.'[11]

MR BLAIR'S DOUBLE U-TURN

As for British reluctance, displayed on a larger scale a year later, there was an interesting hidden story which casts a curious light on the Anglo-American war of 2003. The *Washington Post* reported that Britain had threatened to pull out of further air strikes against Iraq because of increasing military concern that it was difficult to see what they were achieving: 'Frustration quickly set in as pilots understood they were taking risks over Iraq for no real military purpose.' 'Britain, the last ally willing to fly with the Americans over Iraq quietly passed the word to Washington that a more focused and effective strategy was needed to justify continued military action.'[12]

Weeks earlier, the *Guardian* had reported that the British government, 'in a policy U-turn', was about to propose to the incoming US administration that the bombing of targets over southern Iraq should be stopped. 'In an attempt to deflect criticism, the British government has been looking behind-the-scenes at the introduction of so-called "smart" sanctions and an end to the southern [but not the northern] no-fly zone.' The MOD, which had spent more than £800m policing the zones, was said to be increasingly uneasy about the possibility of an RAF pilot being shot down, while 'the bombing has led to public concern, especially after evidence that victims have included civilians.'[13]

Two weeks later, days after the Bush inauguration and three weeks before the major bombardment of 16 February, the Ministry of Defence was reported as saying that 'threats posed to British and US aircraft patrolling the no-fly zones had diminished' with 'fewer threats to the patrolling jets' in the last year. 'Although the official said that Britain's "overall strategic objectives" remained the same, the change in tone may reflect a realisation in Whitehall that US and British tactics have not swayed President Saddam.'[14]

In the six weeks before the major airstrikes on Iraq, then, the British government made it known that it favoured the end of the southern no-fly zone; the threat to British aircraft from Iraqi air defences had diminished; (rather contradictorily) Britain was expressing 'increasing unease' about the possibility of an RAF pilot being shot down in the southern no-fly zone; it was adopting a 'change of tone' towards Iraq; it was realising that its previous tactics had failed to 'sway' Baghdad; and it was hinting to reporters that the southern no-fly zone no longer served any purpose.

THE BACK CHANNEL TO BAGHDAD

In the aftermath of the 16 February air strikes, it was revealed that British officials had 'opened behind-the-scenes channels to Iraq in an attempt to reach a compromise' that would lead to the return of UN arms inspectors to Baghdad and the suspension of sanctions.[15] Peter Hain, a junior Foreign Office minister with responsibility for the Middle East at the time, actually admitted as much in November 2000, expressing the desire to find a solution consistent with Iraq's 'dignity'—a rare concern for a British minister over the past decade.[16] British officials said that these comments represented 'a markedly different, more conciliatory message about Iraq—though not a change of policy.'[17]

THE POLITICAL COST OF SANCTIONS

In this connection, it is worth noting that Liberal Democrat foreign policy spokesperson Menzies Campbell, condemning the British government's 'undeclared war' on Iraq on 10 November 2000, also reiterated his party's call for the lifting of non-military sanctions against Iraq. The *Guardian* reported, 'His remarks, coming at a time when sanctions against Iraq are crumbling fast, are particularly significant since Mr Campbell is close to the Foreign Office establishment. There are many in the FO who believe that the government's policy towards Iraq is unsustainable.'[18] This seemed to be confirmed in the aftermath of the US/UK strikes by the report in the *Telegraph* that, 'Foreign Office officials have been privately rethinking the sanctions policy given the growing difficulty of defending it in the Arab world, and even at home.'[19]

According to the *Guardian*, in an attempt to 'turn foreign and domestic opinion around', ministers were 'actively considering a dual track strategy': they were looking at plans for 'smart sanctions' combined with 'a new propaganda drive highlighting the repression carried out by the Iraqi regime.' The aim was to 'refocus the public debate', according to a British official.[20] This was a goal shared in the State Department. Incoming US Secretary of State Colin Powell said in February 2001 that he believed the West could 'keep the box as tightly closed' on Iraq as it had in the past decade, 'without receiving on our shoulders all the baggage that goes with it.'[21] The 'baggage' was the outrage and condemnation and isolation caused by the US/UK hard line adherence to economic sanctions on Iraq. Sanctions would be focused more tightly on stopping imports that could be used by the Iraqi military or in weapons programmes, and on damaging the finances and freedom of movement of President Saddam Hussein and his coterie.[22] The 'smart sanctions' policy developed in the latter stages of President Clinton Administration was being continued and affirmed by President Bush's new Secretary of State.

The reforms in the sanctions regime were superficial. The *Economist* noted: 'although the country would be able to import more, it would still be denied the free movement of labour and capital that it desperately needs if it is at last to start picking itself up . . . Iraq needs massive investment to rebuild its industry, its power grids and its schools, and needs cash in hand to pay its engineers, doctors and teachers. None of this looks likely to happen under smart sanctions.' In brief, the proposed 'smart sanctions' offered 'an aspirin where surgery is called for.'[23] The goal was to minimise not the human cost, but the political cost of US/UK sanctions policy.

HUMILIATING MR BLAIR

Given that the February 2001 strikes were a U-turn on an emerging British U-turn towards Iraq, it is intriguing to inquire to what extent Britain was involved in the decision-making over the strikes. It later transpired that neither the heir to the British throne, arriving in Saudi Arabia for a state visit, nor the Prime Minister's war cabinet—let alone the whole British Cabinet—were informed of the decision beforehand. 'We're only the bloody cabinet. What are these damned pagers supposed to be for?' complained one cabinet minister, who did not hear of the raids until called by the *Sunday Times* three hours later. 'Bombs before polling day. How cynical can you get?' said another minister (Britain was in the run-up to a spring General Election).[24] In a portent for the future, European allies were not informed by the British government, which had in the past proclaimed its desire to be 'at the heart of Europe'. The US also failed to warn the United Nations that it was about to launch attacks on military targets near Baghdad, although there were more than 100 UN staff in the region, despite the fact that Colin Powell met UN Secretary-General Kofi Annan the day before the strikes.[25]

President Bush sought to play down the 16 February 2001 attack as 'routine'; he described the attacks as 'routine' three times in his initial statement on the raids. White House press secretary Ari Fleischer, earlier in the day, used the word 'routine' five times. National Security Adviser Condoleezza Rice used the words 'routine' or 'routinely' four times.[26] If the bombing had been 'routine', then operational decisions would have been made automatically at lower levels in the Gulf, according to the 'rules of engagement' agreed by London and Washington. Edward Luttwak, a fellow at the right-wing Centre for Strategic and International Studies in Washington DC, commented, 'If it had been routine, it would have been targeted on locations inside the no-fly zones' instead of on Baghdad. Local US and British commanders did not have to ask permission to mount 'routine' missions, but this raid, said Mr Luttwak, was personally authorized by both President Bush and Tony Blair: 'If this raid was "routine" then so was President Clinton's "Operation Desert Fox".'[27]

Was the attack 'personally authorized' by Mr Blair? It has been reported that the President approved the strikes after a briefing on the morning of Thursday 15 February. White House and Pentagon officials then apparently called their opposite numbers in the UK 'to confirm that President Bush had given the Pentagon the go-ahead', and British Defence Minister Geoff Hoon spoke to US Defense Secretary Donald Rumsfeld. In one version of events, Mr Hoon was only contacted by the Pentagon on Thursday night, London time: 'He spoke to the Prime Minister and consultations with the Americans and British defence staff continued through the night.'[28] Unease about Britain's role in the raids grew after it emerged that President Bush had failed to call Mr Blair on a special hotline before the strikes commenced. 'The absence of the courtesy call was in marked contrast with the warm relations enjoyed by Blair when Bill Clinton was president. Both men spoke each time before the two countries went into battle in the Gulf, Bosnia and Kosovo.'[29] US officials said that because the air strike was 'routine', it therefore did not require any conversation between President Bush and Prime Minister Blair before the USAF and RAF launched their attack.[30]

It seems reasonable to characterise the 24-hour notice of the air strikes given to Mr Blair and Mr Hoon, the lack of a hotline conversation, and the disruption of British policy towards Iraq, as the British Government being bounced into what was potentially a politically costly use of force. It also seems reasonable to suppose that this bombing raid was entered into reluctantly by the Prime Minister, that it was not mounted for electoral gain in the forthcoming General Elections, and that in fact it robbed him of some hopes he may have entertained of minimizing rather than sharply escalating the politically damaging confrontation with Iraq. These hopes were dashed by the magic formula of the impatient hawks within the US Administration.

DERAILING EMERGING US/UK POLICY

As the new US Administration came into power, then, British policy seemed to be moving in the direction of lifting the southern no-fly zone; re-focusing the sanctions regime to be slightly more targeted and slightly less damaging to Iraqi civilians; coaxing Baghdad into re-admitting the weapons inspectors; and pushing for the 'suspension' (not lifting) of economic sanctions. State Department policy seemed to be in concert with this agenda, as Colin Powell's public remarks demonstrated considerable continuity with the later stages of President Clinton's policy towards Iraq. There were grounds for believing that this new line towards Iraq might bear fruit: at the time of President Bush's inauguration, mere weeks before the air strikes, the Iraqi regime 'put out clear feelers to the Bush administration', saying that Baghdad did not threaten 'legitimate American interests'.[31]

The softening of the British hard line, and the continuity of US foreign policy towards Iraq were both sharply disrupted by the 16 February bombardment. Britain's secret attempts to negotiate with Iraq were 'effectively buried' by the air strikes, the *FT* commented.[32] The bombardment was a clear and definite answer to the Iraqi 'feelers', and had the predictable effect of hardening Iraqi attitudes, demonstrated ten days later in the failure of talks between Iraq and the UN Secretary-General. Iraq, which had requested the talks in New York to try to negotiate a new solution to the deadlock over inspections, now used the occasion to raise the stakes considerably. Iraqi Foreign Minister Mohammed Saeed al-Sahaf told reporters no inspectors would return to Iraq. If they did return, they would have to visit all countries in the region and 'first Israel because they have atomic arsenals and all other arsenals.' The Foreign Minister added defiantly, 'There will be no return for any inspectors to Iraq—even if the sanctions are totally lifted.'[33]

It is difficult to avoid the conclusion that the decision to strike was the result of the domination of foreign policy, at that moment, by Mr Rumsfeld and Mr Cheney. At the time of the bombing, White House officials admitted privately that work on forging a new approach to dealing with the Iraqi leader was still not finished inside President Bush's new National Security team.[34] The *FT* commented, 'Although it is tempting to read Friday's attack as signalling a new assertive policy towards Iraq, in fact the Bush administration's approach is still under review. The task of running background checks on every new appointment means the people who would craft such a strategy have not yet started.' The *FT* also noted that 'Some clues about administration thinking have come from Colin Powell, secretary of state, the senior administration official who has spoken most extensively about Iraq [who has] depicted the Iraq issue as essentially an arms control problem'.[35] While Mr Powell framed the Iraq issue as 'essentially an arms control problem,' the hawks were in favour of a more aggressive policy. The Rumsfeld-Cheney-Wolfowitz axis took the opportunity, while policy was unformed and the 'National Security team' still unfinished, to push their own agenda and fill the policy vacuum. They succeeded in stamping their authority on US foreign policy, disrupting State Department policy continuity with the Clinton era, derailing the softening British policy towards Baghdad, and establishing a new confrontational attitude towards Iraq.

CHAPTER IV
Sickly Inhibitions

The Political Significance
Of 11 September

THE VIETNAM SYNDROME

Mr Bush entered power with a bombardment of Baghdad. He made clear to his staff his visceral determination to 'dig Saddam Hussein out of power'. However, the new Administration faced several obstacles in its mission to escalate US military intervention against Baghdad. The most significant was US public opinion.

During the US wars in Indochina in the 1960s and early 1970s, the US people had seen enormous destruction inflicted on defenceless peasant societies. Hundreds of thousands of North Americans had responded by organising a movement of protest and resistance, leaving a lasting mark on the public mind. The unwillingness of the people of the United States to engage in further wars in the Third World became known in élite circles as the 'Vietnam Syndrome'. Noam Chomsky, professor of linguistics at the Massachusetts Institute of Technology and a leading critic of US foreign policy for nearly forty years, notes that the term 'syndrome' was a way of stigmatising public repugnance as a diseased political condition. Professor Chomsky describes the Vietnam Syndrome more accurately as 'the reluctance on the part of large sectors of the population of the West to tolerate the programs of aggression, subversion, massacre, and brutal exploitation that constitute the actual historical experience of much of the Third World.' This reluctance is an annoying domestic barrier to military intervention to defend what are called 'our interests'. These guiding interests are in reality, Professor Chomsky observes, 'the interests of those whose power in the private economy gives them a dominant influence over policy formation, and who believe that they stand to gain (though "we" may not) by maintaining a world system in which they are free to exploit human and material resources.'[1]

Returning to the Vietnam Syndrome, two decades ago, right-wing commentator Norman Podhoretz, editor of the journal *Commentary*, condemned the 'sickly inhibitions against the use of military force' that had developed after Vietnam. He hoped that these inhibitions had been cured by the heroic conquest of Grenada by President Reagan's 6,000 elite troops in 1983 (facing a few dozen Cubans and a few Grenadan militiamen).[2] In fact, there have been many hopeful cures for the Syndrome. The US Embassy hostage crisis in Iran that began in November 1979, and the Soviet invasion of Afghanistan that same year, were both seen in this light. The Reagan Administration believed that it was in a position to step up direct US military intervention in Central America, allocating $25 million worth of arms and ammunition to El Salvador, and despatching twenty more US military 'advisers' on 2 March 1981. In response, an enormous Central America solidarity movement grew up to oppose deepening military involvement in what was dubbed America's 'second Vietnam'. Congressional sources reported, for example, that letters from constituents were twenty-to-one against the military aid programme. On 3 May 1981, a mere two months after the aid package was announced, 100,000 people marched on the Pentagon in the largest anti-war demonstration since Vietnam, in parallel with a march of 25,000 people in San Francisco.[3] The Reaganites were forced to scale back their plans.

Professor Chomsky observed in 1992 after the collapse of the Soviet Empire, 'I don't think the US is going to intervene more than it did in the past. It's not deterred any longer by Soviet power, but it's deterred internally.' He cited a National Security Policy Review document drawn up during the administration of President Bush Sr which concluded that in the future 'much weaker enemies' had to be defeated 'decisively and rapidly', because domestic 'political support' was so thin.[4]

11 SEPTEMBER 2001

With the terrorist attacks of 11 September 2001, US public opinion changed dramatically. The President's approval ratings shot into the stratosphere. The Stars and Stripes flew everywhere. David Frum, a right-wing speechwriter for President Bush, has commented, 'It will someday be difficult to describe to people who did not live through the 9/11 attacks the blood-red fury that swept the country in the days afterward.'[5]

To select just one out of the dozens of similar opinion polls, *USA Today* and CNN conducted a Gallup poll in late November 2001 which found that 87 per cent of respondents approved of the way in which President George W. Bush was handling his job. 62 per cent of Americans believed that the United States should respond to terrorism by mounting a long-term 'war against terrorism' (up from 49 per cent in early October) as opposed to just punishing the specific terrorists involved in particular acts of terrorism (31 per cent, down from 43 per cent). The 'war on terrorism' was expected to be long (87 per cent), and difficult (95 per cent). Only 5 per cent of people felt the US should not take any military action in response to terrorism. There was 92 per cent approval of the war in Afghanistan, 91 per cent approval of the presence of US ground troops in that country, and 74 per cent support for sending US troops to the Persian Gulf in order to remove Saddam Hussein from power in Iraq.[6]

On the dissident fringes of society, African-American rappers, more often than not hostile to the US authorities in the tradition of Malcolm X, followed the movement of opinion. A noted MC known as Canibus released a song called 'Draft Me', supporting the war in Afghanistan: 'Draft me! I wanna fight for my country/Jump in a humvee and murder those monkeys/Draft me! I'm too dedicated to fail/Justice must prevail, justice must prevail.' The well-known New York collective, the Wu-Tang Clan inserted a verse into their new album that included the line, 'America, together we stand, divided we fall.' Suge Knight, head of Death Row Records, told the *Washington Post*, 'We're supporting the USA. At this moment, there's no such thing as ghetto, middle class or rich. There's only the United States.'[7]

In the North American heartland, among the thousands of young people who did join the US armed forces was Pat Tillman, a star player with the Arizona Cardinals American football team, who gave up his $1.2 million a year paycheque to join the US Army. Arizona Senator John McCain, the Vietnam veteran who challenged George W. Bush for the Republican presidential nomination, expressed his admiration for Mr Tillman's sacrifice and commented, 'Perhaps the last vestiges of the Vietnam War have disappeared in the rubble of the World Trade Centre.'[8]

THE 'OPPORTUNITY'

Recall the wistful desire of US hawk Kenneth Adelman: 'Ideally, the first crisis [of the George W. Bush administration] would be something with Iraq. It would be a way to make the point that it's a new world.'[9] The airstrikes signalled something, and they achieved the disruption of foreign policy continuity with the Clinton era, but they did not by themselves make it clear that it was a 'new world', or, to use a phrase adopted by the elder Mr Bush, a 'new world order'. Something more vigorous would be needed to decisively break with the 'sickly inhibitions' hobbling US power.

In its letter to President Clinton in January 1998, the Project for the New American Century urged Mr Clinton to adopt a 'new strategy', and a new 'willingness to undertake military action' in order to 'protect our vital interests in the Gulf'.[10] However, the idea of 'forceful intervention in the Gulf to secure US vital interests' did not play very well with the voters—as it effectively meant 'war for the control of Middle Eastern oil'. The public were not enthusiastic about the idea of invading Iraq (even by proxy), and reluctant to concede even their acquiescence in large-scale military action against Iraq. The initial assault on Baghdad in February 2001 did not change this reality. The public relations problem remained unsolved. Then came the terrorist atrocities of 11 September.

As noted already, Defense Secretary Rumsfeld responded the next day, before any evidence was available as to the perpetrators, with the question: 'Why shouldn't we go against Iraq, not just al-Qaeda?' Veteran reporter Bob Woodward notes that Rumsfeld was speaking not only for himself when he raised the question: 'His deputy Paul D.

Wolfowitz, was committed to a policy that would make Iraq a principal target of the first round of the war on terrorism.' 'Rumsfeld was raising the possibility that they could take advantage of the opportunity offered by the terrorist attacks to go after Saddam immediately,' writes Mr Woodward.[11]

Mr Rumsfeld was not the only one thinking of 11 September as an 'opportunity'. The President himself, earlier on 12 September, had said in a Cabinet meeting, 'This is a great opportunity. We have to think of this as an opportunity.'[12] While in Bob Woodward's account Mr Bush made this statement in the context of confronting Afghanistan and Pakistan, and 'improving' relations with major powers such as Russia and China, rather than attacking Iraq,[13] the thinking was the same: these atrocities could be politically useful on the international field.

As US leaders sat down to discuss their response to 11 September, Donald Rumsfeld was forced to admit that it could take up to two months to put together a major strike on Afghanistan, because the Pentagon had no plans for attacking the country and no forces in the immediate area. As far as Iraq was concerned though, even before 11 September, 'the Pentagon had been working for months on developing a military option for Iraq.'[14] The hawks in the Administration had a commitment to build on the bombing raid carried out on 16 February 2001, and now they had their 'opportunity'.

THE COUNTER-CURRENT

It is worth pointing out that the 'blood-red fury' that David Frum observed apparently grew more intense the further one went from the sites of the attacks themselves. The *New York Times* reported (somewhat reluctantly) a week after the attacks that 'the drumbeat for war. . . is barely audible on the streets of New York', and that calls for peace 'far outnumber demands for retribution', even at the main outdoor memorial to loss and grief for the victims of the World Trade Centre bombing.[15] Relatives of some of those killed in the World Trade Centre and the Pentagon actually formed an anti-war group named 'Peaceful Tomorrows' to press for a lawful and non-military response to the atrocities, as opposed to massive retaliatory violence.[16] An opinion poll just over a week after the attacks found that given a range of options the overwhelmingly popular choice of people in the US was for targeted strikes against the terrorist group which carried out the attacks, 'even if it takes months to identify them' (62 per cent of respondents in the US, 82 per cent in the UK). The US Government position (subsequently implemented) to take action against known terrorists 'even if it is not clear who caused the attacks', received the support of only 23 per cent of people in the US (13 per cent in the UK).[17] There were strong counter-currents in the United States to the blood-red tide of 'patriotism' which was harnessed by the Bush Administration.

The Vietnam Syndrome may not yet be entirely cured.

CHAPTER V
George Bush Lied

Misconnecting Iraq, WMD And Terrorism

THE FLUCTUATING RATIONALE

Vice-Admiral Sir Nicholas Hill-Norton noted less than a week before the war that Cabinet Ministers had 'failed to persuade their own electorate' of the threat from Iraq and the necessity for war:

> Joe Public (UK), without access to the sensitive technical and human intelligence that informs our decision-makers, cannot but be bemused. The 'war on terrorism' (mostly al-Qaeda) suddenly changed abruptly to 'Iraq and weapons of mass destruction' without any convincing linkage between the two and, despite intensive intelligence focus and months of inspection, no hard evidence (at least in the public domain) that these weapons exist.

Sir Nicholas, who served as Deputy Chief of the British Defence Staff from 1992 to 1995, suggested that, 'Our brave and loyal men and women in the front line deserve more objective and persuasive evidence and analysis before they are committed to battle for this cause. So do the rest of us.'[1]

The same charge of inconstancy had been made a month earlier by retired Marine General Anthony Zinni, the former commander-in-chief of US Central Command:

> Initially, there was at least an implication that [Iraq] was linked to terrorism. When that link couldn't be made, it was possession of weapons of mass destruction. When that case couldn't be made, it was lack of cooperation. Right now, it's down to 'You won't let us talk to your scientists' as the reason for going to war. And 'We know what the Iraqis have, but we can't tell you.' I just think it's too confusing.[2]

FROM 'TERRORISM' TO 'IRAQ'

Let us return to the beginning of this tangled trail of justifications. In his January 2002 State of the Union address, President Bush broadened the 'war on terror' initiated in response to 11 September. Mr Bush said that the US would pursue 'two great objectives': 'First, we will shut down terrorist camps, disrupt terrorist plans, and bring terrorists to justice. And, second, we must prevent the terrorists and regimes who seek chemical, biological or nuclear weapons from threatening the United States and the world.' Three countries were mentioned in the latter category, the famous 'axis of evil'. While Iran and North Korea were dismissed with a mere sentence each, Iraq received rather more emotionally charged treatment:

> This is a regime that has already used poison gas to murder thousands of its own citizens—leaving the bodies of mothers huddled over their dead children. This is a regime that agreed to international inspections—then kicked out the inspectors.'[3]

(In fact, Baghdad did not kick out the inspectors.[4]) Interestingly, Mr Bush did not demand the return of the UN weapons inspectors, demonstrating a lack of real interest in disarmament, an important issue we will return to. Continuing with the speech, the President then produced his famous phrase to capture Iran, North Korea and Iraq and their alleged allies in the world of international terrorism:

> States like these, and their terrorist allies, constitute an axis of evil, arming to threaten the peace of the world. By seeking weapons of mass destruction, these regimes pose a grave and growing danger. They could provide these arms to terrorists, giving them the means to match their hatred. They could attack our allies or attempt to blackmail the United States.[5]

In his January 2003 State of the Union address, Mr Bush stated that 'the gravest danger in the war on terror, the gravest danger facing America and the world, is outlaw regimes that seek and possess nuclear, chemical, and biological weapons'. The 'regimes' had moved centre stage.

The danger from Saddam Hussein was that, 'Secretly, and without fingerprints, he could provide one of his hidden weapons to terrorists, or help them develop their own.'[6] The field had narrowed down to one country: Iraq 'could' provide a weapon of mass destruction to anti-Western terrorists, or it 'could' help those groups to develop their own weapons of mass destruction. This was the rather tentative connection.

MISCONNECTING IRAQ: 11 SEPTEMBER

11 September was a low-technology attack involving a group of 19 non-Iraqi hijackers, only eight of whom appear to have known that they were on a suicide mission.[7] No weapons of any sort appear to have been passed to the hijackers from any state. The attacks did not involve the use of chemical, biological or nuclear weapons. It seems

difficult at first sight to weave together the World Trade Centre and Pentagon attacks with the supposed threat from Baghdad. Nevertheless, this public relations triumph was accomplished to a significant degree. A national opinion poll in the US in January 2003 found that half of those surveyed said (wrongly) that one or more of the 11 September hijackers were Iraqi citizens. Nearly a quarter of respondents thought the Bush administration had publicly released evidence tying Iraq to the planning and funding of the 11 September attacks. More than a third didn't know or refused to answer the question. In its report on the poll, the *Miami Herald* added, 'No such evidence has been released.'[8]

No funding trail for the atrocities has ever been discovered leading back to Iraq. No Iraqi involvement in the plot has ever been uncovered. The strongest alleged link was the supposed meeting in Prague between Mohammed Atta, the 11 September ringleader, and an Iraqi diplomat named Ahmad al-Ani, later expelled from the Czech Republic for spying. But in the spring of 2002 the Bush Administration finally accepted that this alleged 'meeting' in Prague never happened.[9] The reluctant US admission came more than four months after Jiri Kolar, the Czech police chief, announced the conclusion of an exhaustive police investigation into the matter, saying that there were 'no documents showing that Atta visited Prague at any time' in 2001.[10]

MISCONNECTING IRAQ: AL-QAEDA

An anonymous former CIA officer remarked within days of 11 September, 'The reality is that Osama bin Laden doesn't like Saddam Hussein. Saddam is a secularist who has killed more Islamic clergy than he has Americans. They have almost nothing in common except a hatred of the US. Saddam is the ultimate control freak, and for him terrorists are the ultimate loose cannon.'[11] US General Brent Scowcroft, former National Security Adviser to President Bush Sr during the 1991 Gulf War, argued before the war that Iraq should not be part of the new war on terrorism at all: 'It's not a terrorist state.' Saddam Hussein was 'primarily a problem of hostile military power.' He might acquire weapons of mass destruction or he might not. 'But it's a pretty traditional enemy.'[12] Veteran Middle East reporter Robert Fisk, who has interviewed the al-Qaeda leader, observed that, 'Mr bin Laden hates Saddam Hussein, regarding him as a Western-created dictator—a not entirely inaccurate description.'[13]

THE ZARQAWI/ANSAR DEBACLE

In his attempts to link the secular Ba'athist regime to the fundamentalist al-Qaeda network, Secretary of State Colin Powell constructed an elaborate intermediary structure, a deadly terrorist network based in northern Iraq headed by one Abu Musab al-Zarqawi, who was said to be 'an associate and collaborator of Usama bin Laden and his al-Qaida lieutenants.' Mr Powell told the UN Security Council that Mr Zarqawi's network was 'teaching its operatives how to produce ricin and other poisons' in a camp in northeastern Iraq, a 'sinister nexus' between Baghdad and al-Qaeda. It was a little difficult, however, to reconcile this claim with the Secretary of State's admission that the 'poison camp' was 'in northern Kurdish areas outside Saddam Hussein's control'.

The alleged poison factory was actually the base of a Iraqi fundamentalist group known as Ansar al-Islam. Mr Powell alleged (without proof) that Baghdad had an agent in the most senior levels of Ansar al-Islam, and that, 'In 2000, this agent offered al-Qaida safe haven in the region.' Furthermore, 'Zarqawi's activities are not confined to this small corner of northeast Iraq. He travelled to Baghdad in May of 2002 for medical treatment, staying in the capital of Iraq for two months while he recuperated to fight another day.' During his stay, allegedly, nearly two dozen extremists converged on Baghdad and established a base of operations: 'These al-Qaida affiliates based in Baghdad now coordinate the movement of people, money and supplies into and throughout Iraq for his network, and they have now been operating freely in the capital for more than eight months.'

'From his terrorist network in Iraq, Zarqawi can direct his network in the Middle East and beyond.' In particular, Mr Powell attributed the assassination of US Government official Laurence Foley in Amman, Jordan, in October 2001 to a Zarqawi network cell, and described the curious 'ricin plot' the police 'discovered' in North London[14] as yet another Zarqawi poison-making cell.

Powell sneered, 'Iraqi officials deny accusations of ties with al-Qaida. These denials are simply not credible.' Credible with who? Security sources in London retorted that both they and the CIA remained unconvinced. According to British and US intelligence sources the 'new' material presented to the UN Security Council originated from Iraqi opposition groups and was not regarded as reliable.[15]

Firstly, let us take the issue of links between al-Ansar and Baghdad. Tariq Aziz, Iraqi Deputy Prime Minister, countered that al-Ansar was based outside Iraqi government control and Baghdad supported the Kurdish group in that area, the Patriotic Union of Kurdistan (PUK), when it was attacked by the Islamists. A British security source said: 'That, indeed, appears to be the case and Jalal Talabani [the PUK leader] has told the Americans about this.'[16] Mullah Krekar, the leader of al-Ansar, lives in Norway: 'I can say to you that this is not true that I am a link between Saddam Hussein and al-Qaeda . . . Our aim has always been the toppling of the Iraqi Baath regime.' Mullah Krekar denied the allegation that Abu Wael, another al-Ansar leader, was an Iraqi intelligence liaison officer to the group. He claimed, to the contrary, that Iraqi agents tried to poison Abu Wael in 1992, and would kill him if they could.

Veteran CIA analyst Melvin Goodman, who heads the National Security Project and maintains contacts with former colleagues, summarized the feelings of many in the intelligence community on both sides of the Atlantic: 'I've talked to my sources at the CIA and all of them are saying the evidence [of a link between al-Qaeda and Saddam] is simply not there.'[17]

What about the 'Zarqawi network'? Rohan Gunaratna, the author of *Inside al-Qaeda*, and a mainstream bin Laden expert, said that Mr Powell had failed to prove that Saddam was supporting the terrorist group. In particular, Dr Gunaratna scorned claims that

Zarqawi could head a terror network stretching from Russia to Britain, as Mr Powell had alleged, pointing out that al-Qaeda is organised into cells whose members know only their immediate comrades.[18] British security sources confirmed that there was no solid evidence to support Mr Powell's allegations. One referred to 'jumping to conclusions', and suggested that the US was making a leap too far. Another added: 'It is all a question of interpretation', and insisted it was far too early to make a proper assessment of the terrorist networks.[19]

What about Mr Zarqawi himself? British journalists interviewed jihadists who knew him in Afghanistan, and discovered that he went to Afghanistan in 1990 to fight the Russians. He stayed on after Taliban arrived, but chose to live in an area ruled by the anti-Taliban warlord Gulbuddin Hekmatyar. Mr Zarqawi apparently formed a close-knit group of Jordanians (not Iraqis) linked to the traditional Islamic resistance group, the Muslim Brotherhood. 'There wasn't even a training camp,' said a former Arab *mujahid*. According to Jordanian intelligence, Mr Zarqawi fled from Afghanistan in late 2001, into Iran, where he was deported. He went on to Baghdad, where he received treatment for his wounds and had his leg amputated.[20]

While Mr Zarqawi received medical treatment in an Iraqi hospital, there is apparently no evidence that he contacted Iraqi officials during his time in the capital. The *Telegraph* reported that the attempt by both the White House and the Pentagon to make a clear and definite link between al-Zarqawi, Ansar al-Islam and Saddam Hussein had 'infuriated many within the United States intelligence community'. One intelligence source said, 'The intelligence is practically non-existent,' adding, 'It is impossible to support the bald conclusions being made by the White House and the Pentagon given the poor quantity and quality of the intelligence available. There is uproar within the intelligence commu-nity on all of these points, but the Bush White House has quashed dissent.'[21]

Mr Powell disclosed that the US had asked via an intermediary for the extradition of Zarqawi, but Baghdad had failed to hand him over. British 'sources with access to intel-ligence' responded that Zarqawi had travelled around the Middle East but was 'not in Iraq' at the time of Mr Powell's Security Council speech. Furthermore, the British sources were not aware Mr Zarqawi had even visited north-eastern Iraq, where his 'network' was supposed to be based.[22]

According to the CIA, Mr Zarqawi's name did not figure on its list of the 22 most wanted Islamic terrorists, and he had never been mentioned in the list of senior al-Qaeda men in bin Laden's entourage in Afghanistan.[23] Mr Zarqawi's prominence does not seem to stem from his powerful position within the al-Qaeda network, a position which does not appear to exist, or from his role as an intermediary between al-Qaeda and Baghdad, a link which also does not appear to exist, or even his allegedly intimate co-operation with al-Ansar Islam, whose northern Iraqi base he does not appear to have even visited.

The only two solid facts in this whole fantasy are that Mr Zarqawi spent time in a Baghdad hospital, and that US aid official Lawrence Foley was killed in Jordan in October 2001. According to Jordanian observers, the Jordanian authorities actually needed a figure like Mr Zarqawi to justify their clamp-down on home-grown Islamists. In particular, Mr Zarqawi made a convenient scapegoat for the killing of Lawrence Foley in Amman. The allegations that Mr Zarqawi was involved stem from confessions of two individuals arrested and 'interrogated' by the Jordanian police, who said that Mr Zarqawi supplied them with weapons and money for attacks. It seems at least possible that these confessions were dictated by the Jordanian authorities in order to taint the Muslim Brotherhood (which Mr Zarqawi is linked with, as already noted) and to help justify their repression of the grouping.[24]

The tissue of fabrications woven so skilfully by Mr Powell has entirely disintegrated. Incidentally, Jordanian sources emphasise Mr Zarqawi's links with Syria, rather than Iraq.[25]

THE BIN LADEN TAPE

What about the evidence of a link between Baghdad and al-Qaeda that appeared to come from Osama bin Laden's own lips?[26] In February 2003, a tape was broadcast by the al-Jazeera television station, in which the al-Qaeda leader proclaimed solidarity with Iraq, in the face of the impending Western invasion. British Defence Secretary Geoff Hoon said this confirmed the link: 'he said it, not us.'[27] Mr Hoon seized on the statement on the tape that 'the interests of Muslims coincide with the interests of the [Ba'athist] socialists in the war against crusaders,' as evidence of close ties between al-Qaeda and the Ba'athist regime.[28] Close ties? Mr bin Laden actually said, 'Regardless of the removal or the survival of the socialist party or Saddam, Muslims in general and the Iraqis in particular must brace themselves for jihad against this unjust campaign and acquire ammunition and weapons.'[29] In other words, Saddam Hussein could drop dead.

Mr bin Laden went on: 'Fighting in support of the non-Islamic banners is forbidden.' This is a clear reference to fighting to defend the secular Ba'ath Party:

> [F]ighting should be for the sake of the one God. It should not be for championing ethnic groups, or for championing the non-Islamic regimes in all Arab countries, including Iraq. . . Muslims' doctrine and banner should be clear in fighting for the sake of God. He who fights to raise the word of God will fight for God's sake. Under these circumstances, there will be no harm if the interests of Muslims converge with the interests of the socialists in the fight against the crusaders, despite our belief in the infidelity of socialists.[30]

The Times had this slightly differently: 'Fighting should be in the name of God only, not [in the name of national ideologies nor] to seek victory for the ignorant governments that rule all Arab states, including Iraq.'[31]

In other words, don't fight for the Ba'athists—they are infidels—but do fight alongside them against their enemies because, in the words of the al-Qaeda leader, 'this crusade war is primarily targeted against the people of Islam'.[32] The interests of Muslims and of the non-Islamic socialist infidels could converge because such things had happened before in history: 'The Muslims' fighting against the Byzantine converged with the interests of the Persians. And this was not detrimental to the companions of the prophet.'[33]

In his most hostile reference to the Ba'athists, Mr bin Laden said, 'whoever supported the United States [in the war in Afghanistan], including *the hypocrites of Iraq* or the rulers of Arab countries... should know that they are apostates and outside the community of Muslims. It is permissible to spill their blood and take their property.'[34]

Interestingly, the speaker on the tape pointedly did not address Saddam Hussein himself, whose demise he clearly would not mourn.[35] If the two leaders had really had a close working relationship, if the Iraqi leader had really been a sponsor of al-Qaeda, if Baghdad had truly functioned as an important operational hub of the international terrorist network, surely there would have been some warm words for the sponsor?

Iraq had an ignorant, hypocritical, infidel, non-Islamic, apostate regime which Muslims should not fight for, nor regret if it failed to survive. With friends like this, who needed enemies? The speech, far from demonstrating Osama bin Laden's close working relationship with Saddam Hussein, actually demonstrated the gulf between them.

MISCONNECTING IRAQ: WMD TRANSFER

The *New York Times* reported in February 2002, 'The Central Intelligence Agency has no evidence that Iraq has engaged in terrorist operations against the United States in nearly a decade, and the agency is also convinced that President Saddam Hussein has not provided chemical or biological weapons to al-Qaeda or related terrorist groups, according to several American intelligence officials.'[36] Richard Butler, former head of the UNSCOM weapons inspectorate, testified to the US Senate Foreign Relations Committee in July 2002 that he had seen no evidence of Iraq providing weapons of mass destruction to terrorist groups outside Iraq: 'I suspect that, especially given his psychology and aspirations, Saddam would be reluctant to share with others what he believes to be an indelible source of his own power.'[37]

In general, such a transfer of powerful weapons to terrorist networks by 'rogue states' seems less likely than the autonomous development of such capacities by terrorist networks. The anthrax attacks in the USA are now recognised to have been the work of a domestic terrorist, and the sarin attacks in the Tokyo underground were the work of a domestic cult. No foreign sponsors appear to have been involved. The authors of these WMD attacks were not even terrorist groups in the conventional sense of the word. Author Felipe Fernandez-Armesto suggests that, 'The threat we face from mad individuals and small, unstable hate-groups is greater than from any international terrorist movement.'[38] This appears to apply *a fortiori* to the risks from Mr Powell's 'sinister nexus'.

The events of the first half of 2003 seem to bear out this judgement. The Iraqi Government, under mortal attack, failed to use whatever weapons of mass destruction it possessed against the invading armies or against Western societies. However, in June 2003, a 45-year-old Iraqi man was arrested in Belgium on charges of premeditated assault and battery, after ten letters containing pesticides and poison were sent to the Prime Minister, and the US, British and Saudi embassies.[39] Whether or not this man was responsible for these attacks, this seems to have been the only chemical weapons revenge attack in response to the war on Iraq. There was no reported state sponsor, and there was no reported link to a state-held reservoir of weapons of mass destruction.

British Foreign Secretary Jack Straw said in January 2003 that the 'most likely sources' of chemical, biological or nuclear weapons for terrorist organizations were 'rogue states' engaged in covert weapons proliferation.[40] The record demonstrates that developing the capacity to produce and deploy chemical and biological weapons does not require the military infrastructure of a state. Given this reality, why would a terrorist group intending to use anthrax or sarin go to the trouble of ingratiating itself with a state sponsor? It would seem to be 'most likely' that a WMD terrorist would attempt to maintain as much secrecy and deniability as possible by involving as few individuals and institutions in the process of acquiring or developing these fearful weapons.

From the other end of the relationship, it is 'highly unlikely' that a rogue state would transfer these kinds of technology and weaponry to a terrorist group. This is the opinion of Daniel Byman, Research Director of the RAND Center for Middle East Public Policy:

> It is also possible that a state actor might provide a nonstate actor with WMD. Such a possibility is highly unlikely, however, because even though developing world militaries sometimes suffer from poor civil-military relations . . . powers that possess WMD typically try to guard its deployment and use, ensuring that special units and hand-picked managers control it. Passing it to a nonstate actor, no matter how close, would go against this tendency.[41]

The conclusions reached in December 1999 by the high-level US panel on these topics, the Gilmore Commission, seem entirely reasonable:

> Although one can never completely discount the possibility that any one of these or other 'terrorist-prone' states (such as Libya and Syria) will deliberately assist a terrorist proxy in its acquisition of a CBRN [chemical, biological, radiological, or nuclear weapons] capability, three main factors appear to militate against such a scenario.
>
> First, governments that have devoted considerable time, effort, and resources to a covert buildup of their CBRN capacity—sometimes at the expense of international legitimacy—are unlikely to want to place these weapons in the hands of groups over which they have no ultimate control. The sponsor in question would likely have no direct ability to influence how the weapons are ultimately used (this, in the final analysis, being the decision of the surrogate group).
>
> Moreover, there would doubtless be grave concerns regarding the security of the weapons once in the hands of the terrorist proxy, the security infrastructure and resources of which are unlikely to match those of the supporting state.
>
> Second, if it were ever discovered that a terrorist CBRN attack had been perpetrated with agents procured from a third party state sponsor, extremely strong, international pressure would build to strike back at the supplier. In this respect, the U.S. cruise missile attack on the al-Shifa pharmaceutical plant in Khartoum, Sudan, following last year's embassy bombings, arguably sent a powerful deterrent message to would-be state sponsors or suppliers of such unconventional weapons to international terrorists.

More important, if the targeted state happened to be a nuclear power, retaliation could well be in the form of a nuclear counterattack, something the U.S. has specifically suggested on a number of occasions.

Third, given the unpredictable nature of the terrorist groups that would be most interested in gaining a CBRN capacity, the possibility of proxies using weapons against the supporting state itself could never be entirely discounted by the terrorists' patron.[42]

The Commission found it significant that there was no evidence of any link between terrorist groups and any state's weapons of mass destruction programmes. The Commission, which included Paul Bremer, later to be imposed on Iraq as de facto US governor in May 2003, quoted a 1997 assessment by the US Defense Intelligence Agency:

> Most of the state sponsors have chemical or biological or radiological material in their stockpiles and therefore have the ability to provide such weapons to terrorists if they wish. However, we have no conclusive information that any sponsor has the intention to provide these weapons to terrorists . . . The likelihood is believed to be low.[43]

The risks for any state passing weapons of mass destruction to a terrorist group would be enormous. To transfer such weapons to representatives of a network such as al-Qaeda would be to effectively hand the survival of your own state to a group of suicidal fanatics. This is hardly the 'most likely' scenario, despite Mr Straw's brave assertions.

THE REAL LINKS: IRAQ AND WMD TERRORISM

We began with President George W. Bush's 'axis of evil' speech, in which he invoked the terrible image of a poison gas attack that left 'the bodies of mothers huddled over their dead children'—a reference to the massacre in the Iraqi Kurdish town of Halabja in 1988. For some reason, President Bush failed to express regret for the response to the Halabja massacre of the United States Government of the time (in which his father served as Vice-President).

In October 1988, staff from the US Senate Foreign Relations Committee issued a report on the Iraqi use of chemical weapons which led the Senate to pass a 'Prevention of Genocide Act'. Peter Galbraith and Christopher Van Hollen, the authors of the report, concluded that chemical weapons were being used to depopulate Iraqi Kurdistan: 'The end result of this policy will be the destruction of the Kurdish identity, Kurdish culture, and a way of life that has endured for centuries.' The key to preventing such an outcome was Western action. Thus far there had been none. The report commented,

> The lack of international response has encouraged Iraq to make more extensive use of chemical weapons. [Saddam may not care much about international opinion, but] the Iraqis do understand more direct forms of pressure. As it seeks to rebuild after eight years of warfare, Iraq will be looking to Western loans, to Western commercial credits, and to Western technology. Sanctions that affected Iraq's ability to borrow or to import Western

goods, including technology, could make the price of continued chemical weapons use and of continuing the slaughter in Iraqi Kurdistan unacceptably high.[44]

No such steps were taken.

Earlier in the Iran-Iraq war, in 1986, when a statement condemning Iraq's 'continued use of chemical weapons' was issued by the country serving as the President of the Security Council, the United States voted against the issuance of this statement. The British Government followed suit.[45]

After Halabja, the US Senate Foreign Relations Committee recommended sanctions against Iraq which would have affected $800 million worth of guaranteed loans. The US Senate passed a 'Prevention of Genocide Act' which would have cut off US loans, military and non-military assistance, credits, credit guarantees, items subject to export controls, and US imports of Iraqi oil. The Reagan-Bush Administration responded by calling sanctions 'terribly premature', and counterproductive for 'billions of dollars of business for US companies' in Iraq.[46]

In the run-up to the war, Tony Blair also exploited the memory of Halabja, noting that it was estimated that 5,000 civilians were murdered and 9,000 wounded in that attack.[47] Unfortunately, Mr Blair also failed to utter any words of regret or remorse for the shameful response of the British Government at the time.

Observer journalist John Sweeney records in his book on British relations with Iraq, *Trading with the Enemy*, that in the five years running up to Halabja (when the Iraqi authorities were using chemical weapons against Iranian troops and Kurdish civilians with abandon), Britain had supplied Iraq with 10,000 nuclear-biological-chemical (NBC) warfare suits; a sophisticated chlorine compressor; and the chemical weapons precursor sodium sulphide—this was exported in January 1988, two months before Halabja. (Recall that during the war in 2003, when the invading forces found NBC suits, this was taken as evidence that Iraq was in possession of weapons of mass destruction.)

After Halabja, the trade continued: three tonnes of nerve gas antidotes were shipped to Iraq a year after Halabja. A senior Foreign Office source conceded in 1991 that 'some of these substances [precursor chemicals for poison gas] were not actually made in Britain, but it was easier for the trade to come through here because of our more favoured trading status with Iraq. In that sense we were a clearing house.'[48]

In the aftermath of Halabja, Labour MP Jeremy Corbyn—later a leading opponent of the 2003 war on Iraq—called on the Conservative Government to institute sanctions against both Iran and Iraq to bring their eight-year war to an end, and to end the use of chemical weapons. Foreign Office Minister David Mellor replied that this would be 'an entirely self-defeating exercise'.[49]

THE REAL SINISTER NEXUS

The real 'sinister nexus' is not between states such as Iraq and loose networks such as al-Qaeda, but between imperial powers such as the United States and Britain, and their clients, such as Colombia, Turkey and Israel, who are granted diplomatic cover and material support as they carry out brutal campaigns against those regarded as powerless and unimportant—a privilege also extended to Iraq during the 1980s.

ANOTHER SINISTER NEXUS

Instead of reducing trade with Iraq, the British Government doubled export credits to Iraq after Halabja, from £175 million in 1988 to £340 million in 1989. Sir Harold Walker, who became Britain's ambassador to Iraq in February 1991, recalled that his brief was to maintain Britain's relations on an even keel with Iraq so that British companies could 'do good business': 'I'm afraid the whole human rights issue was brushed under the carpet. The main priority was trade.'[50]

As for Washington, US Assistant Secretary of State, John Kelly, visited Baghdad almost a year after Halabja to tell Saddam Hussein, 'You are a force for moderation in the region, and the United States wants to broaden her relationship with Iraq.'[51] Massive financial support continued via US agricultural credits to Iraq. In contrast to the Senate Foreign Relations Committee investigation, the British Foreign Office drew up a briefing paper in September 1988 which said that, 'Punitive measures such as unilateral sanctions would not be effective in changing Iraq's behaviour over chemical weapons, and would damage British interests to no avail.'[52]

After Halabja, Iraq managed to shock the world once more with the hanging of *Observer* journalist Farzad Bazoft on 15 March 1990, after being found guilty in an Iraqi court on trumped-up charges of spying. The British ambassador was recalled from Baghdad, but diplomatic ties were not broken, and the £250 million trade credits granted to Iraq in November 1989 were honoured in full. An anonymous Conservative MP was quoted in a British newspaper on the day after Farzad Bazoft's execution: 'I came to the House [of Commons] thinking politics was about ideas. Politics is about money. You decide about the money, and then make the ideas fit.'[53]

'British interests.' 'Doing good business.' 'The main priority was trade.' 'Billions of dollars of business for US companies.' Another real and dangerous 'sinister nexus': profit, power and politics.

THE DISTANT THREAT

Returning to the propaganda campaign carried out to justify war against Iraq, where did the fluctuating rationale finally end up? What was the final resting place of the 'just cause'? In the case of Britain, the final destination of Tony Blair's moral certainty was in his passionate declaration that Iraq posed—not a vivid and immediate danger, but—a nebulous and 'very remote' risk.

In a press conference on 13 January 2003, the British Prime Minister spoke of 'a direct threat' to British national security from those engaging in 'the trade in chemical, biological and nuclear weapons':

And I tell you honestly what my fear is, my fear is that we wake up one day and we find either that one of these dictatorial states has used weapons of mass destruction—and Iraq has done so in the past—and we get sucked into a conflict, with all the devastation that would cause; or alternatively these weapons, which are being traded right round the world at the moment, fall into the hands of these terrorist groups, these fanatics who will stop at absolutely nothing to cause death and destruction on a mass scale. Now that is what I have to worry about. And I understand of course why people think it is a very remote threat and it is far away and why does it bother us. . . [I]t is a matter of time unless we act and take a stand before terrorism and weapons of mass destruction come together, and I regard them as two sides of the same coin.[54]

So the danger was not that Iraq was known to be planning to use its (suspected) weapons of mass destruction in the near future against either its neighbours or the West, nor that Baghdad was known to be intent on transferring such weapons to a terrorist network in the near future, nor even that there was an imminent risk that Iraqi unconventional weapons would 'fall into the hands' of a terrorist group. Mr Blair conceded on the night before war began that, 'At the moment, I accept fully that the association between [rogue proliferators and international terrorist networks] is loose', though he claimed that it was 'hardening'.[55] (Incidentally, how could they be 'two sides of the same coin' on 13 January 2003 if their associations were only 'loose' on 18 March? How dangerous is a loosely constructed coin?)

The danger was that 'one day' some proliferator state, not necessarily Iraq itself, might pass its WMD to a terrorist group. This danger could be reduced by demonstrating resolve now, by attacking Iraq now, and that was why the war was necessary. The 'very remote' danger would become still more remote when states who might potentially transfer their WMD to terrorists saw what happened to Iraq, a state suspected of holding hidden stocks of weapons of mass destruction.

This doctrine of 'attempting to reduce still further a very remote danger from loosely associated enemies of the UK' was the argument advanced by Tony Blair to help him win the crucial vote in the British House of Commons on 18 March to go to war the next day.

This was the final form of the 'sinister nexus' rationale first advanced by George W. Bush in January 2002. This was the official justification for the death and destruction meted out to the ordinary people of Iraq.

CHAPTER VI
The First Ultimatum

The Five Demands

THE DECISION TO GO TO WAR

In a debate in the House of Commons on 26 February, the former Conservative Chancellor of the Exchequer, Kenneth Clarke, spoke out against the impending war on Iraq. The *Guardian* suggested in fact that 'it was Mr Clarke who rose to the occasion best.'[1] The Tory backbencher said, 'I cannot rid myself of doubts that the course to war we are now embarked on was actually decided on many months ago, primarily in Washington, and we've seen a fairly remorseless unfolding of events since that time.' That was why 'middle England' and 'a lot of very moderate political opinion' had such doubts about the war.[2]

An article in the *FT* asked, 'Just when *did* Mr Bush decide to go to war? Critics argue that the decision by the president to go to the United Nations Security Council was little more than a charade.'[3]

Columnist Stephen Fidler assembled three suggestive pieces of evidence. A report in *Time* magazine that the President 'poked his head into the office of Condoleezza Rice, his national security adviser, in March 2002 and told three senators sitting there: "[Expletive deleted] Saddam. We're taking him out."' Secondly, Richard Haass, policy planning chief at the State Department, revealed that he was told the war was inevitable by Condoleezza Rice in the first week of July 2002: 'She said, essentially, that the decision's been made, don't waste your breath.' Thirdly, and the immediate trigger for these ponderings, US General Tommy Franks, Commander of US Central Command, and head of the war effort in Iraq said, a week into the war, 'the fact of the matter is that for a period of about a year, a great deal of intense planning and a great deal of what-iffing by all of us has gone into this so that we prepare ourselves and prepare our subordinates in a way that we minimise the number of surprises.' Mr Fidler observes that this would point to serious thinking in the Pentagon about an invasion from March 2002. This was unlikely to have been simply the perpetual round of contingency planning: 'the discomfiture at the White House suggests there may be more to it than that'.[4]

Of course there was more to it. How could Mr Fidler have forgotten, for example, the war planning inside the Administration reported in the *New Yorker* in December 2001?[5] There was the Presidential order to prepare for an invasion of Iraq, signed on 17 September 2001.[6] In April 2002, the *New York Times* reported that senior officials acknowledged that any offensive 'would probably be delayed until early next year, allowing time to create the right military, economic and diplomatic conditions.'[7] In July 2002, a Whitehall source said, 'President Bush has already made up his mind. This is going to happen. It is a given. What we are waiting for is to be told the details of how and when and where.'[8]

President Bush's former speechwriter, David Frum describes not only how the war had become a certainty by January 2002, but how it had become the dominant factor governing the fate of the entire presidency. The President summoned his writers for a preview of the coming year in early January, in which he made clear that nothing major was to be expected on the home front until November:

> We're finished on taxes, except maybe for capital gains—if we win the war, we'll get our recovery. We're finished on education, too—we have three years to see how the new reforms work. . . One idea after another for a major domestic or economic speech was thrown at him: Health care? Trade? He shot them all down.
>
> It took us a while to get the message, but get it we eventually did. There was no more domestic agenda. The domestic agenda was the same as the foreign agenda: Win the war—then we'll see.[9]

By January 2003, it had become unthinkable for Mr Bush to accept the inspections route for disarming Iraq. Gary Schmitt, head of the Project for the New American Century, said, 'There would be open revolt within his own ranks, but also his own credibility would go down the tube. You would see the end of his presidency. It would be the foreign policy equivalent of his father saying, "read my lips, no more taxes".'[10]

TIMETABLE FOR WAR

One obstacle to war was the caution of the professional military men, including the former head of the US Joint Chiefs of Staff, Colin Powell, now leading the State Department.[11] In December 2002, alienated Pentagon officials joked that they still regarded General Powell as their chief of staff.[12] Eventually the professionals surrendered, agreeing a compromise war plan with the Wolfowitz faction in August 2002.[13]

At that point, serious timetabling of the war could begin. The war had to be won by the time the next US Presidential election cycle started in the autumn or winter of 2003. The other immovable limit was the need to avoid fighting during the heat of the summer.[14] These kinds of factors led Pentagon officials to say in late October 2002 that the optimal period to start military action in the Gulf would come some time between late November 2002 and early February 2003.[15] One element in the calculation was how long the conflict was anticipated to last. According to General Franks, the final war plan anticipated that the war could take as long as four months (though curiously this was not publicized before the war began, when the public was given to understand that it would be all over within days).[16]

COLIN POWELL TURNS THE PRESIDENT

In August 2002, the hawks' schedule for war still had to deal with the breadth and depth of international hostility to the idea of war on Iraq, particularly in the states neighbouring Iraq itself (the countries supposedly most at risk from Baghdad's alleged weapons of mass destruction).[17] According to Bob Woodward's well-informed account (he has long had the inside track with Mr Powell's camp), on 5 August the Secretary of State went—with some trepidation—to have a two-hour heart-to-heart with the President.

In 1990, as Chair of the Joint Chiefs of Staff, General Powell had had serious reservations about the intended war against Iraq over the invasion of Kuwait. He had expressed those reservations to President Bush Sr, 'perhaps too mildly', according to Bob Woodward's account of his feelings about the incident. Now, as Secretary of State, Mr Powell had decided 'he had to come down very hard, state his convictions and conclusions so there would be no doubt as to where he stood.' Warning Mr Bush about the possible consequences of the war on friendly Arab regimes, on the possible economic implications via changes in the supply and price of oil, the cost and difficulties of the post-war occupation of Iraq, the difficulties of finding Saddam Hussein, and the danger of Baghdad responding to invasion by using whatever weapons of mass destruction he possessed, the United States' top diplomat steered his argument towards a multilateral approach: 'It's nice to say we can do it unilaterally, except you can't.' The war effort would require access to bases and facilities in the region, and overflight rights over Iraq's neighbours. The US would need a coalition, and the UN was one way to do it.[18]

The end result of the Powell briefing was a decision to go down the UN route, using the emotionally and politically powerful occasion of the President's address to the UN General Assembly in New York on the day after the anniversary of 11 September. It was agreed at the last minute—on the night before the speech was delivered!—that the President would actually ask the UN for a new resolution on Iraq, as a tool for bringing together a coalition. For some reason, this wording was not inserted into the TelePrompTer set up for the President to read from, and Mr Bush was forced to ad lib the sentence, 'We will work with the UN Security Council for the necessary resolutions.'[19] The plural 'resolutions' was to bedevil US relations with the Security Council for some time.

Yet again, Mr Bush failed to demand the return of UN weapons inspectors to Iraq, which logically should have been the centrepiece of his speech to the UN itself. What made the omission even more striking was that the President made a point of drawing attention to Iraq's past failure to co-operate with UN weapons inspectors. The Security Council demanded the resumption of full co-operation with the inspectors in 1994; 1996; three more times in 1997; yet three more times in 1998; 'And in 1999, the demand was renewed yet again.' But in 2002, Mr Bush did not himself 'renew the demand' for inspections.

DESIGNED TO BE REFUSED

Instead, Mr Bush set out five quite different demands:

> If the Iraqi regime wishes peace, it will immediately and unconditionally forswear, disclose, and remove or destroy all weapons of mass destruction, long-range missiles, and all related material.
>
> If the Iraqi regime wishes peace, it will immediately end all support for terrorism and act to suppress it, as all states are required to do by UN Security Council resolutions.
>
> If the Iraqi regime wishes peace, it will cease persecution of its civilian population, including Shi'a, Sunnis, Kurds, Turkomans, and others, again as required by Security Council resolutions.
>
> If the Iraqi regime wishes peace, it will release or account for all Gulf War personnel whose fate is still unknown. It will return the remains of any who are deceased, return stolen property, accept liability for losses resulting from the invasion of Kuwait, and fully cooperate with international efforts to resolve these issues, as required by Security Council resolutions.
>
> If the Iraqi regime wishes peace, it will immediately end all illicit trade outside the oil-for-food program. It will accept UN administration of funds from that program, to ensure that the money is used fairly and promptly for the benefit of the Iraqi people. [20]

The depth and breadth of the demands were calculated to make Baghdad despair of ever satisfying Washington. Iraq would have to complete herculean tasks completely unrelated to its suspected chemical, biological or nuclear weapons in order to avoid war.

The final nail in the coffin of Iraqi hopes was the President's promise that if the five tests *were* met, 'it could open the prospect of the United Nations helping to build a government that represents all Iraqis—a government based on respect for human rights, economic liberty, and internationally supervised elections.'[21] So Saddam Hussein's reward for total co-operation with the UN Security Council would be 'regime change' in the shape of a US-style free market capitalist economy and internationally-supervised elections. The United States was not putting forward a genuine programme for action, but a provocative bundle of demands which was designed to be refused. Iraq's refusal of the US proposals would put the Iraqi government in the wrong. The same strategy was employed with the first 'oil-for-food' deal in 1991,[22] and was shortly to be followed once more in Security Council Resolution 1441, as we shall see.

The purpose of President Bush's General Assembly speech was not to sketch out a roadmap for the Government of Iraq to come into compliance with the UN's demands, but to drive the Government of Iraq headlong down a dead-end road, in an attempt to force Baghdad into refusal and confrontation.

Then disaster struck.

CHAPTER VII
Disaster Strikes

Iraq Accepts The Weapons Inspectors

A CHILLY RESPONSE

To the consternation of the Bush Administration, the Iraqi Government responded to the provocative ultimatum delivered at the General Assembly on 12 September 2002 not with angry words of rejection, but by unconditionally accepting the re-admission of UN weapons inspectors. Four days after President Bush's speech, Iraqi Foreign Minister Naji Sabri wrote to the United Nations announcing that Baghdad would allow the return of UN weapons inspectors to Iraq 'without conditions'.[1]

In Britain, Foreign Secretary Jack Straw gave a chilly response, saying that this 'apparent offer' needed to be treated with 'a high degree of scepticism'.[2] The White House issued the following statement:

> As the president said, the UN security council needs to decide how to enforce its own resolutions, which the Iraqi regime has defied for more than a decade. This will require a new, effective UN security council resolution that will actually deal with the threat Saddam Hussein poses to the Iraqi people, to the region, and to the world. That is the course the security council is on, and the United States is engaged in consultations with council members and other partners in New York at this time.
>
> This is not a matter of inspections. It is about disarmament of Iraq's weapons of mass destruction and the Iraqi regime's compliance with all other security council resolutions. This is a tactical step by Iraq in hope of avoiding strong UN security council action. As such, it is a tactic that will fail. It is time for the security council to act.[3]

'This is not a matter of inspections'. There had been no call in the President's speech for a return of the inspectors. There was no welcome now for the re-admission of the inspectors. The Administration's response to the offer to the impending return of UN weapons inspectors was to express its determination to press ahead with military action ('strong UN security council action') regardless of the degree of Iraqi co-operation. This was a barely concealed declaration of war.

REASONS TO BE SUSPICIOUS

The world was taken by surprise by the Iraqi offer, not least because some of the vehement statements of rejection made by Iraqi officials over preceding weeks and months. The Iraqi offer was also striking because of the deep-rooted and justified suspicions Iraq had developed regarding the inspection regime.

Firstly, Iraq had experienced the political use of the inspection regime, with changing conditions for the lifting of economic sanctions. Paragraph 22 of UN Security Council Resolution 687, which re-imposed economic sanctions on Iraq in April 1991, after the war in Kuwait and Iraq, had said that the sanctions on Iraq's oil exports and related financial transactions would be lifted once UN inspectors verified the disarmament of Iraq's nuclear, chemical and biological weapons programmes, and long-range missile systems, and after a long-term monitoring system had been set up.[4]

In April 1994, however, US Secretary of State Warren Christopher wrote in the *New York Times*, 'The US does not believe that Iraq's compliance with Paragraph 22 of Resolution 687 is enough to justify lifting the embargo.'[5] In March 1997 this position was reaffirmed by US Secretary of State, Madeleine Albright, who said that even if Iraq disarmed, economic sanctions would not be lifted as long as Saddam Hussein remained in power. Former UN weapons inspector Scott Ritter later commented bitterly, 'This violated the provisions of the Security Council resolution governing the sanctions regime and undermined the very framework of UNSCOM's existence.'[6]

In the autumn of 1998, Baghdad wrote to the Security Council asking for a reaffirmation of Paragraph 22. Britain, as the then President of the Security Council, replied on 30 October 1998 with a letter which refused to re-confirm this vital Paragraph. The next day the Iraqi Revolutionary Command Council halted co-operation with UN weapons inspectors (though co-operation resumed within weeks).

The *Financial Times* observed that 'Mr Saddam's decision to cripple UNSCOM was triggered by the US refusal explicitly to commit itself to lifting the oil embargo if Iraq complied with disarmament requirements—as stipulated by' Paragraph 22 of Resolution 687. In the Security Council letter of 30 October, the *FT* commented, 'the US [had] rejected proposals by Russia, France and China that would have clearly committed the security council to a lifting of the oil embargo if Iraq complied with requirements to eliminate its weapons of mass destruction.' The *Economist* observed, 'Iraq interpreted this as confirmation of its long-held—and plausible—belief that, even if it did come clean on all its weapons, no American administration would lift the oil embargo so long as Mr Hussein remained in power.' The *Independent* commented, 'Saddam had some reason for anger—the integrity of Article 22 is crucial for him.'[7]

A TOOL OF US FOREIGN POLICY

Then there was the fact that the first UN weapons inspection agency had, under the leadership of Australian diplomat Richard Butler, become a willing tool of US foreign policy. The head of the UN Special Commission (UNSCOM) helped to precipitate the US and British bombardment of Iraq in December 1998, by arranging a confrontational inspection of a civilian headquarters building at a time convenient to the United States; by writing an excessively negative report on Iraqi non-co-operation; and by withdrawing UNSCOM inspectors from Iraq at a time convenient to Washington.[8] This last event has been the subject of relentless propaganda from the Government and from the mass media. It has been said time and time again that UN weapons inspectors were expelled from Iraq in December 1998. True, but Washington, not Baghdad, was responsible.

Tony Blair, the master of evasion, was finally cornered on this issue and exposed by the renowned BBC interviewer Jeremy Paxman during the run-up to the war. Mr Blair asserted that UNSCOM were 'put out of Iraq'. Under enormous pressure he finally conceded that in fact, 'They were withdrawn because they couldn't do their job'.' The Prime Minister had been caught out in a bald lie (though he did slip in another lie about the inability of the inspectors to do their work).[9]

It was necessary to withdraw the inspectors in order to build a political case for military action. So UNSCOM was 'put out of Iraq' by the United States, leading to its subsequent collapse, in order to facilitate the four-day bombing campaign that took place in December 1998, known as 'Operation Desert Fox'.[10]

A TOOL OF US INTELLIGENCE

There was another major factor in the collapse of UNSCOM. UNSCOM had been penetrated by US intelligence for the purpose of spying on the leadership of Iraq, acquiring targeting data, and as a channel of communication to possible coup leaders within the Iraqi military. Barton Gellman of the *Washington Post* learned in 1999 that in March 1996 a US military intelligence officer working for UNSCOM had secretly inserted special scanners into UNSCOM monitoring cameras, enabling US intelligence to spy on important nodes of Iraqi military communication, without the knowledge of UNSCOM staff.[11] As for targeting, the Pentagon admitted after Operation Desert Fox in December 1998 that 'it was inevitable that information supplied by the [UNSCOM] monitors had played a part in the careful selection of targets.'[12]

In 1998, according to former UNSCOM weapons inspector Scott Ritter, several of the inspectors working under him were actually US intelligence officers gathering information on the Iraqi leader in order to assist an assassination attempt. 'Several of the inspectors were gathering intelligence on where Saddam lived, worked and probably took shelter in air raids—not so they could eliminate his weapons, but to eliminate him,' as *Newsweek* summarized his claims. Embedded in Mr Ritter's team was a British MI6 officer, 'whose job was to recruit a senior Iraqi official'. Also in the team were CIA officers, 'whose job was to do a structural-intelligence analysis of Saddam Hussein's bunkers, and to pinpoint the residences and offices of every senior Iraqi government official.' The recruitment effort failed, but in December 1998, Operation Desert Fox targeted 'every residence and every office occupied by senior Iraqi government officials,' according to Mr Ritter: 'The only way that information was gathered was through the process of inspector access to those facilities.'[13] According to the official UN report of the inspection of the presidential palaces in 1998, 'The Iraqi authorities expressed serious concerns about the confidentiality of the information being gathered by the UNSCOM and IAEA experts, who for their part maintained that the information was totally safe in the hands of UNSCOM.'[14]

Finally, Mr Ritter has revealed his unwitting role as the leader of an UNSCOM mission in June 1996 that the CIA tried to use to link CIA paramilitary officers in Mr Ritter's team with potentially rebellious Iraqi army officers in the super-elite Special Republican Guard charged with defending the Iraqi President.[15]

For all these reasons: the uselessness of co-operation with inspectors in securing a key goal of the regime in the past (the partial lifting of economic sanctions, as promised in a UN Resolution, no less); the willing subservience of past inspectors to US foreign policy; and the evidence that past inspectors had been used as extensions of US security-intelligence agencies, all gave reasonable grounds for Baghdad to be extremely wary of re-admitting the inspectors. In the event, the new inspectorate, UNMOVIC, did not function (so far as we know) as adjuncts of US intelligence (though they may have been used unknowingly[16]), and they did not integrate themselves into US foreign policy or co-operate in the US timetable for war, but they did prove almost entirely useless once more in securing a key goal of the regime, which was also the wish of the international community and the bulk of the Security Council: the preservation of international peace, and the prevention of an Anglo-American invasion.

PREVIOUS IRAQI OFFERS REBUFFED

Despite all this, Iraq made a number of conciliatory offers during 2002, in between bursts of defiant bombast. As noted in the opening paragraphs of Iraqi Foreign Minister Naji Sabri's letter to Kofi Annan, Iraqi delegations had met with the UN Secretary-General in New York on 7 March and 2 May 2002, and in Vienna on 4 and 5 July 2002, to discuss the resumption of inspections.[17] There had also been public invitations to the British Government in March 2002, and to US Congress in August 2002, suggesting that officials and representatives bring their own technical experts to inspect whatever sites they had identified as suspect.[18] Days before the offer to Congress, there was an Iraqi invitation to the new chief UN weapons inspector, Dr Hans Blix, head of the UN Monitoring, Verification and Inspection Commission (UNMOVIC), to come to Baghdad for technical talks.[19] Burhan Chalabi, an Iraqi-born British businessman with contacts in Baghdad, insisted that the Iraqi offer was 'very serious'. Iraq was willing to let the inspectors back, he said. 'All they are worried about is that the Americans might move the goalposts.'[20] A valid fear, as President Bush demonstrated in the General Assembly just a month later.

All of these invitations and offers met with the same response in London and Washington: sneers, rebuffs, and threats, if they were not ignored entirely. For example, when congressional representatives were invited to Iraq on 5 August 2002, UN National Security Council spokesperson Sean McCormack dismissed the offer, saying, 'There's no need for discussion. What there is a need for is for the regime in Baghdad to live up to its commitment to disarm.'[21] As a logical and legal reality, however, Iraq could not live up to its commitment to disarm without permitting international verification. The hostility to discussion of such possibilities spoke volumes about the real nature of US concerns.

A few days earlier, US Under-Secretary of State John Bolton (a Wolfowitz-Rumsfeld appointee forced onto the State Department) said that Baghdad's invitation to the chief UN weapons inspector for technical talks made no difference to America's demand for 'regime change': 'our policy . . . insists on regime change in Baghdad. That policy will not be altered whether the inspectors go in or not.'[22] The Iraqis 'understand what is required of them and there is no need for further clarification or discussion,' said Mr Powell, adding that the US continued to insist on regime change in Baghdad.[23] 'Nothing's changed,' George W. Bush told reporters.[24]

The message from all levels of the US Administration was the same: we will attack Iraq, whatever happens on the inspections front.—a threat that was carried out. This was clearly intended to undermine efforts to secure the return of the inspectors.

In March 2002, Iraq asked a series of nineteen questions of the UN Security Council, via UN Secretary-General Kofi Annan. The central issue was whether permitting inspections to return would grant immunity from attack. Iraq pointed out that sites inspected by the previous inspection teams were attacked during Operation Desert Fox, 'including the presidential sites.' These attacks took place although the inspectors confirmed these sites did not contain weapons of mass destruction. 'Moreover, the United States and Britain bombed all the industrial sites that were under constant supervision based on information provided to them by the spy inspectors.'[25] When this point was transmitted to the Security Council by Kofi Annan, he phrased it thus: 'What are the guarantees that UNMOVIC would not use the same inspection formula which led to the bombing of Iraq in 1998?'[26] The US refused to answer this question, or to offer a guarantee that while the inspectors were at work in Iraq there would be no military assault.

The real US response to these reasonable concerns was to leak, during the July negotiations between Iraq and the UN in Vienna, the outline of a five-inch-thick dossier on the 'concept' of war against Iraq, with precise details of Iraqi bases, surface-to-air missiles, air defence networks and fiber-optics communications to be targeted. The UN-Iraq negotiations promptly broke up without making headway. A participant in the Iraq-UN talks said the leaked war plan 'did not help.'[27]

DEALING WITH DISASTER: PALACE INTRIGUE

All of which serves as background to understanding the extraordinary (and desperate) nature of Iraq's 16 September offer to unconditionally re-admit the weapons inspectors.

The response of the United States was to immediately to try to undermine and then to strangle the Iraqi offer at birth.

After Foreign Minister Naji Sabri's offer to allow the inspectors back in, there was a follow-up letter from Saddam Hussein himself, which said, 'Iraq was, and still is, ready to co-operate with the Security Council and international organisations, but rejects any digression by whosoever at the expense of its rights, sovereignty, security, and independence, that is in contradiction with the principles of the Charter and the international law.'[28] Colin Powell responded by saying, 'Saddam is already walking back, he is already stepping away from the "without conditions" statement.'[29] This was the impression given by virtually every British newspaper—that Iraq was 'stepping away' from the offer of unconditional re-admission of the inspectors. Tim Trevan, a former UNSCOM inspector, and a man who knew better, referred to this language from Baghdad as 'code for no inspections of palaces or government ministry buildings'.[30]

Mr Trevan included the following item in the chronology to his book *Saddam's Secrets: The Hunt for Iraq's Hidden Weapons*: '19-22 June 1996—[UNSCOM chief] Rolf Ekeus visits Baghdad, and agrees with Iraq a joint programme of action to conclude investigations into Iraq's past programmes, and establishes inspection modalities for "sensitive sites" in order to take into account Iraq's legitimate security concerns whilst allowing UNSCOM the access necessary for its inspection activities.'[31] Iraq had objected to UN weapons inspections of what it called 'sensitive sites'. The headquarters of intelligence agencies, Government ministries, and so on, had been off-limits. The 1996 Ekeus agreement allowed inspection of these 'sensitive sites', but only four inspectors would be permitted entry. This agreement was subsequently amended by Dr Ekeus's successor, Richard Butler, who forced the Iraqis to accept the principle that at larger sites more than four inspectors would be permitted onto the premises. However, even after this amendment, Iraq refused to permit inspection of presidential palaces. This led directly to the inspection crisis of February 1998, when only the direct intervention of Kofi Annan, flying into Baghdad, averted a US/UK military assault.

Tim Trevan records the following account in his chronology: in February 1998, the UN Secretary-General succeeded in obtaining an agreement from Iraq on the inspection of the these palaces; from 15–18 February 1998, a UN survey team assessed the size and scope of the eight sites; on 9 March 1998, the Security Council endorsed this new UN–Iraq agreement; and finally, on 4 April 1998, 'Access to the presidential palaces is obtained'.[32]

In the run-up to the 2003 war on Iraq, the British Government actually lied about the fact that there had ever been inspections of the eight 'sovereign' presidential palaces. In the British Government's first weapons dossier, published on 24 September 2002, the Government claimed that 'Iraq consistently refused to allow UNSCOM inspectors access to any of these eight Presidential sites.'[33] Mr Blair said explicitly on British television that the UN weapons inspectors had been effectively thrown out of Iraq because they had been prevented from inspecting presidential palaces.[34] Yet, as Richard Butler, chief UN weapons inspector at the time, wrote in his memoirs, 'Our inspections of the Presiden-

Regime Unchanged

tial sites were eventually conducted over a period of ten days, and on April 15 [1998], a report on these "entries" (in the UN vernacular) was presented to the Security Council.[35] This was confirmed in November 1998, by the Prime Minister himself, in a written answer to a parliamentary question from Tam Dalyell MP.[36]

The claim that Iraq had blocked inspections of its presidential palaces was one of the few independently verifiable assertions in the first weapons dossier. It was immediately picked up by the anti-war Labour MP John McDonnell, who questioned Mr Blair on this point as he presented the weapons dossier to the House of Commons on 24 September 2002 (after allowing MPs mere hours to digest the document).[37] By endorsing this claim in the dossier, the Prime Minister attempted to deceive the House of Commons, a relatively minor element in the campaign of lies leading up to the war.

Incidentally, the section of the September 2002 weapons dossier referring to the history of inspections relied heavily on Tim Trevan's account in the main body of his book. Two key sentences were lifted verbatim from *Saddam's Secrets* (p. 364),[38] a foreshadowing of the large-scale plagiarism to come in the Government's 'dodgy dossier'.[39] It seems that the Joint Intelligence Committee (or some part of the Number 10 machine) having read some portions of Mr Trevan's book, did not check the chronology section at the end of *Saddam's Secrets*, or read Richard Butler's account of these same events.

PRAISING THE ANNAN RULES, 1998

To sum up, after three rounds of negotiations between UN officials and Iraq—with Mr Ekeus in 1996, Mr Butler in 1997, and Mr Annan in 1998—a number of rules had been drawn up for the 'sensitive' and 'presidential' sites: 'sensitive sites' were to be inspected by a maximum of four inspectors; large 'sensitive sites' might have more than four inspectors; and at 'presidential' or 'sovereign' sites the inspection teams were to be accompanied by senior foreign diplomats drawn from a 'Special Group' set up by the UN Secretary-General.[40] The agreements, which made an effort to respect Iraq's sovereignty, did not hinder, but facilitated and enabled the inspection of locations that the Iraqi Government had been extremely loath to open up. Given this history, it is extraordinary that Mr Trevan should say that the language from Baghdad in September 2002 was 'code for no inspections of palaces or government ministry buildings'.

The Ekeus and Butler agreements were not Security Council positions, but arrangements between UNSCOM and the Government of Iraq. In contrast, the Annan agreement of February 1998 regarding the inspection of palaces was adopted by the Security Council, and affirmed in a Resolution in March 1998. Resolution 1154 did two things simultaneously: in Paragraph 3 it stressed that Iraq had to 'accord immediate, unconditional and unrestricted access' to UNSCOM and to the International Atomic Energy Agency (IAEA), and, in Paragraph 1, it also 'endorse[d] the memorandum of understanding signed by the Deputy Prime Minister of Iraq and the Secretary-General on 23 February 1998'.[41] This is very important for what comes next: the special procedures for inspecting the 'presidential' sites (and by implication the other 'sensitive' sites) were not regarded by the Security Council as diminishing or contradicting the 'immediate, unconditional and unrestricted' access rights due to the inspectors.

The February 1998 Memorandum of Understanding between Kofi Annan and Tariq Aziz said, 'The Government of Iraq undertakes to accord to UNSCOM and IAEA immediate, unconditional and unrestricted access.' It also said (in the very next sentence), 'In the performance of its mandate under the Security Council resolutions, UNSCOM undertakes to respect the legitimate concerns of Iraq relating to national security, sovereignty and dignity.'[42] For the Government of Iraq to invoke the latter commitment on 16 September 2002 as it offered to live up to its access obligations was not a threat to 'unconditional' access for the inspectors, despite the claims from Colin Powell and Tim Trevan. The two elements were a negotiated whole.

The New Labour Government in Britain was not only aware of this 1998 agreement; the Prime Minister actually lauded this wonderful achievement of the United Nations at the time. While acknowledging that the Special Group overseeing inspections of presidential palaces would work under 'some extra specific procedures related to the nature of the sites', Mr Blair welcomed the agreement, paid tribute to Secretary-General Kofi Annan's achievement in securing it, and declared, 'It has been an important demonstration of the value of the United Nations and its absolutely vital role in the world.'[43] The then Foreign Secretary Robin Cook added, 'The agreement represents a success for our strategy and, if properly carried out, will enable us to halt [Saddam Hussein] in developing weapons of mass destruction.'[44] Challenged in Parliament, the Foreign Secretary explicitly disagreed with the notion that the Annan agreement had compromised the work of UNSCOM, pointing out that, 'The agreement led the way for UNSCOM to carry out intrusive inspections on presidential sites.'[45]

RIPPING UP THE ANNAN RULES, 2002

Having lauded the Annan agreement in 1998, the British Government in September 2002 turned with alacrity to the task of erasing the agreement from the history books, and supporting the United States in burying the agreement. For the next stage in the US campaign against the UN weapons inspectors was to try to derail the impending return of the inspectors by changing the nature of the deal that Iraq had just accepted.

Paragraph 11 of Security Council Resolution 1284 stated that the new inspection agency, UNMOVIC, inherited all the existing arrangements and agreements between UNSCOM and the Government of Iraq. This included the Ekeus, Butler and Annan agreements. So when Iraq accepted the return of UN inspectors 'unconditionally', it accepted the return of the inspectors subject to the same agreements and rules of inspection that UNSCOM had worked under and which UNMOVIC had inherited. This was certainly the understanding of Dr Hans Blix, the head of UNMOVIC.[46] 'We understand the MOU [the 1998 Annan Memorandum Of Understanding] to still be valid,' said UNMOVIC spokesperson Ewen Buchanan in the aftermath of the Iraqi offer to re-admit the inspectors. A senior US official responded that no conditions, including those relating to presidential sites, would be acceptable: 'This is a high barrier . . . inspections have to be truly unconditional.'[47]

The United States, shocked and dismayed by Iraq's agreement to re-admit UN weapons inspectors, was trying to derail the inspection process before it even started, by ripping up the existing agreements, and demanding 'anyone, any time, anywhere' inspection rights. British journalist Rupert Cornwell commented soon after the Iraqi offer on what was 'emerging as the key issue of the Iraq crisis—US insistence that United Nations inspectors cannot return until the UN has passed a stern new resolution spelling out the consequences if Baghdad fails to cooperate.'[48] Colin Powell told a US Congressional committee, 'There is standing authority for the inspection team but there are weaknesses in that authority which make the current regime unacceptable. And we need a new resolution to clean that up and put new conditions on the Iraqis . . . if somebody tried to move the [inspectors'] team in right now, we would find ways to thwart that.'[49] The inspectors were blocked from returning to Iraq for weeks not by the Ba'athist regime of Saddam Hussein, but by the Republican Administration of George W. Bush. This stand was supported by the British Foreign Secretary Jack Straw, who said in early October 2002, 'The UN weapons inspectors have to work under existing security council resolutions,' but these were 'defective.'[50]

The inspection process in Iraq was divided between two agencies. UNMOVIC dealt with chemical and biological weapons, and long-range missiles. The International Atomic Energy Agency (IAEA) was charged with disarming Iraq's nuclear weapons capability. The day after Iraq's offer to allow inspectors to return, the IAEA spokeswoman said, 'We could start work tomorrow. We have a plan in place.'[51] On 16 September itself, Dr Blix said on behalf of UNMOVIC that the agency could have inspectors on the ground within days, but it would take his teams several weeks before they could begin monitoring Iraqi sites.[52] The United States and Britain instead demanded radical changes in the inspection rules, to be confirmed in a UN Resolution which took weeks to negotiate. Instead of entering Iraq to work within days or a few weeks, IAEA and UNMOVIC inspectors were not to arrive in Baghdad until the third week of November, and did not carry out their first inspection until 27 November 2002—over two months after the Iraqi offer to re-admit them.

The US and UK drew up a new resolution, with new rules, but delayed tabling it at the Security Council, so that the first meeting between the chief UN weapons inspector, Hans Blix, and the Iraqi authorities took place without a clear idea of what the framework of inspections was to be. The *Guardian* reported that Britain and the US were afraid that this would allow Iraq to agree a new inspections regime on the basis of existing UN resolutions 'which allow Baghdad to block access to its so called "presidential palaces".'[53] This was a flat out lie by the two Governments, and one of innumerable examples of subservience on the part of the mass media.[54] A few days later, the *Guardian* (one of the most anti-war of the British newspapers) repeated the lie: Dr Blix and an Iraqi delegation had announced that the inspections would be resumed under existing UN guidelines 'which exclude access for the arms inspectors to eight presidential sites in Iraq.'[55] This was the supposed 'defect' in the existing inspection regime—that it barred inspections of palaces that had actually been surveyed and inspected four and a half years earlier, under precisely these same 'defective' rules.

In fact, the joint press release issued by UNMOVIC and the Iraqis had this to say on the inspection rules:

> On the question of access, it was clarified that all sites are subject to immediate, unconditional and unrestricted access. However, the Memorandum of Understanding of 1998 establishes special procedures for access to eight presidential sites.[56]

Special procedures, yes. A ban on inspections, no. On 1 October, the White House spokesman was asked the following question: 'a 1998 resolution embraced an agreement between Secretary General Kofi Annan and Saddam Hussein that told them they would give prior notice and they would be accompanied by inspectors. Is that one of the reasons that you have to have a new U.N. resolution?' Ari Fleischer replied, 'Absolutely. This is one of the reasons that the existing inspection regime has not worked.'[57] A contention that was about to be disproved comprehensively: when the palaces were inspected under the new rules, nothing was found.

In 1991, UN Security Council Resolution 687 had promised to lift a considerable part of the economic sanctions on Iraq in return for co-operation with UN weapons inspectors. That promise was effectively broken by the United States and Britain. In 1998, UN Security Council Resolution 1154 had promised to observe new rules on inspecting presidential compounds in Iraq. That promise was now being ripped up by the United States and Britain. How much should Baghdad expect from the new Resolution being prepared by Washington and London?

CHAPTER VIII
The Minefield

Resolution 1441:
Designed To Be Refused

REASONABLY REJECTABLE

The ideal for the US was to devise a UN Resolution that seemed reasonable enough to be passed by the Security Council, but that was objectionable enough to be rejected by Baghdad, so that Iraq would withdraw its offer to re-admit the inspectors. A secondary goal, if a sufficiently objectionable resolution could not be agreed, was to write into the Resolution some 'trigger' language which would lend legitimacy to US military action in the event that inspectors did return to Iraq. This would have two benefits: the 'trigger' language itself would be objectionable to Iraq, thus reducing the chances of the inspectors being re-admitted. At the same time these clauses would enhance the prospects for an internationally-acceptable US invasion of Iraq further down the line.

MAKING RESOLUTION 1441 OBJECTIONABLE[1]

The first step in making the Resolution difficult for Baghdad to swallow was to rip up the previous 'sensitive sites' inspection rules or 'modalities': UN weapons inspectors were to have the right to inspect any sites and buildings, 'including immediate, unimpeded, unconditional, and unrestricted access to Presidential Sites equal to that at other sites, notwithstanding the provisions of resolution 1154 (1998) of 2 March 1998.' This was only one of nine sections in Paragraph 7 of Resolution 1441.[2] Another provocative demand was that the inspectors should have the right to import any materials or equipment they wanted to bring in, or export any equipment, materials or documents they took during inspections—without the Iraqi Government being able to search their baggage on leaving the country. UNMOVIC and IAEA were also given the power to declare, for the purposes of 'freezing' a site to be inspected, 'exclusion zones', including surrounding areas and transit corridors, in which Iraq would have to suspend ground and aerial movement so that nothing was changed in or taken out of a site being inspected. The 'exclusion zones' were not limited in size. Given the past history of Western intelligence penetration of the inspection teams, and CIA coordination of inspections and US coup efforts, these were rather difficult concessions for the Iraqi authorities to make.

A second line of attack centred on the personnel suspected of being involved in the prohibited weapons programmes. Paragraph 7 of Resolution 1441 said that UNMOVIC and the IAEA should be provided with the names of all personnel currently and formerly associated with Iraq's chemical, biological, nuclear, and ballistic missile programmes and the associated research, development, and production facilities. Paragraph 5 said that Iraq had to provide the inspectors with 'immediate, unimpeded, unrestricted, and private access to all officials, and other persons who they wished to interview' in the mode or location of the inspectors' choice.' Paragraph 5 also stated that UNMOVIC and the IAEA could 'at their discretion' conduct interviews inside or outside of Iraq, could 'facilitate the travel of those interviewed and family members outside of Iraq', and could conduct such interviews 'without the presence of observers from the Iraqi Government.' This also proved to be a very difficult procedure for the authorities to accept, though private interviews were conducted.

Paragraph 3 also demanded a 'currently accurate, full, and complete declaration' of all aspects of Iraq's programmes to develop chemical, biological, and nuclear weapons, ballistic missiles, and other delivery systems. This declaration was to include the 'precise locations' of such weapons, components, sub-components, stocks of agents, and related material and equipment, the locations and work of its research, development and production facilities, as well as 'all other chemical, biological, and nuclear programmes, including any which it claims are for purposes not related to weapon production or material'. This was to be an inventory of all equipment which could possibly be used for chemical, biological or nuclear weapons programmes—including every fermenting vat in the country—compiled in a month. Chief UN weapons inspector Hans Blix commented that while it was feasible to expect the authorities to compile a report on Iraq's past and present chemical, biological and nuclear weapons programmes within 30 days, '[t]o declare all other chemical programmes in a country with a fairly large chemical industry, as well as other biological programmes might be more problematic in a short time.'[3]

Resolution 1441 was passed on 8 November 2002. The weapons declaration was handed over early on 7 December. It would have been surprising if it did not contain some errors of some kind. According to the language of the Resolution, any errors could count towards a 'material breach' of Iraq's disarmament obligations, even if the errors only concerned fermenting vats in a small brewery.

THE TRIGGER LANGUAGE

A critical concept in the lead-up to the war was that of the 'material breach'. It was widely understood that if Iraq was found to be in 'material breach' of its obligations, war would follow. It was also widely assumed that in such circumstances, military action against Iraq would receive some kind of blessing from the UN itself, or from a UN Resolution. A headline in the *Guardian* put the matter well: 'What will be the trigger for war? As inspectors begin checking Iraqi sites, peace hinges on the interpretation of one phrase: "material breach".' Curiously, the article that followed did not actually explain what this phrase meant, saying only that, 'there are conflicting views not only among Washington, London, Paris, Moscow and Beijing, but also within the British and US governments'.[4] The official line in the US and UK was that if Iraq was found in a further 'material breach' of its disarmament obligations, the two warrior states were empowered by past UN Security Council Resolutions to use force unilaterally against the government in Baghdad.

The important questions then seemed to be: What was a 'material breach'? Why was it important? In this case, what constituted a 'material breach'? Who was authorized to make a judgement as to whether a 'material breach' had occurred? And, the heart of the matter, if a competent authority had found Iraq in 'material breach' of its obligations under UN Resolutions, would this have legally justified the war?

One critical issue was whether there had to be a new UN Resolution finding Iraq in 'material breach' and authorizing military action—these were two separate decisions—before war was permitted. If there didn't have to be a new Resolution, Britain and the US might have been able to argue that they were justified in their unilateral invasion simply by claiming that Iraq was in 'material breach'.

The British Government did not help matters adopting a policy of not being clear on this critical point. In response to a legal case brought by the Campaign for Nuclear Disarmament (CND), Peter Ricketts, the director general for political affairs at the Foreign Office said, 'It would be prejudicial to the national interest and to the conduct of the Government's foreign policy if the Government were to be constrained to make a definitive statement of its legal position under international law in relation to issues concerning the international relations of the United Kingdom.'[5] Mr Ricketts added that, 'The UK's international alliances could be damaged by the incautious assertion of arguments under international law which affect the position of those other states.' He went on: 'it is frequently important for the successful conduct of international affairs that matters should not be reduced to simple black and white, but should be left as shades of grey and open for diplomatic negotiation.'[6] In other words, while diplomacy with Iraq which could lead to a peaceful resolution was to be avoided, diplomatic trickery should be available in order to exploit any possible legal loopholes to help justify war.

THE SIGNIFICANCE OF A 'MATERIAL BREACH'

According to Article 60 of the 1969 Vienna Convention (which governs the Law of Treaties), 'A material breach of a bilateral treaty by one of the parties entitles the other to invoke the breach as a ground for terminating the treaty or suspending its operation in whole or in part.'[7] By March 2003, the US/UK argument was that by (allegedly) failing to comply with its disarmament duties as laid down in UN Security Council Resolution

687—and expanded in Resolution 1441—Iraq had so seriously breached these Resolutions or 'treaties', that other aspects of Resolution 687 could also be terminated or suspended—including the Gulf War ceasefire. According to Washington and London, Iraq's allegedly incomplete disarmament allowed them to resume the 1991 Gulf War.

However, Paragraph 33 of Resolution 687 said that the ceasefire came into effect between Iraq and its enemies 'upon official *notification* by Iraq to the Secretary-General and to the Security Council of [Iraq's] acceptance of the provisions above.'[8] Resolution 687 did not say that the ceasefire depended on Iraq remaining in a continuing state of compliance with the terms of the Resolution. There was no provision in the Resolution for the ceasefire to be revoked after that one-off notification.

THE TWIN TRIGGERS

Resolution 1441 stated that Iraq was already in 'material breach' of its disarmament obligations (Paragraph 1), and would be found in 'further material breach' if it failed to comply with, or co-operate fully with the implementation of, other provisions of the Resolution (such as the right of UN weapons inspectors to remove Iraqi scientists and their families from the country for questioning).

The exact wording is important. Paragraph 4 said that 'false statements or omissions in the declarations submitted by Iraq pursuant to this resolution *and* failure by Iraq at any time to comply with, and co-operate fully in the implementation of, this resolution shall constitute a further material breach of Iraq's obligations' (emphasis added).

These were two conditions, as a British 'source' pointed out in December 2002: 'The resolution talks about a false declaration or omission plus non-co-operation or compliance. Plus is the important word. . . The document itself is not a trigger for war.'[9] The *Guardian* reported, 'The use of "and" rather than "or" was intensively debated by the security council, and was a condition for its unanimous support for the resolution.' Despite hints to the contrary by both Mr Bush and Mr Blair, most senior officials in both Washington and London agreed that the wording meant that the 8 December declaration alone could not provide a justification for military action.[10] What was needed was verified omissions or deceit in regard to the declaration, and what one report described as a 'pattern of delays or outright refusal to provide access to a site or an official'—a single act of non-co-operation was insufficient, according to the understandings reached within the Security Council.[11]

British Foreign Secretary Jack Straw said in Parliament on 25 November 2002,

> I reassure the House that material breach means something significant: some behaviour or pattern of behaviour that is serious. Among such breaches could be action by the Government of Iraq seriously to obstruct or to impede the inspectors, to intimidate witnesses, or a pattern of behaviour where any single action appears relatively minor but the actions as a whole add up to something deliberate and more significant: something that shows Iraq's intention not to comply . . . Operational paragraph 4 makes it clear that a material breach is a failure of disclosure and other failure to comply—there are two parts.[12]

THE COMPETENT AUTHORITY

Some Washington hawks pushed for there to be a single trigger. US Vice President Dick Cheney took up the most belligerent position, insisting to the President that any omission—no matter how minor—would constitute a material breach.[13] The problem was that the United States was not empowered to decide what constituted a 'material breach': only one of the parties to a treaty can make such a judgement, and in the present case the party was either the Security Council as a whole, or Kuwait together with all of its 1991 allies (a grouping that had long ago fragmented).[14]

WHAT 'AUTHORIZATION FOR WAR'?

According to international lawyer Dr Glen Rangwala, if Iraq were to declared to be failing to comply with its disarmament obligations, this would have entitled the Security Council to move on to state that Baghdad was in 'material breach'. There was nothing automatic about this process, however. The Security Council was *entitled* to make this declaration, it was not *obliged* to do so. The Security Council could have declared Iraq to be guilty of a lesser form of breach.

Even if the Security Council had declared Iraq in further 'material breach' of Resolution 687, this would not have meant that it was entitled to somehow tear up the 1991 ceasefire and resume war. Dr Rangwala points out that since the introduction of the UN Charter, there has been a general prohibition on the use of force in international relations, as stated in Article 2.4 of the Charter. Therefore, a ceasefire cannot simply be revoked and war re-started if the terms of a ceasefire treaty are violated. Dr Rangwala comments, 'the standard view in international law—both from academics and from states—has been that a ceasefire returns the parties to a state of peace, and any prior right to use force is terminated.'[15] The invasion of Egypt by Israel in 1956, for example, was not interpreted as a licence for Egypt to revoke the ceasefire agreement of 1949 between the two countries, and to 'resume' the war of 1948.

In short, Resolution 1441 did not empower the US and Britain unilaterally to find Iraq in material breach of its obligations; if Iraq were found to be non-compliant, this did not immediately translate into a finding of 'material breach'; this was a judgement that could only be made by the Security Council as a whole; and even a properly authorised finding of 'material breach' could not in and of itself authorize the use of force since the 1991 'ceasefire' could not be revoked by such a finding. The 1991 ceasefire was a one-off event triggered by a single action by Iraq (notification), not something dependent on Iraq remaining in a state of compliance. Furthermore, the UN Charter's prohibition on the use of force meant that the 1991 ceasefire was a permanent reversion to a state of peace between all the parties, not a temporary suspension of hostilities which could be lifted at any moment. Therefore, quite apart from any questions about the legitimacy and legality of the use of force in 1991, the words 'material breach' were irrelevant to the legality or legitimacy of a new war on Iraq in 2003.

THE SECOND RESOLUTION AMBIGUITY

Paragraph 12 of Resolution 1441 stated that in the event of a report from one of the inspection agencies that Iraq had engaged in 'any interference' with their inspection activities, or had failed to comply with its disarmament obligations, the Security Council would 'convene immediately.' The majority of the permanent members of the Security Council—Russia, France and China—wished this session of the Security Council to consider and to pass an explicit 'authorization' Resolution before any military action could be taken. The United States and Britain had no wish to be so constrained. The wording of the Paragraph said only that this meeting of the Security Council would 'consider the situation and the need for full compliance with all of the relevant Council resolutions in order to secure international peace and security.' There was no explicit requirement for there to be a second, enabling, Resolution explicitly authorizing the use of force.

There was also no authorization for the use of force in Resolution 1441. There was a hint of such a threat, when the Resolution recalled that the Security Council had in the past 'repeatedly warned Iraq that it will face serious consequences as a result of its continued violations of its obligations.' Thus, under Paragraph 2, Iraq was to have 'a final opportunity' to comply with its disarmament obligations. No time limit was set on this 'final opportunity'.

US Ambassador to the UN John Negroponte declared to the Security Council when the Resolution was passed, 'As we have said on numerous occasions to Council members, this Resolution contains no "hidden triggers" and no "automaticity" with respect to the use of force. If there is a further Iraqi breach, reported to the Council by UNMOVIC, the IAEA, or a member state, the matter will return to the Council for discussions as required in paragraph 12.' Mr Negroponte also made it clear, however, that whatever the judgement of the Security Council might be, the US was going to war: 'one way or another, Mr. President, Iraq will be disarmed. If the Security Council fails to act decisively in the event of a further Iraqi violation, this resolution does not constrain any member state from acting to defend itself against the threat posed by Iraq, or to enforce relevant UN resolutions and protect world peace and security.'[16]

Russia, China and France had another interpretation of the Resolution's significance. In a joint statement, the three permanent members of the Security Council said: 'the resolution fully respects the competences of the Security Council in the maintenance of international peace and security, in conformity with the Charter of the United Nations'.[17] The Security Council was still in charge, and no authorization for the use of force had been devolved to any individual member states, in their view. The fact that the Resolution was passed unanimously, with even Syria voting for it, masked the fact that it failed to resolve the central issue of authorization.

Michael J. Glennon, Professor of International Law at the Fletcher School of Law and Diplomacy at Tufts University, suggests that, 'As surely as Resolution 1441 represented a triumph of American diplomacy, it represented a defeat for the international rule of law.'

In Professor Glennon's view, the language of the resolution could be said to lend support to both the US and the majority interpretations. 'The UN's members have an obligation under the charter to comply with Security Council decisions. They therefore have a right to expect the council to render its decisions clearly. Shrinking from that task in the face of threats undermines the rule of law.'[18] This was is what happened on 8 November 2002, in the professor's view.

A CONSIDERED JUDGEMENT

There were other interpretations. After a number of citizen initiatives to bring the issue of war on Iraq under legal scrutiny,[19] BBC Radio 4's *Today* programme held an inquiry into the legality of war against Iraq in the absence of a second UN Resolution explicitly authorizing the use of force. Professor Vaughan Lowe, Chichele Professor of Public International Law at Oxford University, and a practising barrister, presided over the inquiry. He warned that 'The statement in paragraph 13 of the Resolution [1441] that "the Council has repeatedly warned Iraq that it will face serious consequences as a result of its continued violations of its obligations" [was] a simple statement of what the Security Council has done in the past. It cannot in my opinion possibly be interpreted as an express or implied authorization to States unilaterally to take military action against Iraq in the future.'[20] Categorical language.

While that Paragraph amounted to an implied threat if Iraq breached its obligations in the future, 'nothing in paragraph 13 suggests that the consequences would be decided upon and taken by anyone other than the body that has, under the procedure established in the immediately preceding paragraphs 11 and 12, been given responsibility for deciding how to respond to material breaches: that is, by the Security Council itself.'

Professor Lowe was equally categorical concerning the issue of authorization: 'Equally, the simple fact that Resolution 1441 does not expressly forbid the use of armed force plainly cannot itself amount to an implied authorisation to use force . . . Most Security Council resolutions do not expressly forbid the use of force: no-one would argue that they therefore all authorise it.' The end result of Professor Lowe's careful examination of the issues was stark: 'My conclusion, therefore, is that under present circumstances it would be contrary to international law for the United Kingdom to engage in military action against Iraq, or assist any other State in taking such action, unless it was expressly authorised to do so by the United Nations Security Council.'

Without a second Resolution explicitly authorizing the use of force, concluded Professor Lowe, in common with the majority of international lawyers to express an opinion, war on Iraq would be illegal. In the event, no such resolution was obtained. (There were those who argued that even if such a Resolution had been passed, this would not have been sufficient to make the war legal, basing their position on the provisions of the UN Charter, but this argument was never tested by the passing of a second Resolution.)

Furthermore, Iraq was never found to be in further 'material breach' of its obligations, nor did either of the UN weapons inspection agencies ever suggest that such a finding was appropriate, despite the severity of the new conditions imposed by the US after Iraq accepted the return of the inspectors. Perhaps most galling of all for Washington, Baghdad made no serious protest as it accepted the Resolution lock, stock and smoking barrel. However objectionable it was, the alternative was worse, and Iraq submitted post haste.

The Resolution did not say that if at any point Washington or London found Iraqi co-operation insufficient, the Security Council would immediately authorise a military invasion of Iraq (the officially-touted interpretation in Britain and the US after the war). Resolution 1441 said that if at any point *UN weapons inspectors* found Iraqi co-operation insufficient, the Security Council would immediately meet to consider the situation.

Resolution 1441, despite its calculated harshness and its cunning ambiguities, turned out to be irrelevant to both the legitimacy and the legality of the war.

CHAPTER IX
No Smoke, No Gun

No Evidence Discovered

INTO THE MINEFIELD

With Iraq's unconditional offer to re-admit the inspectors, and unconditional acceptance of Resolution 1441, the long-feared return of the UN weapons inspectors was unavoidable. The US pinned its hopes on two immediate crisis points. The weapons declaration that Iraq was required to submit by Resolution 1441 might throw up a self-incriminating *casus belli*. Alternatively, Iraq might hinder or block some of the inspections.

THE DECLARATION

The weapons declaration was something of a no-win situation for Saddam Hussein: if Baghdad admitted possessing weapons of mass destruction, the United States would claim to be justified in going to war; but if the declaration failed to admit the existence of such weapons, Baghdad would be said to be failing to co-operate with Resolution 1441, which would also be said to justify war. President Bush told a NATO summit on 20 November 2002, 'Should he again deny that this arsenal exists, he will have entered his final stage with a lie, and deception this time will not be tolerated.'[1] 'If the Iraqis stick with a declaration of "nil", then it's war,' said Dr John Chipman, the director of the London-based International Institute of Strategic Studies.[2]

When the declaration was handed in on 7 December 2002, there was no gaping hole that could be demonstrated to the outside world. There was also no admission of prohibited activities or materials. On 19 December, after intensive study of the declaration, US ambassador to the UN John Negroponte said that Iraq had 'spurned its last opportunity to comply with its disarmament obligations.' There were 'material omissions that, in our view, constitute another material breach.'[3] No other country, not even Britain, agreed with the US that the declaration amounted to a 'material breach',[4] though the UK did say the declaration was faulty (a necessary step for the launching of any future war). Tony Blair, in one of his many breaches of collective Cabinet decision-making, said 'should it be found that that declaration was dishonest, then that most certainly would be a material breach,' contradicting a statement by British Foreign Secretary Jack Straw on the same day.[5]

THE ALUMINIUM TUBES FIASCO

The head of the International Atomic Energy Agency (IAEA), Mohamed ElBaradei, suggested that the declaration was defective because it had failed to account properly for Iraq's attempt to buy thousands of aluminium tubes that the US alleged were suitable for enriching uranium.[6] On 7 March 2003, however, Dr ElBaradei announced the results of months of intensive investigation. The IAEA concluded that the suspiciously tight manufacturing tolerances and high-strength materials specified for the tubes were the result of an incompetent attempt to copy some conventional rockets Iraq had imported. Having assessed copies of design documents, procurement records, minutes of committee meetings and supporting data and samples, and after interviewing Iraqi personnel involved in the effort, Dr ElBaradei's team failed to uncover any evidence that Iraq intended to use the 81mm tubes for any project other than the 'reverse engineering' of rockets. The project had languished for long periods during its lifespan, and had become the subject of several committees, which resulted in specification and tolerance changes on each occasion. 'Iraq's efforts to import these aluminium tubes were not likely to have been related to the manufacture of centrifuges,' said the IAEA. Moreover, 'it was highly unlikely that Iraq could have achieved the considerable re-design needed to use them in a revived centrifuge programme.'[7]

US Secretary of State Colin Powell had made a great deal of the tubes issue in his presentation to the Security Council on 5 February 2003, saying that they could be adapted for centrifuge use.[8] Now the IAEA was saying that the re-design needed to make the tubes fit for this purpose was 'highly unlikely'. The Secretary of State had no answer to the detailed investigation the IAEA had carried out, only more accusations and discredited speculations. What was most interesting about his intervention was the perhaps inadvertent revelation that US intelligence on the tubes was not automatically shared with the inspectors, part of a larger pattern of US non-co-operation with the inspection effort, despite the injunction in Resolution 1441 that all countries should share information with the IAEA and UNMOVIC.[9]

THE INSPECTIONS

The declaration failed to provide a killer blow. Unfortunately for the US, the inspections also proceeded without a hitch. Chief weapons inspector at UNMOVIC, Dr Hans Blix, warned in mid-November 2002, 'A denial of access, or delayed access, or trying to put something off grounds for us—this would be very serious.'[10] However, as his counterpart at the International Atomic Energy Agency, Mohamed ElBaradei, observed at the Security Council on 19 December, Iraq had so far 'co-operated well in terms of access.'[11]

Recall that the US had delayed the return of the inspectors for nearly two months in order to hammer out new inspection rules, tearing up the previous conditions placed on inspections of 'sensitive sites' and the presidential palaces in particular. It was the US which had delayed the re-entry of the inspectors, arguing that only instant access to the palaces could enable the inspectors to discover the truth about Iraq's weapons. The palaces were built up into a major threat. A *Newsweek* cover story asked, 'Is there really reason to believe Saddam is hiding horrific weapons, or the plans to make them, in his presidential residences?' The answer given was: 'Good reason, yes. Hard evidence, no.'[12] The article noted that the palaces had been inspected in 1998—this was mere weeks after the British Government had officially denied any such inspections had taken place—and that 'after months of haggling and the specter of war, when the inspections finally were carried out, nothing was found.' There is a little more to the story.

Former UNSCOM weapons inspector Scott Ritter, revealed in 2002 that no sampling for the presence of biological weapons was conducted inside the presidential palaces in 1998. Richard Spertzel, head of the UNSCOM biological weapons inspection effort in 1998 (and a former biological warfare officer for the US Army according to Mr Ritter), simply refused to carry out the tests. While tests were carried out for chemical and nuclear weapons in the palaces, the biologists were prevented from conducting any. 'When the Iraqis confronted Dick Spertzel about this, he said he'd never expected biological weapons to be there, and hadn't wanted to give them the benefit of a negative reading.'

According to Mr Ritter's account, 'The Iraqis repeatedly asked him to bring in sophisticated sensing equipment to test for biological weapons. He consistently said he wasn't going to carry out investigations that provide circumstantial evidence to support Iraq's contention they don't have these weapons.' Mr Ritter records that he challenged Mr Spertzel over this refusal, 'But he was in charge of biology. My job was to look for concealment. And I never found any evidence of concealment of biological weapons.'[13]

The *Sunday Telegraph* reported in mid-November 2002 that 'British and American intelligence have developed a plan for the weapons inspectors that meets a timetable for attack early next year.' Washington and London wanted the inspectors to search roughly 1,000 sites: 'About 10 are considered certain to contain evidence of illegal activity.'[14] A number of sites had been identified in US and British Government documents as sites of prohibited activities. For example, in the September 2002 British weapons dossier, the following sites were marked as suspicious: the chlorine and phenol plant at Fallujah 2 near Habbaniyah; the Ibn Sina Company at Tarmiyah; the al-Qa'qa' chemical complex; a large new chemical complex, Project Baiji, in north-west Iraq; the Castor Oil Production Plant at Falluja; the al-Dawra Foot and Mouth Disease Vaccine Institute; and the Ameriya Sera and Vaccine Plant at Abu Ghraib.[15]

At a press conference on 13 January 2003, Mr Blair said confidently, 'I think again we should wait and see what the inspectors find, and 27 January is the first time they will make a full report and then I think things will be a little clearer.'[16] Mr Blair apparently almost broke into a smile while urging reporters to give the UN more time to do its job properly, hinting that a major find was just around the corner. These hopes were dashed. All the suspect sites, including supposedly suspicious presidential sites, were investigated by the UN weapons inspectors. An editorial in the *Guardian* newspaper commented on 27 January 2003: 'the WMD sites pinpointed in Mr Blair's dossier last year have now been inspected; nothing incriminating has been found.'[17]

THE EMPTY WARHEADS

In mid-January 2003, there was finally some good news for Washington. On 16 January, UN weapons inspectors made their first discovery of materials or equipment connected with Iraq's weapons of mass destruction programmes. Inspectors from UNMOVIC found what the UN described as '11 empty 122mm chemical warheads and one warhead that requires further evaluation' (later found to be empty also) at the previously-inspected Ukhaider ammunition dump, 75 miles south of Baghdad. 'They were in excellent condition and were similar to ones imported by Iraq during the late 1980s,' said a UN spokesperson.[18] The White House experienced near-jubilation as aides realised that the warheads represented 'the political equivalent of manna from heaven'.[19]

Before discussing the warheads themselves, it may be worthwhile recalling that the real issue was not whether Iraq possessed weapons of mass destruction: it was whether Iraq posed a threat to the region or to the wider world. Even if a very large number of fully loaded chemical warheads had been found (rather than a very small number of completely empty warheads), this would not have justified military action. Earlier we noted the observation of British Vice-Admiral Sir James Jungius KBE (before the warheads were discovered) that, 'Even if the weapons do exist, where is the evidence of intent to use them? War is too important and unpleasant a business to be undertaken on the basis of a hunch, however good that hunch may be.'[20]

Also relevant here are comments quoted earlier from former Tory Cabinet Minister Douglas Hogg: 'The real question is not whether he's got weapons of mass destruction, but rather whether—if he has got those weapons—he is a grave and imminent threat to the rest of us.' There were many other countries in the world that possessed weapons of mass destruction, or were likely to acquire them, 'but we don't necessarily conclude that they are a grave and imminent threat sufficient to justify war': 'So even if he had these things, unless he's a grave and imminent threat there isn't a moral basis for war, because the doctrine of self-defence isn't properly invoked.'[21]

The 122mm warheads that were discovered seem to have been for an Egyptian Saqr-30 multi-barrelled rocket launcher (based on a Warsaw Pact system known as the Katyusha) which had range of up to 20 miles. While there was initial speculation that the warheads might have been deliberately hidden, and moved recently, this suspicion was discounted after investigation by the inspectors.[22]

The White House viewed the find as 'troubling and serious.'[23] In contrast, Charles Heyman, editor of *Jane's World Armies*, a highly-respected mainstream military publication, said that given the state of the Iraqi armed forces, the official response from Baghdad that the missile warheads had been forgotten was entirely credible. Mr Heyman pointed out that it would make no sense to hide the warheads in an ammunition dump which the inspectors were sure to inspect: 'For once the Iraqis are probably telling the truth.'[24]

Matthew Meelson, a weapons expert at Harvard's International Security Programme, said that the US had in the past lost track of chemical and biological weapons from abandoned programmes and that warheads had turned up from time to time. 'If these canisters are new and show signs of recent machine-shop work, then that is one thing, but if not, it's less than trivial,' said Mr Meelson. 'It would be unfortunate if they go to war over bad book-keeping.'[25] No suspicious marks were found by the inspectors.

One of Dr Blix's predecessors as chief UN weapons inspector, Rolf Ekeus, described the discovery of the warheads as 'militarily insignificant'.[26] Dr Blix himself was equally dismissive, describing the warheads discovery as 'no big deal'.[27] Dr Blix summed the matter up thus: 'Some 12 empty shells have been forgotten and that, evidently, is not very good. But it is not a very big quantity. It's not a smoking gun.' 'Shells are not' weapons of mass destruction.[28]

Interestingly, the Bush Administration did not declare the warhead find a 'material breach' of UN Resolutions. The White House had decided to present the find as a 'building block' in the case for war, not as a 'breakthrough'. Opinion polls showed most Americans were uneasy about the idea of war on Iraq, and Washington was about to experience the biggest peace march since the Vietnam War. President Bush was deterred from making too much of the empty warheads by the strength of the US anti-war movement.[29]

PRO-ACTIVE CO-OPERATION

The British Government was soon reaching the desperate position of arguing that though Iraq was cooperating 'passively' by allowing inspectors to go where they wanted and inspect whatever they liked, Baghdad was still not really cooperating because it was not co-operating 'pro-actively' with the UN inspectors. A British official admitted in January that the Government was increasingly resigned to the fact that Dr Blix and Dr ElBaradei would fail to uncover significant evidence of nuclear, biological or nuclear weapons. The Prime Minister would now have to start making the case that an 'incremental breach' was enough to trigger military action. 'An absence of co-operation and a pattern of obstruction does constitute a breach,' said another Downing Street official. 'As each day goes by and he doesn't satisfactorily answer these questions [on weapons of mass destruction] then it becomes clear that we may not need a smoking gun—but we know there is the whiff of cordite.'[30] Absence of evidence was evidence of presence.

The *Guardian* commented accurately,

> Despairing of conclusive proof and losing the battle for public opinion, the US and Britain are not just moving the goalposts. They are widening the goalmouth and doubling the size of the penalty area . . . while there is much that remains unsatisfactory, nothing that

remotely justifies a resort to war has been uncovered. It is certainly not helpful or convincing to claim an absence of proof is itself proof. It is certainly not helpful for the US to crow that, whatever Iraq does, Saddam is doomed.'[31]

London and Washington had delayed the return of the inspectors, ripped up previous agreements with Iraq, and forced the Security Council to pass a new resolution in order to gain instant access to the presidential palaces, on the basis that the lack of such access had fatally compromised the previous inspection regime, and prevented it from uncovering the hidden weapons. Well, the palaces were inspected. They failed to yield up the treasure expected of them.

London and Washington moved on. They had threatened war if Iraq did not allow complete and instant access for the inspectors. Now they were to say that the complete and instant access that Iraq granted the inspectors was an irrelevant sideshow, an 'empty concession', and certainly not evidence of Iraqi cooperation or compliance.

Blocking access meant war. Granting access still meant war.

CHAPTER X
Colin Powell Lied

Turning On The Inspectors

MATERIALS UNACCOUNTED FOR

The issue of 'pro-active co-operation' was not just a recent and desperate invention of the US and British Governments. There was a real and long-standing issue. In his last report to the UN Security Council, Richard Butler, head of UNSCOM, placed great emphasis on documentation held by the Iraqi authorities which could help to 'close remaining gaps and achieve acceptable confidence in Iraqi declarations.'[1] There were materials and weapons which the Iraqi authorities admitted they had produced or possessed before January 1991, which they claimed had been destroyed or lost, and for which no solid evidence of destruction had been found by the inspectors.

It was a common device of the Bush and Blair Governments to refer to these 'unaccounted for' items as though it had been proven that they still existed. On the eve of war, Mr Blair used this gambit skillfully:

> When the inspectors left in 1998, they left unaccounted for 10,000 litres of anthrax; a far-reaching VX nerve agent programme; up to 6,500 chemical munitions; at least 80 tonnes of mustard gas, and possibly more than 10 times that amount; unquantifiable amounts of sarin, botulinum toxin and a host of other biological poisons; and an entire Scud missile programme. We are asked now seriously to accept that in the last few years—contrary to all history, contrary to all intelligence—Saddam decided unilaterally to destroy those weapons. I say that such a claim is palpably absurd.[2]

(This last sentence, of course, came back to haunt Mr Blair in May 2003 when various officials, including Donald Rumsfeld, began floating the 'weapons-were-destroyed-by-Saddam' theory to cover the embarrassing lack of evidence after the war.) Mr Blair moved seamlessly from the accurate statement that certain materials and weapons had not been 'accounted for', to the unsubstantiated claim that these materials and weapons had definitely existed in the recent past.

Let us consider the '6,000 chemical bombs'. In July 1998 inspectors saw but were prevented from retaining a document which indicated that Iraq had dropped 6,000 fewer air-dropped chemical bombs than it had told UNSCOM. This did not mean that the bombs still existed, it meant there was a question mark over them. When Iraq finally handed over the six-page 'Air Force' document to UNMOVIC on 30 November 2002, it was found not to be helpful in clearing up the discrepancies.[3] On 14 February, Dr Blix said, 'One must not jump to the conclusion that they exist.'[4] According to Baghdad, the 'Air Force' document did not count the chemical bombs used at three airbases which had been occupied in 1991, and where the records in the bases had been destroyed.[5] Of the 6,000 'unaccounted for' weapons, 450 aerial bombs contained mustard gas, and could still have been viable in 2003. The other bombs, containing the nerve agents sarin and tabun, would no longer be useable according to UNMOVIC, because they would have deteriorated long ago.[6] So, it may be that the famous 6,000 chemical bombs were used up in the 1980s, but the records to prove this were destroyed as a result of the 1991 war. If these chemical weapons did survive the 1991 war, only 450 of the 6000 would be of any concern to anyone in 2003.

Iraq declared that 127,941 WMD bombs existed just before the 1991 war—filled and unfilled. UNSCOM accounted for 108,761 of these bombs—they were either destroyed under UNSCOM supervision, or credible evidence of their destruction was provided. Over 85 per cent of the WMD bombs were thus taken care of to UNSCOM's satisfaction. This didn't mean that the other 20,000 or so bombs existed in 2003. It meant there were question marks about these weapons.[7] Yes, there were questions about the anthrax (which would probably have deteriorated by 2003[8]), mustard gas, and other poisons. But these were questions, not evidence. Former UN weapons inspector David Albright remarked in March 2002, 'The evidence produced so far is worrying. It is an argument for getting the inspectors back in as fast as possible, but not for going to war.'[9] Hence the need for 'pro-active co-operation', and the need for inspectors on the ground.

THE NIGHTMARE SCENARIO

The problem was that the United States was opposed to the work of the weapons inspectors. The January 1998 letter from the Project for the New American Century—signed by Mr Rumsfeld and Mr Wolfowitz—argued that, even if inspections were to resume, 'experience has shown that it is difficult if not impossible to monitor Iraq's chemical and biological weapons production.' The hawks wrote that, 'As a result, in the not-too-distant future we will be unable to determine with any reasonable level of confidence whether Iraq does or does not possess such weapons.'[10] When the new Bush administration came to power, the hawks arranged a major bombardment of Iraq in February 2001. Informed observer Dilip Hiro, author of *Desert Shield to Desert Storm*, remarked at the time that, 'Inadvertently or otherwise, Bush and Blair have destroyed any chance Kofi Annan had of working out a plan for UN inspections when he meets the Iraqi Foreign Minister later this month.'[11] Inadvertently or otherwise.

Seymour Hersh, the investigative journalist reported in December 2001, 'Inside the Administration, there is general consensus on one issue, officials told me: there will be no further effort to revive the UN inspection regime withdrawn in late 1998.'[12] President Bush scrupulously avoided calling for the return of UN inspectors in the State of the Union address in January 2002 (or in his address to the General Assembly on 12 September 2002). *Time* magazine reported in April 2002 that the 'principals' in the Bush Administration 'fear that Saddam is working his own UN angle for the return of weapons inspectors to Iraq, whose presence could make the US look like a bully if it invades.' 'The hawks' nightmare is that inspectors will be admitted, will not be terribly vigorous and not find anything,' a former U.S. official said: 'Economic sanctions would be eased, and the US will be unable to act . . . and the closer it comes to the 2004 elections the more difficult it will be to take the military route.'[13] A senior US Senate foreign policy aide was frank in May 2002: 'The White House's biggest fear is that UN weapons inspectors will be allowed to go in.'[14] When the July 2002 talks between the UN and Iraq broke down, the *Daily Telegraph* commented, 'The UN's failure will come as a relief to many in the Pentagon, where senior officials fear that inspectors might be granted some form of access, then give Saddam a clean bill of health he did not deserve.'[15] The talks failed in part because of a well-timed leak to the *New York Times* spelling out US war plans.

In August 2002, Vice-President Dick Cheney was let off the leash.[16] He launched a vitriolic attack on the inspectors' record, saying that 'the inspectors missed a great deal'. The return of UN weapons inspectors to Iraq would provide 'no assurance whatsoever'. On the contrary, said the Vice-President, there was a great danger that it would provide 'false comfort' that Saddam Hussein was somehow 'back in his box'.[17]

The reporting was consistent and unmistakable: inspections were the hawks' 'nightmare scenario'. The inspectors might declare Baghdad free of weapons of mass destruction, removing a justification for war. Or the inspectors might push war back into the autumn of 2003, much too close to the start of the US Presidential election cycle.

MR POWELL GOES ONTO THE ATTACK

The outburst from the Vice-President seems to have caused Secretary of State Powell a great deal of anguish. Bob Woodward, something of a Powell confidant, records that Mr Powell was 'astonished' by the speech, and embarrassed that the BBC was simultaneously releasing excerpts of an earlier interview with him, in which he said that it would be 'useful' to restart the inspections.[18] Mr Powell was a team player, however.

In late January 2003, the former general said, 'The question isn't how much longer do you need for inspections to work. Inspections will not work.'[19] (A month later, Sir Jeremy Greenstock, the British ambassador to the UN, was saying much the same thing: 'The inspectors cannot in these circumstances disarm a resistant Iraq'.[20]) Much earlier, in May 2002, the Administration's dove had made it clear that the US was intent on military action: 'US policy is that, regardless of what the inspectors do, the people of Iraq and the people of the region would be better off with a different regime in Baghdad. The United

States reserves its option to do whatever it believes might be appropriate to see if there can be a regime change.' The issue of the inspectors was a 'separate and distinct and different' matter from the US position on Saddam Hussein's leadership, said Powell.[21]

On 5 February 2003, Colin Powell became the point man for the entire war effort, leading an assault on the Security Council. Later, British and US officials were to look back on his presentation as the 'high water mark' of their campaign for a second Resolution.[22] Mr Powell tried to prove that Iraq had hidden weapons of mass destruction; and to prove that the UN weapons inspectors were incapable of discovering these weapons. Before Mr Powell's address 59 per cent of people in the US wanted UN inspectors to be given at least 'several months' to do their work—41 per cent were willing to give the inspectors as long as they needed. After the presentation, however, 52 per cent of people wanted inspectors out of Iraq within a month or less, and support for the war had risen 10 points to 70 per cent. 69 per cent of respondents said they had found Mr Powell's UN presentation either 'very' or 'somewhat' convincing.[23] In his barnstorming briefing to the Security Council, the US Secretary of State said, 'The issue before us is not how much time we are willing to give the inspectors to be frustrated by Iraqi obstruction, but how much longer are we willing to put up with Iraq's non-compliance before we, as a council, we, as the United Nations, say, "Enough. Enough".'[24] Mr Powell convinced most of the US public that the inspections were futile. The 'evidence' he used was deceitful, however.

THE TAJI SHELL GAME

The most striking images used in the 5 February presentation were of the Taji military base, which Mr Powell said contained both conventional weapons bunkers and active chemical weapons bunkers. A satellite photograph from 10 November 2002 showed two shapes by a bunker—allegedly a decontamination vehicle and a security building for monitoring leakages from the chemical weapons supposedly stored in the bunker. A second photo taken on 22 December, showed UN weapons inspectors' vehicles passing two nearby structures referred to as 'sanitized bunkers'—the original 'chemical weapons bunker' with its 'security building' was not pictured, despite being only a short distance away.[25] Jonathan Ban, a chemical weapons expert at the Washington-based Chemical and Biological Arms Control Institute, raised the critical question: 'what happened to the active bunkers when the weapons inspectors showed up?'[26] The unspoken purpose of the slides was to dramatise the alleged inability of the inspectors to detect Iraqi deception, but they failed to prove either that any of the bunkers had contained chemical weapons or that they had been 'sanitized' in a way that inspectors could not detect.

Taji had been repeatedly inspected since 1991. Baghdad must have expected it to be inspected again. Therefore, Dr Blix pointed out on 14 February, it was an unlikely location for hiding chemical weapons.[27] As Dr Blix noted, 'The reported movement of munitions at the [Taji] site could just as easily have been a routine activity as a movement of proscribed munitions in anticipation of an imminent inspection'.[28]

Regime Unchanged

THE AL-MUSSAYYIB MISDIRECTION

Mr Powell showed a second set of satellite images, this time of the al-Mussayyib weapons facility, allegedly involved in shipping chemical weapons from production facilities out to the field. The first picture, from May 2002, showed a bunker surrounded by what the US said were three 35-tonne cargo trucks, along with an alleged decontamination vehicle—showing, according to Mr Powell, that the site was being used for chemical or biological weapons activity. A second image, taken two months later, showed that part of the site had been bulldozed and the earth freshly 'graded'—allegedly to conceal banned weapons activity from UN inspection teams. Mr Powell said an Iraqi human source had stated that chemical weapons had been removed at that time. On 13 December 2002, inspectors went to al-Mussayyib and found only ready-to-use pesticides.

Chemical weapons expert Jonathan Ban again: 'I find it very difficult to believe that if there was chemical weapons contamination in the area that the Iraqis would be able to completely get rid of that contamination. The image shows that there are some areas of ground on the site that haven't been graded and I think the inspectors would be able to take samples from there to prove conclusively whether or not there has been recent chemical weapons activity.'[29] Sounds like a job for those 'false comfort' inspector types.

The Powell presentation, which was highly effective in the US heartlands, actually demonstrated the importance and relevance of having UN weapons inspectors on the ground. Grainy photographs of suspect 'security buildings' and freshly-turned earth were only useful in identifying possible targets of inquiry by the inspectors.

Mr Powell himself acknowledged the photos were 'sometimes hard for the average person to interpret, hard for me.'[30] Only one expert in space imaging was consulted by the British newspapers to examine the Powell evidence. Mark Monmonier, of Syracuse University in the USA, was unconvinced by the photographs, saying, 'The Bush administration either has little, or is playing its cards very close to the vest.' The evidence being sought was 'not easily revealed on high-resolution space imagery'—'So much depends on intelligent inference, but inference nonetheless.'[31]

Incidentally, Paragraph 10 of UN Resolution 1441, asked all Governments to 'give full support to UNMOVIC and the IAEA in the discharge of their mandates, including by providing any information related to prohibited programmes or other aspects of their mandates'. The Resolution was passed on 8 November 2002, but Mr Powell's dramatic photos taken in May, July, November and December 2002 were not handed over to UNMOVIC—they were kept secret and then publicly displayed on 5 February 2003. Robert Fisk, noting this delay, asked, 'Were the Americans, perhaps, not being "pro-active" enough?'[32]

THE MOBILE CONFIDENCE TRICK

A major weapon against the inspectors was the story of the 'biological weapons factories on wheels and on rails' which were 'designed to evade detection by inspectors.' Mr Powell's punch line: 'It took the inspectors four years to find out that Iraq was making biological agents. How long do you think it will take the inspectors to find even one of these 18 trucks?'[33] However, biological warfare experts consulted by *Newsweek* stated that truck-mounted labs would be all but unworkable: 'The required ventilation systems would make them instantly recognizable from above, and they would need special facilities to safely dispose of their deadly wastes. A routine highway accident could be catastrophic. And US intelligence, after years of looking for them, has never found even one.'[34] The vehicles discovered in Iraq after the war, and trumpeted as a major discovery by Mr Blair were found not to be mobile weapons labs, but vehicles for filling artillery balloons with hydrogen. They were sold to Iraq by Britain's Marconi Command & Control.[35]

THE TRUST ISSUE

We have already noted the fiasco over the 'uranium-from-Niger' claim repeated by Mr Powell in his Security Council presentation, and the anger in US and British intelligence organisations over the misuse of the available evidence on links between al-Qaeda and Iraq.[36] Richard Beeston of *The Times* observed that, in fact, most of Mr Powell's presentation was open to interpretation: 'There was no named high-ranking defector prepared to substantiate the allegations. There was no visual evidence of soldiers or scientists handling weapons such as chemical or biological weapons, nor even attempting to conceal huge items such as Scud missiles.' Mr Beeston's colleague Michael Evans noted that there were no pictures of the inside of any of the alleged mobile biological weapons laboratories, nor any photographic evidence of a chemical weapons programme.[37] The *Guardian* homed in on the 'heart of the matter', which was that that the US claims had to be accepted on trust: 'Mr Powell's sources were mostly anonymous defectors, detainees, third country spooks and US intelligence.'[38]

Joseph Cirincione, senior associate at the Carnegie Endowment for International Peace in Washington DC, warned that, 'We should never go to war based on a defector's tale. There's a long history of defectors' tales being erroneous . . . It is a problem that detectives have all the time; somebody comes to them hoping to get something in exchange.'[39] Dr Blix made similar cautionary remarks: 'Defectors have a natural wish to make themselves interesting and provide things that are sensational. It increases their chances of asylum. And the CIA and everybody knows that. And a lot of it comes in as nonsense.'[40]

The US Secretary of State barraged the members of the Security Council with questions: 'Who took the hard drives? Where did they go? What's being hidden? Why?' Yet he offered few solid answers. Egyptian political scientist Emad Shahin observed wryly, and accurately, 'The speech was long on accusations, and short on evidence.'[41]

Many Western observers were convinced by intercepted conversations between Iraqi military officials. But doubts remained in some quarters about the credibility of the tapes, not least because many observers doubted that senior Iraqi officers would speak so carelessly on open telephone or radio conversations. The conversations were also open to interpretation. Much was made of the recordings of Iraqi officers straining to 'evacuate' any 'forbidden ammo' and a 'modified vehicle.' Jonathan Ban, the chemical weapons specialist, was sceptical: 'what do they mean by a "modified vehicle"? That could mean absolutely, anything as could "prohibited ammo".'[42] Once again, there was an issue of interpretation and judgement, of speculation presented as incontrovertible fact.

Dr Blix remarked tartly, 'Intelligence, "actionable" intelligence, is useful. We can send our inspectors anywhere. But we are interested in sites. We cannot do analysis of telephone conversations.'[43]

Mr Powell repeated the claim that Iraq had sought uranium from Niger. He said, 'Since 1998, [Saddam Hussein's] efforts to reconstitute his nuclear program have been focused on acquiring the third and last component: sufficient fissile material to produce a nuclear explosion.'[44] As noted earlier, the International Atomic Energy Agency (IAEA) said, after looking at the documentation offered as evidence, that the claims were baseless. The fabrication was transparently obvious and quickly established, IAEA sources said, suggesting that British intelligence was either easily hoodwinked or a knowing party to the deceit.[45] Mr Powell effectively lied to the Security Council on a very serious matter, and he was caught out. When confronted with the IAEA refutation of the documents, Mr Powell said, 'It was the information that we had. We provided it. If that information is inaccurate, fine.'[46] Mr Powell told a US television reporter, 'if that issue is resolved, that issue is resolved.'[47] No, the issue was not resolved. The issue was that the forgery on which Mr Powell relied was transparently obvious, which made the US and British Governments either easily hoodwinked (which was not a credible suggestion, given the publicly revealed scepticism of US intelligence) or knowing parties to the deceit.

On the al-Qaeda issue, Mr Powell advanced a number of confident claims of links between Iraq and the terrorist network, reviewed earlier.[48] As we have seen, the US and British intelligence agencies were furious at this misuse of the available evidence. 'The intelligence is practically non-existent', said one 'exasperated' US intelligence source.[49] Again, the claims made were distortions of the available evidence. They were lies, peddled to the Security Council and to the world by a desperate man seeking to build support for a war his political master was determined to wage.

Thus also the deceitful insinuation by Mr Powell (holding up a small vial) that Iraq might be about to use dried anthrax against the US Government, when there was no evidence that Iraq had ever dried anthrax, there was nothing to link Iraq to the attacks on the Senate in 2001, and the estimates of Iraq's 'unaccounted for' anthrax stocks rested on extremely rickety foundations.[50]

THE ADLAI STEVENSION MOMENT

There was much talk of the 'Adlai Stevenson moment' of 1962, and whether Mr Powell could replicate the thrill that came when President John F. Kennedy's Ambassador to the UN presented satellite photographs of Soviet nuclear missiles deployed in Cuba, during the Cuban Missile Crisis. There was at least one crucial difference, of course. Arthur

Schlesinger, a former adviser to President Kennedy, who watched Ambassador Stevenson's dramatic revelations to the Security Council in 1962, pointed out that Mr Powell 'didn't have the definitive evidence that Stevenson had then, particularly on the relationship with al-Qaida.'[51] Adlai Stevenson Jr, a former US senator himself, pointed out that his father had presented the Security Council with irrefutable and incontrovertible proof that a nuclear superpower was placing nuclear missiles 90 miles off the US shore, so that 'The balance of terror and containment and the international community swung behind us'. With Iraq, however, the evidence was 'murky' and the purpose different. The Bush administration rejected containment and the purpose was war.[52]

The *Financial Times* found Mr Powell's presentation to the UN Security Council 'effective', though the 'evidence' required 'a high degree of trust' and was mostly 'old information'. However, the *FT* pointed out, many members of the Security Council already believed that Iraq retained a residual armoury of weapons: their scepticism revolved around whether war was the best way of dealing with it.[53] The *Independent* also found the presentation 'impressive'—a 'bravura performance'. However, the newspaper pointed out that, 'The policy of containment and sanctions, pursued for 12 years, has been frustrating and messy; but it has constrained Saddam. General Powell did not tell us why we must abandon it.'[54]

Even if all of Mr Powell's allegations about the presence of Iraqi weapons of mass destruction had been true, this would not have justified the resort to force. There were two planks to his argument that Mr Powell failed to establish: that Iraq posed an imminent threat either to a neighbour or to any country further afield; and that non-military means of resolving the conflict had been exhausted.

Perhaps a better analogy for Mr Powell's performance is with a previous 'Adlai Stevenson moment'. In 1961, Ambassador Stevenson was sent to the UN with what he thought was conclusive evidence that the US had not been involved in the abortive Bay of Pigs invasion by Cuban exiles. It turned out the evidence was forged and that the invasion had indeed been orchestrated by the CIA.[55]

Washington regarded the inspectors not as part of the solution, but as part of the problem, a hindrance and an obstacle on the way to war. President Bush had refused to call for the return of the inspectors and issued an ultimatum that was little more than a declaration of war. When Iraq nevertheless offered to re-admit the inspectors, the US blocked and delayed, ripping up previously-agreed rules of inspection. The US drafted a Resolution designed to provoke Iraq into withdrawing its offer to re-admit UNMOVIC and the IAEA. When the inspectors returned despite all these efforts, the most moderate and authoritative figure in the Cabinet was sent out to damage and undermine the credibility of the inspectors using lies and distortions, and forged evidence.

Referring to the Vietnam War, Colin Powell wrote in his autobiography, *My American Journey,* 'Many in my generation vowed that when our turn came to call the shots, we would not quietly acquiesce in half-hearted warfare for half-baked reasons that the American people could not understand.'[56] Some vow.

CHAPTER XI
Inspection Was An Option

Qualitative Disarmament

THE FORGOTTEN ROLE OF THE INSPECTORS

The UN weapons inspection system in Iraq was always intended to carry out two quite distinct tasks. The first was to render harmless, or to verify the disarmament of, all elements of Iraq's nuclear, chemical, biological weapons and long-range missile programmes. This was the intrusive, sometimes confrontational and certainly the most public face of both UNSCOM and UNMOVIC. The second task of the inspectors, much quieter, but perhaps even more important, was to establish and maintain a system of 'Ongoing Monitoring and Verification' (OMV), which could give the international community confidence that Iraq was not rebuilding its prohibited weapons capabilities.[1]

QUALITATIVE DISARMAMENT

The original UNSCOM approach, driven largely by Britain and the United States, was backward-looking and quantitative. It was focused on locating, destroying, removing or 'rendering harmless' all weapons of mass destruction, all long-range missiles, and all the equipment needed to produce them. The aim was to establish a 'material balance' for the equipment and weapons in the various programmes. UNSCOM also prioritised the location of all documents relating to the weapons and missiles programmes, to build up a complete history of the various programmes. Many of the most notorious confrontations between UNSCOM and Baghdad actually revolved around documents, not weapons or components.

However, there was a fatal flaw in the quantitative approach. The goal of the inspectors was to establish what had existed in January 1991, before the war, and then to determine what the fate of these different weapons and materials had been. But the baseline was an Iraqi declaration of what it possessed on 15 January 1991 (the deadline for war). This baseline figure was generally supported by some documentation, but it did not hide the fact that the whole 'unaccounted for' strategy relied in the first place on what had been declared. It was possible that materials or weapons had been manufactured or acquired by 15 January 1991 without being subsequently declared. Thus the wisdom of UN Secretary-General Kofi Annan's famous remark in September 1998, 'I personally believe—as I think a lot of the Security Council members believe with 100 per cent certainty—that Iraq being fully disarmed is never going to be possible. At the end of the day, the Security Council must decide whether Iraq is disarmed to the extent that it is not a threat to its neighbours, that it has no weapons of mass destruction, and that it has no capacity to make weapons of mass destruction.'[2]

Dr Blix, head of UNMOVIC, said in mid-2000,

> There will always be a residue of uncertainty, and that was a concept that eventually was accepted by the Amorim report and by the Security Council and I think by most people. There may be computer programs, engineers, scientists, and maybe even a prototype centrifuge lying around. You can never guarantee that such things do not exist. We tell the members of the council how far we have come, and it is then for them to decide whether that satisfies the resolution's articles about neutralizing Iraq's weapons of mass destruction. Because there will always be that residue of uncertainty concerning Iraq's WMD programs, I do not think it is fair, nor was it supported by the resolution, for the IAEA or for UNSCOM to determine what level of uncertainty should be tolerated. That is for the Security Council to do. I think I am inclined to feel the same way about UNMOVIC, but there I would like to defer until there has been some discussion, because these are matters that could very well be politically sensitive.[3]

One major problem with the 100% 'materials balance' process was that if weapons had been destroyed unilaterally by Iraq in a way that could not be verified (if all that was left were some lumpen ingots that used to be bombs, for example), or if the documentation to prove the non-production or destruction of the weapons was itself lost or destroyed, there was no way for Iraq to prove a negative. The second problem, already noted, was that even if a 'materials balance' could be compiled of all declared weapons and materials, there could never be a 100% guarantee that Iraq did not have undeclared items.

An alternative approach was suggested by Scott Ritter in a ground-breaking article in *Arms Control Today* in June 2000. Instead of looking backwards, the international community should look forwards. The aim should be to prevent Iraq being able to develop, produce and use weapons of mass destruction in the future, not to find every single component accumulated in the past. According to Mr Ritter, who was a leading UN weapons inspector, and the head of UNSCOM's counter-concealment unit, it would be possible to prevent Iraq from assembling missiles and weapons of mass destruction even if it still possessed some of the necessary components and materials. Instead of concentrating on quantities and 'materials balance'—every nut and every bolt (and even every document)—the UN Security Council should focus on preventing the reconstitution of Iraq's weapons development capabilities: 'qualitative disarmament'. Mr Ritter defined 'qualitative disarmament' as 'the elimination of a meaningful, viable capability to produce or employ weapons of mass destruction'.

Quantitative disarmament used intrusive inspections to focus on verification and guaranteed disarmament. Qualitative disarmament would instead build on the achievements of past intrusive inspections to focus on prevention and a high level of confidence and security. The quantitative approach of demanding verification of a 'materials balance' was 'a formula for disaster', said Mr Ritter, 'perpetuating the cycle of conflict with Iraq':

> Given the comprehensive nature of the monitoring regime put in place by UNSCOM, which included a strict export-import control regime, it was possible as early as 1997 to determine that, from a qualitative standpoint, Iraq had been disarmed. Iraq no longer possessed any meaningful quantities of chemical or biological agent, if it possessed any at all, and the industrial means to produce these agents had either been eliminated or were subject to stringent monitoring.
> The same was true of Iraq's nuclear and ballistic missile capabilities. As long as monitoring inspections remained in place, Iraq presented a WMD-based threat to no one.[4]

That last sentence deserves repetition and emphasis: 'As long as monitoring inspections remained in place, Iraq presented a WMD-based threat to no one.'

MONITORING

The monitoring process concentrated on 'choke points' in the weapons production process. The nuclear team used isotope detectors in rivers to detect the discharge of any radioactive material. The chemical team used monitors in chemical factories to detect key precursors and chemical agents. The biological weapons team installed temperature sensors to check if factories were operating equipment at a suspiciously high temperature. Under UNSCOM, the system, initiated in 1994, monitored more than 250 sites. Video cameras were installed in 150 locations to ensure that 'dual-purpose' equipment (which could be used for civilian as well as military purposes) was not misused. The cameras were linked by a series of transmitters and repeaters to UNSCOM's Baghdad Monitoring and Verification Centre, and to the UN in New York. Monitoring was also done through weekly U-2 high-altitude reconnaissance flights (the aircraft were owned and operated by the United States, and intelligence went directly to the US) and through helicopter photography. This aerial reconnaissance was intended to detect fresh construction, new power lines, or other signs of renewed activity at suspect sites.

Monitoring covered present capacities in terms of buildings and plant and skilled personnel with previous experience in the research or production of banned weapons and missiles. It also covered any future introduction of new building, equipment or senior scientists and engineers.

We should note in passing that the monitoring equipment brought into Iraq in late 2002 was of a different order to the technology available four years earlier. Before the inspectors re-entered Iraq, it was reported that they would be able to measure, for instance, the percentage of nickel alloy in corrosion-resistant equipment at chemical facilities: a high percentage could indicate a weaponization program.[5] UNMOVIC also had an ultra-sensitive detector known as 'the Ranger' that could pick up gamma rays even through 13-mm steel plating, and about a dozen shoebox-size, $30,000 digital cameras that, once installed in a facility, could alert the inspectors to any movement of stored materials. The cameras, known as 'auroral large imaging systems', were coated in a special powderized paint to deter tampering.[6]

The function of the inspection process was distinct and different from the monitoring regime. The inspection process, especially in the aggressive and intrusive form developed by Scott Ritter during his service in UNSCOM, was focused on uncovering hidden components, materials and documents related to the weapons programmes, or verifying their destruction. The monitoring process, on the other hand, was designed simply to freeze Iraq's unconventional weapons programmes, and to prevent them from re-starting. Together, the two sides of UNSCOM had successfully disarmed Iraq by 1997, according to Mr Ritter: 'through its extensive investigations, UNSCOM was able to ensure that the vast majority of Iraq's WMD arsenal, along with the means to produce such weaponry, was in fact eliminated. Through monitoring, UNSCOM was able to guarantee that Iraq was not reconstituting that capability in any meaningful way.'

Let us recall that the UNSCOM monitoring effort was terminated by the United States, when the US discredited the agency by using it for spying purposes, used the agency to stage a confrontation over the Ba'ath Party headquarters in Baghdad, and then collapsed the inspection and monitoring effort by ordering the withdrawal of the inspectors to pave the way for Operation Desert Fox.

COLIN POWELL LIED—REPRISE

Secretary of State Powell said in his 5 February presentation to the Security Council,

> We know that Iraq has embedded key portions of its illicit chemical weapons infrastructure within its legitimate civilian industry. To all outward appearances, even to experts, the infrastructure looks like an ordinary civilian operation. Illicit and legitimate production can go on simultaneously or on a dime. This dual-use infrastructure can turn from clandestine to commercial and then back again.
>
> These inspections would be unlikely, any inspections at such facilities, would be unlikely to turn up anything prohibited, especially if there is any warning that the inspections are coming. Call it ingenious or evil genius, but the Iraqis deliberately designed their chemical weapons programs to be inspected. It is infrastructure with a built-in alibi.[7]

This was an astonishing attack on UNMOVIC. Mr Powell was saying that the inspectors were incapable of noticing when Iraqi chemical factories turned from producing pesticides, say, to chemical weapons—a flat lie, given UNMOVIC's monitoring capacity. Washington's top diplomat was saying that Iraq's chemical weapons production capacity was 'inspection-proof'. (Incidentally, on the issue of Iraqi sites having advance notice of inspections, Dr Blix reported to the Security Council nine days after Mr Powell's statement that, 'In no case have we seen convincing evidence that the Iraqi side knew in advance that the inspectors were coming.'[8]) In reality, Iraq's chemical weapons production capacity was completely vulnerable to the monitoring process.

Scott Ritter noted in 2000 that questions remained over several hundred 155mm shells filled with mustard gas, which remain unaccounted for. However, he argued that such a small number of shells had little military value on the modern battlefield and therefore 'cannot be viewed as a serious threat'. 'Far more important to assuring Iraq's qualitative disarmament is disabling its production capability—a task that at first glance seems almost impossible.'

However, Mr Ritter referred to a 1998 UNSCOM document which laid out all the possible ways Iraq could conceal a chemical weapons (CW) production capability: 'The document noted that Iraq could either bury precursor chemicals or distribute them throughout its commercial chemical industry to disguise their true use. Likewise, it could distribute empty dual-use munitions to depots under the cover of legitimate use, bury them, or continuously move them around in trucks. The documents required to resume CW activity could, if microfilmed, be stored in a single briefcase.' The possibilities for concealment seemed considerable. Most disturbingly of all,

> the 1998 UNSCOM document noted that Iraq could readily distribute the main pieces of equipment needed for CW production throughout its commercial facilities, meaning that equipment that had a legitimate use in commercial chemical-related activity could also be used for CW manufacture. As long as this equipment was maintained at legitimate facilities, any hidden intent by Iraq to use it for illicit purposes would go undetected. 'There is no single-use CW equipment, all pieces are dual use and could be justified at different locations,' the document noted.
>
> There was absolutely no evidence that Iraq was trying to hide CW production equipment. In its monitoring capacity, UNSCOM carried out extensive inspections of all of Iraq's civilian chemical manufacturing infrastructure and found no evidence of illicit stores of CW precursor chemicals. Precursor chemicals are difficult to hide from inspectors because the minimum amount required for any viable CW-agent production run is several hundred tons. Inspections of dozens of Iraqi munitions depots by UNSCOM also failed to turn up any illicit unfilled munitions.
>
> However, the key to the qualitative argument is that individual pieces of CW production equipment are worthless unless they are assembled in a specific configuration, a unique combination that would be readily discernible to weapons inspectors. 'Only the proper combination of different pieces of equipment in a particular configuration gives to . . . these pieces of equipment the status of a CW production facility,' the UNSCOM document noted.
>
> The point is that all of UNSCOM's speculative fears concerning reconstitution of an Iraqi CW capability can be laid to rest as long as a viable monitoring inspection regime, one that would detect any specialized configuration of dual-use equipment, is in place—the kind of regime that existed prior to the withdrawal of inspectors in December 1998.[9]

Once again, a sentence deserves emphasis: 'the key to the qualitative argument is that individual pieces of CW production equipment are worthless unless they are assembled in a specific configuration, a unique combination that would be readily discernible to weapons inspectors'. As long as the cameras were rolling, the international community would have been able to see, in real time, whether Iraq's chemical industry was turning 'on a dime' to produce weapons. As long as the cameras were rolling, the international community would have been able to detect, by the configuration of the equipment in the factory, whether illicit and permitted production were going on 'simultaneously'. Mr Powell's statements to the contrary to the Security Council on 5 February were among the most important and the most brazen of the lies he told on that day.

Dr Blix said in February 2003 that inspections were not meaningless even if Iraq refused to co-operate. 'This would amount to containment,' he said. Asked about containment, he conceded: 'President Bush has no confidence in that.'[10] Or perhaps President Bush had a great deal of confidence in the effectiveness of inspection and monitoring, and that was why he pressed ahead with the collapse of UNMOVIC before they showed their worth.

CHAPTER XII
Blitzing Dr Blix

UNMOVIC Resists

EJECTING THE INSPECTORS, 1998

President Bush famously said of the Iraq crisis in January 2003, 'This looks like a re-run of a bad movie and I'm not interested in watching.'[1] There were indeed many familiar aspects to the crisis, but also some significant discontinuities. The central relationship in many ways was that between Washington and the UN weapons inspectors. Richard Butler, who headed the first inspection body, UNSCOM, in its terminal phase, writes in his memoirs, 'If one uses the test of looking rationally at outcomes, without ascribing motives, it could be argued that the death of UNSCOM also became US policy because that is what has happened.'[2] In 2003, the death of the second inspection agency UNMOVIC was also US policy, and the death of UNMOVIC was what happened.

It is instructive to recall the sequence of events in 1998. In November 1998, President Clinton explained that he had called off a missile attack on Iraq because it would have 'mark[ed] the end of UNSCOM.'[3] A few weeks later he went ahead with the same attack. Elementary logic suggests something.

Shutting down the inspectors, in order to pave the way for a four-day aerial bombardment known as Operation Desert Fox, required a three-pronged effort. Firstly, the US used UNSCOM to create an atmosphere of crisis. One important confrontation was precipitated by sending a large group of UNSCOM inspectors to inspect a Ba'ath Party regional headquarters in Baghdad, and to be barred from entering. This particular mission had been initially proposed by former US Marine Scott Ritter, and scheduled first for July, and then August 1998. According to Mr Ritter, the mission was cancelled on both occasions because of pressure from the US Government to delay until 'a more opportune time'. Mr Ritter resigned in protest at the way that UNSCOM was being subordinated to US foreign policy needs.[4] The 'more opportune time' came on 9 November 1998, when twelve inspectors were sent to inspect the party headquarters, despite the fact that UNSCOM had previously agreed that only four inspectors would enter such sites.[5]

The second element in the US programme of shutting down the inspectors was Richard Butler's highly negative UNSCOM report for the Security Council of 14 December 1998. Mr Butler's central conclusion was that Iraq's conduct over the previous month had ensured that 'no progress' was made either in disarmament or in accounting for its prohibited weapons programmes, despite the fact that, as Mr Butler himself conceded, 'In statistical terms, the majority of the inspections of facilities and sites under the ongoing monitoring system were carried out with Iraq's co-operation.'[6] The London *Independent* noted that the harshness of Mr Butler's report 'appeared to have taken all sides by surprise.'[7] A fairer assessment was in Kofi Annan's covering letter which described the Butler report as presenting a 'mixed picture'.[8]

Mr Butler notes in his memoirs that before completing his report he met with US National Security Adviser Sandy Berger.[9] Mr Butler is reported to have given a draft of his report to senior US diplomats at the UN, who transmitted it instantly to President Clinton, who apparently found it too 'weak'. According to the *Washington Post*, US officials thereafter played 'a direct role in shaping Butler's text during multiple conversations with him at secure facilities at the US mission to the United Nations.'[10] The final result of these US interventions was a disproportionately harsh report which helped to create an atmosphere of futility and confrontation conducive to US/UK military strikes.

The *coup de grâce* came when Washington simply ordered UNSCOM out of Iraq. After Mr Butler's December report had been circulated to members of the Security Council on 15 December 1998, the chief weapons inspector was called in by US Ambassador Peter Burleigh, who urged him to be 'prudent' with the safety and security of UNSCOM staff. 'Repeating a familiar script, I told him that I would act on this advice and remove my staff from Iraq,' Mr Butler later wrote.[11] UNSCOM inspectors were withdrawn within hours, never to return. The British mass media have consistently misreported this event. For example, the *Guardian* suggested in February 2003 that UNSCOM 'left Iraq because it had been blocked in its attempts to complete its mission.'[12]

UNSCOM was formed by the UN Security Council; it was funded by the Security Council (out of revenues sequestered from Iraqi oil sales); it was directed by the Security Council; and the officials of UNSCOM were employed by the Security Council. Yet the organization was shut down at the behest of a single member of the Security Council, without reference to or consultation with the Security Council.

EJECTING THE INSPECTORS—MARCH 2003

Having failed to prevent the re-entry of the inspectors in November 2002, the United States had a number of goals. It needed confrontations between Baghdad and the inspectors; outright condemnation of Iraqi non-co-operation in an official inspectors' report; and, ideally, co-operation from the inspectors in withdrawing from Iraq. Creating an atmosphere of crisis and confrontation was made more difficult by the fact that the new chief UN weapons inspector, Dr Hans Blix, was less malleable than Richard Butler. Dr Blix was less enthusiastic about manufacturing confrontations with Baghdad, and he generally failed to inject the necessary harshness and negativity into his public statements or his official UNMOVIC reports to the Security Council.

MOVING THE GOALPOSTS, 2002–2003

One real hope for a crisis was the issue of the interviews. Resolution 1441 gave the inspectors the power to remove Iraqi scientists and their families from Iraq for interviews, as well as the power to interview Iraqi scientists without the presence of an observer from the Iraqi Government. The Resolution contained no requirement to obtain the consent of the Iraqis involved, but Dr Blix made it clear that it would in fact be UNMOVIC policy to only remove people from Iraq with their consent.[13] Dr Blix said the organization was not a 'cloak-and-dagger agency to put people in the trunk of the car and drive them out'; 'nor do I think that we are an abduction agency'.[14] One practical difficulty was that of defining a scientist's 'family' in a country with large, extended families.

The issue of interviews was important, no doubt, but the US was merely stoking the atmosphere of crisis. In explaining the genuine significance of interviews, Dr Blix explained the difference between 'process' co-operation (passively allowing inspectors to go wherever they wanted) and co-operation on 'substance':

> if a state, which has used such weapons, is to create confidence that it has no longer any prohibited weapons, it will need to present solid evidence or present remaining items for elimination under supervision. Evidence can be of the most varied kind: budgets, letters of credit, production records, destruction records, transportation notes, or interviews by knowledgeable persons, who are not subjected to intimidation.[15]

If documentary evidence was not available, Iraq ought to find individuals, engineers, scientists and managers to testify about their experience.[16] On 20 January, Baghdad agreed to encourage scientists to accept interviews, whether inside or outside Iraq, without a tape recorder or a Government 'minder' being present. Three individuals who had previously refused private interviews accepted such interviews at the beginning of February 2003.[17]

There was considerable pressure, it appears, on Dr Blix to demand interviews outside Iraq. In early January, the Foreign Minister of Cyprus, where UNMOVIC had an administrative centre, said, 'It seems they will be coming.'[18] Two months later, Dr Blix told the Security Council that, 'It is our intention to request such interviews shortly.' At this point, on 7 March, 38 individuals had been asked for private interviews, 'of which 10 accepted under our terms, 7 of these during the last week.'[19] Iraq had bent, and allowed uncontrolled interviews, and the inspectors had bent by not demanding interviews outside Iraq. The third landmine in Resolution 1441 had been avoided.

However, there were still attempts to use the issue. British Foreign Secretary Jack Straw said, 'Why has not a single person felt free to go for interviews abroad? Because they have been terrorised and so have their families.'[20] The absence of interviews abroad was turned into incriminating evidence of Iraq's weapons capabilities.

Incidentally, the US even cast doubt on the interview process which they had done so much to champion. In his all-guns-blazing presentation to the Security Council on 5 February, Colin Powell repeated President Bush's allegation that key figures had been hidden and decoys provided for interviews with UN inspectors.[21] What made this repeated claim all the more striking was that Dr Blix had already responded to this allegation, saying that there was no evidence that government agents had been posing as Iraqi scientists.[22] If UNMOVIC officials really were taken in by impostors in the way Mr Bush and Mr Powell alleged, they must have been guilty of incompetence and *naïveté* on a grand scale, sufficient to discredit their entire effort. This was precisely the purpose of such allegations. Mr Powell provided no evidence. The point was not to *prove* that the inspectors were incompetent, but to build this impression in the public mind.

PRESSURE ON DR BLIX

One of the curiosities of the US campaign against the inspectors was that it very much focussed on UNMOVIC, and on Dr Blix in particular. The International Atomic Energy Agency seems to have been left largely alone, perhaps because even the US hawks accepted that Iraq's nuclear weapons programme was long dead. Whatever the reason, the IAEA conducted only 10 interviews between December and late February—all with a tape recorder or an Iraqi witness—but this does not seem to have been remarked on by the US.[23] Dr Blix was forced to meet leading figures in the US and Britain repeatedly, once being subjected to a reportedly tough talking-to by Condoleezza Rice, President Bush's National Security Adviser. In early February, Ms Rice flew to New York to see Mr Blix, where 'she urged him to report the facts', according to Ari Fleischer, the White House press secretary. An insult to Dr Blix's competence and integrity, one might think. A US official added that Ms Rice wanted to make clear that 'a certain kind of language might be a problem.'[24] Russian Foreign Minister Igor Ivanov said on 20 February, 'According to our information, strong pressure is being exerted on international inspectors to provoke them to discontinue their operations in Iraq, as happened in 1998, or to pressure them into coming up with an assessment that would justify the use of force.'[25] This impression was confirmed in private by other UN diplomats, who suggested that pressure on Dr Blix had become 'a fact of life'.[26]

This pressure does not seem to have been exerted in the same way on Dr ElBaradei, the head of the IAEA. After the first major reports to the Security Council on 27 January 2003, *The Times* commented that 'Hans Blix and Mohamed Elbaradei have adopted different policies on interviewing Iraqi scientists, given different assessments of the discovery of hidden documents, taken a different approach to seeking scientists' names and made quite different cases about the need for more time.' At their presentation to the Security Council, 'Dr Blix sounded the alarm about the discovery of a cache of 3,000 pages of documents about uranium enrichment but Dr Elbaradei dismissed their significance. While Dr Blix failed to ask for more time for inspections, Dr Elbaradei made an impassioned appeal for a few more months.' What made the divergence between the two inspectors more poignant was the fact that it was Dr Blix, when he was the head of the IAEA, who hired Dr ElBaradei, who promoted him to become head of the organisation's legal department and then its director of external relations, and who may even have groomed the Egyptian lawyer as his successor.[27]

In 1998, as noted earlier, the co-operation of UNSCOM chief Richard Butler was a crucial ingredient in the US drive to the mini-war—or rather, the long-distance assassination attempt—of Operation Desert Fox. In 2003, the indications at first were that Dr Blix might be similarly co-operative. However, as the months went by and the pressure mounted, Dr Blix paradoxically became more and more independent, and more and more resistant to US demands, and his position converged steadily with that of his protégé Dr ElBaradei.

CO-OPERATION=NON-CO-OPERATION

US attempts to provoke a confrontation with Iraq at first centred on the issue of access. Then came the switch to issues of 'substance'—interviews being a perennial topic. At the end of January, there was also a great deal of fuss made about U2 overflights of Iraq. It was commonly reported that Iraq had 'refused to allow inspectors to use a spy plane.'[28] More scrupulous reports said Iraq had imposed 'too many conditions on the use of the plane.'[29] Sometimes it was even reported accurately: 'Iraq has refused to guarantee the safety of a U-2 plane placed at UNMOVIC's disposal for aerial imagery and for surveillance during inspections.'[30] The *Guardian* said, 'Iraq has set impossible conditions on their use.'[31] 'US officials said yesterday that Iraq had placed unacceptable conditions on flights by U2 surveillance aircraft, such as giving notice of flight schedules, speeds and call signs.'[32] The problem seems to have been that Iraqi air defences reserved the right to fire on illegal US and British incursions into Iraqi air space, and Baghdad at first refused to guarantee the safety of the UNMOVIC U2 aircraft, if clear advance information was not given about the flight path of the U2s. By the end of February, however, the issue had faded away as Iraq permitted overflights, and gave the appropriate guarantees of safety.[33]

Another focus for attention was the al-Samoud missile. In mid-February 2003, 'the White House floated a new idea in the press, telling journalists that a draft resolution might include three tests of Iraqi intentions. Baghdad would be given an ultimatum of a few weeks to provide unfettered interviews with its scientists, destroy its al-Samoud missiles, and allow overflights by spy planes providing data to the inspectors'.[34] Under Resolution 687, the disarmament resolution which re-imposed economic sanctions on Iraq after the 1991 war, Iraq was not permitted to develop long-range missiles, with a capacity over 150km. The al-Samoud was declared by the Iraqis as a sub-150km system. It had been tested to 183km.[35] Baghdad argued that the rocket would fall within accepted ranges once it was loaded with a warhead and a guidance system.[36] The Iraqi Government wrote to the UN inspectors asking for technical discussions on the issue, and invited them to observe a static-testing of the missile, in what might have been an attempt to prove that at least some components should be saved from destruction. However, Dr

Blix ignored these overtures and ordered the elimination of the weapon, a process to be started by 1 March.[37] The Iraqi position appeared reasonable—the excess range seemed marginal—but this was actually an atypical and curious instance of the media under-reporting Iraqi machinations.

The critical issue was not the range *tested*, but the range *possible*. Crucially, the diameter of the missile had been increased from 500mm to 760mm in contravention of a directive from UNSCOM in 1994, enabling Iraq to equip the missile with two engines. The Volga SA2 engines also violated a 1997 UN order: with two Volga engines instead of one, the missile's range could be increased by a factor of two or even three, according to Tim McCarthy, a former UN missile inspector now with the Monterey Institute of International Studies, which had studied the al-Samoud 2. Israel is 300 km away from Iraq, and Tehran just over 500km away.[38]

The general director of the al-Haytham plant in the suburbs of Baghdad, where the missiles were made, complained bitterly about the UNMOVIC order to destroy them. 'We are being threatened by the Americans and even now they are bombing our country,' said Eowayed Ahmed Ali. 'And yet they want to take away our only defensive weapons.'[39] Despite these bitter feelings, the process of destruction began on schedule. Dr Blix described this to the Security Council on 7 March as 'a substantial measure of disarmament—indeed, the first since the middle of the 1990s.' He added, 'We are not watching the breaking of toothpicks. Lethal weapons are being destroyed.' By 7 March, 34 al-Samoud 2 missiles, including four training missiles, two combat warheads, one launcher and five engines had been destroyed under UNMOVIC supervision. Two casting chambers used in the production of solid propellant missiles had also been destroyed.[40]

Along with a rush of other Iraqi initiatives, designed to clear up long-standing questions about anthrax and other unaccounted for materials or weapons, the destruction of the al-Samoud missiles was a significant measure of co-operation on matters of 'substance', and not just in terms of 'process'. Dr Blix said at the Security Council on 7 March, 'the numerous initiatives, which are now taken by the Iraqi side with a view to resolving some long-standing open disarmament issues, can be seen as "active", or even "proactive".' On the other hand, 'these initiatives 3–4 months into the new resolution cannot be said to constitute "immediate" cooperation.'[41] For those concerned with security, non-proliferation, international law and peace, the fact that Iraq was being somewhat tardy was less important than that there was real co-operation and real disarmament going on. For those concerned with war, the focus was elsewhere.

The more Iraq co-operated with the inspectors, the more hostile the US and Britain became to the inspection process. 'It would not surprise the US if Saddam Hussein pretends all of a sudden to have change of heart and allow the U2 to fly or to show up with some of the weapons he promised he never had,' a White House spokesperson said. 'But it wouldn't change the fact that Saddam Hussein is not co-operating.'[42] Co-operation equalled non-co-operation. This was helpfully spelled out, at length, by the dove-turned-hawk, US Secretary of State Colin Powell on 5 March 2003:

Regime Unchanged

Process is not performance. Concessions are not compliance. Destroying a handful of missiles here under duress, only after you're pressed and pressed and pressed and you can't avoid it, and you see what's going to happen to you if you don't start doing something to deceive the international community once again, that's not the kind of compliance that was intended by UN Resolution 1441.

In recent weeks, we have seen a dribbling out of weapons—a warhead there, a missile there—giving the appearance of disarmament, the semblance of cooperation. And in recent days, they have promised more paper, more reports. But these paltry gestures and paper promises do not substantially reduce Saddam's capabilities . . .[43]

What Dr Blix described as 'active', even 'pro-active', co-operation, and a 'substantial measure of disarmament' became 'process', 'the semblance of co-operation,' and 'paltry gestures'. Mr Powell told the Security Council on 7 March, 'Nobody wants war but it is clear that the limited progress we have seen, the process changes we have seen, the slight substantive changes we have seen come from the presence of a large military force': 'Now is the time for the council to tell Saddam that the clock has not been stopped by his strategems and his machinations.'[44] Nobody wanted war, but the UN should tell Iraq that however much co-operation it offered, however much disarmament it engaged in, the war would begin anyway, relentlessly and unavoidably.

In February, Mr Powell had put the matter thus before the Security Council: 'The issue before us is not how much time we are willing to give the inspectors to be frustrated by Iraqi obstruction but how much longer are we willing to put up with Iraq's non-compliance before we, as a council, we, as the United Nations, say, "Enough. Enough".'[45] The inspectors could only face frustration and obstruction—in fact, they came to the Security Council within weeks to report 'active co-operation' and a 'substantial measure of disarmament'. Within weeks, Iraq had allowed instant access to presidential and other sensitive sites, private interviews with weapons scientists, unconditional U2 overflights, and the destruction of 34 al-Samoud missiles.

The definitive statement of US contempt for the inspectors had come earlier, in late January 2003, when Colin Powell said, 'The question isn't how much longer do you need for inspections to work. Inspections will not work.'[46] (This was an almost verbatim repetition of an opinion rendered anonymously by a hawkish senior Pentagon official two months earlier: 'The inspections cannot work. Period. Military power works. Period. All this is a side-show which, the longer it drags on, the greater the need to break the cycle becomes and the need to get involved militarily.'[47] At this time, in November 2002, US hawks had made it clear that they would be happiest of all if the full inspection teams never made it to Iraq.[48]) In early March 2003, Colin Powell said,

Iraq's too little, too late gestures are meant not just to deceive and delay action by the international community, he has as one of his major goals to divide the international community, to split us into arguing factions. That effort must fail. It must fail because none of us wants to live in a world where facts are defeated by deceit, where the words of the

Security Council mean nothing, where Saddam and the likes of Saddam are emboldened to acquire and wield weapons of mass destruction.[49]

In other words, if Saddam Hussein were to co-operate and be disarmed of weapons of mass destruction by non-military means (or to have his lack of weapons verified by UN inspectors), he and his ilk would be emboldened to acquire and use weapons of mass destruction in the future. If Saddam Hussein were to tell more of the truth and allow his scientists to tell the truth in private, lies would rule the world.

The intrusive inspections (of palaces, arms dumps, and the sites identified in British and US dossiers); the flight of U2 aircraft to spy on Iraq's military capacities; Iraqi co-operation of all sorts (whether 'passive', 'active' or 'pro-active'); and actual Iraqi disarmament of missiles capable of being converted to carry weapons of mass destruction, these were all 'empty concessions'. Why? Because Iraqi co-operation was an obstacle to war, and therefore it could not exist. It did not exist.

Across the Atlantic, the British Government played its part in rubbishing Iraqi co-operation. In February, Foreign Secretary, Jack Straw said, 'Instead of open admissions and transparency, we have a charade, where a veneer of superficial co-operation masks wilful concealment . . . there is only one possible conclusion: Iraq is in further material breach as set out in resolution 1441.'[50] There was only one possible conclusion. Mr Blair said a few weeks later, 'Resolution 1441 called for full, unconditional compliance—not 10 per cent, not 20 per cent, not even 50 per cent but 100 per cent. Anything less will not do'.[51] Not 75 per cent, not even 95 per cent. After the destruction of al-Samoud missiles began, the Prime Minister said, 'We always thought this was likely to be part of the drip feed of concessions. This is how Saddam plays the concession game. It is not the full, immediate co-operation that the UN demands.'[52]

What of the leader of the war effort, President Bush? 'Saddam Hussein has learnt the lessons from the past. He asked for more time so he can give the so-called inspectors more runaround. He is interested in playing hide-and-seek in a huge country. He is not interested in disarming.' The contemptuous reference to the 'so-called inspectors' speaks volumes.[53] After the al-Samoud missiles began to be broken up, the President said, 'He will say words that sound encouraging. He's done it for 12 years. He has got a lot of other weapons to destroy, why hasn't he destroyed them yet?'[54]

Whatever weapons Iraq destroyed, the US would always say that there were more being concealed which should be destroyed.

The definitive George W. Bush statement on Iraqi co-operation came early in February, over a month before the war began: 'Saddam Hussein can now be expected to begin another round of empty concessions, transparently false denials. No doubt he will play a last minute game of deception. The game is over.'[55] The 'game' of inspections, the 'game' of disarmament, the 'game' of non-proliferation was over. Whatever Iraq did, whatever co-operation was afforded, it was all a 'game of deception'.

Asked about Mr Bush's crushing comments, Hans Blix responded defiantly:

Q: Is the game over, as US President Bush said?
Blix: We are still in the game.[56]

Not for much longer.

DR BLIX'S EVOLVING REPORTS

At first, the US and Britain had been hopeful that Dr Blix would produce the goods for them. At the 27 January meeting of the Security Council, Hans Blix flashed the thumbs-up sign to John Negroponte, the US Ambassador to the United Nations.[57] He delivered the soundbite that the hawks needed: 'Iraq appears not to have come to a genuine acceptance—not even today—of the disarmament which was demanded of it.'[58] Just as with Richard Butler's condemnatory report in December 1998, Hans Blix's judgement of Iraq was 'unexpectedly tough'.[59] The *Guardian* reported, 'Iraq yesterday tried to overcome its surprise at the severity of the UN weapons inspectors' report . . . one of Saddam Hussein's closest advisers said openly that Iraq was caught off guard by the speech'.[60] Richard Beeston, Diplomatic Editor of the London *Times*, commented in a report headed, 'Blix report swings the balance in favour of US-led invasion': 'International opinion shifted noticeably against Baghdad yesterday, after world leaders digested Hans Blix's report. From Europe to the Middle East and beyond, some of the strongest critics of the US-led campaign against Iraq appeared to soften their positions after Dr Blix accused Baghdad of concealing its weapons programmes and hampering the work of inspectors.'[61] 'If Iraq starts hampering the work of the inspectors then Russia may change its position and agree with the United States on the development of different, tougher UN Security Council decisions,' said President Putin of Russia.[62]

The next major 'update' from the inspectors came on 14 February. It was of an entirely different character. As the *Observer* reported, 'There was no more talk of "dark caves" that still needed to be checked. No more talk of the Iraqi dictator not really understanding that compliance with 1441 meant more than simply opening a few gates to former military sites . . . As Blix continued, Powell's expression was icy . . . There was almost an audible gasp in the chamber as Blix turned to the "clinching" evidence that Powell had presented to the Security Council the previous week. It was ambiguous and unconvincing, Blix said. . . Blix described the inspectors brief as theoretically "open-ended".'[63] Dr Blix's new soundbite was: 'Inspections are effectively helping to bridge the gap in knowledge that arose due to the absence of inspections between December 1998 and November 2002.'[64]

'It wasn't exactly a bag of goodies, was it?' remarked one senior British diplomat after Mr Blix had finished speaking.[65] A key Number 10 official described the speech as a 'disappointment'—'We thought he would be tougher. It's not been the best of days.'[66] In London, Tony Blair told his advisers that the search for a second resolution would continue, but it would now have to be 'Blix-proof': the weapons inspector could no longer be 'relied on' to tilt the scales towards military action.[67] Weeks earlier, a British minister had grumbled to *Sunday Telegraph* political correspondent Matthew d'Ancona, 'Beware the foreigner speaking English, even if he is a Swede.'[68] Such pessimism had been borne out. Dr Blix refused to be a tool of US foreign policy, and refused to be the trigger for war. Dr Blix was not Mr Butler.

In January, Dr ElBaradei had said, 'Barring exceptional circumstances and provided there is sustained co-operation by Iraq, we should be able within the next few months to provide credible assurance that Iraq has no nuclear weapons programme. These few months, in my view, would be a valuable investment in peace because they could help us to avoid a war.'[69] Dr Blix had made no similar statement in January, but on 7 March he pressed the case for 'months' more to be given to the inspectors to do their work:

> How much time would it take to resolve the key remaining disarmament tasks? While cooperation can and is to be immediate, disarmament and at any rate the verification of it cannot be instant. Even with a proactive Iraqi attitude, induced by continued outside pressure, it would still take some time to verify sites and items, analyse documents, interview relevant persons, and draw conclusions. It would not take years, nor weeks, but months.[70]

As was pointed out by the hawks, this was a conditional statement. The priority tasks involved in disarming Iraq could be carried out within months, *if* Iraq continued to have a 'pro-active attitude' of co-operation. Nevertheless, the clear import of Dr Blix's statement was that, in the absence of evidence of an overwhelming danger of an Iraqi WMD attack within the next few months, there was no case for an immediate military assault on Iraq. Non-military alternatives had not been exhausted.

The *Wall Street Journal* observed, 'As each day passes, the evidence mounts that the UN inspections regime is not about containing Saddam; it is about containing America'.[71] That is how the hawks saw the inspectors, certainly. World opinion seems to have seen the inspectors as containing both Iraq and the world's remaining superpower.

As for the inspectors themselves, Dr Blix was adamant and consistent in his preference for non-military forms of disarmament. In late January, meeting with Iraqi officials in Baghdad, Dr Blix said, 'We do not think that war is inevitable. We think that the inspection process that we are conducting is the peaceful alternative.'[72] As *The Times* reported in early February, the chief UN weapons inspector often contrasted the cost of inspections, conducted with 250 officials and $80 million a year, to the possible $100 billion price-tag of a war involving a US force of 250,000 military personnel.[73] Dr Blix told the *New York Times*, also in early February, 'I think it would be terrible if this comes to an end by armed force, and I wish for this process of disarmament through the peaceful avenue of inspections.'[74]

Dr Blix refused to bow to the US agenda. He refused to stage unnecessary confrontations, and he refused to tailor his reports to suit Washington. Closing down the inspectors was going to require more than just smears and pressure.

CHAPTER XIII
The Censored Document

Destroying The Inspectors

WRITTEN OUT OF HISTORY

There is one crucial document in the history of the second Anglo–American war against Iraq, a document which could have—and should have—prevented the war from taking place. This document, however, has been written out of history. It may even qualify as The Most Censored Document Of 2003. BBC Television's detailed instant history of 'The Road To War' omitted this document from its rendition of the US and British drive to war.[1] The *Guardian* newspaper's 'Special Investigation' into 'Blair's road to war' also failed to mention this dramatic intervention.[2] It is not recorded in the *Guardian*'s own instant book on the war, *The War We Could Not Stop*, or in the *Telegraph*'s instant history *War On Saddam*, or in the BBC's *The Battle For Iraq*. It seems safe to predict that this potentially pivotal document in what is widely regarded as a defining moment of our times will be effectively erased from history, and relegated to the peripheral realm of footnotes and obscure specialist studies. Nevertheless, on the very eve of war, there was an event that could have changed the course of history, and a document that should have halted President George W. Bush in his tracks.

This explosive yet virtually unknown document was the 'Draft Work Programme' of the UN weapons inspectors, the United Nations Monitoring, Verification and Inspection Commission (UNMOVIC), submitted to the UN Security Council on 17 March 2003. This document should have heralded a new and decisive phase in the inspection process, allowing the UN by solely peaceful means to extract definitive answers to the lingering questions around Iraq's suspected weapons of mass destruction—and to determine whether Iraq had failed the 'final opportunity' to disarm offered in Resolution 1441.

The UNMOVIC alternative was not explored. The peaceful route of inspections was shut down on 17 March mere hours after Dr Hans Blix, head of UNMOVIC, submitted the Draft Work Programme in writing to the UN Security Council. At 8pm that night (US time), President George W. Bush announced an ultimatum to Iraqi President Saddam

Hussein to leave Iraq. Mr Bush included an ultimatum to the UN weapons inspectors. They were given even less time to leave Iraq:

> All the decades of deceit and cruelty have now reached an end. Saddam Hussein and his sons must leave Iraq within 48 hours. Their refusal to do so will result in military conflict, commenced at a time of our choosing. For their own safety, all foreign nationals—including journalists and inspectors—should leave Iraq immediately.[3]

The inspections came to an end not because they had been blocked or frustrated by Baghdad, or because the inspectors had finished their work. Indeed, the drawing up of the Draft Work Programme should have signalled the opening of a new and more significant phase of the inspectors' work, if only they had been allowed to implement the plans contained within that document.

The truth seems to be that the inspections were shut down by President Bush precisely because the inspectors were about to launch a new series of tasks, interviews and inspections. A peaceful route to disarmament was opening up, and this presented a threat to President Bush's determination to go to war. That was why the inspections route was blocked off, and the inspectors ejected from Iraq by the United States—for the second time in five years.

THE KEY REMAINING DISARMAMENT TASKS

A year after UNSCOM withdrew from Iraq on US instructions in December 1998, the Security Council passed Resolution 1284 in December 1999, creating a new replacement inspection agency UNMOVIC and a new set of procedures for the inspectors to follow if and when they ever returned to Iraq. Paragraph 7 of Resolution 1284 says that the Security Council

> Decides that UNMOVIC and the IAEA, not later than 60 days after they have both started work in Iraq, will each draw up, for approval by the Council, a work programme for the discharge of their mandates, which will include. . . the key remaining disarmament tasks to be completed by Iraq . . . and further decides that what is required of Iraq for the implementation of each task shall be clearly defined and precise'.[4]

After four months of co-operation, according to Paragraph 33, economic sanctions could be suspended temporarily (on a rolling basis).

The defining characteristic of the 'key disarmament tasks' was that the Security Council, for the first time, would set out in black and white, 'clearly' and 'precisely' what Iraq had to do in order to get economic sanctions first suspended, and then eventually lifted. The tasks were to be 'clearly defined and precise' in order to stop the US and UK from 'moving the goalposts', as they had consistently done since 1991. This critical element of the inspection system, a fundamental cornerstone of the inspectors' procedures in relation to Iraq, has been systematically erased from history. The *Guardian*'s instant history book on the war against Iraq remarks in passing that, 'Hans Blix and his team suggested establishing "tasks" for Iraq to carry out which were due to be listed on 27 March.' True, but misleading. This was not just a suggestion from Dr Blix and his colleagues, but a legal duty required by a US and British-sponsored UN Security Council Resolution only three years old.[5]

A CURIOUS TIMETABLE

Importantly, Resolution 1284 did not set a deadline for inspectors to finish their work in Iraq, because when Britain and the US drew up the Resolution, they wanted a way of stringing out the inspection process in order to maintain the economic sanctions on Iraq indefinitely. In 1999, London and Washington wanted inspectors to have all the time in the world. In 2003, they wanted the inspectors to roll up their operations ASAP.

As the extract quoted makes clear, while there was no deadline for the inspectors' work to end, there was a deadline for work to start. As the inspectors returned to Iraq on 27 November 2002, one would have expected them to have presented their work programme on 27 January 2003, 60 days later. If this had been done, and if the 'key remaining disarmament tasks' had been defined and approved on that day, it is possible that war would have been put off until the autumn, or perhaps derailed entirely.

The definition of the 'key remaining disarmament tasks' would have initiated a new, intensive and definitive process of inspections by UNMOVIC, lasting some months. During this time, it would have been politically impossible for Washington to demand that the inspectors leave Iraq mid-mission so that the US and UK could invade the country to detect weapons which the inspectors were only weeks away from definitively pronouncing on. If the tasks had been defined in January or March, it is quite likely that the process of carrying out and evaluating the tasks would have taken us into the summer, and Washington would have had to wait until the autumn to see whether the inspectors came out with a negative verdict that could be used to justify war. From the US point of view, it was too risky to hope for Iraqi obstruction and/or a negative report from the inspectors. The war had to begin before the key remaining disarmament tasks were approved by the Security Council. Thus the projected date for the presentation of the Draft Work Programme effectively became Washington's deadline for war.

The 'key disarmament tasks' weren't defined on 27 January, and the war effort wasn't derailed. For a very peculiar reason. According to UNMOVIC spokesperson Ewen Buchanan, although inspectors returned to Iraq on 27 November and started carrying out activities then—clearing up the long-deserted office, carrying out inspections, and so on—the agency decided not to define this as 'starting work', but as a 'build-up period'. The inspectors had decided to date the 'start of work' as 27 January, so the 60 day deadline moved back another 60 days, and the key remaining disarmament tasks had to be defined by 27 March.

What made this decision so odd was that Resolution 1441 asked the inspectors 'to resume inspections no later than 45 days following adoption of this resolution' (on 8

November 2002). So inspections had to 'resume' by 23 December. UNMOVIC decided that it had 'resumed inspections' in Iraq by 23 December, but that it did not 'start work' until 27 January 2002. Agency spokesperson Ewen Buchanan acknowledges that the inspectors could be said to be 'having their cake and eating it.'[6]

It is hard to believe that the inspectors were not pressured to define the two start dates differently by the superpower which was intent on going to war with Iraq by mid-March 2003, and which therefore needed to make sure the disarmament process mandated by Resolution 1284 was kicked into the long grass beyond any likely date for the start of war. On the other hand, Dr Blix did say in mid-2000 that there would have to be some 're-baselining' with initial inspections before the Draft Work Programme was worked up: 'So, work in Iraq cannot mean the moment when you send in the first inspector.'[7] It is possible that some odd bureaucratic procedure devised years earlier delayed the drawing up of the Draft Work Programme and the key remaining disarmament tasks by two crucial months. If so, this might qualify as one of the most tragic bureaucratic delays in recent years.

THE DREADED BENCHMARKS

The concept of key disarmament tasks surfaced in the negotiations around a second UN resolution. One intermediate stage in drawing up the key disarmament tasks was the 'clustering' of 'unresolved disarmament issues'. On 24 February 2003, Dr Blix presented a list of more than 35 outstanding issues to the UNMOVIC 'College of Commissioners', an advisory group of experts. Seeking a way through, some countries pushed for clear benchmarks for measuring Iraqi co-operation in relation to these 'clusters'. The US was unenthusiastic: officials said even those benchmarks could be manipulated. The *FT* doubted whether an ostensibly technical solution could bridge a fundamentally political question.[8] A perceptive remark.

The problem with the benchmarks, as far as the US was concerned, was that they could *not* be manipulated. The danger was that they might be met.

Recall that at one point Washington had apparently toyed with the idea of making the destruction of the al-Samoud missiles, private interviews with weapons scientists and U2 flights the three key demands which would have to be met within days.[9] These demands *were* met, which must have given Washington a shock. If an ultimatum—with clear benchmarks for measuring Iraqi cooperation—was issued and then *met*, the momentum for war would disappear. This could not be allowed to happen.

The *Telegraph* reported in late February,

In private, British officials fear that Mr Blix's 'benchmarks' for Iraqi compliance may make their uphill struggle to win the resolution even more difficult. Mr Blix's questions could be seized upon by opponents of war—France, Germany, Russia, China and Syria—to string out the UN process on grounds that the UN must be given time to provide clear answers. Diplomats said America and Britain will resist any attempt to insert the benchmarks into the resolution as part of a formal ultimatum to Iraq.[10]

Some countries suggested that the unresolved disarmament issues could be used to formulate specific tasks, possibly with a deadline, which could clarify matters for the Security Council's middle ground as decision time approached. The US argued that Resolution 1441 was all the benchmark it needed, 'amid fears that a list of tasks could be used to string out the process': 'The chances of [benchmarks] being put forward by the US or the UK is close to nil,' said one Council official, but 'around the debate there will be a lot of trying to find measures by which to judge Iraq.'[11] In other words, there would be some members of the Security Council trying to implement Resolution 1284, despite US/UK obstructionism. 'The US has so far resisted setting benchmarks, amid fears they could sow further ambiguity and string out discussions.'[12] The real danger to the US was quite the opposite: unambiguous 'benchmarks' could have helped Iraq to demonstrate that its co-operation and its disarmament were full and complete, thus denying the US the war it sought for other reasons.

In early March, a reporter put to Colin Powell the idea of 'very specific benchmarks with very specific deadlines, almost in the form of ultimatum, focusing on specific items, such as the VX, or the anthrax, or the biological labs, with the presumption that if there is not a concrete response on these specific items, as to some extent there has been on the rockets, then there would be common action for the purpose of disarming Iraq'. The Secretary of State dismissed such proposals:

> I don't think it's a question of additional benchmarks. All of these benchmarks have been out there for years . . . [Saddam Hussein] knows what they are, and he has not demonstrated a willingness to answer the questions that have been out there for so many, so many years. . . that's the reason we are reluctant to yet see another resolution come forward that starts listing benchmarks in that resolution as a new measure of merit.[13]

Prime Minister Blair repeated this theme in the House of Commons: 'He knows, and the world knows, what he has to do. The world has been patient. If we go to war it will not be because we want to, but because we have to in order to disarm Saddam.'[14] Foreign Secretary Jack Straw complained, 'You don't need to treat [Saddam Hussein] like a child. He does not need to be provided with a list of things he knows he's got to do in any event.'[15] 'The Iraqis have the answerbook already . . . it may take time to fabricate further falsehoods, but the truth takes only seconds to tell.'[16]

Mr Powell told the Security Council on 7 March that it was 'a question of intent' on the part of the Iraqi leadership:

> It's not a question of how many unanswered clusters of questions are there, or are there more benchmarks that are needed, or are there enough unresolved issues that have been put forward to be examined and analyzed and conclusions reached about. The answer depends entirely on whether Iraq has made the choice to actively cooperate in every possible way.[17]

Mr Straw pounded the same point home: 'What we need is an irreversible and strategic decision by Iraq to disarm, to yield to the inspectors all of its weapons of mass destruction and all relevant information which it could and should have provided at any time in the last 12 years.'[18]

If the benchmarks had been there for years, if they were so patently obvious, if it was patronizing to the Iraqis to set out the questions they had to answer, why then did the Blair Government propose the 'key remaining disarmament tasks' process in Resolution 1284 in December 1999? Why did the US Government of the time support it? Why did Tony Blair and Jack Straw (a member of the Cabinet in December 1999, though in another post) propose a Resolution which gave the weapons inspectors 60 days after re-starting their work in Iraq to draw up the 'key remaining disarmament tasks'? Why did they think it would take so long to draw up?

The truth was that defining 'clearly and precisely' what Iraq needed to do to prove its innocence was a complex and challenging task, requiring an assessment of the new situation on the ground after the inspectors returned to Iraq. Hence the need for 're-baselining'.

As for the suggestion that 'it may take time to fabricate further falsehoods, but the truth takes only seconds to tell', Mr Straw had just heard Dr Blix tell the Security Council,

> While co-operation can and is to be immediate, disarmament and at any rate the verification of it cannot be instant. How much time would it take to resolve the key remaining disarmament tasks? Even with a proactive Iraqi attitude, it would still take some time to verify sites and items, analyse documents, interview relevant persons, and draw conclusions. It would not take years, nor weeks, but months.[19]

Mr Straw was correct to say that the truth only takes a second to tell, but he was lying when he implied that the world could know in that same instant whether or not the truth had been spoken. The truth of Iraq's 'answerbook' could only be determined by painstaking and detailed work—over months—as in the case of the aluminium tubes, which the US had alleged were sought as part of a nuclear weapons programme.

Resolution 1441 gave Iraq a 'final opportunity' to disarm. It 'set up an enhanced inspection regime with the aim of bringing to full and verified completion the disarmament process established by resolution 687 (1991) and subsequent resolutions of the Council'—including Resolution 1284. Mr Straw said days before the war started, in March 2003, 'He was given this final opportunity in resolution 1441, and the overwhelming evidence is that he has failed to take it.'[20] But the truth was that there had been substantial and increasing cooperation between Baghdad and UNMOVIC in mid-March 2003, cooperation on matters of substance as well as on matters of process/access, cooperation signalled in the destruction of al-Samoud missile delivery systems.

The truth was that Iraq could not have failed its 'final opportunity'. You cannot fail a student when the exam board has not yet approved the examination paper; when you have not given the student that exam paper; when you have not told them the duration of the exam; and when their work has not been evaluated by a competent independent authority. Iraq did not fail the test. Washington locked out the exam board, dismissed the invigilators, and drove a tank through the examination hall.

THE LUNATIC SCHEDULE FOR WAR

In late January, a European official noted that, 'The pressure comes from President Bush and it is felt all the way down. They're talking about weeks, not months. Months is a banned word now.'[21] There was considerable nervousness in London at the haste in Washington. 'There's no point in going down the UN route if we shut it down just two weeks after giving them intelligence,' said one British official in January.[22] A US diplomat in London was tolerant: 'Sure, the Brits are one or two degrees to the left of us.' There was 'daylight' between the two allies. The diplomat said, 'The question is, is it constructive or destructive daylight? I think it's constructive. It's analogous to the old good cop/bad cop routine. Plus, when it really counts, they're with the program.'[23] True, London would always obey in the end—though Roger Stone, Secretary of the Poodle Club of Wales, condemned the analogy between Tony Blair and a poodle: 'I have no time for the man . . . Comparing him to a poodle was a damn insult to the poodle.'[24]—but there was enormous unease in Whitehall over the war, as there was throughout British society.

A senior British official said in January 2003, 'There is an assumption that there will be a campaign before the summer because of the heat. The autumn would be just as sensible a time and in the meanwhile Saddam would be thoroughly constrained by the inspectors.'[25] An entirely practical approach, but one that ran unacceptable risks. By the autumn the inspectors might have given Iraq a clean bill of health—removing the justification for war. Alternatively, any further delay in the autumn would crash into the preparations for the year-long presidential re-election campaign.

Back in October 2002, well-informed British journalists were given the impression from military sources that the optimal period to start the war was between November and February, with something of a preference for the January–February period.[26] Due to enormous political pressures inside and outside the Labour Party, the British Government was forced to pursue a second UN Resolution which could be presented as authorising military action. The Bush Administration reluctantly acquiesced in this process, and the timetable for war drifted back and back until it hit the double brick wall of the start of the summer and the looming presentation of the Draft Work Programme.

In February 2003, Sir David Manning, Mr Blair's Foreign Policy Adviser, in conversation with Condoleezza Rice, US National Security Adviser, 'argued for a short delay to give diplomacy three more weeks—until mid-March—as the French had suggested.' Ms Rice was extremely reluctant, wanting to make 1 March the cut-off date, but Washington acquiesced, perhaps in part because of the disruptive effects on war planning and logistics of the refusal of the Turkish Parliament to permit the use of Turkish territory for the land invasion of northern Iraq.[27]

The best time to start the war would be on a moonless night when the night-fighting technological advantages of the US Air Force would be at their maximum. This meant either 4 March or 1 April. The 1991 war on Iraq and the 2001 war on Afghanistan both started on moonless nights. 4 March was preferred by the military: 'The Pentagon has the date ringed in its diary,' it was reported at the beginning of February.[28] However, the strategic decision was taken to wait until after the inspectors reported to the Security Council on 7 March, and then to press for a vote on a new Resolution. This would seem to move the war back to the latter stages of March, when there was beginning to be less moonlight at nights. Hence the prediction by former US General Wesley Clark that the war could start on 24 March,[29] and the prediction by Rupert Cornwell, Washington correspondent of the *Independent on Sunday*, that war might begin on 23 March.[30] Bronwen Maddox, Foreign Editor of *The Times*, commented on 11 March that the US and UK were trading in three kinds of currency at the Security Council in order to achieve their second Resolution: 'More time, a list of tests by which to judge Saddam Hussein—and cash or other favours for those voting "yes" ... cash may prove the one that the US finds easiest to give.' By then, the US and Britain were giving least ground of all on the question of timing: 'perhaps a week beyond March 17 but no more'.[31]

So informed observers were under the impression, as late as 10 March that the war was due around 23 March, despite the fact that moonlessness would favour 1 April as a start date. That is one mystery. A second mystery is why the war was advanced almost a week, and the ultimatum was issued on 17 March. One possible explanation is that Washington was stampeded by the inspectors. Dr Blix had been firm in his determination to press ahead with the Draft Work Programme in his 7 March address to the Security Council: hence the need to start the war before 27 March. The US must also have been aware of the frantic efforts by UNMOVIC to move the presentation of the Draft Work Programme forward; to circulate it on 17 March and formally present it to the Security Council for approval on 19 March. This may have been a major factor, perhaps even the decisive factor, in Washington's decision to shift the start of the war to just about the least technically advantageous period of the month.

KILLING UNMOVIC

Dr Blix expressed confidence that the Security Council would accept whatever UNMOVIC put forward in the Draft Work Programme—when interviewed in the summer of 2000: 'Because the report has to go to the Security Council for approval, what we say could theoretically be modified by the council. But I would imagine that our professional judgment will carry some weight with the council. At least I hope so.'[32] In the event, UNMOVIC's professional judgement, as embodied in the key disarmament tasks listed in the Draft Work Programme, carried no weight whatsoever with the Security Council's decisive member. UNMOVIC itself was blasted off the political stage, and its crucial contribution erased from history, by sheer US power.

On 16 March, the US told the UN privately to leave Iraq, as Kofi Annan revealed the following day: 'Yesterday UNMOVIC, the [International] Atomic [Energy] Agency and myself got information from the United States authorities that it would be prudent not to leave our staff in the region. I have just informed the Council that we will withdraw the UNMOVIC and Atomic Agency inspectors, we will withdraw the UN humanitarian workers, we will withdraw the UNIKOM troops on the Iraqi–Kuwaiti border who are also not able to operate.'[33] So here is another measure of the world's progress towards legality over the previous five years. In 1998, the US only ordered out the inspectors, in a private arrangement. The rest of the UN staff working in Iraq were not informed and the bombing began with them *in situ*. There was no advance warning for the Secretary-General. In 2003, however, all UN staff were told to get lost at the same time, and the Secretary-General received the courtesy of being given advance notice of his own irrelevance.

Addressing the Security Council in the aftermath of war, Dr Blix remarked, 'while I have at no time suggested that the war was a foregone conclusion, I have stated as my impression that US patience with further inspection seemed to run out at about the same time as our Iraqi counterparts began to be proactive in proposing new investigations, supplying more explanations and names'. He added diplomatically, 'I did not imply that there was any causal link.'[34] There was clearly such a causal link, however, just as there seems to have been a causal link between the US schedule for war and the introduction of the Draft Work Programme.

On 9 March, the Prime Minister's official spokesperson said, 'We believe the Blix process is now complete.'[35] The following week, on 17 March, this barefaced lie was contradicted when UNMOVIC made the Draft Work Programme available to members of the Security Council in writing, setting out Iraq's key remaining disarmament tasks, and the steps that could be taken to settle the outstanding weapons issues. That evening, President Bush shut down the weapons inspectors, as well as the UN humanitarian programme in Iraq. On 19 March, Dr Blix went through the formality of officially presenting the Draft Work Programme to the Security Council in person. He said, 'I naturally feel sadness that three and a half months of work carried out in Iraq have not brought the assurances needed about the absence of weapons of mass destruction or other proscribed items in Iraq, that no more time is available for our inspections and that armed action now seems imminent.'[36] The depth of hostility in Washington and London towards the Draft Work Programme and its potential was revealed by the fact that while the foreign ministers of France, Germany, Syria, Guinea and Russia attended the 19 March Security Council meeting, their British and American counterparts stayed away.[37]

The enemy had finally been defeated. The inspections were dead. The key disarmament tasks were dead. Resolution 1284 was dead. The threat of peace had been averted.

THE COMPREHENSIVE REVIEW

In late 1998, Washington had reason to fear the looming threat of a 'comprehensive review' of Iraq's disarmament process. This initiative, spearheaded by UN Secretary-General Kofi Annan in August 1998, initially seemed to offer Iraq a time-limited review process which might lead swiftly to the lifting of the embargo on Iraq's oil exports and the revenues it derived from those exports (fulfilling Paragraph 22 of 1991's Resolution 687). Iraq proposed that the comprehensive review should lift economic sanctions progressively as disarmament was verified, an entirely rational approach. Baghdad also asked for a clear statement that no additional non-weapons-related demands would be made of Iraq before sanctions were suspended or lifted. Again, a rational approach, which could have prevented the 'moving of goalposts' which had been a constant feature of the sanctions regime. While these proposals were not accepted by the Security Council, the generally held perception was that the decision to authorize the review would come shortly after Richard Butler's report in mid-December 1998. The Secretary-General confirmed this feeling by noting that, barring any hitches, the comprehensive review would begin in early January.[38] Instead, the road to disarmament and the lifting of sanctions was comprehensively torn up by the bombing raids of Operation Desert Fox. It is intriguing to speculate whether, once again, there was a 'causal link' between the threat of a decisive period of inspections and the use of violence.

NOT MR BUTLER

In 1998, chief weapons inspector Richard Butler helped to stage confrontations with Iraq, building an atmosphere of crisis. In 2003, chief weapons inspector Hans Blix neatly side-stepped numerous explosive situations, and Iraqi cooperation robbed Washington of several potential 'justifications' for war. In 1998, Mr Butler (and US officials) wrote a damning report on Iraqi non-cooperation, which helped create the political conditions for war. In 2003, Hans Blix refused to slant his reports in favour of the US position, and accurately reflected the degree of cooperation he was receiving from Baghdad, denying Washington a vital propaganda weapon. In 1998, Richard Butler obeyed a private US instruction to withdraw his personnel from Iraq in order to help create the conditions for war. In 2003, Hans Blix was forced to obey a televised, public demand to withdraw his personnel from Iraq for their own safety.

Dr Blix was not Mr Butler.

Despite the many differences between these two international civil servants, the end result was the same. War. Death. The breaching of procedures laid down in a UN Resolution. The re-writing of history. The undermining of world order.

CHAPTER XIV
Authority And Power

US–UK Versus The UN

BREAKING DOWN RESOLUTION 1284

As just noted, UN Resolution 1284 required the Security Council to approve a Draft Work Programme to guide the work of UN inspectors on their return to Iraq. The Resolution 1284 process was, however, dismissed from history on 17 March 2003.

Back in December 1999, however, the British Government was enthusiastic about its new approach. Peter Hain, then a Foreign Office minister, wrote in the *Independent* on 7 August 2000, 'If Saddam Hussein were to allow a new disarmament body into Iraq, he could quickly move towards suspension [of economic sanctions] if he cooperated with the weapons inspectors.' A month later, on 11 September 2000, Mr Hain said, '1284 is the way forward.' It was 'a win-win for everybody': 'UN inspectors could return, Iraqi people get relief, Iraq's neighbours feel safer with Saddam Hussein's weapons under some measure of control.'[1] British Ambassador to the UN, Sir Jeremy Greenstock, spoke to the Security Council on behalf of the Blair Government on 17 December 1999, praising the Resolution 1284: 'The Council now has the policy which it needs; and this resolution is now the law of the globe.' If the Resolution was implemented, it would be 'to the advantage of the people of Iraq and of the region, in the interests of the future authority of the United Nations, and to the great credit of this Council.'[2]

In March 2003, the majority of the members of the Security Council struggled to find ways to fulfil the provisions of Resolution 1284, and to defend the weapons inspectors against Washington and London. If they had succeeded, it would indeed have been 'to the advantage of the people of Iraq and of the region, in the interests of the future authority of the United Nations, and to the great credit of the Security Council.' Instead, the promise contained in Resolution 1284 was broken, the 'law of the globe' was broken (in several ways), and the inspection system set up by Resolution 1284 was broken, by the exercise of sheer brute power.

Goodbye, Resolution 1284.

BREAKING DOWN RESOLUTION 1154

In February 1998, there was a world crisis over the access rights of weapons inspectors. After the crisis passed, the UN Security Council passed Resolution 1154 in March 1998, which warned that unless Iraq allowed 'immediate, unconditional and unrestricted access' to UN weapons inspectors, it 'would have the severest consequences for Iraq'. However, the final paragraph of the Resolution said that the Security Council '[d]ecides, in accordance with its responsibility under the Charter, to remain actively seized of the matter, in order to ensure implementation of this resolution and to secure peace and security in the area.'[3] In other words, further violations of the inspection regime would be dealt with by the Security Council. No authority to use force was delegated to any member of the Security Council.

Despite this clear reservation of powers to the Security Council itself, in December 1998, the US and Britain launched a unilateral assault on Iraq—as the Security Council sat down to consider a report on Iraqi co-operation from the weapons inspectors. Just as the Security Council was about to fulfil its responsibilities under Resolution 1154, and to deliberate on the proper course of action towards Iraq, news came of the first bombs falling in Iraq.[4]

Goodbye, Resolution 1154.

BREAKING DOWN RESOLUTION 687

The ceasefire resolution, UN Security Council Resolution 687 of April 1991, was fundamental to the British and US case for war against Iraq in 2003. Paragraph 22 of Resolution 687 said that when UN inspectors found Iraq had disarmed its weapons of mass destruction and its long-range missiles, and had set up a long-term monitoring programme, then sanctions on Iraq's exports and 'financial transactions related thereto' would be lifted. The Government of Iraq would then be allowed access to foreign exchange. However, it was a cardinal goal of the United States to prevent Iraq from getting direct access to foreign exchange, which could help to revive the Iraqi economy, while Saddam Hussein was still in power in Baghdad.

In April 1994, three years after Resolution 687 was passed, US Secretary of State Warren Christopher wrote in the *New York Times*, 'The US does not believe that Iraq's compliance with Paragraph 22 of Resolution 687 is enough to justify lifting the embargo'. This message was reinforced time and again by US Administrations.[5]

Goodbye, Resolution 687.

'SUPPORTING' THE UN

Even if we restrict ourselves only to the Security Council Resolutions concerned with Iraq, we find time and again that the Resolutions have been defied or broken by Britain and the United States. The authority of the UN was undermined over and over again by the reckless and unilateral exercise of power by Washington and London.

This hostility to the UN was disguised by propaganda and media servility. The rhetoric of both British and US leaders in the run-up to the war emphasised the need to 'support' the United Nations—by going to war with Iraq in defiance of the will of the UN Security Council and the provisions of the UN Charter.

There was political benefit in accommodating pro-UN feeling even in the United States. An opinion poll immediately after Colin Powell's presentation to the Security Council on 5 February found that 51 per cent of the US public supported military action only with the support of the UN. 37 per cent said the US should invade regardless.[6] A poll less than a month before the war was to begin, found 56 per cent of the US public willing to wait in order to secure a second UN Resolution endorsing US military action against Iraq. On the other hand, at that point half the country believed that the US should move against Iraq even over the objections of the United Nations.[7]

In Britain, support for the UN was much stronger. A poll in the UK in late February found only 21 per cent of the public would support war without a UN Resolution—though 59 per cent would have supported war if there was a UN Resolution endorsing military action.[8] This was a pivotal issue in Britain—almost a life-and-death issue for Tony Blair's political career. The pro-UN rhetoric was also designed to play well on the international stage, as the US and UK attempted to secure a Resolution which could be presented as authorising war on Iraq.

President George W. Bush said this was 'a moment to determine, for [the UN], whether or not it is going to be relevant as the world confronts the threats of the 21st century. Is it going to be a body that means what it says?'[9] Eminent British historian Correlli Barnett observed, 'Clearly, "relevant" for Bush means subserviently useful to his administration's global policies.' While the Bush Administration might be the most militarily powerful state in the world, 'only the collective voice of the UN enjoys global moral authority,' wrote Mr Barnett: 'It is for the collective voice to define the meaning of relevance in terms of the UN's future.'[10]

At the last council of war in the Azores on 16 March, Mr Blair said that Saddam Hussein was playing the same old game: 'Disarmament never happens but instead the international community is drawn into some perpetual negotiation.'[11] But disarmament *was* happening, UNMOVIC was destroying weapons systems in Iraq as the Prime Minister was speaking. Two of Iraq's al-Samoud missiles were broken up on the day he spoke bringing the total number of missiles destroyed to 70.[12] The UN system was actually in the process of disarming Iraq, as Mr Blair and Mr Bush made their sneering remarks.

RESOLUTION 1441: THE THREAT OF FORCE

Ah, but in Resolution 1441 the UN demanded immediate and total disarmament or the use of force, suggested the Prime Minister. At the beginning of February, Mr Blair warned, 'Show weakness now and no one will believe us when we try to show strength in the future. If having made a demand backed up by a threat of force we fail to enforce that demand, the result will not be peace or security.'[13] But was Resolution 1441 'a demand backed up by a threat of force'? The Resolution said that the UNMOVIC and the IAEA should report 'immediately' any interference by Iraq with inspection activities, as well as any failure by Iraq to comply with its disarmament obligations. If such a report was received, the Security Council would convene 'immediately' to 'consider the situation.' The sentence that Britain and the US focussed on comes next, in Paragraph 13, where the Security Council 'Recalls, in that context, that the Council has repeatedly warned Iraq that it will face serious consequences as a result of its continued violations of its obligations.'[14] As noted earlier, Professor Vaughan Lowe, Chichele Professor of Public International Law at Oxford University, and a practising barrister delivered a judgement on these issues to BBC Radio 4's *Today* programme. On this point, the professor said,

> The statement in paragraph 13 of the Resolution that 'the Council has repeatedly warned Iraq that it will face serious consequences as a result of its continued violations of its obligations' is a simple statement of what the Security Council has done in the past. It cannot in my opinion possibly be interpreted as an express or implied authorization to States unilaterally to take military action against Iraq in the future.
>
> Certainly, paragraph 13 amounts to an implied threat of 'serious consequences' if Iraq breaches its obligations in the future. But nothing in paragraph 13 suggests that the consequences would be decided upon and taken by anyone other than the body that has, under the procedure established in the immediately preceding paragraphs 11 and 12, been given responsibility for deciding how to respond to material breaches: that is, by the Security Council itself.
>
> Equally, the simple fact that Resolution 1441 does not expressly forbid the use of armed force plainly cannot itself amount to an implied authorisation to use force . . . Most Security Council resolutions do not expressly forbid the use of force: no-one would argue that they therefore all authorize it . . .
>
> My conclusion, therefore, is that under present circumstances it would be contrary to international law for the United Kingdom to engage in military action against Iraq, or assist any other State in taking such action, unless it was expressly authorized to do so by the United Nations Security Council.[15]

War was not the only way to enforce the demands of the UN. It was not 'weakness', but wisdom, for the Security Council to consider the situation in Iraq, and to make the appropriate intervention in accordance with international law. The true 'weakness' of the Security Council lay in its powerlessness to enforce the UN Charter, which forbids the use of force except in the case of self-defence while under attack. The 'weakness' of the Security Council lay not in its reluctance to endorse a US/UK invasion, but in its inability to prevent this lawless act.

THE SIX TESTS

The unfortunate reality for Mr Blair was that while Iraq had undoubtedly failed to give 'immediate' co-operation to the UN inspectors, it was giving considerable amounts of co-operation at the time of his speech, including the destruction of medium-range missiles which UNMOVIC had only just found to be prohibited. That was one of the reasons why the British Government had to move into dangerous waters in its attempt to secure a second Resolution from the Security Council.

In the final stages of the negotiations, this involved the setting of a number of tasks for the Government of Iraq, including the demand that Saddam Hussein should admit on Iraqi national television that he had hidden weapons of mass destruction, and promise to hand over all hidden prohibited weapons and materials.[16] Despite official denials,[17] this was not about co-operation, as the *Financial Times* pointed out, this was about 'the public humiliation of Mr Hussein through an appearance on national Iraqi television to confess the error of his ways.'[18] The point of this demand was not to advance the disarmament agenda, but to advance the war agenda. Saddam Hussein would either plead guilty, and therefore appear to justify war, or he would fail to comply with the demand, and therefore appear to justify war.

BLAMING THE BRITISH

The six tests or 'benchmarks' failed to persuade the Security Council to back the British draft Resolution. The negotiations then broke down under the weight of US impatience. In February, a senior administration official rejected long negotiations over the Resolution because, 'A delay so protracted that people in the region begin to question our resolve is a much, much bigger loss than the kind of thing that might be gained by adding a few additional fence-sitters who think a few more months might get them to change their minds.'[19] 'We've had enough. The UN doesn't matter. A veto won't stop us. Our patience has run out.' That was an anonymous presidential aide on 22 February.[20] By mid-March, hawks in the White House were criticising Tony Blair for his persistence in seeking a second UN Resolution. A Bush administration official said, 'Blair is hurting himself by dragging this out.' Another official added, 'This is just masochistic. We're just haemorrhaging for no purpose.'[21] On the eve of war, a State Department official said anonymously, 'More and more people are saying "enough already". We're the US for chrissakes. We don't plead. We don't beg. You're either with us or not.'[22]

On 16 March 2003, the leaders of the US, Britain and Spain agreed to issue an ultimatum to Saddam Hussein the following day. The negotiations were over and the draft Resolution was withdrawn. There were still plenty of ideas on the table in New York, but the US had run out of patience (and may well have been frightened of the impact on Security Council members and the public of the UNMOVIC Draft Work Programme about to be presented for approval).

BLAMING THE FRENCH

One important propaganda tool in the British Labour Government's struggle to win votes among Labour MPs was a drastic misrepresentation of the position of the French Government. For a Resolution to pass at the Security Council, it needs nine out of fifteen votes in favour, and it needs the five permanent members of the Security Council to hold back from casting any vetoes. The Anglo–American strategy at the Security Council had been to try to neutralize the threat of a French veto by promising to go to war even if there was an 'unreasonable' veto. The original idea seems to have been to get nine positive votes from the minor countries first, then to pressure Russia, China and France not to get in the way. When both France and Russia made clear their intention to veto the Resolution, the objective evolved into securing a 'moral victory' by lining up nine positive votes for the resolution so that the war could be presented as fufilling the will of the Security Council, which had been blocked by two 'unreasonable' permanent members.

For the six smaller undecided countries on the Security Council—the U6 or 'undecided six'—there were pressures at home, from powerful anti-war movements; and there were pressures in New York, from major powers competing with inducements and threats. The announcement by President Chirac on 10 March that Paris would veto the draft British Resolution, come what may, reversed the Anglo–American U6-first strategy. France never had to cast its veto, because whatever support for the Resolution existed among the U6 crumbled. Why take the political punishment at home when the Resolution was sure to be lost in any event?

The British Government was incandescent with rage. This rage was channelled effectively into lobbying and spin by a range of ministers, including the Foreign Secretary Jack Straw. Mr Straw solemnly quoted Mr Chirac verbatim: 'Quelquefois les circonstances, France votera non.' The Foreign Secretary said, 'I sadly take that to be an announcement by France they were abandoning enforcement of [Resolution] 1441.' The Prime Minister said in the House of Commons in the crucial debate on 18 March, 'The French position is that France will vote no, whatever the circumstances. Those are not my words, but those of the French President.' If not for that veto, 'had the UN come together and united—and if other troops had gone there, not just British and American troops—Saddam Hussein might have complied.' 'The choice was not action now or postponement of action; the choice was action or no action at all,' because of the French position.[23]

Let us return to reality. Firstly, Iraq *was* complying. Iraq *was* co-operating. Missiles were being destroyed on a daily basis. Secondly, in the interview he gave on 10 March 2003, President Jacques Chirac actually made it clear that he supported war in the event of a breakdown in Iraqi compliance. If, after a few more months of investigation the inspectors were to say Iraq was not co-operating, 'In that case it will be for the Security Council and it alone to decide the right thing to do.' In that case, 'regrettably, the war would become inevitable.'[24]

Asked about the likely voting in the Security Council, Mr Chirac said, 'I firmly believe, this evening, that there isn't a majority of nine votes in favour of that resolution including an ultimatum and thus giving the international green light to war.' Therefore a negative vote by France would not be a veto, because the Resolution would not have attracted enough positive votes to survive into the veto stage of proceedings. However, if there were nine positive votes, France would veto the Resolution. Asked, 'And, *this evening*, this is your position in principle?' M Chirac replied, 'My position is that, regardless of the circumstances, France will vote "no" because she considers *this evening* that there are no grounds for waging war in order to achieve the goal we have set ourselves, i.e. to disarm Iraq.'[25] The words 'this evening' were never included in the British Government's frequent quotations of this exchange.

One curious sidelight on this was the relationship between France and the undecided six small countries. 'They do not seem to be prepared to let the U6 take responsibility,' said a Whitehall source. 'That is both arrogant and an affront to multilateralism.'[26] According to an account in the *Financial Times*, though, it was the U6 who asked for the Chirac statement. Apparently, at a meeting in New York on 8 March, the U6 agreed they could not support the British resolution. The next day Vicente Fox, Mexico's president, explained the position to President Chirac, and said that he was eager for the permanent members to say that they would veto the resolution. With this cover, responsibility for the defeat of the plan would not fall on Mexico or Chile, and they would not feel the wrath of Washington.[27] This may explain the confidence with which Mr Chirac expressed his opinions about the state of play in the Security Council, and the laborious way in which he explained the French veto.

Regardless of the details, the basic fact was that President Chirac did not say that France would veto any Resolution authorising the use of force 'in any circumstances'. Less than a week later, on 16 March, President Chirac modified his position, and he made it clear that he was prepared to accept a deadline which was set by the UN inspectors: 'One month, two months, I am ready to accept any accord on this point that has the approval of the inspectors.'[28] Despite this explicit statement, the British Government continued to use their misrepresentation of his earlier 'whatever the circumstances' quotation to persuade wavering MPs to vote in favour of war two days later.

AUTOMATICITY

What France objected to was the introduction of 'automaticity' in an ultimatum to Iraq. This would mean abandoning inspections, and, in the French President's words, saying instead, 'in so many days, we go to war'. The draft British Resolution said,

> Iraq will have failed to take the final opportunity afforded by resolution 1441 (2002) unless, on or before 17 March 2003 the council concludes that Iraq has demonstrated full, unconditional, immediate and active co-operation in accordance with its disarmament obligations under resolution 1441 (2002) and previous relevant resolutions, *and* is yielding possession to UNMOVIC and the IAEA of all weapons, weapon delivery and support systems and structures, prohibited by resolution 687 (1991) and all subsequent relevant resolutions, *and* all information regarding prior destruction of such items.[29]

The burden of proof had been reversed. In order to avoid war, on or before 17 March 2003, a Resolution would have to be passed by the Security Council accepting that Iraq was behaving perfectly. Given the unremitting hostility of the United States to the Iraqi regime, a veto from this quarter was certain. The draft Resolution was actually setting 17 March as an unmovable deadline for war.

'Without that automaticity we would have been locked into a never-ending series of Security Council discussions,' said a senior British official after the war.[30] Again, untrue. The French position on 10 March was that the inspectors should be given their 'months'. If Iraq did not comply, war would become 'inevitable'. The French position on 16 March was that they would accept a deadline for war, so long as it was more than a few days, as already noted.

On 19 March, Dr Blix alluded to these proposals, observing that 'specific groups of disarmament issues could be tackled and solved within specific time lines.' For example, UNMOVIC could 'aim at addressing and resolving the issues of anthrax and VX in March and Unmanned Aerial Vehicles (UAVs) and Remotely Piloted Vehicles (RPVs) in April'.[31] But thirty days was too long for the US, and benchmarks were too dangerous.

THE AUTHORITY OF THE UN

Foreign Secretary Straw said in February 2003, 'If the Security Council were to demonstrate that it was incapable of tackling the new threats of WMD and terrorism, it would risk doing as much damage to the UN as that suffered by the League of Nations when it failed to face up to the challenges of the 1930s.'[32] The UN *was* capable of tackling the new threats of WMD. It was actually tackling them in Iraq when President Bush issued his ultimatum. The damage to the UN was done by US and British bullying. The *Independent* pointed out correctly, 'The test of the UN's relevance cannot be the extent to which it comes into line with US policy. On the contrary, the test must be the extent to which it encourages US policy to come into line with the concept of international law.'[33] A columnist in the *Financial Times* observed that, 'The UN would have fatally undermined its authority had it accepted that one nation (the one that just happens to be militarily the most powerful) could pre-empt its decisions.'[34]

The real problem for the authority of the UN was the attitude of the Bush Administration, summed up by John Bolton, the third most senior official at the US State Department, who said in January 2003, 'There is no such thing as the United Nations. There is only the international community, which can only be led by the only remaining superpower, which is the United States.'[35] This was not a war to support the authority of the United Nations, but a war to reinforce the dominance and power of the United States, the country which had, in the period 1971–1990 vetoed more Security Council Resolutions (66) than the other four permanent members of the Security Council put together (64).[36] All 'reasonable' vetoes, of course, the 29 vetoes to protect Israel from international condemnation; the 18 vetoes to protect apartheid South Africa from censure; and the nine vetoes cast to protect Washington from condemnation of its own military adventures abroad.

CHAPTER XV
Regime Reloaded

Re-Nazifying Iraq

THE THREE-MAN ULTIMATUM

On 17 March, President Bush ordered the President of Iraq and his two sons to leave Iraq.[1] It seemed that the war was just about Saddam Hussein, Uday Hussein and Qusay Hussein. Mr Bush said even if the three leaders left Iraq, US forces would still enter Iraq:

> It is not too late for the Iraqi military to act with honor and protect your country by permitting the peaceful entry of coalition forces to eliminate weapons of mass destruction. Our forces will give Iraqi military units clear instructions on actions they can take to avoid being attacked and destroyed . . . all Iraqi military and civilian personnel should listen carefully to this warning . . . Do not destroy oil wells, a source of wealth that belongs to the Iraqi people. Do not obey any command to use weapons of mass destruction against anyone, including the Iraqi people. War crimes will be prosecuted.[2]

No military or legal action would be taken against the Iraqi military so long as they did not fight the invaders, use weapons of mass destruction, or damage Iraq's oil wells. The Iraqi political and military leadership would be permitted to survive. The political and military machine which invaded Iran and waged a decade-long war involving missile attacks on Iranian cities and the use of chemical weapons, could remain unchanged. The political and military machine which carried out the al-Anfal campaign against the Kurds of Iraq in the 1980s, killing 50,000 civilians in what Human Rights Watch describes as 'genocide', could remain unchanged.[3] The political and military machine responsible for Halabja could remain unchanged. The political and military machine which invaded Kuwait could remain unchanged. The political and military machine which brutally cut down the March 1991 uprisings in southern and northern Iraq, under the gaze of US occupation forces, could remain unchanged. The political and military machine which had turned Iraq into one huge prison for decades, could remain unchanged.

Regime change? Regime unchanged.

IMMUNITY FOR SADDAM

White House spokesperson Ari Fleischer was questioned further on the ultimatum:

> Q My question is that since President Bush has given an option of choice to Saddam Hussein to leave the country by tomorrow night, that means we are not interested to capturing him? And how about the crimes he has committed against his own people, so we will never know about them, and he will never be brought to justice.
>
> MR. FLEISCHER: The President has said that he hopes Saddam Hussein will leave, and he's given him that period of time in which to do so.

Asked if the US would seek to have the Iraqi leader prosecuted for war crimes, Mr Fleischer once again avoided the issue: 'That would be a question for the international community to consider.'[4] The dirty work was left to Jack Straw, British Foreign Secretary, speaking on the day of the ultimatum. If Saddam Hussein went into exile, said Mr Straw, 'we would support a United Nations Security Council resolution to provide Saddam Hussein with immunity from prosecution so that he could go into exile and enjoy a retirement of the kind that he has denied to so many of his own people.'[5]

So the preferred outcome of the Iraq crisis was for the Iraqi leader to go into exile, where he would be granted immunity; for there to be no more UN inspections; for there to be a 'peaceful' invasion of Iraq to deal with the weapons issue; and for the military and political system in Iraq to continue in place, under a new leadership.

MR RUMSFELD DEFINES THE REGIME

The exile option was expressed publicly and forcefully by Donald Rumsfeld on a number of occasions. In January 2003, Mr Rumsfeld said, 'To avoid a war, I would, personally, recommend that some provision be made so that the senior leadership and their families could be provided haven in some other country. I think that would be a fair trade to avoid a war.'[6] A few weeks earlier, the US Defence Secretary told a Congressional committee, 'One choice he [Saddam Hussein] has is to take his family and key leaders and seek asylum elsewhere. Surely one of the 180-plus countries would take his regime—possibly Belarus.'[7] Please note the reference to 'the regime', defined by by one of the most senior figures in the Bush Administration as being composed of Saddam Hussein, his family, his 'key leaders' and their families. This certainly fits with the even more circumscribed list given by the US President on 17 March. The problem was not the system of government in Iraq, or the institutions of power more generally, or the ruling Ba'ath Party, it was one man and his entourage.

Colin Powell, speaking to a Congressional Committee, said in February 2003 that the Administration was 'in touch with a number of countries that have expressed an interest in conveying this message to the Iraqi regime.' He noted that, 'It would ultimately require some kind of United Nations participation in order to make sure that we can do it in a way that would actually entice him to seek asylum.' This was an 'attractive' option which avoided a lot of problems, but 'it would have to include him [Saddam Hussein] and it would have to include his top level. We would have to get the whole infection out and then get on with the healing process.' According to Mr Powell, the right message to convey was that 'time's up and one way to avoid a lot of suffering is for the regime to step down.'[8] The 'regime'—the 'infection'—was just Saddam Hussein and his 'top level'.

A Foreign Office spokeswoman stated in January 2003: 'The key issue is for Iraq to comply with its international obligations whatever group of people forms its leadership.'[9] But the real aim was 'leadership change'.

THE BA'ATHIST COMEBACK

This is rather as if Britain and the United States had said in the final stages of the Second World War that the problem was Adolf Hitler and his inner circle, but that the Nazi Party could continue to rule, and the totalitarian political-military-judicial-police-bureaucratic-academic system created by the Nazi Party could continue to function unchanged, if only the Supreme Leader and his immediate entourage went into exile (where they would be granted immunity). In fact, after the war de-nazification procedures were carried out against all the institutions of power in Germany, including the civil service and those corporations which were pillars of the fascist order, a subject we return to shortly.

In Iraq, the first weeks of 'liberation' saw the restoration of many Ba'athists to power by the US and British occupation forces. Hence the headlines: 'British spark protests by reappointing Ba'athists' (*Telegraph*, 18 April 2003, p. 13); 'Concerns grow as Ba'ath old guard takes reins of power' (*Telegraph*, 7 May 2003, p. 11); 'Shia clerics urge faithful to attack returning Ba'athists' (*Financial Times*, 10 May 2003, p. 6); and 'Saddam's poachers become America's gamekeepers' (*Financial Times*, 24 June 2003, p. 11).

The first month after the fall of Saddam Hussein's statue in Baghdad was summed up accurately in the 'After Saddam' section of the BBC News Online website. In 1 July 2003, this site had a corner entitled 'Baathist Comeback':

> in many cities former Baath Party officials are taking leading roles in the administration the US and British forces are attempting to establish. It is mainly the middle and lower ranks of officials that are taking up where they left off under the old regime, but there are reports that senior bureaucrats and ministers at the oil and health ministries have been offered their jobs back by the US military. In Baghdad and Basra, thousands of policemen under the old regime have been recruited for the new police forces, and have been going out on joint patrols with coalition troops.[10]

This was a fair rendition of the events of the first month of 'liberation.'

'BA'ATHISM WITH AN AMERICAN FACE'

In mid-February 2003, Kanan Makiya, a professor of Middle East studies at Brandeis University in Massachusetts, and the author of the classic anti-Ba'ath text *The Republic of*

Fear, excoriated US plans for postwar Iraq. As reported in the *Observer*, the US blueprint foresaw a US military governor ruling post-war Iraq for up to a year. The infrastructure of the ruling Ba'ath party would remain largely intact, with the top two officials in each Iraqi ministry replaced by US military officers.[11]

Professor Makiya described this as using 'an unknown number of Iraqi quislings palatable to the Arab countries of the Gulf and Saudi Arabia as a council of advisers to this military government.' The Professor warned that this plan was guaranteed to turn the Iraqi opposition into an opponent of the United States on the streets of Baghdad the day after liberation. The driving force of this plan was the 'appeasement of the existing bankrupt Arab order,' and 'ultimately the retention under a different guise of the repressive institutions of the Baath and the army.'[12] Professor Makiya described the US plan as 'bizarre'—'Baathism with an American face'.[13]

Faced with this withering critique, President Bush's special envoy met the Iraqi opposition. Zalmay Khalilzad promised an 'accountable and representative government' based on 'justice and the rule of law'. Iraq would 'ultimately' become a democracy.[14] Mr Khalilzad also 'appeared to offer a role in government to the Iraqi army, traditionally a power base in politics, by insisting that the armed forces "will be part of the future of Iraq".'[15] The opposition quietened down, unwisely.

AN IRAQI FACE: THE HEALTH MINISTRY

Instead of 'Ba'athism with an American face', after the fall of the Iraqi regime, the US moved to impose 'Ba'athism with an Iraqi face'. Instead of removing the top two Iraqi officials in each ministry and imposing a US officer, Washington removed the top two Iraqi officials and imposed the third-ranking Iraqi official in each ministry as the effective Minister of the interim Iraqi Government .

For example, in the Health Ministry, the first new Minister appointed by the US was Dr Ali Shenan al-Janabi, an optometrist and formerly the third highest ranking official in the ministry. Asked to renounce his membership of the Ba'ath Party, Mr al-Janabi refused: 'I'm not an active member of the Baath Party anymore. But if you ask someone to change their personal ideology, that is something different.'[16] Mr al-Janabi said, 'I did believe in the party, but that did not affect my work.'[17] This was not the view of his fellow doctors. When Dr al-Janabi was presented to an all-day conference of doctors in Baghdad, his appointment was greeted with disbelief and charges of corruption from many doctors. Dr Hussein Harith, a senior registrar at the al-Mansour teaching hospital, said the new appointee was one of a group of senior Ministers who asked the directors of hospitals to report that they did not need more drugs and medicines (supplied to Iraq under the oil-for-food programme), even though they were desperate for them.[18] Hundreds of Iraqi doctors in white lab coats took to the streets of Baghdad, insisting they would not accept Mr al-Janabi as the Health Minister. Before the war, Mr al-Janabi 'was a faithful servant of Saddam,' said Imad Saud, a resident in cardiothoracic surgery. 'How can we trust him?'[19]

Steven Browning, the Bush administration's 'adviser' to the Health Ministry, said the new Minister was 'not associated with criminal activities or human rights abuses or weapons of mass destruction. So we are happy to work with him.'[20] But the protests forced the US eventually to effectively sack the new Minister.[21]

AN IRAQI FACE: CULTURE AND OIL

Haider Mnather is an Iraqi playwright who was intimidated for turning out plays considered disrespectful of Saddam. The London *Sunday Times* reported in early May 2003: 'Imagine then his horror on discovering that the Americans were offering the job of cultural overlord in the new Iraqi administration to the man who had held it before, a figure despised by Baghdad's artists'. Mr Mnather said, 'We will not accept it. This man made victims of all of us.' Louai Haki, known as the Iraqi President's favourite poet, harnessed Iraq's artistic creativity for the glorification of Saddam Hussein. He said that the US forces had been very 'polite' in asking him to resume work as Director-General of Iraqi cinema and theatre. The Minister expressed some concerns at the administrative ethos that Washington might try to impose, however. 'Iraq is not suited to democracy,' he said, describing his countrymen as a 'herd of sheep' whose totalitarian traditions made them incapable of obedience to more than a single shepherd.[22]

At the oil ministry, famously one of the two Government buildings preserved by the US during the chaos of 'liberation', a senior Iraqi technocrat was appointed to run the oil industry 'amid growing unease at the number of former officials of the Baathist regime securing key posts in the post-war administration,' reported the *Independent*.[23] The new chief executive of the Oil Ministry was one Thamir Abbas Ghadhban, previously the head of the ministry's directorate of studies and planning.[24]

At the end of April 2003, senior sources at the US Office of Reconstruction and Humanitarian Assistance proclaimed their success in developing agreements with leading officials just below ministerial rank in several pre-existing government departments.[25] The plan was to leave the central civil service intact, and to 'decapitate' each ministry, promoting the third-ranking official to the top position.

AN IRAQI FACE: THE BASRA AUTHORITY

In mid-May 2003, British historian and Iraq specialist Charles Tripp suggested that the British army in Basra appeared to be making a better fist of finding and encouraging Iraqi leaders than the Americans in Baghdad: 'They are consulting widely and choosing the people they deal with and draw into leadership and administration more carefully. In Basra there is a local leadership emerging that is ready to co-operate pragmatically with the British forces.'[26] In mid-April, however, the right-wing *Daily Telegraph* reported,

> British forces struggling to assemble an interim authority in Iraq's second city, Basra, are facing criticism for re-appointing officials from Saddam Hussein's Ba'ath Party. At an

inaugural city council meeting, half of the dozen members on show were said to have held prominent places in the fallen regime. One of them, Ghalib Cubba, a rich businessman known in Basra as 'Saddam's banker', once held soirees at which the leader known as Chemical Ali was a regular guest. Others included the imam of Saddam's mosque and a university lecturer who had a reputation for converting students to the Ba'ath cause.

Brigadier Graham Binns, head of 7th Armoured Brigade, and the effective military governor of Basra, said he had spent time with each member of the interim council: 'I feel confident they are acting as a force for good. Anyone with influence was a member of the Ba'ath Party.'[27] True. Just as you had to be in 'the Party' in Germany in the early 1940s.

As for the wide 'consultation' Charles Tripp lauded, the *Telegraph* reported in mid-April that the make-up of the Basra interim advisory council was 'carefully withheld from the public.' A former Iraqi brigadier-general, Sheikh Muzahim Mustafa Kana al-Tamimi, had been appointed head of the interim administration, but then had to be 'quitely dropped from the line-up' after public protests. Learning of the remaining composition of the council, Mohammed al-Shatti, a Basra language teacher said, 'There will be great anger among the people when they find out who these men are.'[28]

AN IRAQI FACE: UMM QASR

The southern port town of Umm Qasr, the first population centre to be 'liberated' by the invading forces, was also the first town to be handed over to self-government, on 15 May 2003, in what military commanders hailed as a huge success story. Yet the *Telegraph* reported that a British soldier who had worked closely with the 12-member, all-male council in the run-up to the hand-over described it as 'a joke' and a 'bloody disaster': 'They're almost all of them on the make.' The soldier, from 23 Pioneer Regiment, said, 'We've worked hard to get where we are today, but there is concern as to just what we're leaving ordinary people with.' Given £6,000 to start up the administration and to begin paying public servants, 'they came back to us and said they still needed money to pay the wages, saying they had lost the original amount'. The councillors were also paying themselves £70 a month, when the average wage in Iraq was around £3 a month. The anonymous British soldier told the *Telegraph* that several of the members were Ba'athists.[29]

Quite a flagship of democracy.

FASCIST JUSTICE RESTORED

On 8 May 2003, Baghdad's courts re-opened. Clint Williamson, US adviser to the Justice Ministry, said that all Iraqi laws would apply except certain laws from the Ba'ath era.[30] These may have been the laws on capital and corporal punishment, which the US banned Iraqi police from applying.[31] Ibrahim Malik al-Hindawi, president of one of the two courts which re-opened in Baghdad, said, 'There'll be punishment for everyone, even if they have high positions. The Iraqi justice system is completely independent and we'll not accept British or American interference.'[32] Noble words. Another relic of the Ba'athist era,

Mr Sami al-Ba'ati, who had been a judge for 16 years, was a little more candid: 'I will do whatever the Americans want. We are ready,' he told a British reporter, without enthusiasm. Mr al-Ba'ati openly admitted to membership of the Ba'ath Party. He inadvertently explained how the 'independent' judiciary had operated under fascism as he boasted of his fearlessness in challenging power by jailing Ziad Aziz, the son of Deputy Prime Minister Tariq Aziz. The younger Aziz had tried to help a friend to leave the country without customs clearance by arranging for an escort of his father's bodyguards. Mr al-Ba'ati boasted, 'We applied the law in the Tariq Aziz case and the decision was just. The president was pleased with our judgement. He gave us presents of 5m Iraqi dinars and a wrist watch.'[33] So much for independence.

FASCIST POLICE RESTORED: BAGHDAD

In early May 2003, there was a flurry of mysterious reports about the first interim police chief appointed by the US in Baghdad. The *Sunday Times* reported, 'Efforts to restore order were dealt a blow when Baghdad's new police chief abruptly resigned yesterday after just nine days in the job. An American army spokesman said Zuhair al-Naimi did not want to implement police procedures suggested by the United States.'[34] The *Independent on Sunday* said the resignation 'remained something of a mystery', without discerning any further details. So far as I am aware, out of the entire British press, only James Drummond of the *Financial Times* reported that Zuhair al-Nuaimi, the interim head of the Baghdad police, was 'a former army general and interior ministry official'.[35] The Interior Ministry in a fascist regime is of course in reality the Repression Ministry.

The US official spokesperson, announcing the resignation, said that Mr al-Nuaimi had handed over more than $380,000 (£237,000) in cash and 100kg of gold recovered from looters.[36] One possibility is that by the time of his resignation, after just nine days in office, General al-Nuaimi had put by enough for a comfortable retirement. A more pressing factor was probably the rising level of popular anger and resistance and protest against the Ba'athist revival, a matter we will examine in greater depth shortly.

In the first weeks of 'liberation,' the people of Baghdad were left to police themselves. In the Shia ghettos of Saddam City (renamed Sadr City after a revered Shia cleric) and Khadamia, where the US forces were reluctant to go even in tanks, the local imams organized local militia to police the hospitals and the Shia areas.[37]

On 4 May, after calls from the occupation forces, hundreds of Baghdad police officers reported for work.[38] They were rarely to venture forth from their offices.[39]

FASCIST POLICE RESTORED: BASRA

The process of re-employing the fascist police force had begun earlier in Basra. In mid-April, some 500 former Iraqi police officers signed up for their old jobs.[40] In early May, Sergeant Euan Andrews of the 7th Parachute Regiment of the Royal Horse Artillery summed up the brotherly atmosphere in Basra by embracing his new friend Ahmed, an officer in the freshly painted Basra police station. 'A month ago we were shooting at each other, now we are on the same side,' said Sergeant Andrews.[41]

Sergeant Andrews was not with 40 Commando Royal Marines in Abu Al Khasib, a suburb of Basra, when they entered the police station on 1 April to discover a row of torture cells: 'In one, a meat hook hung from the ceiling, in another a thick line of hose pipe sat on the floor, with no water taps for it to attach to anywhere in sight.' It became abundantly clear that 'the building in this captured suburb of Basra was, in fact, a house of torture used to inflict pain and suffering on possibly hundreds of civilians.' The soldiers also found car tyres and a live electric lead in another room, used for electrocution, and a pile of ID cards of the 'disappeared'. A Marine explained, 'This is something we came across a lot in Bosnia. The interrogator would stand on the tyres while prodding the captive with the live cable. His own feet were insulated from the high voltage by the rubber.' Later an Iraqi told the troops that the secret police, the Mukhabarat, worked in the building. Corporal Dominic Conway of the Royal Marines remarked, 'They weren't policemen in there, not like we understand the term. They weren't even animals because animals aren't that cruel. I'm just sorry a few of them didn't decide to hang around a little longer to meet us. That would have been very interesting for them.'[42]

Within a fortnight, however, instead of meting out summary justice to the functionaries of the torture state, the British occupation authorities were re-employing them to patrol the streets of Basra.

RE-NAZIFICATION

When Umm Qasr was handed over to its interim authority, the *Telegraph* reported that 'Members of the police force, currently under the supervision of the Royal Military Police, have allegedly been using "old-style techniques" to beat confessions out of those they have arrested.' The newspaper reported that across the southern zone of occupation, there was widespread disgruntlement among British troops over the choice of re-hired police officers, many of them former Ba'athists. 'They're all murdering bastards,' said one lieutenant at a police station in Basra, where military police officers withdrew to leave the former police in charge.[44] Not just a matter of a few 'rotten apples', then.

They were 'murdering bastards' during the time of Saddam Hussein. They remained 'murdering bastards' after the fall of Saddam Hussein. Barrels and barrels of rotten apples were rolled out on the public payroll by the British and US occupation authorities, on the instruction of their political masters in London and Washington.

The war on Iraq was not a war of liberation. For the people of Iraq, it was intended to be little more than a re-branding exercise. The first month of the 'liberation' of Iraq saw not 'regime change' and 'de-nazification' by US and British authorities, but widespread attempts at 're-nazification' by the invaders.

When we turn back the pages of history, we find, shockingly, that this also was largely true in Germany and Japan after the Second World War.

CHAPTER XVI
Hitler Won

False De-Nazification

THE MYTH AND THE REALITY

President Bush exploited the mythology of the de-nazification of Germany and Japan to help build the case for war against Iraq:

> After defeating enemies, we did not leave behind occupying armies, we left constitutions and parliaments. We established an atmosphere of safety, in which responsible . . . local leaders could build lasting institutions for freedom. In societies that once bred fascism and militarism, liberty found a permanent home.'[1]

The reality was somewhat less uplifting.

THE RE-NAZIFICATION OF JAPAN

General Charles Willoughby, head of intelligence in the US Occupation Government, wrote later that the bloodless invasion of Japan was accomplished by 'the shatteringly simple formula of utilising the existing Japanese Government, the person of the Emperor, and the psychic force of tradition. No other formula was practicable.'[2] (Note that it was the refusal of the US and British Governments to concede the position of the Emperor until *after* Hiroshima and Nagasaki that prolonged the Pacific War.[3]) At first over a thousand members of the administration were purged, along with many business people, local government officials, journalists, and so on. 8,000 people were barred from political office; 600 from key positions in business; and 200 from public information work. The Justice Minister Yoshio Suzuki expressed gratitude, contrasting the purge to the 100,000 Germans in jail, and the 1,000,000 Germans suffering fines, confiscations and menial labour.[4] The purges were soon reversed, however. By 1949, 10,090 individuals had been de-purged. By 1951, the figure had reached 177,000. The bulk of those who remained banned from influential occupations were by this time past retirement age.[5]

General MacArthur, US ruler of Japan, said of the Japanese combines known as *zaibatsu*, their integration with government 'was complete', 'their influence upon government inordinate', and they 'set the course which ultimately led to war and destruction.'[6] Initially, a US mission drew up a plan for breaking up the combines into small firms, but this plan was ignored and then repealed.[7]

Turning to the fascist military, General Willoughby (quoted above) neglected to mention in his writings about post-war Japan that he himself recruited high-ranking Japanese war criminals. On 5 September 1945, days after the Japanese surrender, General Willoughby, the director of US counter-intelligence, recruited Lieutenant-General Arisue Seizo, the director of Japanese Military Intelligence—along with many of his associates—to continue his anti-Soviet work, now under US direction. A domestic Japanese intelligence agency was reconstructed under the leadership of the former Deputy Chief of the General Staff, and a hundred other senior officers and politicians. General Willoughby also set up another secret organization, ostensibly to write a history of the Pacific War, which formed the nucleus of Japan's future army, including Colonel Hattori Takushiro, who had been Chief of the Operations Section of the Imperial General Staff.[8] By January 1946, there were 190 Japanese admirals and generals under General Willoughby.[9] Japanese experts in chemical and biological warfare, who had experimented on POWs, were also given immunity in return for access to their research results.[10]

The British Government approved. The Foreign Office rejected calls for a second series of trials for Class A war criminals still in custody after the Tokyo Tribunal (the equivalent of the Nuremberg Tribunals) had settled the first wave of cases.[11]

A US researcher who worked in the Occupation Government summed up in 1954:

> The purge had been abandoned and forgotten, except by victims who resented its unfairness; police and bureaucrats regained their old control if, indeed, they ever really had loosed their hold. Zaibatsu firms revived under their once proscribed names; political and gang bosses flourished; decentralization of schools and local government reversed itself and old-line thought and methods reappeared in editorial offices, movie studios, and courts of law. Americans who had hailed Japan's constitutional renunciation of armed force were offering as gifts large fleets of warships, munitions in huge quantities, money to rebuild an army, and skilled instructors to teach Japan to fight.[12]

The economic, financial, political, cultural and military centres of Japanese fascism had returned to power. Japan was in the hands of those who ruled during the fascist period.

RE-NAZIFYING GERMANY: US ZONE

Postwar Germany was divided into four zones, controlled by the four occupying powers—Russia, France, Britain and the US. The Soviet zone saw a thorough-going social revolution, in large part a matter of revenge for the German invasion. Of the remaining three zones, the harshest of the Western powers was the US, as the result of a secret decision by the US Joint Chiefs of Staff in April 1945 to pursue the strict de-nazification and de-industrialization of Germany. In Bavaria alone, by August 1945, 100,000 top Nazis had been fired from the municipal administration, the postal and telephone services, and so on. The US employed a detailed, 131-item questionnaire to detect Nazis. By March 1946, 1.4 million of these *fragebogen* had been filled out.[13] Then the Law of Liberation passed in March 1946 replaced the old form and set out five categories for the de-nazification process: I) major offenders; II) offenders; III) lesser offenders; IV) followers; V) non-offenders. Thirteen million questionnaires were filled out under these new rules. Three million required hearings by de-nazification courts.

Then, in 1947, the US Defence Secretary ordered the US Occupation Government to halt de-nazification. On 31 March 1948, de-nazification was officially ended in the US zone of occupation, around the time that the purges in Japan were being put into reverse. The timing was interesting. The easy cases, involving lower category offenders, had been dealt with. 600,000 cases involving Categories III to V had been settled. On the other hand, 30,000 cases involving alleged Category I and II war criminals remained pending. Historians Dennis Bark and David Gress summarize the situation: 'proportionately far more of the "smaller fry", most of whom would not have been re-employed anyway, were fined, while categories I and II escaped more lightly because OMGUS [the US Occupation Military Government] abandoned the whole enterprise before their cases could be processed': What began life as a grandiose plan to purge all Nazis from leading roles in public life and to punish severely persons who had held responsible positions in the Third Reich was, in practice, transformed into a procedure by which major offenders were slapped on the wrist and minor offenders exonerated. There were more former members of the Nazi Party in the civil services of local counties or Länder in the US zone in 1949 than there had been under Adolf Hitler.[14]

RE-NAZIFYING GERMANY: BRITISH ZONE

In the British zone, things were worse. The British occupation authorities had been much less enthusiastic about de-nazification, in part because of their 'concern about the results of dismissing most of the country's trained personnel,' according to the *Daily Telegraph*'s correspondent in the British zone.[15] A familiar theme in Iraq today. There were other considerations. One British diplomat remarked in June 1945 that 'Bomber Harris must have got more victims on his conscience than any individual German General or Air Marshal.'[16] This was regarded as an argument for restricting the number of war crimes trials in Germany, rather than for instituting them in Britain.

The British authorities reinstated the Nazi police in their zone, including SS officers, a scandal uncovered by the veteran British reporter Tom Bower in his meticulously documented study *Blind Eye to Murder*. After being vetted twice, SS Lieutenant-Colonel Adolf Schult was chosen by the British to be the Chief of Police in Hanover. The colonel's records, in the possession of the British, clearly demonstrated that he had been a member of the Nazi Party since 1933, and as an SS officer had been the chief of personnel of the German police in Nazi-occupied Holland. Colonel Schult had been fired from the SS when his illegal profiteering became too notorious—an event also recorded in his file. Once appointed Chief of Police, the former SS colonel naturally appointed former comrades to work for him. In this, Hanover was only one of a number of towns and cities where the British employed Nazi police. One German police officer, stationed in Göttingen, complained in February 1946 that Nazi officers were 'astonished to find that they were not dismissed after the German defeat, and some have become quite arrogant,' especially as they had been promoted by the British. The British administration recruited former SS officers who had served in Poland and Russia—scenes of extraordinary barbarity—and those whose names appeared as security suspects on official lists.[17]

In April 1946, the Foreign Office noted that 'if denazification of the police is carried to extremes there would be no police force left': 'With conditions in our zone as they are, it would perhaps seem that the essential is to have a reliable police force and this cannot be achieve without some sense of security.'[18] Never mind the insecurity of the fascists' surviving victims. What was needed was a group of 'reliable' Nazis, as in Iraq today.

RE-NAZIFYING GERMANY

In the universities, Nazi professors continued to teach—in the US, French and British zones. In November 1947, the British authorities admitted that of 121 key positions in the judicial system in their zone, over thirty per cent of posts were held by former members of either the Nazi Party or the Nazi SA group. The majority of these Nazis had not even been through British de-nazification procedures. In industry, no directives were ever given to the British military government to enable them to remove Nazi businesspeople. Sir Percy Mills of the British Control Commission reappointed committed Nazi supporters to run German industry, and permitted them to retain the fabulous wealth they had stolen from other European countries. Britain refused to co-operate with US proposals for decartelization of German industry along the lines of the (fleeting) moves planned against the Japanese *zaibatsu*. Key figures in German financial institutions were also left in place.[19]

Much of the Nazi civil service survived the various de-nazification regimes. For example, Hans Globke, the civil servant who wrote the commentary to the Nuremberg race laws, was employed by Konrad Adenauer, first Chancellor of West Germany, as his personal assistant.[20] Other top civil servants in Herr Adenauer's administration were Franz Thedieck (who betrayed a group of anti-Nazis to the Gestapo in 1933); Dr Gunther Bergmann (who supervised the plunder of Serbia during the war); Ludger Westerick (who employed a workforce which was 80 per cent slave labour when he managed the wartime aluminium industry); Rudolf Senteck (who served in the Race and Resettlement Main Office as a senior SS officer); and Herbert Blankenhorn (who, as well as being a member of the SS and the Nazi Party, was an active and aggressive Nazi propagandist while serving in the German Embassy in Washington DC between 1935 and 1939).[21]

The chief of the Special and Denazification Branch of the US Occupation Government, William E. Griffith, wrote in 1950 that the de-nazification programme had 'failed to achieve any objective, German or American, and in particular failed to realize the American effort to construct democratic foundations from German society and thus to prevent a recrystallization of its traditional authoritarian social structure.'[22] Reviewing this judgement in 1993, Mr Griffith wondered whether de-nazification had not been successful after all, combating political attitudes in the media and *classe politique*. Insofar as evidence exists, however, it does not support this revisionism so far as popular attitudes were concerned. Opinion polls in 1951 found that only 32 per cent of West Germans believed that Nazi Germany was responsible for the outbreak of war, a rise from 20 per cent in November 1945.[23] Hardly a decisive break with the past. In 1955, 48 per cent of West Germans believed that Hitler without the war would have been one of the greatest statesmen. Similarly, in November 1945, 50 per cent of people had thought that National Socialism was a good idea badly carried out.[24]

Analysis of the poll results from the 1950s suggest that perhaps a quarter of the population was composed of consistent supporters of democracy, while perhaps a fifth were strongly pro-Nazi. This picture may not be all that different from the period of Nazi rule. British historian Ian Kershaw has shown that the opinion polls carried out by the Nazis themselves indicated that by the end of the war there was a silent majority disgusted with the Nazi regime, but willing to obey.[25] An earlier survey, in 1942, showed that only five per cent of Nazi Party members approved of the shipment of Jews to 'labour camps', 70 per cent were indifferent, and the rest showed some concern.[26] Among the general population, support for the Holocaust would surely have been even less.

These sketchy indications do not support the notion that the false de-nazification in the US and British zones of occupation somehow managed to dislodge Nazism from West German culture.

TAKING UP WHERE THE NAZIS LEFT OFF

In early 1947, General Brian Robertson, deputy military governor of the British zone, explained that the British interest in de-nazification was quite different from that of the Germans: 'Apart from war criminals, we are chiefly concerned with security, i.e. we wish the German administration and German industry to be staffed with people who are not dangerous to the aims of the occupation. For the Germans, however, the question is largely one of justice and retribution upon individuals who have oppressed and persecuted their fellow citizens and brought disaster upon their country.'[27]

Security versus justice. What kind of 'security' and what were the 'aims of the occupation'? The practice of the British (and US) authorities suggests that a major aim of the occupation was to reconstitute the authoritarian political-bureaucratic-economic-judicial-educational structures of the Nazi era, without the formal trappings of the former ruling Party, and deprived of the state terrorism of the earlier period.

The Allies' commitment to 'security' went far beyond re-instating Nazi police officers. As in Japan, the Western Allies recruited Nazi torturers and war criminals for their own purposes. Noam Chomsky observes that the most important of the post-war networks founded by the Nazi–US alliance was the 'Gehlen' organization, constructed by General Reinhard Gehlen, who had headed Nazi military intelligence on the Eastern Front. This was the equivalent of the near-simultaneous recruitment of Lieutenant-General Arisue Seizo, the head of Military Intelligence in Japan. General Gehlen was placed in charge of the official espionage and counter-espionage service of the new West German state.[28]

Another notable recruit was Klaus Barbie, known as the 'Butcher of Lyons', who was employed by US intelligence in Europe, then sent to Bolivia, where he introduced the concentration camp; lectured on the use of electrodes in interrogation; and helped to organize a violent coup in 1980. Herr Barbie was a central figure in an international fascist network which assisted the formation of Nazi-like National Security States throughout Latin America. Noam Chomsky draws the connection—through Klaus Barbie and his ilk—between the death camps of Nazi Europe and the death squads of Nazified Latin America. This connection was created and sustained by decisions made in Washington.[29]

After Herr Barbie was extradited to France in 1982, a retired US colonel, Eugene Kolb, wrote to the *New York Times* to defend the decision to recruit the 'Butcher of Lyons'. The torturer's 'skills were badly needed': 'To our knowledge, his activities had been directed against the underground French Communist Party and Resistance, and just as we in the postwar era were concerned with the German Communist Party and activities inimical to American policies in Germany.'[30] Noam Chomsky observes that this comment was entirely apt: 'The US was picking up where the Nazis had left off, and it was therefore entirely natural that they should employ specialists in anti-resistance activities, whose "atrocities" were not considered real atrocities, given the nature of the targets.'[31]

The right-wing British newspaper, the *Daily Telegraph*, commented in early April 2003, 'To leave the Ba'athists in any serious form of power in Iraq would be like leaving the Nazis in charge of Germany in 1945.'[32] The record shows that much of the Nazi system *was* left in charge of Germany in the aftermath of 1945, and within days of this editorial being published, the British and US Governments were straining every nerve to re-nazify Iraq and to leave Ba'athist leaders in very serious forms of power.

Juan Jose Arevalo, an advocate of liberal capitalism, was elected president of Guatemala in 1944. His administration, though it was in many ways modelled on the New Deal policies of the pre-war US Government, quickly incurred US hostility. Señor Arevalo did not repress the Communist Party, because of his commitment to democratic values; he adopted a liberal labour code that harmed the interests of the United Fruit company; and he hesitated to grant oil concessions to US oil companies. By the time he left office in 1951, the rift was complete. Senor Arevalo recalled the noble wartime rhetoric of President Roosevelt. He commented sadly, 'Roosevelt lost the war. The real winner was Hitler.'[33]

CHAPTER XVII
Coup d'État

The US Wanted A Coup

THE OPEN SECRET

The story of the war on Iraq is a story of open secrets, kept not by official censorship, but by media self-censorship. George Orwell wrote, in an unpublished foreword to *Animal Farm*, 'The sinister fact about literary censorship in England is that it is largely voluntary. Unpopular ideas can be silenced, and inconvenient facts kept dark, without any need for any official ban.' The desired effect is achieved in part by the 'general tacit agreement that "it wouldn't do" to mention that particular fact', and in part as the result of the concentration of the media in the hands of 'wealthy men who have every motive to be dishonest on certain important topics.' The result is that, 'Anyone who challenges the prevailing orthodoxy finds himself silenced with surprising effectiveness.'[1]

Thus far, we have documented several major hidden scandals, including the disruption of the 'key disarmament tasks' process, and the attempted re-nazification of Iraq in the first month of 'liberation'. The documentation has drawn on the media, but the understanding developed has come in spite of the outpourings of the media system, not because of them. Noam Chomsky and Edward Herman remark,

> That the media provide some information about an issue . . . proves absolutely nothing about the adequacy or accuracy of media coverage. The media do, in fact, suppress a great deal of information, but even more important is the way they present a particular fact—its placement, tone, and frequency of repetition—and the framework of analysis in which it is placed.

There is so much information in the media system, some error and leakage is inevitable. Professor Chomsky says, 'the enormous mass of material that is produced in the media and books makes it possible for a really assiduous and committed researcher to gain a fair picture of the real world by cutting through the mass of misrepresentation and fraud to the nuggets hidden within':

That a careful reader, looking for a fact can sometimes find it, with diligence and a skeptical eye, tells us nothing about whether that fact received the attention and context it deserved, whether it was intelligible to most readers, or whether it was effectively distorted or suppressed.[2]

Why was the regime restored in Iraq? Was this an inadvertent or accidental outcome of the chaos of war? No, it was premeditated and long-planned and deliberate. The restoration of the regime was in fact a major goal of the campaign. Throughout the long Iraq crisis, it was possible to discern in the flood of propaganda nuggets of a suppressed truth: the US Administration were set on triggering a military coup in Baghdad.

The reports began early. In March 2002, the London *Guardian* reported that 'Top of the US wish list would be a coup by an Iraqi officer . . . The US might, from its point of view, even get lucky with an air strike on the centre of Baghdad that killed Saddam' (which is, of course, exactly how the US opened the 2003 war).[3] *Newsweek*, on 25 March 2002, reported that, 'At the CIA, State Department and among the uniformed military, specialists are trying to find the proverbial Man on a White Horse, a respected officer who can ride in, take control and unite Iraq's fractious tribes and religious groups': 'the US will need some kind of military strongman to foment a coup, or head a rebel army that could work alongside US forces, or run the Iraqi military after Saddam is gone.'[4] The US magazine surveyed a number of possible candidates for the position of 'Man on a White Horse', including Brigadier-General Najib al-Salhi, who served Saddam Hussein until he defected in 1995. The *Sunday Telegraph* noted that the general was being 'actively courted by the State Department as a potential conduit between rival groups,' a man who claimed to be able to get rid of Mr Saddam 'at very low cost'. In the spring of 2002, the Brigadier-General gave an idea of the kind of 'multiparty democratic system' he intended for Iraq by stressing 'the need to encourage Iraqi military leaders to switch sides by promising that no more than 20 of Saddam's closest henchmen would be treated as criminals by an incoming Iraqi government.'[5] Again, this was very much the shape of eventual US policy, as we have seen.

In May 2002, *Time* magazine commented, 'The smoothest regime-change scenario—a coup within Saddam's own military ranks—is the least likely.'[6] This illustrated the real meaning of 'regime change' in elite circles. In August 2002, *Time* reported that 'the war party is looking for a silver bullet strategy—a lucky first strike on Saddam, say, or a manufactured coup by Iraqi dissidents—that would forestall an old-fashioned deployment of hundreds of thousands of troops and tanks.' (US military professionals discounted such 'dream schemes.')[7]

The experts were agreed on the preference for a coup: Daniel Neep of the Royal United Services Institute in London said in November 2002, 'Once the military campaign starts, Saddam has to go. The ideal scenario is someone within Iraq, preferably within the army, killing Saddam and taking control. That would mean that entering Baghdad would not be necessary and would also solve the problem of who will govern once he has gone.'[8] Another military dictator, someone who had served Saddam Hussein faithfully.

OPERATION FORCE ON MIND

From July 2002 onwards, there was a steady stream of well-sourced and substantial leaks concerning US war plans towards Iraq. These leaks were themselves part of the coup-making strategy. In November 2002, the *Observer* reported that, 'analysts say the repeated leaks of war plans by American and British defence sources are part of a concerted strategy to put pressure on Saddam and his supporters within the army and, despite the bullish talk, the prospect of allied troops being sucked into combat in cities, where they would sustain heavy casualties, is worrying military planners.'[9] In January 2003, Richard Norton-Taylor of the *Guardian* observed,

> Our diplomats and military commanders are clinging to the hope that pressure on Iraq from the build-up of American military force in the Gulf will lead to an 'implosion' of Saddam Hussein's regime without a war. They want the organs of the Iraqi state, including the Republican Guard, to remain in place, to maintain law and order with the help of American and British forces and prevent the oil-rich nation's disintegration.[10]

In February, the *Observer* reported again that leaks of military plans, especially those targeted at Saddam Hussein's home region of Tikrit, were 'clearly part of an increasingly vigorous propaganda effort designed to further persuade Saddam and his key commanders that it is not worth fighting and that exile is the best option.'[11] *The Times* reported a few days later, 'America is hoping that its massive show of force will prompt a "palace revolt".'[12] Also in February 2003 came this report in *Newsweek*:

> Until now, most other countries believed that the Bush administration was mainly pursuing a strategy of 'force on mind'—a combination of tough talk and a theatrical military buildup that would place unbearable psychological pressure on Saddam's regime. Operation Force on Mind is what the Brits are calling their Army buildup in the Gulf . . .[13]

In mid-March, Britain's 'order of battle,' a rundown of the military hardware that was then in place, was revealed, reportedly 'to increase the psychological pressure on President Saddam Hussein.'[14] However, by this point the British, at least, had begun to lose heart, concluding that while senior members of the regime were 'preparing their bolt-holes', they were unlikely to risk staging a coup until a war began, according to one report: 'America and Britain have long hoped that the build-up to war might break the regime without the need for military action . . . The British assessment is that a coup is unlikely before a war, but it is possible once hostilities begin.'[15]

THE MOTHER OF ALL COUPS

Under the headline 'US seeking to foment the mother of all coups,' the *Financial Times* reported in February 2003, 'A coup would be a dream solution to many of those involved in the Iraq drama, despite the US administration's insistence that one of its objectives is to sow the seeds of democratic change in Iraq.'[16] The most dramatic expression of the desirability of this 'dream solution' came from the lips of the White House spokesman Ari Fleischer on 1 October 2002. Asked the Congressional Budget Office estimate that the war in Iraq would cost between $9 billion and $13 billion, Mr Fleischer replied, 'I can only say that the cost of a one-way ticket is substantially less than that. The cost of one bullet, if the Iraqi people take it on themselves, is substantially less than that.' Another reporter followed up: 'I'm asking you if you intend to advocate from that podium that some Iraqi persons put a bullet in his head?' The President's spokesperson responded, 'Regime change is welcome in whatever form it takes.'[17] One bullet could achieve 'regime change', as defined in the White House.

DECODING THE EXILE OFFER

It appears now that the exile offers also were a form of code for encouraging a military coup. The *Financial Times* reported in February 2003, that the hope in the Administration was that offers to allow Saddam Hussein to leave the country 'would either convince the Iraqi leader to seek exile or provoke his removal.'[18] This seems also to have been the thinking behind the 17 March ultimatum. Roula Khalaf, writing in the *FT* under the headline 'Bush speech seen as urging coup', observed that, 'With his ultimatum to Saddam Hussein and his sons to leave Iraq or face war, President George W. Bush appeared to be encouraging a last minute coup more than the Iraqi leader's departure from Baghdad, diplomats and analysts said yesterday.' Western diplomats in the region said the ultimatum was designed to raise the internal pressure on insiders in the regime to move against the Iraqi leader. One senior diplomat in the region said, 'exile might be read as another form of exit.'[19]

Newsweek reported in January 2003 that Arab Governments were attempting to 'checkmate Saddam with his own pawns': 'If there is ultimately a message of amnesty, perhaps through a new UN resolution, it will be directed at the small clique of relatives and cronies, generals and secret-police officials who might actually force Saddam from office with a cup of poison or a palace uprising. Many in the Bush administration say privately they'd be more than happy with that outcome.'[20]

BLITZ-COUP

With the ultimatum, we reach the brink of war. Did the coup strategy extend into the period of war itself? Did the coup strategy form part of the war strategy? Yes.

Before considering the war plan, it may be useful to recall the first blow of the war, an attempt to strike Saddam Hussein and his two sons on the first night of the war. This was a last-minute change to the plan, as the CIA claimed to have reliable intelligence on the whereabouts of the Iraqi leader. (Mr Blair was apparently not consulted—shades of February 2001.[21]) An old military saying had to be revised. 'No plan survives contact with the enemy, but in this case it appears it didn't even survive no contact with the enemy,' said retired US Admiral John Sigler.[22] The meaning of the war was laid bare in this cruise missile assassination attempt. It was a war for 'leadership change', not 'regime change.' It was a war for 'decapitation', not 'democracy'.

Turning to the actual conduct of the war, the *Financial Times* noted that some analysts speculated that the US had raised expectations that the war would open with an overwhelming campaign 'in the hope that it would never have to wage it': 'The pause before the shock and awe was an attempt to get a coup as they move[d] to Baghdad from the south,' said Toby Dodge, an Iraq expert at the University of Warwick. The point was 'to put pressure on the second league of generals and push them against Saddam's inner circle so the US would not have to fight for Baghdad.'[23] When Donald Rumsfeld talked of a 'shock and awe' assault, he spoke of striking 'on a scope and scale that makes clear to Iraqis that [Saddam Hussein] and his regime are finished. With the start of the air war it may be that we find people responding.'[24] What kind of 'response'? Mr Rumsfeld was hoping for troops to surrender, and for military leaders to mount a coup attempt.

According to one report, the original war plan was to send a massive armoured column of US tanks speeding through Iraq's Western Desert to the outskirts of Baghdad within three days. The column was likely to stop outside the city of Karbala while US airborne units secured the numerous bridges around Baghdad, sealing off the city. If by this time Saddam Hussein was still resisting, military planners had 'factored in a short political pause to allow his capitulation. If no white flag was seen, the assault on Baghdad [would] begin.'[25]

Note the innocuous phrase, 'a short political pause'. The meaning of this concept was spelled out in the *Daily Telegraph* before the war started. Patrick Bishop had been briefed by a senior British officer in Kuwait:

> The war in Iraq is expected to be a two-stage operation with a pause to allow time for Saddam Hussein to be toppled by his own people ... Troops [invading from the south] are under orders to do everything to minimise military casualties and damage to civilian infrastructure in order to consolidate good-will and apply further pressure on the Baghdad regime to turn on Saddam and remove the need for an attack on the capital. A senior British army officer said: 'No one's going to go charging into Baghdad. Fighting in urban areas is a hugely risky business.' If the regime does not fall under the shock of the initial assault, a stand-off around Baghdad is 'a very likely scenario.' The Allied planning appears heavily weighted towards an incremental strategy that applies mounting pressure and allows time for Saddam's henchmen to decide their self-interest lies in risking a move against him. 'This is all about getting someone to tip him over,' said the source.[26]

PSYCHOLOGICAL WARFARE

Mr Rumsfeld said on 21 March, 'there are communications in every conceivable mode and method, public and private, to the Iraqi forces, that they can act with honour and turn over their weapons and walk away from them and they will not be hurt.'[27] Presumably they were also receiving hints and suggestions that they not merely turn over their weapons, but that they turn their weapons on the ruling family. *The Times* reported, 'Surrender talks beween coalition forces and Iraqi chiefs have gathered pace in recent days, and a senior American official said yesterday that General Tommy Franks, the US commander in the Gulf, would scale the intensity of the bombardment in accordance with progress in those talks. If they did not reach a successful conclusion, the bombing would go "full-throttle".'[28] It was also reported that Western military intelligence chiefs stepped up their e-mail and mobile phone contacts with generals about laying down their arms, and that these conversations encouraged American officials 'to believe that Saddam was losing his grip on power'—in other words that they were closer to achieving the long-desired coup. 'Saddam's inner circle is starting to collapse,' one official told *The Times* on 21 March. The newspaper commented, 'The American claims were impossible to verify and may simply be part of the intense psychological campaign being waged by CIA and US military chiefs to sway Iraqi generals.'[29] Mr Rumsfeld said that surrender discussions between US officials and some Iraqi military leaders had intensified: 'They're beginning to realize the regime is history. And as that realization sets in, their behavior is likely to begin to tip and to change.'[30] This was the famous 'tipping point', like 'implosion' a euphemism for 'military coup'.

While the US strategy was touted as a new 'effects-based' form of warfare, Christopher Bellamy, formerly the military correspondent for the *Independent*, and now professor of military science and doctrine at Cranfield University, Bedfordshire, pointed out that behind it all lay a 'medieval concept': 'You offer talks. You negotiate. The opposition does not play. So you apply a bit of torture, a bit of terror. You up the ante. Then you offer to talk again. The tactics would be familiar to Caesar, to the Sheriff of Nottingham, to Genghis Khan, to Edward I, to Stalin.'[31]

Michael Evans, Defence Editor for *The Times*, observed that, 'From the moment Operation Iraqi Freedom was launched, the focus of every military action has been aimed at undermining the leadership in Baghdad . . . the overarching purpose was to put maximum pressure on Baghdad, to cause confusion in the leadership and to undermine the morale of the so-called elite forces guarding Saddam in the capital. They know what is coming and the pressures on them are growing by the hour.' Mr Evans had an extraordinary revelation: 'The whole point of "embedding" 700 reporters in American brigades and divisions was to ensure that Saddam and his regime would watch the progress of the coalition force as it advanced towards Baghdad. It is the most blatant form of information warfare ever devised. The Americans may have brought with them to the Gulf the familiar array of weapons systems, such as the B52s, the B2 Stealth bombers and Tomahawk cruise missiles. But the most potent weapons have been psychological.'[32]

The war on Iraq is better thought of as an unusually destructive psychological warfare campaign than as a conventional military campaign of conquest.

USING THE FASCIST POLICE AND ARMY

Only an understanding of the real objectives and strategy of the US provides an explanation for one of the mysteries of the invasion and occupation—the patent inability of the

US forces to control the country in the wake of their successful overthrow of the Government. Why did the US invade with light forces that it must have known would be incapable of securing and administering a nation of over 22 million people? According to a senior aide to President Bush, speaking in August 2002, the British Government kept asking how the United States proposed to keep law and order the day after victory; 'And when there's no concrete answer, the question comes back: "OK, how long are we going to be occupying Iraq?" ' 'No one has any answer to that question,' said the aide.[33] There was a very simple answer, though it may not have been transmitted to London at that point. Or ever. In May 2003, a British official said, 'It's difficult to imagine how this could have happened. But it appears that there was no planning whatsover.'[34] Actually, there was. It was just that the plans did not work out. *Time* magazine reported after the war, 'Few had expected the US to have this much trouble bringing order to Iraq': 'The Pentagon had expected the postwar transition in Iraq to be orderly and quick, without requiring a major, long-term commitment of US forces and other resources.' How was this to be done? US Army Major General Buford Blount, commander of the 3rd Infantry Division said, 'We half expected the police force to still be functional, but they were not.'[35] The US was expecting to use the 'shatteringly simple formula of utilizing the existing Iraqi Government', following the Japanese precedent, with the notable discrepancy that this time the 'Emperor' was to die. That was the whole point of the conflict.

Before the war took place, Sir Timothy Garden, formerly an Air Marshal of the RAF, a former Director of the Royal Institute for International Affairs, and now head of the Royal College of Defence Studies, pointed out:

> The desired end state is key to determining the way the military phase is tackled. There appears to be a political consensus to preserve Iraq as a single entity . . . To US planners the simplest way to keep Iraq together after a war may be to use the current Iraqi security forces, but under new management. This would need a very specific direction: that the security apparatus be disabled but not destroyed during conflict. This is not an easy military option.[36]

'Leadership change', not 'regime change'. 'Decapitation', not 'democracy'. The fascist system was to be taken over lock, stock and barrel, along the lines of Japan and Germany. It was not an easy military option, and in the end the US failed to maintain the cohesion of the system. In pursuit of leadership change, the US destabilized the regime, which fell apart and dispersed, politically and militarily, just when Washington was hoping for a smooth hand-over to the Ba'athists.

One important goal was to secure the surrender of the military in order to have a force to hand power over to. That is why, before the war, it was reported that the first raids on Iraq 'would follow heavy aerial leafletting of Iraqi forces in the field and broadcasts encouraging them not to resist.' Sources said the aim was not to neutralise the Iraqi army in combat but to make it 'come over' so it could be used to 'police the country after Saddam had gone.'[37] Earlier we quoted from Donald Rumsfeld. Here is the rest of his warning/appeal to the Iraqi army: the assault 'will be of a force and scope and scale that has been beyond what has been seen before. The Iraqi soldiers and officers must ask themselves whether they want to die fighting for a doomed regime or do they want to survive, help the Iraqi people in the liberation of their country and play a role in a new free Iraq?'[38] The military were being offered the chance to retain their dominant role in Iraq.

Explaining the process of vetting captured Iraqis at the end of March, a senior US official said, 'There's going to be an enormous amount of case-by-case, especially early on.' The intelligence services would be razed to the ground, but the military was 'a tricky one'. The official stated, 'Our bias will be toward forgiving as much of the past as possible.'[39] This suggested that 'only a tiny handful of the worst of the worst will actually be prosecuted.' While this outraged human rights activists, *Newsweek* suggested, 'as the United States tries to foster a coup or a quick surrender by the people around Saddam, it's practical.'[40] Once again, a passing reference to the centrality of the coup in US war plans.

A few days into the war, a source at the British Army's HQ in Kuwait, said, 'If local ceasefires can be negotiated as we take ground, we will be relieved of the huge logistical problem of having to build camps for all of the PoWs.' The source added, 'The plan is to keep the military largely intact to maintain the security of the country after Saddam falls.' Those who capitulated before firing a shot could expect to be invited to join the 'new army of Iraq'.[41] The implication was that whatever crimes a soldier or officer had committed in the past, the 'bias' would be 'toward forgiving as much of the past as possible,' to use the US formula, and so long as the individual had not actively resisted the invaders they would have the opportunity to bear arms in the near future in a new army sponsored by Britain and the US.

Whitehall had examined the legalities and believed that allied commanders had the right to force Iraqi POWs to work in ports unloading aid supplies, or assisting in the urgent rebuilding of water and sanitation plants.[42] There was other work on the agenda also: Major Eric Murray of the US 3rd Infantry said in late March, that 'the majority of the low-ranking POWs would probably land on the white list—that is, Iraqis who pose no threat to allied forces. These soldiers may simply be set free or even converted into a post-Saddam peacekeeping force.'[43] Recall that before the war, British sources said that the aim was not to neutralise the Iraqi army in combat but to make it 'come over' so it could be used to 'police the country after Saddam had gone.'[44]

'Our plan is basically to put them into a constabulary force. We are not going to make them POWs,' said a senior US official before the war. There were complications, the *FT* noted, as 'occupying powers are governed by the Fourth Geneva Convention of 1949, and troops cannot be made to fight their own people.'[45] This was a broad hint of the real meaning of the terms 'constabulary' or 'peacekeeping' force. The US was preparing itself, if necessary, for a re-run of March 1991, once again assisting Iraqi forces in putting down insurgent movements. In 1991 the assistance was largely tacit and discreet; this time it might have to be overt and directive.

In the event, such was the disarray that most Iraqi POWs were just freed. On 8 May, the Pentagon said that 7,000 of the prisoners captured in the war had been released, leaving only 2,000 in US–UK hands.[46] It was reported in early May that US forces would retain control over security for at least two years 'as they rebuild the Iraqi army.'[47]

THE REPUBLICAN GUARD

The elite military unit the Republic Guard, and the super-elite Special Republican Guard, were widely seen as the crucial actors in any coup scenario. Entrusted with protecting the Iraqi President, the Republican Guard formations were the best-trained, the best-equipped, the best-paid and the most loyal elements of the Iraqi armed forces. They were also the most dangerous to the leading family. An officer in US Central Command, which was to conduct the war against Iraq, said in late 2001,

> Our question was, 'What about the day after?' For example, do you take the Republican Guard and disarm it? Or is it preferable to turn it from having a capability to protect Saddam to a capability to protect Iraq? You've got Kurds in the north, Arab Shia in the south, and the Baath Party in the middle, with great internal tribal divisions. There's potential for civil war. Layer on external opposition and you've got a potential for great instability. I'm a military planner and plan for the worst case. As bad as this guy is, a stable Iraq is better than instability.[48]

'Stability' versus 'justice,' to use the dichotomy identified in post-war Germany. The fate of the Republican Guard was a matter of great puzzlement during and after the war. John Keegan, the Defence Editor for the *Daily Telegraph*, wrote in early April, during the closing stages of the war,

> One of the most mysterious aspects of this highly mysterious war is the absence of casualties . . . the great riddle of the Second Gulf War: where have all the Iraqi soldiers gone? Have they gone home and hidden their uniforms? Have they drifted across the border into Iran or Syria? Are they refugees in the northern no-fly zone? No answers. Unless they materialise soon, this war will fizzle out for lack of an enemy.[49]

After the war, *Time* magazine conducted an investigation into the fate of the Republican Guard. It was discovered that four Republic Guard divisions had been deployed south of the capital in two defensive arcs involving between 16,000 and 24,000 troops. *Time* also established that of the 28,000 bombs and missiles dropped by US pilots in the war—70 per cent of them smart—'about half were directed against the Republican Guard.'[50] Despite this, relatively few members of the Republican Guard were actually killed in the fighting. According to accounts collected by *Time*, the Iraqi forces for the most part survived aerial bombardments by keeping their distance from their armour, which US pilots targets with great precision. When US ground troops approached, the Republican Guard generally fled. In Baghdad, according to a high-ranking Republican Guard officer interviewed by *Time*, troops were actually instructed to desert. 'This may help explain why the members of the Special Republican Guard, deployed within Baghdad as the Iraqi regime's ultimate defenders, put up virtually no resistance to the American takeover of the city, as they felt the entire elite-forces structure collapsing around them.'[51]

MR WOLFOWITZ AND PEOPLE POWER

The Pentagon hawks fought a long hard battle for de-Ba'athification—at a verbal level. In reality, however, the hawks' commitment to the democratic Iraqi opposition was shown by their deeds. The offers of exile to Saddam Hussein by Donald Rumsfeld; the ceaseless encouragement of a military coup; the Pentagon's psychological warfare strategy of leaking war plans in order to provoke the Iraqi military into acting against Saddam Hussein; the search for a 'silver bullet' solution; the two-stage war plan to allow a coup to take place; and the calibration of the bombardment to the surrender/coup-mindedness of Iraqi military leaders, all point to one conclusion.

The hawks were as committed to 'regime stabilization and leadership change' as anyone else in the Bush Administration.

The point man for the hawks was, and remains, Paul Wolfowitz, deputy to Donald Rumsfeld. Mr Wolfowitz says that the pivotal moment in his early political career came in 1985 when, as assistant secretary of state for Asia, he helped to shape Reagan Administration policy towards President Ferdinand Marcos of the Philippines. Apparently, when Mr Wolfowitz talks about building democracy in Iraq after the overthrow of Hussein, he often does so through the prism of his own experiences in Asia. Stephen Bosworth, who was ambassador to Manila at the time of Marcos's overthrow, and who is now dean of the Fletcher School of Law and Diplomacy at Tufts University, observes that, for a long time, Mr Wolfowitz and other senior Reagan Administration officials took the view that the dictator President Marcos was a major part of the problem, 'first we must make him part of the solution': Mr Wolfowitz's 'initial instinct' was to work with Marcos. 'There did not seem to be any alternative.'[52] This is the torch-bearer of democracy in the Arab world.

AFTER ME, THE COUP

US and British leaders were quite frank about their desire for a coup d'etat to depose Saddam Hussein and his inner circle, frank enough for this aim to surface repeatedly in the US and British mass media. They pinned their hopes on the Iraqi military. When a list of 14 wanted leaders was circulated in the run-up to the war, none of those named were from the army. The fascist military leadership would be at the heart of the new/old regime.[53] The mass media colluded in hiding this open secret from the general public, by the placement, tone and lack of repetition given to the insights collated here, in addition to the general framework of analysis which the media worked to.

CHAPTER XVIII
Why 'Regime Stabilization'?

Saudi Arabia and Turkey Need Saddamism

THE SAUDI FACTOR

Why would the United States commit itself to 'regime stabilization, leadership change' rather than real 'regime change'? To understand, it may be useful to revisit that moment before the war, when Kanan Makiya issued a bitter attack on US intentions towards the people of Iraq, charging betrayal. President Bush sent in his special envoy Zalmay Khalilzad to meet the Iraqi opposition delegates gathered in Iraqi Kurdistan in late February 2003. Mr Khalilzad gave a pledge that the US intervention in Iraq would last 'not one minute' after Iraq had been furnished with an 'accountable and representative government' based on 'justice and the rule of law.' Iraqis should control their own affairs as soon as possible, he said.[1] Mr Khalilzad said, 'The coalition will not depart Iraq one minute before this job is done. But nor will it stay one minute after the job is done.' He insisted that Washington was now in favour of de-Ba'athification, and reaffirmed the US commitment to transforming Iraq 'ultimately' (a useful qualifier) into a Western-style democracy: 'Some have said it is impossible for Iraq to become a democracy. The US government disagrees.'[2] Kanan Makiya announced that he was now broadly reassured: 'There is a new emphasis on democratisation that was missing before.'[3] An emphasis which proved in the first weeks after 'liberation' to be a propaganda smokescreen rather than a real commitment.

While Mr Makiya was reassured, others were not. The *Guardian* reported that, 'Mr Khalilzad's remarks are also likely to alarm Saudi Arabia, which wants Iraq's traditional minority Sunni elite to remain in power.[4] Earlier in the month Prince Saud al-Faisal, the Saudi Foreign Minister, had lobbied world leaders on the need to preserve Iraq's military and Government in order to maintain stability for a post-Saddam regime. *The Times* noted that, 'The Saudi move received a sympathetic hearing at Downing Street [in the first week of February 2003]. British officials said they were open to any plan that helped restore stability in post-conflict Iraq.' Both Riyadh and London favoured installing a UN civilian leadership 'but keeping much of the country's bureaucracy intact.' Both parties also agreed that the Iraqi opposition leadership was too weak and divided to be considered as an alternative government.[5] Prince Saud told the Saudi daily newspaper *al-Riyadh* that his plan for Iraq envisaged 'preserving the present administration in Iraq' in order to 'safeguard internal security, the state's sovereignty and prevent the break-up of Iraq.'

'The idea is that the Iraqi head be severed from the Iraqi body,' said one Saudi official. 'We do not see why removing the current leadership means destroying the whole country as well.'[6] For a paranoid dictatorship like Saudi Arabia, dismantling the structures of fascism was tantamount to destroying the entire nation.

SAUDI FEARS OF SHIA ISLAM

Saudi Arabia had a number of different concerns. As a rather fragile dictatorship with a restive population, a vibrant Arab democracy breaking free from decades of repression right on the northern border was a frightening prospect, with potential for a threatening 'demonstration effect.' More particularly, Saudi Arabia, like all the Arab Gulf states, is dominated by Sunni Muslim leaders. An Iraq in which democracy flourished, or in which the violent constraints of the Ba'athist era were loosened significantly, would mean a real voice for the Shia majority in Iraq. Shia Muslims make up over 60 per cent of the population of Iraq. If they were to have representation in proportion to their numbers, Iraq's social and political order would be imbued with, and informed by, Shia Islam. The Arab princely states fear the extension of influence from Iraq's Persian neighbour, Shia Iran. Throughout the Gulf there are numbers of Shia Muslims who might be encouraged to challenge their suppression and exploitation. In Bahrain, as in Iraq, the Shia Muslims make up the majority of the population. In Saudi Arabia, the proportion is relatively small, but discrimination against the Shia has created considerable potential for friction. The 2001 Human Rights Watch annual report noted that, 'Shia Muslims, who constitute about eight percent of the Saudi population, faced discrimination in employment as well as limitations on religious practices.'[7]

The rulers of Saudi Arabia fear both the encouragement of the Shia populations of the region, and the extension of Iranian political influence into southern Iraq, dominated by the Shia majority population. While it is facile to suggest that Iraq's Shias are in thrall to Tehran, there is certainly a substantial proportion of the Shia population which feels some sense of allegiance to the only Shia Islamic state in the world. On the other hand, hundreds of thousands of Iraqi Shias fought in the war against Iran in the 1980s. Yitzhak Nakash, author of the ground-breaking *The Shi'is of Iraq*, points out that while in Iran Shia Islam is recognized as the force which for centuries held Iranian society together, in Iraq Shia Islam is a recently acquired identity for the majority population: 'at the core of Shi'ism in Iraq [is] a society whose strong Arab tribal value system was encapsulated by Shi'i religion, not permeated by it'. Professor Nakash argues persuasively that the tribal Arab societies of southern Iraq adopted Shia Islam in the nineteenth century as a solution to the displacement, disorder and fragmentation caused by the move from a nomadic to a settled agricultural life, a transition forced on an unwilling population by Ottoman colonialism.

Shia Islam was a dissident, anti-colonial, anti-Government, anti-elite, anti-oppression identity congenial to bewildered peoples at the receiving end of a forced 'modernization' which dismantled their existing relationships:

> It is the fragmentation of tribal systems, which generated an identity crisis among the settled tribesmen, as well as their need to relocate themselves on the social map of their surrounding environment, that can fully explain the motivation of the tribesmen . . . The conversion was a compensation for the tribesmen's loss of their former way of life and an indication for their pursuit of stability . . . Nonetheless, the conversion to Shi'ism did not pervade the former social and moral values of the tribesmen.[8]

While not quite 'skin-deep', it seems that 'conversion' did not mean 'transformation'. Shia Islam was of value to the tribes who converted in the mid- to late-nineteenth century as an identity of resistance. This has sadly been appropriate for more recent chapters in their historical experience.

However, despite their suffering at the hands of the modern Iraqi state, Iraqi Shias have continued to have a strong identification with the Iraqi nation-state. The settlement of the nomads 'marked the beginning of a process of Shi'i state formation in southern Iraq, which was aborted following the British occupation in 1917 and the subsequent formation of the Iraqi monarchy in 1921.' The establishment of modern Iraq pulled many Arab Shi'is toward Baghdad, so that 'the Iraqi state emerged as the major focus of identity for Shi'is.' The policies of successive Sunni Iraqi governments, supported by Iran's Pahlavi rulers, reduced the ties between Shias in Iraq and Iran, and accelerated the decline of Shia financial and intellectual institutions in Iraq.[9]

There is no natural convergence between Iraq's Shia population and Iran, then, and nationalism has long been an important element in the Shia identity—which goes some way to undermining the fears of those who warned before the war that the south of Iraq might secede. The firing of a rifle or a pistol in the air, an act often used by the Western media to emphasise Saddam Hussein's militaristic and aggressive character, is actually 'an act which symbolised a kind of traditional Iraqi tribal celebration (the *hosa*)', according to Yitzhak Nakash.[10] It was one of the devices used by the Ba'athist leadership to emphasise and strengthen the tribal and national identities of the Shia population, and to undermine the political significance of their religious affiliation.

Incidentally, some of the early emissaries who advanced the cause of Shia Islam among the Arab tribes were driven out of the Saudi peninsula by the Wahhabi fanatics who now dominate Saudi Arabia. The Wahhabis invaded Iraq several times in the eighteenth and early nineteenth century, besieging Najaf twice, and sacking Karbala in 1801. 'The Wahhabi attacks of Najaf and Karbala reinforced the sectarian identity of the Shi'i ulama [clergy] and increased their motivation to convert the tribes.'[11] The present hostility of Saudi rulers to Shia Islam in Iraq has deep historical roots.

THE TURKISH FACTOR

Similar concerns in the north motivate US policy. Turkey has been pursuing a brutal war of suppression against the Kurds of south-east Turkey for decades, disguised as a counter-insurgency war against the Kurdish Workers' Party (PKK). In 1995, Human Rights Watch observed that the war's toll over the previous 11 years had been estimated at over 19,000 deaths, 'including some 2,000 death-squad killings of suspected PKK sympathizers, two million internally displaced, and more than 2,200 villages destroyed, most of which were burned down by Turkish security forces.'[12]

As a result of public outrage in the West in the aftermath of the 1991 war against Iraq, the US and Britain were forced to intervene in Iraqi Kurdistan, and as a result the Kurds of northern Iraq were able to carve out their own autonomous zone, outside of Baghdad's control. This was deeply troubling for the Turkish authorities, in part because of the unwelcome encouragement this gave the Kurds of Turkey, in part because the autonomous zone provided a safe haven not only for the Iraqi Kurdish organizations, but also for the Turkish Kurdish PKK. The Turkish authorities sought and gained permission from London and Washington to intervene in northern Iraq in 'hot pursuit' of PKK groups, and to attack the organization.

The first major attack came in August 1991. From 1991 onwards, the Turkish army continued to shell and bomb border areas, periodically resorting to large-scale ground offensives backed by air strikes. The no-fly zone barred Iraqi, but not Turkish, aircraft from attacking Kurds in northern Iraq. The first major ground invasion came in October 1992, involving 20,000 Turkish troops. In March 1995, 35,000 troops invaded. In May 1997, 50,000 soldiers invaded.[13] These are only some of the larger invasions Turkey has mounted—without a peep of protest from the West.

In the run-up to the 2003 war on Iraq, Turkey once again feared the de-stabilizing consequences of political change in Iraq. If the Iraqi Kurds were able to secure a federal constitution, with considerable autonomy, and a border secure against the Turkish military, this would have a most undesirable inspirational effect on Turkey's Kurdish population. The Turkish military secured permission from Washington to invade northern Iraq simultaneously with the US invasion from Turkish territory. Before the war took place, Turkey deployed an estimated 5000 troops inside northern Iraq, and the Government indicated that up to 80,000 Turkish troops could invade the Kurdish enclave, alongside some 40,000 US forces.[14] Regional analysts expected Turkey to move in 'to ensure that any attempt at independence by the Iraqi Kurds is quashed.'[15]

The threat was the source of enormous fear and anger in Iraqi Kurdistan, already facing the threat of attack by Ba'athist forces, possibly with whatever chemical or biological weapons the Iraqi Government possessed. Students demonstrated against the threat of a Turkish invasion.[16] Hoshyar Zebari, the head of foreign relations of the Kurdish

Democratic Party, warned of clashes: 'It would be a nightmare for us because the Turks could easily cut our communications with the outside world. Our people are terrified by the prospect.'[17]

Ankara had drawn up a plan for Turkish troops to deploy along a nearly 200 mile-long, 20 to 25 mile-deep 'buffer zone' on the Iraqi side of the border, from the Kurdish town of Zakho eastwards. It was reported in late February that the deal was part of a quid pro quo with Turkey for allowing US troops to use Turkish bases.

Congressman Jim Moran, a senior Democrat who had recently met the Kurdish ambassador to Washington, said on 27 February, 'If we sell out the Kurds for the third or fourth time, that's wrong.'[18]

Astonishingly, the Turkish invasion did not take place, because the Turkish anti-war movement forced the Turkish Parliament to turn down a multi-billion-dollar bribe and refuse Washington access to Turkish bases for the US invasion of northern Iraq. As in the case of France and the UN, US arrogance and contempt for lesser powers created an unexpected backlash in the nation concerned, resulting in a severe problem for US war plans. Once the Turkish Parliament had voted the wrong way, the US then withdrew permission for the Turkish invasion against the Kurds. Turkish democracy, in a bizarre and convoluted way, had protected the Iraqi Kurds from destabilization and assault by the Turkish Government.

THE BIG PICTURE

In February 2002, the *Financial Times* commented, 'Washington's calculation is that a break-up of Iraq would fundamentally alter the balance of power in the Middle East, especially if it led to the creation of an independent Kurdistan. Turkey, a steadfast US ally with a large Kurd minority, would be destabilised. Iran could exploit the vacuum.'[19] Sir John Moberly, who had been British ambassador to Iraq between 1982 and 1985, said that after a major war, there would be such instability in the country that 'there would be a great temptation to replace Saddam with another Saddam—another iron-fisted military man.'[20] 'Instability' meant 'independence' from the US, the real danger.

It is just these kinds of concerns that have driven US policy since 1991. Thomas Friedman, Diplomatic Correspondent of the *New York Times*, explained in mid-1991 that the economic sanctions against Iraq would continue until there was a military coup within Iraq, which would create 'the best of all worlds': 'an iron-fisted Iraqi junta without Saddam Hussein'. This would be a return to the days when Saddam's 'iron fist . . . held Iraq together, much to the satisfaction of the American allies Turkey and Saudi Arabia.' In March 1991, this prospect was described by Ahmad Chalabi (now leader of the Iraqi opposition group the Iraqi National Congress) as 'the worst of all possible worlds' for the Iraqi people.[21]

The basic philosophy was stated starkly and clearly at the time by Richard Haass, then Special Assistant to President George Bush Sr, and Senior Director for Near East and South Asian Affairs on the staff of the National Security Council. Mr Haass told Peter

Galbraith, senior advisor to the Senate Foreign Relations Committee who was doing his best to assist the Iraqi opposition in March 1991, 'You don't understand. Our policy is to get rid of Saddam, not his regime.'[22] Later that year, Mr Haass was awarded the presidential Citizens Medal for his contributions to the development and articulation of US policy during Operations Desert Shield and Desert Storm.[23] (During the 2003 war on Iraq, Mr Haass was head of Policy Planning, with Ambassador status, in the State Department.)

The regime was useful in securing the rule of the Turkish and Saudi Governments. Why were these Governments so important to the United States? Because the Saudi regime is an essential component of US control of Middle Eastern oil. Because Turkish military power is an essential component of US 'support' for the brittle princely states in the Persian/Arabian Gulf.

Iraq's Sunni-dominated anti-Kurd military dictatorship was useful to US and British vital interests in the region, hence the diplomatic, financial and military support extended to Saddam Hussein's regime by Washington and London during the invasion of Iran, and the worst years of the near-genocidal campaign against the Kurds in the 1980s. The mass murdering Ba'athist fascists were then useful to British and US commercial interests and could kill with impunity as they committed the crimes which fifteen years later were transformed into justifications for a war for 'leadership change', to create 'Saddamism without Saddam', the 'best of all worlds' for Washington and London.

CHAPTER XIX
Crushing The Resistance

After WWII:
Betraying The Anti-Fascists

THE PARALLELS WITH GREECE

In May 2003, the respected journalist Robert Fisk observed that, 'Iraq today resembles not some would-be democracy but rather the tragedy that greeted the British when the German occupation of Greece ended in 1944.' George Papandreou played the part that Pentagon hawks would have liked Ahmad Chalabi to play in Iraq, a local figurehead for external power. Mr Fisk surprisingly follows conventional mythology that the problem in Greece was that 'the Elas Communist guerrillas wanted power': 'They had fought the Nazis since Germany's 1941 invasion, and, like many of the Muslim Shia of today feared that they were going to be excluded from power by a new pro-Allied regime.' This is why the 'liberation' of Athens 'quickly turned into a pitched battle between British troops (for which read the Americans in Iraq) and the Communists.' The veteran Middle East correspondent recalls that Winston Churchill told the British commander in Greece, 'do not hesitate to act as if you were in a conquered city'. 'In the event, Churchill was able to restore order only because he had secretly obtained Stalin's agreement that Greece should remain in the Western sphere of Europe.' The difference in Iraq is that the nation which could help Washington, as the Soviets helped London, is Iran. 'And Iran, far from being an uneasy ally, is part of President Bush's "axis of evil", which fears that it may be next on America's hit list.'[1] The parallels with Greece are indeed striking, but they extend far beyond Greece to the entire zone of liberation after the Second World War.

NORTH AFRICA

In November 1942, General Eisenhower avoided war during the invasion of North Africa by reaching an agreement with Admiral Jean Darlan, commander-in-chief of Vichy

France's domain in North Africa (Vichy France being that part of France not occupied by the Nazis but collaborating intimately with Berlin). Darlan was the bitterly anti-British author of Vichy's anti-Semitic laws, and had been a willing collaborator with the Germans. In return for his co-operation in ordering Vichy French forces to lay down their arms, Admiral Darlan was installed as Governor-General of the territory by the Allies. A respected US historian has commented,

> The result was that in its first major foreign-policy venture in World War II, the United States gave its support to a man who stood against everything Roosevelt and Churchill had spoken out against. As much as Göring or Goebbels, Darlan was the antithesis of the principles the Allies were defending.[2]

Darlan was conveniently assassinated in murky circumstances in December 1942, but the regime he had created outlived him. His US-nominated successor, General Henri Giraud kept anti-semitic laws on the statute book and appointed a former Vichy Minister of the Interior—a man who had been in charge of political arrests and anti-semitic laws—as Governor-General of Algeria. President Eisenhower (privately) justified General Giraud's appointment on the basis that there was 'a great paucity of qualified men to fill the highly specialized posts . . . Abrupt, sweeping or radical changes, bringing into office little known or unqualified administrators, could create serious difficulties for us.'[3] That there might have been 'serious difficulties' for the victims of the collaborators and anti-semites as a result of appointing General Giraud was of no moment. The parallels with Iraq in the first month after 'liberation' are striking.

ITALY

On 16 July 1942, President Roosevelt and Prime Minister Chuchill issued a manifesto to the Italian people which declared, among other things, that the Allied leaders were 'determined to destroy the false leaders and their doctrines which have brought Italy to her present position'.[4] In fact, they accepted the continued rule of King Victor Emmanuel and Prime Minister Marshal Pietro Badoglio (the conqueror of Ethiopia), the latter chosen by the Fascist Grand Council to replace Mussolini.[5] The main organisation of the Italian Resistance, the Committee of National Liberation (CLN), refused to enter the Badoglio Cabinet, demanding that the compromised King step down.[6] The USSR then intervened decisively, recognising the Badoglio government, and despatching Palmiro Togliatti, the leader of the Italian Communist Party, to engineer what is known as the *svolta di Salerno* (the 'reversal at Salerno'), ending Communist opposition to Badoglio and offering to participate in his Cabinet without requiring the abdication of the king. The rest of the Resistance was forced to fall into line.[7]

In July 1944, the Allies encountered thousands of partisan fighters for the first time when they took Florence. They insisted on the immediate disarmament of the guerrillas and refused to transfer intact Resistance units into the Italian army, as the partisans had requested. The Allies also replaced the local Resistance nominees for key administrative positions with more pliable types from the South.[8] The Allied administrators were 'emasculating the political [and military] force of the resistance as it came into contact with it.'[9] Large sections of the northern Resistance, particularly supporters of the Socialist and Action Parties, had argued for the seizure of administrative power after liberation, and the conversion of the organs of the Resistance, the CLN Committees, into bodies of local government. The Action Party, which led about a quarter of the partisans in the North, had similar political principles to the Socialists, stressing industrial democracy, land reform, republicanism, and political decentralization—non-doctrinaire libertarian socialist ideas which were very much the spirit of the times.[10] Under enormous pressure from Nazi persecution, the northern Resistance agreed in December 1944 to surrender their ideals in return for financial subsidies, food, clothing and arms from the Allies.[11]

When the final offensive was launched on 9 April 1945, Resistance groups launched insurrections in Genoa, Milan, and other towns and cities in the north, creating local Resistance governments which generally prioritized 'a speedy and violent purge of leading Fascists'.[12] Though their administrations were dispersed by the Allies, the Resistance continued to demand a thorough purge of fascists and collaborators; a constituent assembly with full powers to reconstruct Italian social and political life; a new army based on Resistance formations; and industrial democracy based on factory councils.[13] This vision of radical democracy was firmly blocked by the occupation forces. The new Minister of Justice in an Allied-imposed Government formulated an amnesty law in June 1946 which granted immunity to all Fascists not actually convicted of crimes, effectively ending the period of 'national renewal'.[14]

The anti-fascist Resistance was politically and militarily dispersed by the Western Allies, and the existing power structure was largely maintained—all with the support of the USSR. After the war, the Italian Communists co-operated in the US-backed neutralization of the radical democratic programme of the Resistance.

FRANCE

The main organisation of the French Resistance, the *Conseil National de Résistance* (CNR) or 'National Council of the Resistance' was a broad church, including groups and political parties ranging from the Christian Democrats on the Right to the Socialists and the Communist Party on the Left. The CNR nevertheless managed to agree a Charter in March 1944 centred around three themes: retribution against collaborators and the Nazi occupation forces; confiscation of the property of 'traitors and black marketeers'; and the transformation of the French economy through nationalization and socialization.

As in Italy, the Resistance launched large-scale insurrections as the Allies invaded and, in the South, often liberated towns before the Allies reached the area. In some areas, Resistance administrations held complete power: 'in the Auvergne in early August, some regions had been virtually operating under Resistance control for weeks before the Liberation'.[15] The main concern of these Resistance administrations, as in Italy, was rooting out collaborators in what was termed *l'épuration* ('the purge'). A high-level Allied summary of 'civil affairs' up to 31 August 1944 concluded that the Resistance was 'much better disciplined in most areas than anticipated and rendering considerable assistance.'[16] The report noted that, 'When difficulties were caused by the Resistance, they seemed largely to be provoked by attempts to track down alleged traitors and pursue personal vengeance.'[17]

General de Gaulle fulfilled the hopes of the British Foreign Office by moving decisively against the indigenous Resistance. Over the next few months, he excluded the national Resistance organisation, the CNR, from the new government (whose members he appointed personally); he disbanded the CNR's military wing and dissolved the 'patriotic militias'; he outlawed the carrying of weapons except by the police and regular army; dismissed calls for the incorporation of Resistance units into the new army; and re-imposed the authority of pre-war regular officers.[18]

On the central issue of collaboration, of the 2,853 collaborators sentenced to death, only 767 were actually executed; of the 38,226 people sent to prison for collaboration, all but 1,570 were released within seven years; and only 1.3 per cent of Vichy government employees were sacked or given lesser punishments for collaboration.[19] Two historians of the period comment: 'What had started off as a renewal had evidently become an adjustment of the more unacceptable and visible aspects of a largely restored system.'[20]

Note that US and British intelligence showed that neither the French Communist Party nor the armed Resistance grouping dominated by the Communists made any attempt to seize power, even at a local level, at the time of the landings in the north.[21] The US Ambassador to the USSR reported in July 1944 that 'Molotov has told me several times since I have been back that it was the Soviet policy to leave the initiative in French policy to the British and ourselves.'[22] General de Gaulle was so confident of Soviet conservatism that he personally granted an amnesty to the leader of the French Communists, allowing him to return to France. On his return, M Thorez lost no time in firmly underlining the legitimacy of the de Gaulle government, and the illegitimacy of the Resistance militias and the other institutions of the indigenous Resistance.[23]

It is now clear from a number of sources, including the prefects imposed by General de Gaulle in different parts of the country on Liberation, that neither the Communists nor the Resistance as a whole had any intention of staging a coup at the moment of Liberation—the Communist strategy was rather 'to place themselves in as advantageous a position as possible from which to fight and win an election, coming to power through the ballot box as a Jacobin party.'[24]

Together, the Allies and General de Gaulle neutralized and dispersed the Resistance, after benefiting in their different ways from its activities. One of the main functions of the Resistance, as in Italy, was to smooth the assumption of power by the new/old regime. A Gaullist prefect who visited different areas during the Liberation remarked that the interventions of the local Resistance governments 'made possible the transition, at minimum cost, from the collapse of Vichy to the new authority. It had saved France from the terror of the void.' 'For those who knew how to use them, [the Resistance organizations] could be brakes on excessive energy as well as powerful means of action.'[25]

Incidentally, those who defend the 'moderate' policy of the French Communists argue that it was faced with only two options: to try to foment a revolution, impossible in conditions of military occupation; or to accept General de Gaulle's rule 'and work within that framework.'[26] There was, however, always a third alternative, which was to maintain the solidarity of the Resistance, and to press for the implementation of the CNR Charter. If the Resistance had remained united, this policy might possibly have forced deep changes in French society—not a revolution but significant reform. The PCF chose instead the path of patriotism, reaction and collaborationism, until ejected from influence. The Soviet Union had once again used its local affiliate to undermine the Left, and to assist the betrayal of the Resistance.

GREECE

In the cases of North Africa and Italy it could be argued that collaboration with the fascistic regimes of Admiral Darlan and Marshal Badoglio was a military necessity in the course of 'total war'. When we turn to the case of Greece, however, 'military necessity' does not begin to explain British behaviour.

Greece was one of the few countries in Europe not liberated by Allied armies. German troops began their evacuation from Greece in October 1944 *before* British soldiers entered the country (though there were a few harrying operations by the British as the Nazis withdrew). There was, then, no need for extensive British military operations in Greece, and troops committed to the liberation could have been kept with the invasion force still ploughing through Italy. Despite this, 10,000 British troops were sent to Greece as the Nazis withdrew, increasing to 75,000 by mid-January 1945. The underlying motivation for the British invasion was explained by a British Special Operations Executive (SOE) officer in mid-1943:

> As I understand it, the aims of the British Government in Greece are two-fold: First, to obtain the greatest military effort in the fight against the Axis and, second, to have in post-war Greece a stable government friendly to Great Britain, if possible a Constitutional Monarchy. Unfortunately, the present state of affairs in Greece makes the prosecution of the two aims almost incompatible . . .

The most significant military force in Greece was the Resistance coalition known as EAM ('National Liberation Front'), a six-party coalition of the Left committed to republicanism and nationalism, in which the Greek Communist Party was the dominant force. As in Italy, Britain demanded that the Resistance enter a royalist government (albeit one in exile). EAM suddenly capitulated and entered a cabinet headed by the British-appointed figurehead George Papandreou, taking only minor and insignificant posts.[27] This equivalent to the Italian *svolta di Salerno* followed the visit of a Soviet military mission in July 1944, which urged the Greek Communists to join Papandreou's cabinet.[28]

After the German withdrawal, Mr Papandreou demanded that EAM's guerrilla army ELAS be demobilized before the demobilization of the elite royalist Third Brigade.

EAM (which, incidentally, had been in effective control of the national territory after the Nazi withdrawal) argued that all regular and paramilitary groups should demobilize simultaneously, and that a new national army should then be created from both royalist and republican forces. Far from ELAS and EAM demanding power, as mainstream Cold War mythology has it, the anti-fascist Resistance was actually prepared to contemplate co-habitation and national reconciliation with the forces of the Right, even though the Resistance was in effective control of the entire country.

EAM ministers resigned from the Government over the issue on 2 December 1944. At an EAM demonstration in Athens the following day, the police fired on the demon-strators, killing several and wounding over sixty.[29] Between 13 and 17 December 1944—while the war against Nazi Germany was still raging—Britain sent two divisions, a tank regiment, two brigades, and other supporting units to Greece in order to crush an anti-fascist Resistance that had merely objected to its immediate demobilization. As already noted, the British Prime Minister instructed the local British commander, 'Do not however hesitate to act as if you were in a conquered city where a local rebellion is in progress.'[30] When the revolt actually began, the Greek Communists received no support whatsoever from the Soviet Union. Churchill commented on the fact that Stalin was keeping his end of their bargain.[31] The Varkiza Agreement of February 1945 ended the conflict officially, but the Right continued its war against the Resistance. By June 1945, the US Ambassador was writing to the Greek regent, Archbishop Damaskinos,

> After the civil war I had always expected a reaction against KKE which would lead to some excesses . . . [but] the National Guard were engaging in some places in what could only be described as terrorism.[32]

The former Resistance was once more forced underground. The Communists were the last segment of the Resistance to join the new underground 'Democratic Army of Greece'. When the Communists were finally forced into the hills to help form a 'Provisional Democratic Government' of Greece in December 1947, they were pointedly ignored by the Soviet Union's international body, the Cominform.[33]

The pattern by now hardly needs restatement. One comment may be in order: 'mili-tary necessity' cannot simultaneously explain the reluctance of the British and Americans to replace the fascist authorities in Italy on the one hand, and the enthusiasm of the British (supported by the US) in rooting out the *de facto* anti-fascist government in Greece on the other, while the war on the European continent was still going on.

USING JAPANESE TROOPS

In Vietnam, the Resistance movement was formed by the Indochinese Communist Party in the shape of a 'League for the Independence of Vietnam', known as the 'Viet Minh'. After the Japanese surrender in August 1945, the Viet Minh and its allies seized control of their country. British Major-General Gracey, Allied commander in southern Vietnam, ordered Japanese troops to disarm the Viet Minh police, to maintain 'law and order' with Japanese forces, and to set a curfew in the main cities of Saigon and Cholon.[34] In late September 1945, General Gracey used Japanese troops to enforce the curfew—apparently they used mortars as part of their efforts against the Vietnamese.[35] Japanese troops were then used extensively in a continuation of their counter-insurgency war against the indigenous Resistance. The British historian of this period in Vietnam's history skates over this disturbing period, contenting himself with the oblique comment that 'Gracey could not wash his hands of the kidnappings and murders of civilians.'[36] The Supreme Allied Commander for South East Asia Command, Lord Louis Mountbatten told General Gracey at the end of September, in Mr Dunn's paraphrase, 'that His Majesty's Government was determined not to repeat the Greek experience, and the British forces must not incur casualties by becoming involved in local affairs.'[37]

A few days later, Lord Mountbatten asked the Chiefs of Staff to delay the repatriation of Japanese troops because of their importance in offensive operations against the Vietnamese Resistance, and because of a delay in the deployment of French colonial forces. He remarked, 'we shall find it hard to counter the accusations that our forces are remaining in the country solely in order to hold the Viet Minh Independence Movement in check.'[38] The British were supposedly engaged in the disarmament and repatriation of Japanese fascist forces. But the disarmament and the repatriation of enemy troops was delayed in order to help restore French colonialism and defeat Vietnamese nationalism.

Fascist troops with a long history of atrocities against civilians were also used by the Allies in post-war Indonesia. After the Japanese surrender, South East Asia Command ordered the Japanese forces to maintain the status quo in Indonesia before the arrival of Allied troops.[39] Japanese troops were then used by the Allied occupation forces on a scale which astounded even Lord Mountbatten in April 1946. He wrote in his personal diary,

> I, of course, knew that we had been forced to keep Japanese troops under arms to protect our lines of communications and vital areas in Sumatra, for which the British Indian troops did not suffice; but it was nevertheless a great shock to me to find over a thousand Japanese troops guarding the nine miles of road from the airfield to the town [of Palembang], and to find them drawn up in parties of 20, presenting arms, the officers saluting with swords which long since should have been our war souvenirs.[40]

Edward Behr, the noted foreign correspondent, served in Indonesia with the British forces at this time. He recalled later that 'on at least one occasion, deplored and hushed up at Mountbatten's express command, Japanese artillery went into action alongside Indian Army troops against the Indonesian rebels.'[41] He also noted that the British were capable of 'reprisals—burned villages, deportations, arrests, and even summary executions—which would have branded us as war criminals had any publicity been forthcoming.'[42]

CONCLUSIONS

The overall pattern of relationships is clear. In the aftermath of the Second World War, the United States and the United Kingdom, despite their rhetorical commitments to anti-fascism, did their best to disarm and neutralise the Resistance, both militarily and politically, and to restore the rule of the pre-war Establishment, including reactionary monarchs and fascist collaborators, in Western and Southern Europe, and in South East Asia. Their reasoning was, as in Italy, that there was 'nothing between the King, with the Patriots (that is, Badoglio and company) who have rallied around him, who have complete control, and rampant Bolshevism' (Winston Churchill). The Western Allies had 'to treat with any person or persons in Italy who [could] best give us, first, disarmament, and, second, assurance against chaos' (Franklin D. Roosevelt).[43]

Among these supposed 'rampant Bolsheviks' were the anti-Bolshevik libertarian socialist Action Party and the conservative Count Carlo Sforza, in other words almost the entire Resistance, internal and external. The supposed purveyors of 'chaos' in Italy actually had, as elsewhere, well-developed plans for the reconstruction of their country, and the military and administrative ability to implement them in the aftermath of Liberation, as they demonstrated in practice in northern Italy. The Resistance in reality provided an invaluable stabilizing force in a period of chaos, as was recognized in France. The problem for the West was that the social and political priorities adopted in, for example, the French Resistance's CNR Charter, were quite unacceptable; therefore they were described as, and perhaps even perceived as, 'chaos'.

The position of the real Bolsheviks was one of complete support for the right-wing rehabilitation of the old social order. The role of local Communist Parties and of the Soviet Union was in general a conservative one. In Italy, France and Greece, Soviet 'advice' led to outright political somersaults, and the breaking of the unity of the Resistance by the local Communist Parties. Where Communist Parties were temporarily permitted access to power in France and Italy, they were impeccably 'moderate', particularly over the abandonment of the anti-collaborationist purges—until their ejection from power. Where the post-war repression of the Resistance lead to the resumption of an armed struggle— in Greece—the Communist Party was the last section of the Left to enter the field of war.

The process of containing and obliterating the Resistance often led to political and military crises, often centring on the issue of lopsided demobilization, where the Resistance was expected to put itself utterly in the hands of reactionaries and unreformed collaborationist security forces who were utterly opposed to the political programme that the Resistance had fought for. As early as December 1940, Labour Cabinet Minister Hugh Dalton noted in his diary, 'There is no place, today, for stupid doctrinaire prejudices against "Fascism" as such. If some Fascist toughs will murder Mussolini and a few more and then join with others, representing the Royal Family, the Army, Industry, the Italian workers and peasants, we must not reject them for the sake of some thin theory.'[44] The 'thin theory' that the Second World War was an anti-fascist war, for example.

The continuity between Hugh Dalton's Old Labour colonialism and Tony Blair's New Labour neo-imperialism is deeply rooted. Just as Japanese troops were used in order to secure a political and economic order that was 'acceptable to British interests', so today Washington and London are prepared to use Iraqi fascists to construct a political and economic order that serves British and US 'vital interests'.

CHAPTER XX
Regime Revolutions

De-Ba'athification?

PEOPLE POWER AND REVENGE ATTACKS

In post-war Iraq, as in post-war Europe, there was a burning urge to punish collaborators and oppressors. However, as with the restoration of the fascists to power, the story of popular resistance to the re-nazification of Iraq received only glancing attention in the Western mass media. Peering through the distorting prism of the British press it is still possible to detect signs of the rage that rose up from the depths of Iraqi society in the aftermath of war. Sometimes, as in the case of Baghdad's doctors, the protest was peaceful (and successful). Apparently this was preceded by an earlier, and equally successful, protest by doctors in Basra over British attempts to restore local medical administrators from the former regime to their previous jobs.[1] Former Iraqi brigadier Sheikh Muzahim Mustafa Kana al-Tamimi, appointed head of the interim Basra administration, was 'quietly dropped from the line-up' because of popular protests over his previous links to the regime.[2] In Umm Qasr, popular protests caused the interim council to resign in early May 2003 but most members were later re–appointed by the British authorities.[3] At the Industry Ministry, the former deputy minister Ahmed Rashid Gailini was appointed Minister, but fierce protests from Iraqi colleagues over his Ba'ath connections led to an election. A landslide against Mr Gailini elected Mohammed Abdul Mujib, apparently a 'less offensive' Ba'athist.[4]

In mid-May, the *Guardian* reported, 'Frustrated Iraqis are beginning to force US officers to remove senior Ba'ath party figures who have tried to return to power.' The US army was forced to sack the Baghdad police chief it was working with, because he was accused of being a senior Ba'athist and running his own mafia in the force. This was Major-General Hamid Uthman, who headed the police under Saddam Hussein. Recall that the first police chief was Major-General Zuhair al-Nuaimi, who, it now turned out, had been the deputy chief of police in the old regime.[5] One of these two police chiefs was called a 'thief' to his face by a subordinate, in front of a reporter from *The Times*.[6]

The Iraqi National Congress (INC) tried to capitalise on popular unrest by insisting on 'de-Ba'athification', and the exclusion of 30,000 senior party members.[7] Zaab Sethna, a senior aide to Dr Ahmad Chalabi, the chair of the INC, described the appointment of Dr al-Janabi as the interim Health Minister as a 'bad mistake.' Mr Sethna said that the occupation forces were leaning too far 'in the interests of expediency' towards appointing former Ba'athists to key jobs. There was 'a whole group of people who were forced to stop doing their jobs because they refused to join the Baath Party.' The INC had been visited by a delegation of 25 former judges and senior police officers who had quit their posts in the late 1970s and early 1980s for just that reason. In other words, there was a pool of relatively uncontaminated professionals who could have been drawn on to dilute if not entirely replace the fascist leadership in the judiciary and police .[8]

THE PEOPLE'S PURGE

Dr Chalabi himself apparently warned of violence if top Ba'athist officials were not 'held to account'.[9] This was merely the Westernized tip of an enormous iceberg of public outrage in Iraq over the re–nazification of the state by the Anglo–American invaders.

In late May 2003, Shia Muslim clerics were engaged in a serious debate on the limits of revenge against former Ba'athists, but there was a general acceptance in the majority community that revenge was permissible. In the Baghdad slum known now as Sadr City, residents said between five and 10 Ba'athists had been hunted down and killed in revenge attacks. Sheik Ali al-Gharawi, one of several community leaders in Sadr City, told a reporter, 'People come to me and say they want to kill such and such Baathist. I tell them to threaten them first. If they don't heed the threat, then they must live with the consequences.' Only officials attempting to return to positions they held under Saddam should be killed–and only after a fair warning, according to Sheik al-Gharawi.[10]

The Shia religious leadership was divided on the question of retaliation. In early May 2003, Qadhim al-Nassiri, a Shia cleric, told tens of thousands of worshippers at Friday prayers outside the Muhsin mosque in Sadr City in Baghdad that a senior religious figure from the holy city of Najaf, Qadhim al-Hairi, had issued a recent edict on the fate of the Ba'athists. 'The message is clear. The *hawza* [the Shia clerical establishment] cannot protect them—these Ba'athis, these Saddamites—who are now coming out [and resuming their positions],' declared the cleric. 'This is unacceptable to the *hawza* . . . It is permissible to kill them.' However, this *fatwa* or clerical ruling was issued by only one cleric and did not necessarily point to a policy by the Shia clerical establishment in Najaf. Grand Ayatollah Ali al-Sistani, considered by many Iraqis the top Shia authority in the country, warned against any resort to violence and cautioned followers to verify any *fatwa* issued by other clerics.[11] The Grand Ayatollah refused to condone the revenge attacks. A statement issued by his office in Najaf quoted Ayatollah al-Sistani in May 2003 as saying that retaliation should be left to Islamic courts.[12]

A typed sign posted outside the al-Hikmah mosque in Baghdad said, 'We demand punishment for those who planted fear in the heart of the innocent.' 'Baathists: There is nowhere to escape,' said graffiti on a main thoroughfare in Sadr City. 'The cursed Saddam and his cowardly Baathist scum have fallen,' declared another. Residents suggested that the killings were not the work of a systematic political movement. Instead, they were motivated by rage—triggered by the loss of a friend or family member at the hands of Saddam's thugs.[13] One well-known Ba'athist to fall victim to a revenge attack was Dawood al-Qais, a singer who became famous with songs praising Saddam that were aired repeatedly on state television. He was shot dead at point-blank range outside his Baghdad home in early May 2003.[14] Down south in Basra, arson attacks against the homes of former Ba'athists multiplied in the second month of 'liberation.' One house that was torched belonged to Nuhad Nahi, a former Ba'ath security official whose husband also held a senior post in the Party. The house, which was empty, was set on fire by a family that had lost two sons, Ahmad and Jawad Kazem, executed in 1999 on the basis of reports drafted by Nahi, according to neighbours.[15]

For its part, the long-persecuted Shia party known as al-Dawa in mid-May 2003 offered a £1,000 reward for each senior Ba'ath Party official found, dead or alive.[16]

MR BREMER'S U-TURN

Under pressure from the Iraqi people, with resignation after resignation coming in, Washington made a 180 degree change of direction. The team in charge of 'reconstructing' Iraq, Jay Garner and Barbara Bodine of the Office for Reconstruction and Humanitarian Affairs (ORHA), were sacked in mid-May 2003, and replaced by one Paul Bremer, a State Department counter-terrorism expert with links to the hawks in the Pentagon. Mr Bremer was appointed with a very different brief to the first occupation administration. He arrived in Baghdad on 16 May announcing a purge of up to 30,000 senior Ba'athists. *The Times* reported, 'Baathists banned from jobs in US policy U-turn'.[17] An ORHA official said the US now intended to 'extirpate Ba'athism' and 'put a stake in its heart'.[18]

The 'De–Baathification of Iraqi Society' order said that senior Party members, holding the ranks of Regional Command Member, Branch Member, Section Member and Group Member were 'hereby removed from their positions and banned from future employment in the public sector'. Everyone in the top three layers of management in national government ministries or institutions, such as universities and hospitals would be interviewed 'for possible affiliation with the Baath party' and 'subject to investigation for criminal conduct and risk to security.'[19]

THE VERY SHORT LIST

The seriousness of US intentions will be measured partly by how de-Ba'athification affects the senior levels of the Party, and, crucially, how it affects the police and the security forces which Mr Bremer dissolved and promised to reconstruct shortly. The extent of the Bremer U-turn can be gauged by the fact that in the run-up to the war the number of top Ba'athists deemed to be unacceptable was extremely small. In early January 2003, it was reported that planners in the State Department had drawn up a list of the 'Filthy Forty' Iraqi leaders who would be unacceptable as replacements for Saddam Hussein because of their records of war crimes.[20] By February, the list had shrunk. A list of 14 wanted leaders, none of them from the army, was given to opposition groups to circulate. It included family members of the Iraqi leader, and key political aides as well as the head of general intelligence and the minister of military industrialisation.[21] *Time* magazine set out the names of the 13 men in Saddam Hussein's inner circle, with the subtitle 'A portrait of the regime Bush is changing,' yet another indicator that 'regime change' meant merely 'leadership change'.[22] Within a fortnight of the start of the war, *Newsweek* was being briefed that, apart from the Iraqi leader himself, and his two sons, there were only six other Ba'athists who were considered 'irredeemable,' as one Bush administration official put it. As the magazine pointed out, this was a 'remarkably short' list: 'Only these few, according to administration officials, are certain to be prosecuted for war crimes and crimes against humanity—if they live that long.' As for the others, if they were implicated in past crimes, they would be subject to immediate detention, 'and then we'd figure out what would happen to them,' said a Bush Administration official.[23]

The list was kept so 'remarkably short', explained a Jordanian official who knew many members of the Iraqi hierarchy, in order 'to convince people they don't have to die for Saddam.'[24] Why was this important? Because it was the senior leadership of Iraq outside this circle of named 'irredeemables' who the United States and Britain were hoping would save them the cost and risks of war, invasion and street fighting in Baghdad by carrying out a military coup against the Iraqi leader. The short lists of war criminals were a signal to those not on the lists that they could expect to be forgiven by the US and allowed to rule in place of Saddam Hussein, if they moved against him. As we have seen, the drive to war and even the war strategy itself was centrally concerned with producing a military *coup d'état*.

ZIG-ZAG

For anyone committed to genuine de-Ba'athification, there were some serious complications. At the end of March 2003, Iraqi exile Kanan Makiya suggested that the 'most insidious presence' of the Party was in the schools, the universities, the trade unions, the women's organizations, the youth groups, the mosques, the police and the army. Professor Makiya noted, 'To further complicate things, seniority in the Baath Party does not always translate into a position of power in government, and conversely, not all officials who are guilty of crimes are high up in the Baath Party hierarchy. How are we Iraqis even going to begin to sort through all that?'[25]

The question was whether the United States was committed to a genuine de-Ba'athification, or whether Mr Bremer's order was merely a tactical retreat in the face of popular anger. In Japan, the rolling back of the purges and other anti-fascist measures in 1947–8 is known as the 'reverse course'. In Iraq, the question is whether the 'reverse course' of May 2003 will itself be reversed in a 'zigzag course'.

CHAPTER XXI
Shia Power

A Looming Confrontation
With The People Of Iraq

SHIA SURPRISE 1: NO UPRISING

On 25 March, a few days into the war, Major General Peter Wall, British Chief of Staff at Allied Central Command in Qatar, claimed that a 'popular civilian uprising' was taking place in the southern Iraqi city of Basra.[1] The following day, the British Prime Minister himself said that there had been 'some limited form of uprising' in Basra.[2] There was disquiet at the lack of any popular uprisings welcoming the invaders. On 18 March, the *New York Times* had reported that 'Military and allied officials familiar with the planning of the upcoming campaign say they hope that a successful and "benign" occupation of Basra that results in flag-waving crowds hugging British and American soldiers will create an immediate and positive image worldwide while also undermining Iraqi resistance elsewhere.' As the BBC pointed out on 26 March, however, 'The fact is that Basra is not undergoing a benign occupation. It has just been declared a military target by British forces which have come under attack from inside.'[3] An Arab television operating inside Basra on 25 March reported no sign of an uprising, saying that the city was quiet.[4] When the British forces finally entered Basra on 7 April, there were indeed cheering crowds (mostly children, with many impassive adults, according to one report[5]), but there had been no uprising.

A high-ranking American official blamed the passivity of the Shia population on the nazified culture of Iraq,[6] despite the fact that in March 1991, rebellions took most of the country. Ahmad Chalabi, head of the opposition group the Iraqi National Congress, charged the coalition with failing to encourage an insurrection—for three reasons: 'Bad intelligence; fear of the political forces of the Iraqi people; and the coalition's desire to shape the future of Iraq entirely on their own, without opposition participation.'[7]

Boris Johnson, editor of the right-wing *Spectator*, commented on 26 March, one week into the war, 'The Iraqis are fighting back more vigorously than some of us expected. To see why, look at yesterday's YouGov poll, showing growing support for the war. The British people have rallied instinctively to their Forces, and a symmetrical phenomenon is taking place, of course, in Iraq.' The Conservative MP wrote, 'No matter how much I might dislike the Blair regime, I would have mixed feelings about a "liberating" force that destroyed the MoD, the Foreign Office, the BBC and Number 10. I might even draw the line if I saw a cruise missile disappear into Alastair Campbell's office. And if I saw an Abrams tank rumbling down Whitehall, I might just go to the cupboard, pull out the ancestral *jezzail*, and have a pop.'[8]

One factor producing caution among the southern Shia population was undoubtedly the folk memory of the 1991 uprisings. Yitzhak Nakash observed long before the war that, 'Like the 1920 revolt in Iraq, the insurrection of March 1991 will become an important event in shaping the national identity of Iraqi Shi'is and their collective memory as the stories and episodes connected with the insurrection are transmitted to younger generations.'[9] BBC reporter John Simpson recalled in July 2002, 'I shall not quickly forget the tears of the Iraqi Shia general who told me in July 1991 how he went to his own base, now occupied by the Americans, to beg them for the Iraqi weapons stored there. They refused; and he and his men had to face Saddam's avenging forces unarmed. The general was one of the very few survivors.'[10]

In 1991, the US spared key elements of the Republican Guard at the war's end; permitted Iraq to use its helicopter forces to put down rebels; withheld arms from Iraqi opposition forces; rebuffed an unwelcome coup attempt linked to opposition forces; and held the rebels at arm's length, refusing to meet with opposition leaders.[11] President George Bush Sr had called on the Iraqi people to take matters into their own hands and to overthrow their leader. When they took him at his word, the US President did everything in his power to support the repression of the uprising, short of ordering US tanks and aircraft to fire into the crowds.

The US National Security Adviser at the time, Brent Scowcroft, later confessed in a television interview, 'I frankly wish [the uprising] hadn't happened. I envisaged a post-war government being a military government.'[12] The US was expecting, and preferred, a military coup which would retain and stabilize the political system in Iraq: not a popular revolution which would unleash nationalist, religious and democratic forces which would destabilize the fascist regime, and which would have been extremely hard to control.

Gerard Baker, columnist with the *Financial Times*, wrote of the Anglo–American victories in southern Iraq in March 2003:

> Instead of Paris 1944, it has looked more like Tokyo 1945; a frightened, cowed, humiliated people sullenly watching a despised victor. With hindsight it is easier now to see why Iraqis—even those who have suffered so much under Saddam—might feel this way. The 1991 experience is obviously relevant. How many of the Shias in Basra and elsewhere

watched as relatives and friends were taken off to be executed once their last US-incited uprising had been quelled. And how many blame it on American perfidy?[13]

The *FT*'s man in Baghdad reported, 'Every civilian death costs the invading forces dearly. Whatever the range of opinions among Iraqis about the government of Saddam Hussein, hostility to American and British interference in their country runs deep.' A baker who gave foreign journalists bags of biscuits warned them emphatically, 'The Americans have to know that they will never have foothold anywhere in Iraq. It is absolutely impossible for us to live alongside colonialists in this day and age.'[14] An Iraqi exile based in London warned that there were deeper memories also: 'Some people have strong nationalist feelings and strong Islamist feelings. They're reminded by their parents of the time of the British occupation and the resistance at that time.'[15]

Down south, before the British forces took Basra, a BBC journalist talked to local Iraqis: 'Those I have spoken to all say the same. They are nervous. They do not like Saddam Hussein, but they do not like the British army either. "We are not Palestine, we are not Palestine!" one Iraqi man shouted. "You can't just occupy us." '[16]

The beginnings of an uprising in Basra came *after* the British took the city. First there were the protests against the Ba'athist revival. Then, when the Ba'athist interim administration was dissolved, a crowd of 5,000 demonstrators took to the streets again, to protest against a British commander being installed as the de facto leader of the city. One of the organisers of the demonstration, Sheikh Ahmed Malki, said, 'We demand an Iraqi governor elected by the people while they are imposing a British governor on us.'[17] The demand for democracy was heard throughout the country, and resolutely resisted by the occupation forces.

SHIA SURPRISE 2: THE SHIA TAKE-OVER

The plan had been to 'decapitate' the regime with a military coup and to hand over power to the same military and political system. Unfortunately, from Washington's point of view, the military and political system disintegrated and key figures fled, leaving a gaping vacuum. This vacuum was filled in many parts of the country by Shia clerics and their local organizations. Shia power was dramatized on 22 April, when over a million Shia Muslims engaged in a long-forbidden pilgrimage in Karbala to commemorate the martyrdom of Imam Hussein, grandson of the Prophet Muhammad.

BBC reporter Fergal Keane observed from the scene that this was 'raw emotion unleashed on a scale that the Middle East has not seen since the heyday of Nasser'. He marvelled at 'the absence of any police or military and still the extraordinary discipline.' Mr Keane suggested that 'For organisational skills they are not unlike Sinn Fein; in terms of marrying faith and politics they are like Hizbollah in Lebanon. Like both Sinn Fein and Hizbollah they have been quick to grasp the importance of social-welfare work in the community. Most important, they are on the ground talking to people every hour of the day. People have not forgotten who was with them during the long darkness of Saddam.'[18]

The *Sunday Times* acknowledged that, 'Despite years of repression under Saddam, Iraq's Shi'ite clerics and their followers, who make up the majority of the country's population, have displayed impressive organisational strength, taking over the running of hospitals and, in the absence of traffic lights, even the direction of traffic.'[19] The *Washington Post* noted that after the Iraqi government's collapse on 9 April, the clergy from the Mohsin Mosque in Baghdad 'raced to fill a chaotic void by delivering sometimes heavy-handed security in the streets, confiscating stolen goods and delivering food and money to Baghdad's poor':

> In lawless streets filled with gunfire, they sent guards armed with AK-47 assault rifles to enforce order. Hundreds of poor came to their mosque for flour or stipends; the mosque claimed to have handed out more than $800 a day. One cleric organized a team to drive two tankers to clear out water mains overflowing with sewage. Another drove an ambulance through the city's deserted streets at night, blaring appeals on its loudspeaker for municipal workers to return to work.[20]

The Baghdad clerics worked closely with a layman, Ali Feisal Hamad, who was instrumental in organizing the committees that dealt with needs ranging from security at hospitals to restoring electricity. Twelve committees, each led by a cleric, took on tasks ranging from running religious schools to setting up what the clerics hoped would become a media conglomerate.

The *Post* reported, 'An undercurrent is the belief that they are competing with the Americans to determine the shape of what follows Hussein's government.'[21] According to another report, Shia clerics became community leaders, 'taking charge of hospitals, schools, welfare, security and even creating an Islamic legal system.'[22]

The world was shocked by the destruction wreaked in Baghdad's hospitals by looters. The world was less aware of the fact that the return of the looters was prevented not by the US forces, but by groups of volunteers organized by Shia clerics. According to Merlin, the British aid organization, between half and three-quarters of the clinics in Baghdad were under clerical control in early May. These popular protection forces were forced out of some hospitals by the US in mid-May. Stephen Browning, the same US 'adviser' to the Health Ministry who appointed Mr al-Janabi as Minister of Health, said on 9 May, 'If the armed thugs who have taken over the hospitals don't stand down we may have to rely on coalition forces to return the hospitals to the ministry of health within the next two weeks.'[23] Washington was angry with the 'thugs' who were protecting the shattered remains of Baghdad's hospitals from looting (while US troops stood aside); but was 'happy' to appoint the fascist thug who had helped to deprive those same hospitals of medicines under the former regime, by forcing doctors to declare that they did not require any more of the medicines they desperately needed.[24]

At the end of June 2003, the World Health Organization estimated that half of the clinics and hospitals in Baghdad were still being guarded by popular militias, mostly Islamist groups.[25]

The Shia clerics even re-organized and re-employed members of the police force in Baghdad, weeks before the US took a similar step. When more than 100,000 people attended Friday prayers at a mosque in Sadr City on 25 April, 'The marshals were joined by police in the green uniforms and black berets of the Ba'athist era but yesterday wearing identification tags issued by the *hawza* Shia clerical establishment based in Najaf . . . Locals said police in Sadr city, formerly Saddam city, were now being paid by the religious leadership.'[26] The police were now under the watchful eye of the popular militia.

THE *HAWZA*

The pattern of Shia control was evident far beyond Baghdad. In Karbala during the pilgrimage, a teacher from Kut named Ali Faraya Hamid told a British reporter, 'The Americans did nothing after the Baath fled, so the religious leaders have started to run things. We are following what the Koran has taught us. We do not need foreigners to tell us what to do.'[27] British journalist Ewen Macaskill reported in early May that there were 'parallel universes operating within Iraq'. There was the US bubble, 'and there is the rest of the country, where the dominant force is Islam.'[28] The *Guardian* reporter warned that any US-imposed provisional government 'could prove short-lived': 'Power now lies elsewhere, with the majority Shia Muslims, who were suppressed by Saddam.'[29] Elections were delayed by the occupation authorities because, 'the process would be open to intervention by extremists,' according to a senior US official in Baghdad.[30] In other words, the wrong people were expected to win, and that was unacceptable.

The Shia administration of much of Iraq was a 'de facto Shia confederacy' centred on the *hawza*, a Shia religious body based in Najaf, which apparently co-ordinated the takeover of the administration of towns and cities by clerics. Predictably the British and US media barely noted the existence of this critical element of the post-war Iraqi scene. A rare interview with a member of the *hawza* took place amidst the crowds in Karbala during the April pilgrimage. Abbas Nahidi told the *Independent*'s Kim Sengupta,

> Our job is to ensure that the people get the message of the Hawza. They should listen and act as our wise leaders advise. We are talking to all our people in our cities to plan the action. The Hawza believe there should be elections so people can decided who should govern us. We want an Islamic state. We do not want to be ruled by any foreign powers including the United States.[31]

At the heart of the Shia popular movement was the conviction propagated by clerics that *al-Hawza al-Ilmiyah*, the supreme Shia scholarly centre in the holy city of Najaf, was the strongest and most popular authority in Iraq. Shia clerics expressed the determination to use all possible peaceful means to show the United States that the *hawza*, rather than exiled opposition groups, wielded real power inside Iraq. Unfortunately, they also recognized that, 'America will not allow those wearing turbans to rule Iraq,' in the words of Sheik Abdel-Rahman al-Showeili, a senior Shia cleric. He urged a change of attitude: 'But we tell America: Let the people choose.' Sheikh al-Showeili insisted in early June that the Iranian system of clerical rule would not be Iraq's model: 'We want an Islamic state based on guaranteeing freedoms.'[32] Democracy is a constant theme.

This seems to have been the feeling during the Karbala pilgrimage. British reporter Ewen MacAskill reported, 'Many in the crowd said they did not want rule in which Shia clerics have the monopoly, but instead wanted to share power.'[33]

Sheik Kazem al-Abadi, in many ways the public face of the *hawza*, stressed the need for nonviolence in a sermon in a Sadr City mosque on 30 May: 'I indeed want immorality and decadence to be fought, but without bloodshed. There are many ways to deter such things [corrupt thoughts brought in by the US occupation] without shedding blood.' The *hawza* representative added: 'Our voice is not the voice of terrorism. We just want to offer guidance to society.'[34]

A DIFFERENT ISLAM

In the early days of the Shia take-over, White House spokesperson Ari Fleischer said the US would not support a regime that was 'an Islamic dictatorship, that does not respect the religious disagreements among the people, that is not tolerant, that is dictatorial, that is closed, that doesn't govern by a rule of law or transparency.'[35] (So much for Saudi Arabia, then.) Mr Fleischer added, 'I think it's a given it will be an Islamic leader—it's an Islamic country. But that's different from an Islamic dictatorship.'[36]

What were the prospects of an Iranian-style revolution? Yitzhak Nakash, an expert on the Shia Muslims of Iraq, had written months earlier,

> The prospect of the Shiites coming to power should not raise the fear that Iraq might be swept away by Islamic radicalism, or that Iran would be able to increase its leverage in the country to a significant extent.
> On the contrary, for more than a decade radical Islam in the Middle East has been largely shaped by Sunnis, many of whom have been influenced by the Wahhabi-Hanbali school dominant in Saudi Arabia. Although the Iranian revolution emboldened Arab Shiites, Iran has failed to reshape Arab Shiism in its own image.[37]

This analysis is echoed by Karen Armstrong, a Western expert in Islam who has been honoured as a bridge builder who promotes understanding among the three Abrahamic faiths. Writing a month after the fall of the Ba'athist regime, Ms Armstrong noted that during the 1970s and 1980s, while Western powers supported the Ba'ath regime, the Shias of Iraq regularly risked their lives in the three-day pilgrimage from Najaf to Karbala, 'braving police bullets, waving the bloodstained shirts of those who had fallen, and shouting: "Oh Saddam, take your hands off the army! The people do not want you!" ' It was not Saddam Hussein's secularist policies, his initial courting of the West, nor his neglect of Islamic law that offended them, according to Ms Armstrong: 'Their resistance to Baghdad was fuelled by a visceral and religiously inspired rejection of tyranny.'

Shia Islam possessed 'a religiously-motivated secularism': 'long before western phi-losophers called for the separation of church and state, Shias had privatised faith, convinced that it was impossible to integrate the religious imperative with the grim world of politics that seemed murderously antagonistic to it.' Every single Shia imam was imprisoned, exiled or executed. By the eighth century, most Shias held themselves aloof from politics and regarded all governments—even those that were avowedly Islamic—as illegitimate. When Iran became a Shia state in the early 16th century, the Shia clergy still refused public office, adopted an oppositional stance to the state, and 'formed an alternative establish-ment that—implicitly or explicitly—challenged the shahs on behalf of the people.' Ayatollah Khomeini's declaration that a mullah should be a head of state actually 'broke with centuries of sacred Shia tradition', according to Ms Armstrong. In 1906, leading mullahs in Iran had campaigned alongside secularist intellectuals for a modern constitu-tion on European lines.'[38]

In the aftermath of the war in 2003, the Shia clergy of Iraq appeared to be following this remarkable tradition by calling for democracy, not dictatorship. Naturally, it would be a democracy shaped and informed by Islam, but nonetheless, in the words of Sheikh Abdel-Rahman al-Showeili, 'we tell America: Let the people chose.' One of the clerics most closely associated with Iran, Ayatollah Mohammad-Baqir al-Hakim, returned to Iraq on 10 May, after 23 years of exile. The Ayatollah told an audience in Tehran the day before returning to Iraq, 'The future of Iraq belongs to Islam. And making efforts to preserve Iraq's independence is our key challenge.'[39] The Supreme Council for the Islamic Revolution in Iraq (SCIRI), the organization headed by the Ayatollah, made it clear on the same day that it did not seek an Iranian-style Islamic state. Iran's priority in relation to Iraq was not religious but political: to prevent a hostile government from taking power in Baghdad.[40]

The *Financial Times* had some pragmatic advice for Washington:

> The speed with which Shia clerics and politicians have taken on security and welfare functions US forces have failed to fulfil has clearly alarmed some officials, who talk menac-ingly of the dangers of an Iranian-style theocracy. Yet if the US and Britain are serious about creating a representative interim Iraqi government, there is no alternative to building it from the ground up—none, at least, that will work. As the *Financial Times* has argued, the success of this risky venture will in great part depend on whether the US chooses to work with the majority Shia, or loses its nerve and starts to work against them ... Across the Arab and Islamic world, where the state has failed to provide health and education, welfare and infrastructure, Islamist forces have stepped into the vacuum. Iraq will be no different.[41]

Religious author Karen Armstrong suggested that, 'If Iraqis choose a Shia government in free and fair elections, we should at least give it the benefit of the doubt.'[42] For its part, Washington has no intention of permitting the majority population to shape the social, political and economic fabric of Iraq, for reasons explored in an earlier chapter. There were two basic strategies open to Washington in relation to the Shia clergy: divide and rule, or counter-insurgency (a euphemism for 'state terrorism'.) The first option involved co-opting elements of the clergy and the Shia community willing to serve US goals in the region. Early efforts were not promising.

GOOD COP: ABDUL MAJID AL-KHOEI

One key player in the Anglo-American co-option strategy was Seyyed Abdul Majid al-Khoei, a London-based Shia cleric. Mr al-Khoei, the son of Grand Ayatollah Abolqassem al-Khoei, the supreme spiritual leader of Iraq's Shia population, fled Iraq in the aftermath of the failed 1991 uprising, settling in London. The son of the Grand Ayatollah developed a close relationship with the British Government. In October 2001, Mr al-Khoei was invited to Downing Street to discuss terrorism, as a representative of Britain's Shia Muslims. Along with the Archbishop of Canterbury, George Carey, the Chief Rabbi, Jonathan Sacks, and Hindu and Sikh leaders, he endorsed Tony Blair's decision to attack the Taliban in Afghanistan.[43] As the war on Iraq approached, Mr al-Khoei agreed to be inserted into southern Iraq by US forces to secure the co-operation of Shia leaders.

Once he was back in Najaf, as his father had done in 1991, the *Guardian* reported, Mr al-Khoei organised a committee of 25 leading citizens from all walks of life 'to help keep order, to stop inhumane acts, and to bring in desperately needed supplies of food, water and medicine.' This was clearly an attempt to compete with the parallel Shia administrations already springing up. Within a week, it was said, Mr al-Khoei's network had extended its influence north to Karbala and east to Diwaniya.[44]

Then, suddenly, the returned exile was dead. Various rumours swirled about his murder. His own al-Khoei Foundation stated that, 'Al Saiyyed Abdul Majid was performing prayer at the shrine of Imam Ali A.S in the city of Al Najaf when he was attacked by the remnants of Saddam Hussein's regime.'[45] The truth was more complex, and rather unsavoury.

Newsweek reported later that 'Al-Khoei was a key figure in U.S. efforts to nurture moderate leaders in post-Saddam Iraq—and a counterweight to radical clerics backed by Iran.' The cleric was flown into Najaf with Marine escorts on 3 April, mere hours after the Ba'athists fled. 'In the busy week that followed, he paid visits to key clerics in Najaf, including his father's successor, the Grand Ayatollah Ali Sistani, who issued a *fatwa* urging followers to co-operate with U.S. troops. Al-Khoei organized a civilian council to get electricity and water flowing and return the police to the streets. The CIA had reportedly given him as much as $13 million, with which he planned to pay workers' salaries and begin reconstructing the city.'

The trouble came when Mr al-Khoei decided to visit the holy shrine of Imam Ali in the company of Haidar Raifee, the principal custodian, or *kelidar*, of the shrine. Haidar Raifee was a religious scholar whose family had served at the shrine for 400 years—and a member of the Ba'ath Party and a delegate to Saddam Hussein's rubber-stamp National Assembly. Mr Raifee held the keys to a gilded cage in the shrine that contained the tomb of the Prophet Muhammad's son-in-law—and access to millions in cash donations left by pilgrims from around the world. Mr Raifee had been accused of stealing precious gifts given to the shrine, and giving them to Saddam Hussein, including a diamond presented to the shrine by the Shah of Iran in the 1930s. The custodian also allegedly diverted many of the donations left inside the tomb to the Ba'ath Party. Such was the scale of the thefts that Shia religious leaders in Najaf were driven to issue a *fatwa* ordering followers to cease leaving donations.

Newsweek also reported that, 'al-Khoei apparently viewed the return of Raifee to his post as a key gesture of reconciliation in the seething city.' Mr al-Khoei escorted Mr Raifee to the shrine, with a dozen men armed with Kalashnikovs. Deputy custodians prevented these bodyguards from entering, claiming that their weapons would violate the sanctity of the site. When Mr Raifee, Mr al-Khoei and a group of supporters entered the shrine, an angry mob armed with hand grenades, swords and assault rifles surrounded the building, denouncing the Ba'athist custodian of the site. Members of the crowd reportedly sprayed the hall with AK-47 fire, fatally injuring a member of Mr al-Khoei's entourage. He himself 'grabbed a gun that the night guards stored inside the building and fired at least one warning shot through the window, to no avail.' The two men were taken outside the building and killed.[46]

The centrepiece of the Anglo-American strategy to penetrate the Shia population of Iraq was flown into Iraq by the US with $13 million of CIA money in his pocket, was guarded by US Special Forces officers, chose to align himself with a hated Ba'athist functionary, and fired a weapon inside one of the holiest shrines in the world of Shia Islam. *Newsweek's* investigation of the murders suggests that the exiled cleric's death was the result of a plot by a rival, Muqtada al-Sadr, also the son of a famous Shia leader. Perhaps. But the son of the Grand Ayatollah seems to have done a great deal to put himself in danger in post-Saddam Najaf without the need of a murderous rival. US and British policy was revealed as both flawed, and, once again, fatally contaminated with collaboration with Ba'athism.

A senior US official said on 22 April, 'We don't want to allow Persian fundamentalism to gain any foothold. We want to find more moderate clerics and move them into positions of influence.'[47] Astonishingly, it appears that senior policymakers at the Pentagon believed that Ahmad Chalabi, the secular Shia leader of the Iraqi National Congress exile opposition group, could have influence over the Shia population: 'They really did believe he is a Shiite leader,' said a US official in late April. 'They thought, "We're set, we've got a Shiite—check the box here." '[48] (In early May, a survey disclosed that many of Iraq's Islamist parties either did not like Mr Chalabi or had never heard of him.[49])

'We've just got to play it well. We'll continue to do what we are doing, trying to elicit those leaders who have a voice that's consistent with what we want to see achieved in Iraq,' said a US official in late April.[50] The US attempts to secure the goodwill of the Shia majority were rather inadequate, it appears. In late May, *Time* magazine reported from Baghdad, 'To show that the US cares about ordinary Iraqis, soldiers are going into a different section of town every day to help with garbage collection and medical care. The

US had unwittingly ceded such basic services to Shi'ite organizations that opposed the American presence.'[51] Collecting some rubbish and providing some medical care, on an occasional and fleeting basis was a pale shadow of the depth and breadth of services that the Shia clergy seems to have provided for the bulk of the population in the frightening days of the interregnum.

In the south, British attempts to co-operate with the Shia majority went somewhat further. In late April, it was reported that British troops had sketched out 'the first tenets of post-Saddam law, involving an amalgam of Sharia, tribal and British law.' The new legal code would be enforced by an interim administration in Basra and Maysan, the two provinces held by the British, and would form the basis for law in a future Iraqi federation, believed British commanders.[52] In late April, at the gates of al-Amara in southern Iraq, the most northerly reach of British Forces, soldiers from the 16 Air Assault Brigade shared checkpoint duties with members of the local Shia militia.[53]

There were certainly divisions between the various Shia religious leaders, especially between those clerics returning from exile and those who had remained with their flocks throughout the era of Saddam Hussein. At the time of writing it remains unclear to what extent the US will be able exploit these divisions for its own purposes. Ewen MacAskill warned perceptively from Karbala the day after the great pilgrimage, 'There is a strong chance that the Shia may yet fragment and that yesterday may yet turn out to have been the last day of Shia unity.'[54]

BAD COP: THE 'WAR ON TERRORISM'

BBC reporter Fergal Keane, musing on the events of Karbala, commented, 'A lot depends now on how the Americans respond to the growing Islamic movement. If they try to crack down, they will face a guerrilla war and will eventually lose. They should realise too that this movement has a distinctly nationalist tone: don't overplay the role of Shia Iran in the growing militancy inside Iraq.'[55]

The signs in early May were not promising. US Defence Secretary Donald Rumsfeld, speaking in Baghdad, promised to 'root out the terrorist networks operating in this country'. Veteran reporter Robert Fisk commented of these 'networks',

> They may not actually exist yet. But Donald Rumsfeld knows (and he has been told by US intelligence) that a growing resistance movement to America's occupation is gestating in Iraq. The Shia Muslim community, now supported by thousands of Badr Brigade Iraqis trained in Iran, believes the US is in Iraq for its oil. It is furious at America's treatment of Iraq's cities; in three days last week at least 16 Sunni demonstrators were killed, two of them less than 11 years old. And it is not impressed by Washington's attempts to cobble together an "interim" pro-American government . . .
>
> Here is a little prediction. Mr Bush says the war is over, or words to that effect. Then Shia resistance begins to bite the Americans in Iraq. Of course, Mr Rumsfeld will have warned of this: it will be characterised as the famous 'terrorist networks' which still have to be fought in Iraq. And Iran—and no doubt Syria—will be accused of supporting these

'terrorists'. The French did much the same in their 1954–62 war against the FLN in Algeria. Tunisia was to blame. Egypt was to blame. So stand by for part two of the Iraq war, transmogrified into the next stage of the 'war on terror'.[56]

If this is at all well-founded as a prediction, and I fear that it is, a likely corollary is some form of confrontation between Washington and Tehran. The easiest way to sell a new war on the people of Iraq (who the last war was supposed to liberate) is to present the Shia nationalist forces of Iraq as agents of an alien Iranian fundamentalism. White House spokesperson Ari Fleischer said in late April 2003, 'We've made clear to Iraq that we would oppose any outside interference in Iraq's road to democracy. Infiltration of agents to destabilise the Shiite population would clearly fall into that category.'[57]

THE SHIA EXPERIENCE

The recent experience of suffering and persecution of the Shia majority has received only fragmentary attention in the Western media, and yet it is one of the most potent political forces at work in post-Saddam Iraq. Roula Khalaf, the outstanding regional correspondent for the *Financial Times*, presented one family's experience.

After the regime assassinated the leading Shia cleric Mohamed Sadeq al Sadr in 1999, there was an uprising in Basra. Bassem Jawad al-Sajed's brother Mustafa was said to have been involved. Bassem and Mustafa were both imprisoned and interrogated. Mustafa was executed. Bassem was released after eight months. Other relatives were also arrested: his mother was held for three months, his father and other brothers were imprisoned for a further four months. During their imprisonment, their house was destroyed by security forces who took the furniture and told the neighbours to help themselves to the remains.

Because they were Shia Muslims, Bassem and his family were excluded by the state: 'His parents knew that their children would not rise through the ranks of the public service or ever secure a decent job in the private sector.' Bassem said in April 2003, 'Each person has his traditions, and our faith prevented us from recognising the Ba'ath. It was secular, atheist and it was not a fair party. But if you're not with them, then you are considered against them.' (An intriguing resonance.) Bassem's father, an English teacher, was given an administrative job because he was considered unfit to teach a new generation of Iraqis. One of Bassem's sisters had a degree in literature, but was never allowed to hold a government job.

Roula Khalaf pondered the situation of the Shia: 'I wonder whether, if the US rebuilds Iraq in its own image, then people such as Bassem and his family, the victims of Saddam's tyranny, might be seen as too devout, too intransigent. I cannot help asking myself if it will end up being the practical people, the ones like Haydar the oil smuggler and Baha'a the colonel who were more willing to compromise with Saddam Hussein's regime, who will also find life easier in the new Iraq.'[58]

The depth and ferocity of the exclusion of the Shia is indicated by these vignettes from secret army files recovered by the Iraqi opposition: 'A party official notes tears in an officer's eyes during a broadcast of a religious ceremony for Shi'ites, the branch of Islam out of favour with Saddam's ruling Sunnis. It is duly noted in his file, and that is the end of his career.' An officer named Khaled al Hayani was punished for making unguarded remarks: 'At a gathering of officers, he was reported by a fellow officer to have said that a Colonel Ahmed had been discharged from the army "because he was fasting and praying and they don't want people like that".'[59] The story of Colonel Ahmed is likely to have been true; the story of Khaled al Hayani, however, is pointed in demonstrating how the regime did not even tolerate a passing reference to the repression of the Shias.

Religious enthusiasm could get you killed. In the aftermath of the war, the bodies of Isa Nama, Mustafa Eyssa, Ibrahim Eyssa, Ali Eyssa, and Mortada Abdel Jaber, young Shia Muslims killed by the Ba'athists in 2000, were recovered from a secret graveyard for the 'disappeared' near to the infamous Abu Ghraib prison. Relatives said the Eyssas and Isa Nama were good young men whose crime was to be seen to go to the mosque too much and wear their beards too proudly. Saddam's secret police accused them of belonging to the banned Shia political grouping al-Dawa ('Islamic Call'). The young men denied the charge. Mortada Abdel Jaber was taken and killed 'simply because he was sitting with the Eyssas when the policemen came.'[60]

The depth of hatred for the Ba'ath Party among the Shia population is virulent, and hence the determination of the clergy and the laity alike to block the re-nazification of the country. There is also, at the time of writing, a building hatred of the US occupation which the *hawza* is hard-pressed to hold back. In Karbala in late April, banners read, 'Bush equals Saddam', 'Down USA', 'Yes, Yes, Islam'.[61] A month later, 25,000 worshippers at a mosque in Sadr City chanted, 'No, no to America! No, no to Satan!'[62]

How much longer until the Basra uprising?

CHAPTER XXII
Sunni Rage

After Falluja

SUNNI DOMINATION

The territories which make up modern Iraq have had a dominant Sunni minority for centuries. Under the Ottoman Empire, the Sunni elite was used to run the country (the Arab tribes in the provinces who were later to convert to Shia Islam were barely seen as Muslims). Britain conquered the three Ottoman provinces of Basra, Baghdad and Mosul during the First World War, and unified them into a new state of Iraq, under a British imperial 'Mandate'. At the beginning of the Mandate period, there were three million Iraqis, of whom more than half were Shia Muslims and a fifth were Kurdish, while eight per cent of the population was composed of the Jewish, Christian, Yazidi, Sabaean and Turkoman minorities. 'Yet the government ministers, the senior state officials and the officer corps of the armed forces were drawn almost exclusively from the Sunni Arabs who formed less than 20 per cent of the population,' as historian Charles Tripp observes.[1] The British buttressed the existing framework by imposing a foreign Sunni king, Amir Faisal, a member of the Hashemite royal family who London had tried but failed to impose on Syria in an earlier debacle. The crucial distinguishing characteristic of this Arab collaborator was that, as Charles Tripp points out, 'he was believed to be amenable to British advice and well aware of the limitations that the reality of British power in the Middle East would place upon his ambitions.'[2] Imperial systems tend to rely on dependent and therefore dependable local clients. King Faisal was an outsider with no roots in Iraq, who understood his subordinate position. The Sunni generals and ministers who ran Iraq were equally aware of their minority position within the new state, and their reliance on British power.

Iraq threw off the colonial yoke on 14 July 1958, with a reformist military coup, but in the 1980s, under the rule of the supposedly nationalist Ba'ath Party, Iraq drifted into the orbit of US power. The task the US took on in 2003, with the intended overthrow of Saddam Hussein, was somehow to reconstruct the imperial relations of yesteryear, and to re-build the traditional patron-client relationship with the Sunni minority. Unfortunately, with the disintegration of the regime during the war, and the ascendancy of a parallel Shia administration on the ground after the war, the Sunni minority was thrown out of its position of dominance, in an enormous psychic upheaval. An (unintended) consequence of the war was a considerable levelling of the military playing field between the different communities, and therefore a dramatic shift in the balance of power to the Shia majority. A shift of power back to the Sunni minority may well require a considerable effort from the US forces along the lines of the British (and later US) intervention in Greece after the Second World War.

If it was the US intention to restore the link to Sunni elites (for reasons discussed earlier), the situation became considerably more complex as a result of the violent Sunni resistance that built up in the first two months of occupation—in response to the unpunished killing of civilian Iraqis by US occupation forces.

FALLUJA

The critical event was the massacre carried out in the largely Sunni town of Falluja, 35 miles west of Baghdad, at the end of April 2003. According to one report, the town had been quiet for two weeks after Iraqi troops and the local Ba'ath party leaders had fled. Local clerics halted the looting and arranged for much of the stolen property to be returned. A new mayor organized the re-opening of the schools, and persuaded the police to return to work. 'Then the Americans arrived, arrested imams, put up roadblocks and occupied a school—all without prior discussion with local leaders,' according to respected British journalist Jonathan Steele.[3] Then came the massacre of 13 civilians (the echoes of Northern Ireland's Bloody Sunday are striking).

Late in the evening of Monday 28 April, a demonstration gathered outside the school being occupied by US troops, demanding that the soldiers leave so that the school could be re-opened. The official US account has it that 25 armed civilians, mixed in with the crowd and also positioned on nearby rooftops, fired on the soldiers of the 82nd Airborne, leading to a 'fire-fight'. A US officer who was at the scene, Lieutenant Colonel Eric Nantz, said immediately after the killings, 'There were a lot of people who were armed and who were throwing rocks. How is a US soldier to tell the difference between a rock and a grenade?'[4] Presumably by whether it exploded or not.

Phil Reeves, a reporter for the British *Independent on Sunday*, conducted a careful independent investigation and concluded that the official story was a 'highly implausible version of events'. Witnesses interviewed by Mr Reeves 'stated that there was some shooting in the air in the general vicinity, but it was nowhere near the crowd, which comprised mostly boys and young men who descended on the school at around 9pm to call for the US troops to leave the premises.' Mr Reeves points out that gunfire in the air is commonplace in Iraq—and the Falluja demonstration coincided with Saddam Hussein's birthday. Colonel Nantz admitted to Reuters that the bloodshed occurred after 'celebratory firing', but he claimed that the firing came from the crowd: 'There were a lot of people who were armed.'[5] However, all the witnesses Phil Reeves could find agreed on two issues: Firstly, there was no 'fire-fight' nor any shooting at the school. Secondly, the crowd—although it had one poster of Saddam and may have thrown some stones—had no guns. The *Independent* journalist observed:

> The evidence at the scene overwhelmingly supports this. Al-Ka'at primary and secondary school is a yellow concrete building about the length and height of seven terraced houses located in a walled compound. The soldiers fired at people gathered below them. There are no bullet marks on the facade of the school or the perimeter wall in front of it. The top floors of the houses directly opposite, from where the troops say they were fired on, also appear unmarked. Their upper windows are intact.[6]

Western journalists were taken to see bullet holes in an upper window and some marks on a school wall, 'but they were on another side of the school building.'[7] US Central Command initially refused to confirm that the civilians killed or injured were unarmed: 'it described the deaths of unarmed people as "allegations" and estimated the toll at seven injuries, all people who were armed.'[8]

Dr Ahmed Ghanim al-Ali told reporters at Falluja Hospital, 'Medical crews were shot by [US] soldiers when they tried to get to the injured people.'[9]

Phil Reeves reported on 4 May that nearly a week after the US military announced an inquiry, commanders had yet to speak to the doctors who counted the bodies. 'Nor, by late yesterday, had US commanders been to the home of a 13-year-old boy who was among the dead, even though it is located less than a mile from the main American base in Fallujah, a conservative Sunni town 35 miles west of Baghdad.'[10]

THE DESTRUCTION OF THE AL-ANI FAMILY

The day after the bloodbath, US soldiers displayed three guns which they said they had recovered from a home opposite, but, as Mr Reeves pointed out, 'this proved nothing. Every other Iraqi home has at least one firearm.'[11]

Let us go to that home opposite, and discover how these events appeared from the wrong end of the guns. Living in two houses opposite the school were the al-Ani family: Mufina al-Ani, her three sons Muthana, Osama and Walid, and their wives and children. The brothers shared a taxi as their means of earning a living for the extended family. Muthana's wife Eptisan al-Ani went out to see what was happening in the demonstration outside their house. She was shot in the leg. Muthana ran out to help her. (Another report says that the couple were trying to pull demonstrators to safety in their house when they were shot.[12]) Walid came from the next house to help his brother and sister-in-law, and was shot dead.

Osama, the third of the brothers, got the family taxi going to take Walid and Eptisan to hospital. As he began to reverse into the street, the taxi was riddled with gunfire. Osama, Eptisan and grandmother Mufina were all wounded. Eptisan's husband, Muthana, said later in hospital of these few minutes, 'our family is destroyed.'

The taxi the brothers had shared to generate income was left looking 'like a cheese-grater', in the words of Ed Vulliamy, who gathered together this account of the destruction of the al-Ani family. The *Guardian* journalist counted 38 rounds to the metalwork alone. He summarized: 'Each of the brothers came out in turn to try and help their families and were each targeted and shot.' Mr Vulliamy asked the inevitable question. Muthana al-Ani answered, 'What do I think of the Americans? Look at where my foot used to be, look at my dead brother and the rest of my family, with which I do not know what to do. I have a wife and seven children who were all right, and now? That is what I think.'[13]

Standing with an unblinking stare by the family taxi, 14-year-old Ahmed al-Ani, son of Muthana, told a Western journalist two days after the massacre, 'I hate Americans. I want revenge. I will wait, I will join a group, and, one day, I will kill Americans.' Muthana's son 'said he now wanted to join al Qaeda because he admired Osama bin Laden, the network's leader and alleged mastermind of the Sept. 11 attacks on America.'[14]

RAGE AND REVENGE

Phil Reeves left Falluja the day after the massacre with another set of 'unforgettable' words ringing in his ears. The quietly spoken headmaster of the occupied school, whose students were among the protesters, injured and in perhaps three cases killed in the shooting, said calmly that he was willing to die as a 'martyr' to take his revenge against the US troops.[15] Hend Majid, a 29-year-old housewife living opposite the US-occupied school, told a Western reporter she was glad Saddam Hussein was gone, but the US occupation which had led to her neighbours' deaths made her feel like a Palestinian under Israeli rule. 'Sitting in her living room where two bullets had pierced the window and flown above the cot of her 7-day-old niece, she vowed to become a suicide bomber. "I will strap explosives to my chest to get rid of them." '[16]

Two days after the massacre, a protest march was held. US troops shot dead two demonstrators. No US soldiers were injured or killed, despite claims that they had been fired on first.[17] Reporters from the British *Daily Mirror* were six feet away when a young boy 'hurled a sandal at the US jeep—with a M2 heavy machine gun post on the back—as it drove past.' The soldier in charge of the machine gun ducked down, 'then pressed his thumb on the trigger' to unleash a 20-second burst of automatic fire at 'a crowd of 1,000 unarmed people.' Reporter Chris Hughes said, 'We heard no warning to disperse and saw no guns or knives among the Iraqis whose religious and tribal leaders kept shouting through loudhailers to remain peaceful.' After the shooting, those in the crowd still standing, 'now apparently insane with anger—ran at the fortress battering its walls with their fists. Many had tears pouring down their faces.'[18]

Khalaf Abed Shebib, a tribal leader in Falluja, said, 'People are ready to die in this battle.' A local imam had had to call off a second demonstration after seeing 'protesters' stuffing hand grenades into their pockets.[19] 'Everyone here was happy at first that the Americans threw out Saddam,' said Ibrahim Hamad, a retired soldier. 'But these killings will make all our children go off with bin Laden.'[20]

Officially, US commanders in Baghdad attributed the problems in Falluja to remnants of Saddam Hussein's Ba'ath Party and his armed militia, Saddam's *fedayeen*. Colonel Vaught, a local US officer, noted, 'There are lots of Baathists, there are some Fedayeen around.' However, he appeared to agree with residents of Falluja that there was a more complex picture of accumulated grievances: 'disappointment with the U.S. occupation, an avalanche of hardship and a lust for revenge.' In some attacks, militants were stirring up religious hostility. In other cases, hooliganism appeared to be at the root. 'In any event, they said, loyalty to Hussein is far from the driving force here.' Riad, a lawyer who declined to provide his last name, said that the killings of local people had prompted relatives to plan revenge attacks against American soldiers: 'This is our culture. Clans are strong here and it is the duty to avenge a wrongful death. People do not forget.'[21] There followed a string of attacks on US forces. The younger generation was apparently proud of Falluja's violent resistance. A group of teenagers outside a kebab restaurant said in early May, 'Of all of Iraq, only Fallujah is resisting the Americans. The Americans have these big tanks. We show everybody that they are just toys.' Riad added, 'I'm afraid taking shots at Americans will become a sport for these types.'[22]

Peaceful protests succeeded in forcing the US to withdraw from the school, first to a local Ba'athist headquarters (entirely aptly). The US forces 'hunkered down in the old Baath Party building, surrounded by barbed wire and a permanent crowd of angry young men.'[23] Then the violent resistance forced the soldiers several miles east of the town. 'We didn't want to stay in the Alamo,' explained a US commander.[24]

When British forces moved into a Ba'ath Party headquarters in the southern town of Zubayr at the end of March 2003, a local person remarked to a British reporter, 'They have come to free us, but instead they move in where the Ba'ath party used to live. We are going to tell them they should take that building down.'[25] The building was not pulled down. Across Iraq, in the weeks that followed, the edifice of fascism was repaired and restored.

Returning to Falluja, the new mayor, Taha Bedaiwi al-Alwani, repeatedly asked US forces to withdraw to the edge of the city. On 3 May, nonetheless, US Captain Bren Workman said, 'He is not asking us to leave.' Khalaf Abed Shebib, the tribal leader quoted earlier, responded, 'If they do not leave, we will make them.'[26] After the troops moved into the Ba'ath Party headquarters, a banner was hung on the mayor's office next door: 'Sooner or later, US killers, we'll kick you out.'[27] In this, the resistance succeeded.

Washington was seen to be reneging on promises to leave the country as soon as possible. 'We are Arab, and we believe a deal is a deal,' said a local cleric. 'Fallujah gave up without a fight, to keep the Americans out. Then they came in. Now, we don't know when Iraqis will rule Iraq . . . Reputation is important here. Even among smugglers, a deal is a deal,' he said with a laugh.[28] (Falluja is a well-known for smuggling.)

The US occupation forces attempted a 'charm offensive' in Falluja a month after the massacre, delivering food to unpaid teachers, cleaning up schools and bulldozing plots into soccer fields. Captain Anthony Butler of the 3rd Infantry Division admitted that it was difficult to switch from 'killing everything we saw to being nice.'[29] By this time, the Falluja massacre had already begun to be erased from history. Reporting 'Operation

Friends and Neighbours' in Falluja, the 'quality' British newspapers reported 'smouldering distrust' in the town, but not one of them mentioned the main reason for the burning hostility to the US forces—the massacre.[30]

THE SUNNI TRIANGLE

In the Sunni heartland north of Baghdad known as the 'Sunni Triangle', there were many incidents that embittered relations between the US occupation forces and the local people. Let us take two incidents at random. On 26 May, in the city of Samarra, US soldiers killed two boys aged 12 and 13 and a 22-year-old man. A 16-year-old boy died later of his wounds. The four were riding in the back of a pickup truck in a convoy of wedding guests when celebratory gunshots went off. US soldiers then fired on the convoy.[31] Two days later in Samarra, Roukan Habib Khalaf was hurrying to get home before the curfew in his battered Toyota pickup. Mr Khalaf came round a sharp turn near a US military checkpoint and swerved to avoid the troops. The soldiers unleashed a fusillade so fierce it decapitated two of his daughters, Nour, 12, and Ghazal, 9, sitting on the front seat by Mr Khalaf. 'There were no screams, no nothing. They died right away,' Mr Khalaf told a Western reporter, surrounded by neighbours who had come to offer condolences. 'Americans,' said one of his visitors, 'are murderers.'[32]

It has long been the practice of US military expeditions to put a premium on the safety of US soldiers, at the expense of local populations. In the age of the suicide car bomber, this posture has become a deadly hair-trigger response to the possibility of threat, with predictable consequences. British practice was somewhat different. After Falluja, British soldiers expressed their fury anonymously: 'Don't talk to me about the US army,' said one British military source. 'Let's just say that they face a very steep learning curve.'[33]

The reaction among Iraqis was also predictable. 'Why can the U.S. Army come here, kill us, destroy our property and we are not allowed to kill them?' asked Yehia al-Motashari, son of a tribal leader in Samarra. 'We don't plan to surrender our arms. With every passing day we have more guns.' 'We are hurting,' said Jassim Mohammed Sultan, a 70-year-old labourer in Ramadi. 'You cannot blame us for what we do.' 'The future is jihad,' said Sheik Mohammed Ali Abbas, a cleric in Ramadi, 65 miles west of Baghdad.[34]

The familiar cycle of atrocity-retaliation-repression-retaliation moved up a notch in the second week of June 2003, with the first major operation against the Sunni resistance. Operation Peninsula Strike involved 4,000 troops scouring an area around the Tigris river near the town of Balad. Task Force Ironhorse, which included air assault teams, ground attack squads, river patrol boats and local Iraqi police, raided suspected guerrilla hideouts from the air, land and river, as other units hunted down fugitives and blocked escape routes. This followed 85 attacks on US forces in May 2003, almost triple the number of the previous month.[35]

In the first two months of attacks after the war, over 40 US soldiers were killed in attacks, or died in accidents. In the first two days of Operation Peninsula Strike in mid-June 2003, US occupation forces reportedly killed 97 Iraqis.[36]

As in the case of the murder of Mr al-Khoei, it was easy to blame 'Saddam loyalists', but much of the insurgency seems fairly unideological. Clerics, tribal leaders and merchants interviewed by one journalist referred to US troops as 'infidels,' 'immoral' or 'dirty animals.' They considered the presence of US servicewomen an insult. They said that the troops' practice of searching homes for weapons or fugitives violated the sanctity of the Muslim home.[37] 'In farming areas, Iraqis speak bitterly of US soldiers entering women's quarters—they also accuse them of spying on women using nightvision equipment.'[38]

According to Sheikh Jamil Ibrahim Mohammed of Falluja, the attacks in Falluja were a simple matter of a blood feud: 'What can you do if a man sees American troops kill his son, and then you see these same men on our streets every day? Of course he will seek revenge, especially if he sees there is no justice from the Americans.'[39] A US army spokesperson in Baghdad admitted on 11 June, 'It would be hard to discount revenge.'[40]

Part of Operation Peninsula Strike was an amphibious assault on a 'terrorist training camp' north of Baghdad involved 800 soldiers and even a Predator drone. Lieutenant Colonel Philip Battaglia of the 4th Infantry Brigade declared the operation 'a great victory': 'We've just taken out one more terrorist training camp, which means one more step towards making Iraq a safe and prosperous country.' When reporters from the *Daily Telegraph* visited the 'compound', however, they found a collection of four family houses on the banks of the river Tigris. A retired teacher sleeping in his garden was reportedly beaten on the head with the butt of a gun until he died. In a nearby house, a farmer named Mohammed al-Juboori, opening the door for soldiers to enter, was hit in the chest and the arm with their guns. When Mr al-Juboori began to have a heart attack, his fifteen-year-old son Zadoon fetched his medicine. A soldier allegedly ground the pills into the earth with his boot. Mr al-Juboori died. Jasim al-Juboori, a lawyer attending Mr al-Juboori's funeral, said of the fighting in Falluja, 'The people who are fighting are only taking action to avenge the murders of their family members. Every day that passes and more blood feuds are beginning.'[41] During Operation Peninsula Strike, 397 suspects were detained; within a week all but 60 had been released for lack of evidence.[42]

The *Financial Times* had another angle. The town of al-Duluiya ('Thuluiya' in the *FT*) where the al-Juboonis lived ('Jbur' in the *FT*) is a largely Sunni village, not far from the mainly Shia city of Balad, which has 'years of pent-up hostility to the surrounding Sunni towns.' The mayor and former police chief of Balad, Nabil Daweesh Mohammed, took credit for directing the US to al-Duluiya, naming the sheikh of the al-Juboonis as the leading Ba'athist in the province. However, despite the deaths of four Iraqis during the raid, the results were meagre: small arms, one mortar and two rocket propelled grenades. No high-ranking Ba'ath Party officials were discovered.[43]

On 13 June, 27 Iraqis were reported killed after a failed ambush on a group of US Abrams M1 tanks outside Balad city. Richard Beeston of *The Times* reported that, 'The size of the attack was particularly surprising as it was carried out the day after 4,000 US troops were involved in a huge sweep of suspected Saddam loyalists in villages on the banks of the Tigris river.'[44] But it was precisely because of the US attacks that family members would mount assaults on the almost-impregnable tanks. Four of the attackers were reportedly killed immediately in this incident. A helicopter gunship and armoured vehicles 'pursued the enemy personnel', killing 23 more Iraqis according to the official US version of events. Patrick Cockburn, co-author of *Saddam Hussein: An American Obsession*, reported, 'It is not clear how many Iraqi casualties really were fighters. In country areas, Iraqi civilians invariably own weapons, which may include rocket-propelled grenade launchers and machine-guns. "A man in Iraq does not think he is really a man unless he has a gun, the bigger the better," said one Iraqi observer.'[45] Mr Cockburn remarks, 'One explanation for American aggression is that their commanders see the possession of arms as hostility to the occupation. But Iraqi farmers are always armed, usually with AK-47 machine guns.'[46] A few days later, it was admitted that actually only seven men were killed in this incident, and five of those were apparently innocent farmers.[47]

THE IMPERIAL DYNAMIC

At the time of writing, it is unclear how the triangular relationship between the Sunni and Shia communities and the occupation forces will develop. The impunity granted to frightened and trigger-happy US soldiers during the early weeks of the occupation has done much to undermine the traditional relationship between the imperial power and the Sunni minority. Given the importance of the traditional arrangements to key client states in the region, however, it seems safe to predict that there will be efforts to resume the process of regime restoration and stabilization. In a word, re-nazification.

How this will feel to 14-year-old Ahmed al-Ani and others who have lost relatives in a hail of US bullets is not clear. Perhaps, even if there is a re-forging of the US-Ba'ath partnership at the elite level of Sunni society, at the grassroots the blood feud will continue to fester, and some of the younger generation of Iraqi Sunnis will indeed become part of the fundamentalist Sunni networks that find their inspiration in Osama bin Laden. The consequences of such a development are unpredictable.

A large share of the responsibility for those consequences must lie with those who proceeded with the war on Iraq, despite warnings from across the political spectrum that the war would benefit al-Qaeda. Field Marshal Lord Bramall, a former Chief of the British Defence Staff, warned before the war that, 'Petrol rather than water would have been poured on the flames, and al-Qaeda would have gained more recruits.'[48] Some of these recruits may be young Iraqis seeking revenge for the deaths caused by US forces— with impunity. The seeds sown in Falluja and throughout Iraq in the first months of the occupation may yet have a harvest much farther afield.

On 31 April the mayor of Falluja asked US officials for compensation for the victims of the massacre that had occurred the day before.[49] I can find no reports of any compensation being offered or paid as of 1 July 2003.

CHAPTER XXIII
Capitalism's War

THE ROOTS OF WAR

How could a Labour Cabinet Minister write in his diary in December 1940 that a takeover by 'Fascist toughs' in Italy would be perfectly acceptable?[1] In 1943, the Conservative Foreign Secretary Anthony Eden submitted a paper to the British War Cabinet which included the following observations:

> I assume that the aim of British policy must be, first that we should continue to exercise the functions and bear the responsibilities of a world Power; and, secondly, that we should seek not only to free Europe, but to preserve her freedom . . . We cannot afford a Europe unfriendly to our interests or antagonistic to our way of life. We cannot afford a Europe which is dominated by Germany.[2]

The problem was not fascism. The problem was a rival power in a commanding position close to the seat of the British Empire. The first priority was clear: 'We have to maintain our position as an Empire and a Commonwealth. If we fail to do so we cannot exist as a world Power.'[3] The second priority was to ensure that Europe was free from domination by an 'unfriendly' power. 'Friendly' dictatorships were not problematic, hence the earlier policy of appeasement.

In an important essay entitled 'Defending the Empire or defeating the enemy: British war aims 1938–47', British historian Michael Dockrill points out that for Britain the war began with limited aims—German withdrawal from Poland, the recreation of an independent Bohemia, and a general agreement on disarmament. There was no mention of overthrowing Hitler or 'overthrowing fascism'. Before the war, the First Sea Lord, Lord Chatfield suggested that if Germany expanded to the south-east, 'we must, in my opinion, accept it.' In the early years of the war, there was, in Michael Dockrill's words, a 'frenzied debate' at the highest levels of the British Government around the proposal to negotiate a peace settlement with Hitler.[4] There was, in his view, no principled opposition to this concept either before or during the war. If the Nazis refrained from posing a threat to Britain's vital interests in the Middle East (one of Lord Chatfield's key concerns), co-existence would have been acceptable.

In public, of course, a very different pose was struck. This was a war in defence of the 'Four Freedoms'—freedom from fear, freedom from want, freedom of speech and freedom of religion. Noam Chomsky remarks bitingly that the real over-riding value was the 'Fifth Freedom': the Freedom to Rob and Exploit. Professor Chomsky observes, 'as the historical record demonstrates with great clarity, it is only when the fifth and fundamental freedom is threatened that a sudden and short-lived concern for other forms of freedom manifests itself, to be sustained for as long as it is needed to justify the righteous use of force and violence to restore the Fifth Freedom, the one that really counts.'[5]

In August 1941, Prime Minister Churchill and President Roosevelt made an eight-point declaration of their peace aims, incorporating the Four Freedoms. The third point of this 'Atlantic Charter' stated that the two leaders 'respect[ed] the right of all people to choose the form of government under which they will live; and they wish[ed] to see sovereign rights and self-government restored to those who have been forcibly deprived of them.'[6] Within a month, Mr Churchill was telling the House of Commons that this only meant 'the restoration of the sovereignty, self-government and national life of the States and nations of Europe now under the Nazi yoke.'[7] Freedom for European nations enslaved by Nazi imperialism, not for Asian and African nations enslaved by British colonialism. Churchill put the matter succinctly in 1942, in his famous statement at the Lord Mayor's Day Luncheon: 'We mean to hold our own. I have not become the King's First Minister to preside over the liquidation of the British Empire.'[8]

CONNECTING 'VITAL INTERESTS'

Earlier in 1942, the Foreign and Colonial Offices summarized 'Essential British requirements': 'From the economic point of view, the things which it is essential for us to preserve in our colonies are . . . access to raw materials, markets for our manufactures, access to ocean ports and opportunities for investment and development.'[9] These were the persistent deep motivations that led to the systematic support of collaborators and fascists around the world in the aftermath of the Second World War, and these are the same motivations that drive US and British foreign policy today.

The 1995 Defence White Paper stated that Britain must be able to deter, or defend against, 'external aggression against the United Kingdom, our Dependent Territories or our vital national interests'. The opening paragraphs of the Defence White Paper went on to identify vital interests abroad as trade, the sea routes used by British trade, raw materials from abroad, and British investments abroad worth an estimated $300 billion.[10]

This strategic assessment of the Conservative Government was adopted by the incoming New Labour Government in 1998, in the Strategic Defence Review (SDR). The SDR affirmed the importance of the security and stability of the European mainland, but went on to say 'our vital interests are not confined to Europe':

> Our economy is founded on international trade. Exports form a higher proportion of Gross Domestic Product than for the US, Japan, Germany or France. We invest more of our income abroad than any other major economy. Our closest economic partners are the European Union and the US but our investment in the developing world amounts to the

combined total of France, Germany and Italy. Foreign investment into the UK also provides nearly 20% of manufacturing jobs. We depend on foreign countries for supplies of raw materials, above all oil.[11]

This is almost the same list of interests as in 1995, and as in 1942. These are the enduring drivers of British foreign policy.

THE GRAND AREA

Returning to the 1940s, Britain's imperial drive to re-conquer the Empire was actually supported by the US Government, contrary to much mythology. US historian William Roger Louis comments at the conclusion of his respected study *Imperialism At Bay: The United States and the Decolonization of the British Empire, 1941 - 1945*, 'in fact, from about 1943 into the period of the cold war the general policy of the American government, in pursuit of security, tended to support rather than break up the British imperial system.'[12] By November 1944, US officials were informing Roosevelt that as the imperial nations of Western Europe would be 'impoverished and weak' without their empires, 'You may therefore expect Britain, France and the Netherlands to disregard the Atlantic Charter and all promises made to other nations by which they obtained support in the earlier stages of the war'.[13] This was deemed acceptable. US planning for the postwar peace had by that stage developed an ambitious global political and economic framework within which the British Empire played an important part.

The 'War and Peace Studies Project', initiated in 1939, brought together State Department planners and the 'foreign policy elite' in the shape of the business-based Council on Foreign Relations (CFR). The focus was on the 'requirement[s] of the United States in a world in which it proposes to hold unquestioned power'—a rather more serious predecessor of the Project for the New American Century, one might say. In the early years it was assumed that some portion of the postwar world would be controlled by Germany. The goal was therefore to develop 'an integrated policy to achieve military and economic supremacy for the United States within the non-German world'. This would require plans and action to 'secure the limitation of any exercise of sovereignty by foreign nations that constitutes a threat to the world area essential for the security and economic prosperity of the United States and the Western Hemisphere.' This 'world area' would consist of the British Empire and the Far East, in addition to the Western Hemisphere, a natural integrated economic unit.[14]

At this point the major threat in the non-German world was actually Britain. Lend-lease aid to Britain had to be calibrated carefully. It had to be sufficient to enable the UK to continue the war against Germany, but insufficient for the re-establishment of British pre-eminence. Historians David P. Calleo and Benjamin M. Rowland observe that while the war exhausted British economic power, 'To a considerable extent, the United States was responsible.' Throughout the War, US Secretary of State Cordell Hull 'had used the leverage of Lend-Lease skillfully and systematically to reduce Britain to a financial satellite.'[15] Noam Chomsky remarks, considering this analysis, 'There was a mini-war between the United States and Great Britain within the context of the common struggle against Germany, where, of course, Britain was on the front line.'[16]

The US-led non-German bloc was entitled the 'Grand Area' in the CFR-State Department studies. With the gradual decline of German military fortunes, the Grand Area expanded to Western Europe. Noam Chomsky has selected some key statements from the CFR planning documents. Participants recognized that 'the British Empire as it existed in the past will never reappear and . . . the United States may have to take its place.' Another stated that the United States 'must cultivate a mental view toward world settlement after this war which will enable us to impose our own terms, amounting perhaps to a pax-Americana.' Another participant argued that the concept of US security interests should be enlarged to incorporate areas 'strategically necessary for world control.' Professor Chomsky remarks, 'It is a pervasive theme that international trade and investment are closely related to the economic health of the United States, as is access to the resources of the Grand Area, which must be so organized as to guarantee the health and structure of the American economy, its internal structure unmodified.'[17]

'Access to resources' was to be carried out on a rather lopsided basis. Oil was the key world resource, clearly. The reserves of Saudi Arabia were recognized by the State Department as 'a stupendous source of strategic power, and one of the great material prizes in world history.'[18] A State Department memorandum of April 1944 described the 'Petroleum Policy of the United States': US oil companies must have equal access everywhere in the world, but there should be no equal access for others where the US held the upper hand. The policy 'would involve the preservation of the absolute position presently obtaining, and therefore vigilant protection of existing concessions in United States hands coupled with insistence upon the Open Door principle of equal opportunity for United States companies in the new areas.'[19] Open Door for us; Closed Door for you.

The management of British decline, and the assumption of a dominant position supplanting that of the UK, was well illustrated in relation to Middle Eastern oil. For example, Britain was displaced from Saudi Arabia by the simple expedient of extending Lend-Lease to the House of Saud, despite the fact that this was supposed to be a programme for assisting allies fighting the Axis powers, hardly the case with King Ibn Saud. US oil companies had told President Roosevelt that direct US Lend-Lease assistance for King Saud was the only way to keep their Arabian oil concession from falling into British hands. The President notified the Lend-Lease administrator, 'In order to enable you to arrange Lend Lease aid to the government of Saudi Arabia, I hereby find that the defense of Saudi Arabia is vital to the defense of the United States.'[20]

To take a later example of the same process, the British were elbowed out of their dominant position in Iran during the course of a CIA-MI6 coup against the elected nationalist Government of Mohammed Mussadiq in 1953. After the US poured in $1 million, and Britain $1.5 million to destabilize the country, General Zahidi, a US–UK favourite, toppled Mr Mussadiq and enabled the re-invigorated Shah of Iran to take control once again. The Shah quickly agreed new oil concession arrangements with the

West, which resulted in Britain's interest being reduced to 40 per cent of the oil, while US oil companies, allowed to hold an interest in Iran for the first time, also received a 40 per cent concession. Thus the CIA's first major covert operation, carried out in co-operation with MI6, enabled US oil companies to penetrate a country which had previously been closed to them by British power, a matter of some bitterness in Whitehall. The US share of total Middle East oil rose from 44 per cent to 58 per cent in the aftermath of the Iranian coup, while Britain's share dropped from 53 per cent to 24 per cent, leading the British ambassador to the US, Sir Roger Makins to ask, 'Are the Americans consciously trying to substitute their influence for ours in the Middle East?'[21] (Incidentally, the Shah's regime set new standards for the systematic use of torture as a means of political control while continuing to enjoy diplomatic and material support from the West.)

London's subservient position within the transatlantic relationship was brutally enforced in 1956, when Britain and France made the mistake of believing they still had an independent political and military role in the Middle East. The Suez invasion (coordinated with Israel) was brought to a speedy and ignominious halt by the use of US financial power. In his study of the Suez Crisis, W. Scott Lucas concludes that the most important factor in the British decision to halt the invasion of Egypt was US pressure on the weak pound: 'In the first week of November [1956], $85 million of the foreign reserves, almost five per cent of the total, was lost.'[22]

From this point on, British policymakers adapted to the role of regional enforcer in the Persian/Arabian Gulf on behalf of Washington, until growing economic weakness forced Britain to withdraw from east of Suez in 1971. The 'vital interests' remained the same. In the aftermath of Suez, in January 1958, British Foreign Secretary Selwyn Lloyd summarised British interests in the Gulf thus:

(a) to ensure free access for Britain and other Western countries to oil products produced in States bordering the Gulf; (b) to ensure the continued availability of that oil on favourable terms and for sterling; and to maintain suitable arrangements for the investment of the surplus revenues of Kuwait; (c) to bar the spread of Communism and pseudo-Communism in the area and subsequently beyond; and, as a pre-condition of this, to defend the area against the brand of Arab nationalism under cover of which the Soviet Government at present prefers to advance.[23]

The supply and pricing of oil were important considerations (adjusted to ensure a 'favourable' rate of profit for British oil companies), as was the re-investment of Kuwaiti oil revenues in the faltering British economy. Fundamental to both goals was the suppression of Arab and Iranian nationalism which might direct the current of oil revenues away from the needs of wealthy and powerful Westerners towards the needs of the people of the region.

Despite the use of Cold War rhetoric invoking the struggle against international Communism in order to legitimise the Western assault on Third World nationalism, the truth was sometimes admitted by policymakers. US Under Secretary of Defence for Policy Robert Komer admitted in 1980 that 'the most immediate threat in the Indian Ocean area is not an overt Russian attack, but rather internal instability, coups, subversion.' President Reagan was clearer: 'Saudi Arabia we will not permit to be an Iran.'[24] The threat was nationalism. The fear was of popular uprisings against the dictatorships imposed by the United States and Britain.

GREECE, ITALY AND THE MIDDLE EAST

In 1944, British policymakers became concerned at the extent of Moscow's ambitions in Europe and beyond. Foreign Minister Anthony Eden worried that 'Russia has vast aims and that these may include the domination of Eastern Europe and *even* the Mediterranean and the "communizing" of much that remains.' British historian John Kent remarks, 'The prime concern was not Russian dominance over Poland, Hungary, Czechoslovakia or Romania (and in Churchill's case Bulgaria), but whether such dominance would be used to undermine British interests in the Mediterranean. More precisely, the British were worried, and increasingly so, that in Greece the military campaigns for the liberation of the country would not enable them to establish the kind of friendly government deemed necessary to preserve their Mediterranean dominance.'[25] Domination of the Mediterranean was necessary to maintain dominance over the oil reserves of the Middle East, and to maintain control of the sea lanes to the Far East, where lay the outlying links of the British Empire.

In June 1944, the Foreign Office recognized in a paper submitted to the British Cabinet that while the partisans of the Resistance might be spreading Communist ideas, the Russians were not. While there was no detectable central organisation out to convert the Balkans to Communism, there was a spread of Russian influence which seemed to be intended to secure a predominant position for the USSR in southeastern Europe 'by forming governments subservient to Russia.' There were different ways of forestalling this outcome. 'The option of an Anglo-Soviet self-denying ordinance in Greece, Yugoslavia and Albania was definitely ruled out,' British historian John Kent observes. Even if the Soviets had agreed to stay out of the region, it would have been 'unacceptable' in the view of the Foreign Office, for Britain not to 'play an active part' in the internal affairs of Greece and Yugoslavia.[26] Britain had to dominate Greece in order to dominate the Mediterranean, all the fine words of the Atlantic Charter notwithstanding. To protect Greece from Russian influence by abandoning hopes of British domination of the country was unacceptable.

In the aftermath of the European portion of the Second World War, Sir Orme Sargent, one of the most influential policymakers in Whitehall, wrote a celebrated memorandum entitled 'Stocktaking on V-E Day', immediately before the Potsdam Conference of the Allies. In order to re-establish the position of the British Empire, Sir Orme proposed that Britain should 'organise under our leadership the lesser colonial powers who have a stake in the Far East' and establish a firm hold in Asia. 'We are perhaps in danger of regarding ourselves as a European Power and tend to overlook the fact that we are still the centre of an Empire. If we cease to regard ourselves as a World Power we shall gradually cease to be one.' In Europe,

> it must be an essential feature of our European policy to maintain close and friendly relations with Italy, Greece and Turkey, so as to secure our strategic position in the Eastern Mediterranean, especially now that Russia, stretching down from the North is once again exerting pressure on this all important link between Great Britain on the one hand, and India, Malaya, Australia, New Zealand and our Persian and Iraq oil supplies on the other.[27]

'Close and friendly relations' was a euphemism for 'maximum political and economic domination', and the termination of independent nationalism. So there was a connection between Iraqi and Iranian oil on the one hand, and the crushing of the Greek Resistance and the neutralization of the Italian partisans on the other.

The problems for Britain and the United States in the aftermath of the Second World War were 'chaos' and 'Bolshevism': technical terms not referring to social disruption or the spread of Communist ideas, but meaning independent nationalism and radical democracy in action. The popular movements developing from the anti-fascist Resistance threatened to re-shape societies in strategic regions in a way that would prevent British and US domination, and the construction of an overarching global framework within which US and British economic and financial interests could thrive.

ELBOW ROOM FOR DOMINANT INTERESTS

The CFR planners who devised the concept of the Grand Area were explicit in recognizing that this 'world area' was required in order to provide 'the "elbow room"'. . . needed in order to survive without major readjustments'. The new imperial domain was not needed in order for the US economy to survive. The US economy would have survived anyway. The re-taking of as much of the British Empire as possible (and the Middle East and the Mediterranean in particular) was not necessary for the survival of the British economy. The British economy would have survived anyway. Survival in a non-imperial framework, however, would have meant 'major readjustments', adjustments that Noam Chomsky points out would have spelled major changes in the distribution of power, wealth, ownership and control in US and British society.[28]

The US and British world empires were built and re-built after the war, the anti-fascist Resistance movements of Greece, Italy, Vietnam and other countries were dispersed, and collaborators and fascists re-installed in power throughout the globe, in order to maintain the power and wealth of those who direct and profit from international trade, those who maintain hundreds of billions of dollars worth of foreign private investment in different countries around the globe, those who own and manage the private empires known as 'transnational corporations'.

Three years after the end of the Second World War, the head of the State Department Policy Planning Staff spoke out frankly as to the path ahead for the United States:

[W]e have about 50% of the world's wealth, but only 6.3% of its population . . . In this situation, we cannot fail to be the object of envy and resentment. Our real task in the coming period is to devise a pattern of relationships which will permit us to maintain this position of disparity without positive detriment to our national security. To do so, we will have to dispense with all sentimentality and day-dreaming; and our attention will have to be concentrated everywhere on our immediate national objectives. We need not deceive ourselves that we can afford today the luxury of altruism and world-benefaction . . . We should cease to talk about vague and—for the Far East—unreal objectives such as human rights, the raising of the living standards, and democratization. The day is not far off when we are going to have to deal in straight power concepts. The less we are then hampered by idealistic slogans, the better.[29]

Noam Chomsky notes that the author, George Kennan, was 'one of the most thoughtful and humane of US planners', who left his pivotal position in US policy formation soon after making this prescription 'because he was considered not sufficiently tough-minded for this harsh world.'[30]

Professor Chomsky also observes that a critical issue for US policymakers was to maintain 'positions of disparity' internally, *within* the United States. Planners 'recognized early on that more egalitarian social arrangements at home might reduce the need to protect the Fifth Freedom abroad.'[31]

CAPITALISM'S WAR

The right-wing British newspaper the *Daily Telegraph* drew a familiar parallel in commenting on the position of Tony Blair a week before the decisive vote in the House of Commons on 18 March on whether to go to war against Iraq:

> Within a month, we should know whether Tony Blair stands comparison with Winston Churchill, or with Ramsay MacDonald. Will his resolution ensure that Britain can successfully take part in a war, renew the most important alliance in its history and rise above the carping short-sightedness of our two main EU partners? Or will an unpopular war break his hold over his party, offer an opening to the Conservatives and leave Britain friendless in a Europe that has decisively thrown off the American yoke?
>
> In 1931, the first Labour prime minister was thought to have capitulated to the needs of capitalism in the slump. Will the latest, and hitherto most successful, of Labour prime ministers be dismissed for having slavishly prosecuted capitalism's war?[32]

The war on Iraq was indeed 'capitalism's war', designed to reinforce positions of disparity internationally, between the Great Powers and the colonial areas, and internally, between US and British ruling elites and the general populations of these two warrior states. Fascism and anti-fascism were not decisive factors for British and US decision-makers in the 1940s; they are not decisive today. What is decisive is the enduring conception of 'vital interests' that in truth are the interests of those who own and manage the private empires that dominate modern capitalism.

CHAPTER XXIV
Regime Unchanged

Politics today begins and ends with 11 September. British and US war leaders attempted to win support for the invasion of Iraq by appealing to the memory of the multiple atrocities carried out on that day. On 15 February 2003, facing the prospect of millions of people demonstrating in Britain and around the world in an enormous popular convulsion against the planned war, the editors of the *Daily Telegraph* asked, 'Will today's protesters spare a thought for the victims of September 11 ... How many protestors can honestly reply "yes" to the question: would I be marching today if the attacks on September 11 had been, not on New York and Washington, but on London?'[1] Musician Michael Stipe, vocalist for the group 'REM', was woken in his New York flat by the first strike on the World Trade Centre. Interviewed during the war on Iraq, Mr Stipe recalled watching events unfold from his window, and said, 'I was so afraid. It was terrifying. At the time it felt like the world was coming to an end. ... I'm not sure I ever will [get over it]. But what happened that day doesn't justify what is happening now in Iraq. To me, there is no connection between the two events.'[2] Mr Stipe joined dozens of other US celebrities such as Gillian Anderson, Lawrence Fishburne, Mia Farrow, and Martin Sheen in signing a petition supporting inspections and rejecting war against Iraq.[3]

In the run-up to war, British Prime Minister Tony Blair engaged in a 'masochism strategy' of appearing on television with opponents of the war. On 26 February 2003, Mr Blair had perhaps his most difficult encounter—with a relative of a victim of 11 September. Facing Joy Bennett, whose son Oliver was one of the British victims of the attacks, Mr Blair said, 'Supposing I'd said in August 2001, a month before September 11, that there was a terrorist network operating out of Afghanistan and we had to take action against it. If we thought they were going to take action against us, don't you think we should in those circumstances be prepared to act?' Mrs Bennett responded firmly, 'I would have far preferred if somehow somebody, who knew there were things going on with terrorism, would have actually protected my son. I don't want anyone to die and I certainly don't want any mother to go through what I've gone through in the last 18 months.'[4] In an online memorial site, Mrs Bennett recalls that her son, killed in the World Trade Centre, was a passionate listener. However, he was not a passive person. 'His withering one-liners,' Mrs. Bennett said, 'could take your breath away.' 'You didn't cross Oli lightly. He let you know just what he thought.'[5] Mr Blair seems to have been rocked by an on-air manifestation of this family trait, which was later compared to the drubbing Margaret Thatcher received over the sinking of the Belgrano at the hands of British home-maker Diana Gould. The *Daily Telegraph* reported, 'Mr Blair appeared surprised and struggled to answer [Mrs Bennett], before insisting: "Look, I do not want to go to war."'[6] Mrs Bennett formed a different view, based on a further half hour's conversation with the Prime Minister after the cameras had stopped rolling: 'He was listening to what we were saying but I don't feel that we, or anybody else really, can change his mind.'[7]

Would military action against Afghanistan in August 2001 have prevented the atrocities of 11 September 2001? The most intensive investigation in history has turned up only hints of operational links between the suicide hijack group and the al-Qaeda leadership based in Afghanistan. To put it mildly, it does not appear to have been established that if the network's leadership in Central Asia had been killed or captured weeks before the attacks were due to begin, Mohammed Atta's small group of suicidal fanatics several thousands of miles away would have been so disoriented and dismayed that it would have abandoned its long-prepared plans for mass killing.

An act of self-defence can only be legitimate in international law if it is capable of warding off an attack; if it is directed towards warding off that attack (rather than being a punitive raid); and if it is proportional to the attack being defended against. Pre-emptive acts of self-defence must, at a minimum, obey the same restrictions (there is a debate about whether or not pre-emption can be legal). A pre-emptive war on Afghanistan in August 2001 would not, on the evidence available in mid-2003, have been capable of halting an attack in September 2001 carried out by what appears to have been a semi-autonomous al-Qaeda affiliate that had already built up its own autonomous leadership, logistics and financial stockpile in the United States. The only way to have prevented that particular attack would have been to have apprehended the leadership of the suicide hijackers before they boarded the aircraft they intended to use as weapons. This required police work, not an invasion.

THE INTELLIGENCE FAILURE

Mr Blair tried to persuade Mrs Bennett that the problem in August 2001 was that the world did not know as much about the threat from the suicide hijackers as it now knew (in February 2003) about the threat from Iraq: 'The difficulty is, we didn't have that intelligence.'[8] The implication was that the world, or perhaps more narrowly the British Government, now possessed compelling 'intelligence' regarding the threat from Iraq.

This was another impressive insinuation from a master of spin. The lies and distortions surrounding the drive to war against Iraq might have defeated Jonathan Swift. It nearly defeated British comedian Armando Iannucci, who admitted he was becoming unable to satirize world events in successive *Daily Telegraph* columns in January 2003, a process which culminated a few weeks later in a heartfelt plea for readers of the most right-wing newspaper in Britain to attend the anti-war demonstration in London on 15 February.[9] In the real world, the distortion of the available 'intelligence' by the British and US Governments was so gross and shameless that intelligence officials on both sides of the Atlantic spoke out repeatedly to repudiate the claims of their political masters.

US intelligence officials mocked the British Government (and by implication their own) for accepting forged letters 'proving' that Iraq had attempted to purchase uranium from Niger, despite 'laughable' and 'childlike' errors. 'These are not the kind of forgeries that you would expect to fool a professional intelligence agency,' said one US official.[10]

The lack of real 'intelligence' was such that the British Government released a supposedly intelligence-based dossier on Iraq's concealment of its weapons which was actually largely copied from an article and Ph.D. thesis by Ibrahim al-Marashi. Dr Glen Rangwala of Cambridge University noticed the unacknowledged plagiarism in what is now known as the 'dodgy dossier'—which included typographical and other errors copied from Mr al-Marashi's work.[11] By late June 2003 it had become clear that the 'dodgy dossier' was not approved by the British intelligence services, and was largely the work of Mr Blair's closest advisers. This admission from the Foreign Secretary Jack Straw (which was coupled with an apology to Mr al-Marashi), and the revelation that the document was unknown to the Foreign Office until three days after it had been distributed to the newspapers, came in hearings of a parliamentary inquiry into the affair.[12] Incidentally, the true significance of the 'dodgy dossier', which was concerned with Iraq's concealment capabilities, was pointed out by Dr Paul Maddrell, lecturer in Intelligence and Strategic Studies at the University of Wales. By describing Iraq's extensive concealment measures, it was designed to discredit UNMOVIC by explaining 'how the inspectors would be bamboozled at every turn.'[13]

The earlier British Government dossier on Iraq's weapons was delayed for months because of concerns in Whitehall that the claims made did not stand up. The *Sunday Times* reported in March 2002 that the dossier, compiled by the Joint Intelligence Committee, the apex of British intelligence, contained little new information worth sharing or publishing 'according to insiders'—insiders with access to top secret intelligence, quite possibly intelligence officials themselves.[14] The *Financial Times* reported that there was considerable resistance from senior Whitehall officials, some ministers, and the secret intelligence service MI6: 'the information on Iraq was judged by some Whitehall officials as insufficient to convince critics within the Labour Party that the full-scale offensive against Iraq was justified'.[15]

The row inside the Government over the first weapons dossier spilled out into public view at the end of May 2003, with the admission by a senior intelligence source involved in the drawing up of the dossier that the document had trumpeted material which the intelligence services had not considered worthy of inclusion:

> It was transformed in the week before it was published, to make it sexier. The classic example was the statement that weapons of mass destruction were ready for use within 45 minutes. That information was not in the original draft. It was included in the dossier against our wishes, because it wasn't reliable. Most things in the dossier were double source, but that was single source, and we believed that the source was wrong.[16]

The BBC reporter who broke this story, Andrew Gilligan, told a parliamentary inquiry that other BBC reporters as well as a host of newspaper journalists were also told by intelligence sources of concern over the 'tone and tenor of the dossier'.[17] Peter Beaumont of the *Observer* confirmed Mr Gilligan's statement: MI6 and the Foreign Office (to which MI6 is attached) briefed journalists, including Mr Beaumont himself, that Number 10, and the Prime Minister's closest adviser Alistair Campbell in particular, 'had gone out of its way to overstate the threat posed by Iraq to make the case for war.' Mr Beaumont was told by a middle-ranking intelligence officer around the time of the 15 February demonstrations that the threat was not really as immediate as was being claimed: 'Instead the threat was—as he described it—philosophical. It was contingent on a chain of events that allowed material into the hands of a group that might want and know how to use it. It was a difficult case to make, he admitted, because of all the ifs.' In late June 2003, Mr Beaumont consulted a friend with a wide range of contacts inside MI6, who reported that there had been a 'massive breakdown of trust between the Secret Intelligence Service [MI6] and Number 10.'[18]

One key issue leading to the breakdown of relations between intelligence services and their political masters on both sides of the Atlantic was the politically necessary, but logically implausible and factually bereft assertion of a connection asserted between Saddam Hussein's secular totalitarian police state and Osama bin Laden's fundamentalist terrorist network. It was this issue which prompted US and British intelligence officials to speak out angrily to deny Colin Powell's claims regarding the fantasy 'Zarqawi network', supposedly headed by the Jordanian Islamist Abu Musab al-Zarqawi. Mr Zarqawi was said by Mr Powell to be 'an associate and collaborator of Usama bin Laden and his al-Qaida lieutenants', but in fact was so unrelated to the terrorist network that even after Mr Powell's 5 February 2003 speech the UN committee investigating al-Qaeda did not even bother to inquire into his involvement.[19]

Let us recall the reckless way in which Mr Powell linked Mr Zarqawi, the Iraqi fundamentalist group Ansar al-Islam (which was based in the zone of Iraqi Kurdistan outside Baghdad's control), and Saddam Hussein's regime infuriated members of the United States intelligence community. One intelligence source said, 'The intelligence is practically non-existent,' adding, 'It is impossible to support the bald conclusions being made by the White House and the Pentagon given the poor quantity and quality of the intelligence available. There is uproar within the intelligence community on all of these points, but the Bush White House has quashed dissent.' The *Daily Telegraph* commented, 'This could all be dismissed as a turf war between rival intelligence agencies were it not for the near unanimity across the British and American intelligence communities, including the Defence Intelligence Agency analysts whose bosses produced the line the White House wanted to hear.'[20] British security sources confirmed there was no solid evidence to support Mr Powell's allegations. One referred to 'jumping to conclusions,' and suggested that the US was making a leap too far. Another added, 'It is all a question of interpretation', and insisted it was far too early to make a proper assessment of the terrorist networks.[21]

Colin Powell made other allegedly 'intelligence-based' claims in his theatrical performance at the Security Council on 5 February 2003. The interpretation he offered of certain satellite photographs was doubted by a US expert in space imaging, Mark Monmonier of Syracuse University, who said, 'The Bush administration either has little, or is playing its cards very close to the vest.'[22] Chief UN weapons inspector Dr Hans Blix responded even more briskly a few days later: 'The reported movement of munitions at the [Taji] site could just as easily have been a routine activity as a movement of proscribed munitions in anticipation of an imminent inspection.'[23]

What the inspectors wanted, said Dr Blix, was not transcripts of ambiguous telephone conversations, but more and better intelligence on sites to investigate. A senior member of the UN weapons inspection team (probably Dr Blix himself) told a British newspaper in late February,

> It took a long time for the US to hand over intelligence in the first place and when they did it has proved to be highly inaccurate. Intelligence is circumstantial, outdated or completely wrong. It's wasting our time and our resources. Frankly we have better things to do than run around the country chasing bogus so-called evidence.

The inspectors said that they had found nothing at an alleged nuclear research site shown in satellite pictures presented to the UN by Mr Powell. They found nothing at one of Saddam's palaces where they were given precise map co-ordinates of supposedly incriminating evidence. The inspectors said they had been fed 'garbage after garbage after garbage' by the US.[24]

The difference between the work of the inspectors and the propaganda of the warrior states was that the inspectors were able to engage in detailed investigation on the ground to provide considered and factual statements, while Mr Powell and other British and US leaders were trading in allegations, insinuations and exaggerations based, if they had any grounding in reality, on the accusations of defectors and oppositionists. The aluminium tubes were a classic example of this divergence. Iraq tried to buy some high-specification aluminium tubes. The US said that they were too good to be used for conventional rockets (as Baghdad claimed) and that they could have been adapted to be used in a nuclear weapons programme, and that this was Iraq's intention. The International Atomic Energy Agency conducted an investigation for over a month, examining the minutes and other documents of a string of Iraqi procurement committees, dating back over many years, and concluded, firstly, that the Iraqis had simply got the specifications wrong, and, secondly, that it was 'highly unlikely' that the tubes could have been re-engineered for the purposes claimed in Washington.[25]

Mr Blair told Mrs Bennett, 'The difficulty is, we didn't have that intelligence' in advance of 11 September that we had concerning Iraq. The 'intelligence' seems to have been fairly clear. The available 'intelligence' was distorted even beyond the tolerance of US and British intelligence officials. What the 'intelligence' amounted to was a case for rigorous inspections. A year before the war began, a former IAEA inspector said, 'The evidence produced so far is worrying. It is an argument for getting the inspectors back in as fast as possible, but not for going to war.'[26] While the next twelve months saw an increase in allegations and claims, there was no appreciable change in the publicly available evidence, and strong indications from the intelligence services that the privately held intelligence was no more conclusive. In April 2003, a 'high-level UK source' was reported as saying that intelligence agencies on both sides of the Atlantic were furious that briefings they gave political leaders were distorted in the rush to war with Iraq. A British intelligence source said, 'What we have is a few strands of highly circumstantial evidence, and to justify an attack on Iraq it is being presented as a cast-iron case.'[27]

It was not sufficient to prove that Iraq had weapons of mass destruction (something that was not proved before the war took place). For there to be a possibility of justifying military action, it had to be shown, firstly, that Iraq was planning imminently to attack another country, and, secondly, that the invasion would and could avert that attack. Neither of these arguments was even assayed.

TORPEDOING THE INSPECTORS

Non-military means had not been exhausted on 17 March 2003. The policy of the Bush Administration was to undermine and frustrate those non-military methods of dealing with Iraq's suspected weapons programmes. President Bush pointedly did not call for the return of the UN weapons inspectors, even when addressing the UN General Assembly on 12 September 2002. A few weeks earlier, Vice-President Cheney had said that the return of the inspectors would risk providing 'false comfort' regarding Iraq's weapons. When the Iraqis unconditionally accepted the return of the inspectors on 16 September, the US threatened to 'thwart' the return of the inspectors until a new Resolution had been passed—that resolution was designed to be objectionable to the Iraqi Government, and to be refused. The US was hoping to prevent the return of the inspectors.

Right-wing commentator Con Coughlin, author of *Saddam: The Secret Life*, wrote on 17 November 2002, 'Many on Bush's team hoped the President would order a devastating bombardment of Saddam's key command and control sites as early as this week. That cannot happen now that Saddam has signed up to the UN Security Council resolution setting out strict terms and conditions for the inspection teams.' Saddam Hussein's decision to capitulate had made an invasion impossible, 'at least in the short term.' Mr Coughlin added, 'The fear now stalking the Bush administration is that Saddam's concession to the UN could put off the day of invasion for ever, thwarting any attempt to bring about the one thing that the President has so often insisted is necessary for world security: regime change in Baghdad.' It was Iraqi compliance that was the problem.

A US official told Mr Coughlin, 'So long as Saddam behaves himself, the inspection process could go on for months. There is only a relatively small window of opportunity for us to take military action early next year before the weather conditions will make it really difficult. So if Saddam can string this out until next spring—he is safe.' Among the hawks, the blame lay not with Saddam Hussein: 'some of these officials seem to think that the real "axis of evil" consists not so much of Iraq, Iran and North Korea, but of Colin Powell, Kofi Annan, the UN Secretary General, and Dr Hans Blix':

Donald Rumsfeld and Dick Cheney wanted to tackle Saddam unilaterally, without bothering with the Security Council or Hans Blix. They agreed to go through the UN only on the assumption that Mr Powell would persuade the UN to pass a resolution whose conditions were so uncompromising, and such a flagrant breach of Iraq's sovereignty, that Saddam simply could not possibly agree to them. The conditions should be designed to be rejected, and so to trigger war—much in the same way that the conditions that the Serbs were offered by the Clinton administration at Fontainebleu were designed to be rejected by Slobodan Milosevic.[28]

While publicly President Bush praised Resolution 1441, '[p]rivately, however, the President's close advisers are saying that Mr Powell made far too many concessions in the final stages of negotiations to secure Security Council support.' The time permitted to Iraq was too long. 'Things would, however, be even worse if the weapons inspectors come back and report that the Iraqi regime has fulfilled the terms of Resolution 1441. The pressure to lift sanctions on Iraq would then start to become irresistible, for the country would have complied with the conditions whose breach led to the imposition of sanctions in the first place.'

It was not Iraqi weapons that were the threat, it was Iraqi compliance. It was not the possible failure of the inspectors that was the fear, it was their possible success. The issue of Iraq's weapons of mass destruction was agreed as the leading propaganda tool for 'bureaucratic reasons', leading US official Paul Wolfowitz confessed after the war. Picking weapons of mass destruction was 'the one reason everyone could agree on.'[29] The war was desired for other reasons.

THE CHALLENGE OF CREDIBILITY

Con Coughlin indicated what some of these other reasons might be in his 17 November 2002 article:

> The inevitable result of Saddam's mere survival in power, never mind flourishing with billions from oil revenues, would be a serious blow to President Bush, who has staked his credibility on removing Saddam. It would also dent US prestige by confirming that the US could be 'defeated' by a sufficiently determined, and flexible, opponent.[30]

While the President's personal prestige was no doubt a major factor in the Administration's policy, there was, as the *Telegraph* columnist points out, the larger issue of US 'credibility'. If Saddam Hussein were able to defy Washington and still survive, and perhaps to win the suspension of economic sanctions by co-operating with UN weapon inspectors, this would be a blow to the image of the United States. The Iraqi President's continued rule of Iraq would be a 'defeat' for Washington, even if the UN weapons inspectors searched out all of Iraq's hidden weapons and concluded that he had no weapons of mass destruction at the ready—even if they installed the most intrusive Ongoing Monitoring and Verification (OMV) system in the history of the world.

Tony Blair explained the need for 'credibility' in his final address to the House of Commons on 18 March, before the crucial motion authorising war against Iraq. He condemned the path of continuing with 'strong language but with weak intentions'. When 'the threat' returned, who then would believe us (when we threatened them)? 'What price our credibility with the next tyrant?'[31]

> That is why this indulgence has to stop—because it is dangerous: dangerous if such regimes disbelieve us; dangerous if they think they can use our weakness, our hesitation, and even the natural urges of our democracy towards peace against us; and dangerous because one day they will mistake our innate revulsion against war for permanent incapacity, when, in fact, if pushed to the limit, we will act. But when we act, after years of pretence, the action will have to be harder, bigger, more total in its impact. It is true that Iraq is not the only country with weapons of mass destruction, but I say this to the House: back away from this confrontation now, and future conflicts will be infinitely worse and more devastating in their effects.[32]

This was not about disarmament, or non-proliferation, or weapons of mass destruction. When the masters of the world have issued a threat, they must carry it through, or be forced to be even more destructive in their response to future acts of disobedience. If Iraq were disarmed by non-military means, and Saddam Hussein survived once again, this would have caused intolerable damage to the fearsome image of the US and Britain.

Noam Chomsky has remarked that the concept of 'credibility' in international affairs is akin to the 'credibility' of the Mafia Don. It reduces the systemic costs of maintaining the system if everyone obeys instantly. If one person defies the Don and survives un-punished, this can cause ripples of resistance and rebellion which requires much greater efforts to subdue. A startling demonstration of the costs of disobedience every so often is a cost-effective way of keeping the machine running smoothly. If the analogy with the Mafia seems far-fetched, it is sobering to be told that one of the favourite sayings of Mr Donald Rumsfeld is, 'You will get more with a kind word and a gun than with a kind word alone.' A quotation from Al Capone. *Newsweek* editor Fareed Zakaria commented on this revelation in March 2003:

> But should the guiding philosophy of the world's leading democracy really be the tough talk of a Chicago mobster? In terms of effectiveness, this strategy has been a disaster . . . Having traveled around the world and met with senior government officials in dozens of countries over the past year, I can report that with the exception of Britain and Israel, every country the administration has dealt with feels humiliated by it . . . The point is to scare our enemies, not terrify the rest of the world.[33]

Some months earlier, *Time* magazine carried a summary of the results of a discussion between the President and Vice-President:

> Both Bush and Cheney had long agreed that US foreign policy had gotten flabby over the years. A clear and aggressive posture, on the other hand, could act as a deterrent to mischief-

makers and compel countries to bend to US pressure. How do you behave enough like a thug to convince your enemies you are serious, but enough like a statesman to bring the allies on board?[34]

The *Daily Telegraph*, ideologically close to the Bush Administration, was frank: 'Opponents of the war are right about one thing. We will not be fighting *only* for the UN; the conflict is also—as Lord Salisbury described the Boer War—about "who is to be boss".' This was 'nothing to be ashamed of,' suggested the *Telegraph*.[35]

UN Resolution 687, which promised the partial lifting of sanctions in return for weapons disarmament, was broken by the publicly announced determination of the US Government to continue with sanctions until Saddam Hussein was deposed. Security Council Resolution 1154, which kept decisions on how to deal with Iraqi non-co-operation in the hands of the Security Council, was broken by the unilateral Anglo-American aerial assault nine months later, in December 1998. Resolution 1284, which set out a procedure for the conduct of inspections, was broken by the ultimatum ordering UN weapons inspectors out of Iraq on 17 March 2003. The founding document of the United Nations, the UN Charter, which forbids the use of force except in self-defence, was set aside as an irrelevance. The Security Council was systematically abused by Washington and London. The UN was praised when useful as a tool of US power, and denigrated or ignored when it became an obstacle to the exercise of domination.

The war on Iraq was also a war against the authority of the United Nations, a war for the thuggish 'credibility' of the Anglo-American boss-states.

DESTROYING THE INSPECTORS

In January 2003, Secretary of State Powell said that, 'Inspections will not work.' Only too true. They were not permitted to work.

The UN inspectors could have done two things. Firstly, they could have investigated the status of Iraq's suspected weapons programmes, disarming whatever weapons and equipment they came across (as happened with 70 al-Samoud missiles in March 2003). Secondly, and more importantly, they could have installed and maintained a new Ongoing Monitoring and Verification system which would have prevented Iraq from re-starting its prohibited weapons programmes. Colin Powell claimed before the Security Council that the Iraqi chemical weapons programme was 'inspection-proof', embedded in the commercial chemical industry. This was the very reverse of the truth, as he well knew. With their high-technology cameras and other sensors in position, relaying images and data live to Baghdad and New York, the inspectors were capable of monitoring in real time the configuration and condition of Iraq's chemical and biological industries. UNMOVIC inspectors in New York would have been able to determine remotely whether Iraq's industries were in a civilian or a military mode of operation.

It was this capacity that was at the heart of former UNSCOM inspector Scott Ritter's proposal for 'qualitative disarmament' in Iraq. If the choke points of the Iraqi weapons programmes were monitored closely, the outside world could have a high level of confidence that Iraq was not reconstructing its arsenal of weapons of mass destruction. This was a threat to US plans for 'leadership change' in Iraq, and had to be swept aside.

Resolution 1284 required the inspectors to propose a plan for the Ongoing Monitoring and Verification system. It also required them to define the remaining 'key disarmament tasks' for Iraq to complete. The Draft Work Programme that contained these two crucial documents was circulated on 17 March 2003, hours before President Bush's ultimatum to Saddam Hussein also ejected the UN inspectors. The Draft Work Programme has been dismissed from history, nullified in every way by the President's ultimatum. It is possible that the schedule for war was advanced precisely because of the imminent publication of the inspectors' blueprint for disarming Iraq, which would have initiated a new and decisive phase of inspections and postponed the war to the autumn.

On 9 March, Tony Blair's official spokesperson said, 'We believe the Blix process is now complete.'[36] Eight days later, the Blix process, far from being complete, was about to be properly launched for the first time, with the definition of Iraq's 'key remaining disarmament tasks', in a Resolution-based process that a British Foreign Minister had once described as 'the way forward', a 'win-win for everybody'. The Blix process was terminated not because the inspectors reported obstruction by the Iraqi authorities, or shocking new finds, or because they had come to the end of the road. The road was opening up: Baghdad was co-operating on an unprecedented scale, and the inspectors said they were mere months away from solid conclusions regarding Iraq's weapons programmes. The road was blown up by Washington.

We now know that the Security Council was on the verge of an extraordinary consensus, which would have given Iraq and the inspectors 30 days to demonstrate the viability of a non-military solution to the inspection crisis. France and Britain were near to making the compromises necessary to secure a second UN Resolution, which would have left the door open for the initiation of the 'key disarmament tasks' process, and which would have broken decisively the fragile unity between London and Washington. This prospect may have been another factor in hurrying President Bush into war, despite the disadvantages of starting the bombing on the moonlit nights of mid-March.

THE RELUCTANT LEADER-FOLLOWER

The Prime Minister nearly did not follow President Bush into war. He was forced to issue threats of resignation to secure a majority of his own Labour MPs in the British Parliament; he had to order the Ministry of Defence to draw up contingency plans to withdraw from the invasion force just days before the expected onset of war; and he nearly broke with Washington and agreed with Paris to set Iraq a 30-day ultimatum.

The Prime Minister had no wish to rely on the UN Security Council for a new Resolution. A year before the war, newspaper reports suggested that while the Foreign Office favoured obtaining some form of authorization from the Security Council, Mr Blair's advisers were unenthusiastic, foreseeing a Russian veto.[37] The Prime Minister was forced reluctantly back to the Security Council by the weight of the anti-war movement, both inside and outside the Labour Party. There he suffered a 'diplomatic trainwreck' which left him almost entirely bereft of legal and political cover.

The Prime Minister had no wish to hold a Commons debate to authorize the use of force. This reluctance reached ridiculous heights with the argument in early February (typically advanced by Defence Minister Geoff Hoon) that the British armed forces needed to preserve the advantage of surprise: 'As has always been the case it would simply not be sensible to signal in advance our intentions to the enemy.' Diane Abbott, a Black Labour MP, responded, 'Given the size of the US and British deployment in the region and the hundreds of thousands of forces amassing on Iraq's borders, the likelihood of any attack being a surprise is remote. You're going to have to come up with something better than that to explain to the British people why the US Congress can have a vote before its troops are sent into action but somehow the British parliament is denied such a vote.'[38] In the end, there were several debates, and one motion of authorization on 18 March. In Turkey, such a parliamentary vote on participation in the war was necessary because of the Turkish constitution. In Britain, the vote was forced on a reluctant premier by the power of the anti-war movement.

TONY BLAIR LIED

The Prime Minister made a fateful promise, expressed in a press conference on 13 January, and on the BBC's *Newsnight* programme on 7 February 2003:

> The only qualification we have added . . . is if you did have a breach, went back to the UN but someone put an unreasonable or unilateral block down on action, now in those circumstances we have said we can't be in a position where we are confined in that way.[39]
>
> If the inspectors do report that they can't do their work properly because Iraq is not co-operating there's no doubt that under the terms of the existing United Nations Resolution that that's a breach of the Resolution. In those circumstances there should be a further Resolution. If, however, a country were to issue a veto . . . If a country unreasonably in those circumstances put down a veto then I would consider action outside of that . . . Firstly you can't just do it with America, you have to get a majority in the security council . . . because the issue of a veto doesn't even arise unless you get a majority in the security council.[40]

The inspectors did not report any obstruction or lack of co-operation. There was no majority in favour of the Resolution. There was no 'unreasonable' veto of the British Resolution. Britain withdrew the Resolution before it came to a vote. Yet the Prime Minister still refused to be 'confined' by international law. He was questioned in the House of Commons:

> Mr. Alex Salmond (Banff and Buchan): The Prime Minister says that the French have changed position, but surely the French, Russians and Chinese always made it clear that they would oppose a second resolution that led automatically to war. [Interruption.] Well they

publicised that view at the time of resolution 1441. Is it not the Prime Minister who has changed his position? A month ago, he said that the only circumstances in which he would go to war without a second resolution was if the inspectors concluded that there had been no more progress, which they have not; if there were a majority on the Security Council, which there is not; and if there were an unreasonable veto from one country, but there are three permanent members opposed to the Prime Minister's policy. When did he change his position, and why?[41]

Mr Blair's only response was to explain why 'the hon. Gentleman is absolutely wrong about the position on resolution 1441.' He refused to deal with the substance of the question, which was unanswerable. Yet this breach of a clearly stated promise was fatal to his claims of honesty and integrity. The mass media and the political system consigned the issue to the memory hole, and protected what has been called the Prime Minister's 'scandal-proof bubble'.[42] His reputation depends on their looking the other way.

When the Prime Minister lied about President Chirac's position, claiming that the French leader wanted to veto military action under any circumstances, the press protected Mr Blair from the consequences of his easily documented deceit, and helped to secure the acquiescence of Labour Party backbenchers.

THE POODLE

Mr Blair had a very uncomfortable year, from the time of the council of war in Crawford, Texas in April 2002 until the war. It was clear that he was most reluctant to go to war with Iraq. In December 2002, a senior Whitehall source said the Prime Minister still hoped to avoid a war: 'Tony Blair has fought hard to go down the UN route and wants it pursued as vigorously as possible. If there is any chance of avoiding a war he will make every effort to seize it.' The *Telegraph* reported then that, 'Despite publicly stating that he will stand alongside America in any action against Iraq, Mr Blair has delayed ordering troops to the Gulf to give diplomacy a chance.' Senior Government sources said the Prime Minister had been reluctant to order the deployment of forces to the Gulf because it was 'politically difficult'. 'The reasons include the "overstretch" in the Army caused by the firemen's strike, the Treasury's reluctance to release the money for a major deployment and the strong opposition in the Labour Party.'[43] The anti-war movement inside and outside the Labour Party was reaching a size and scale that was seriously worrying Downing Street.

The *Daily Telegraph* reported that the resumption of inspections had 'raised hope among some British officials that the process would stretch out over several months and that America would revert to a policy of containment rather than "regime change" through military force.' According to authoritative sources, the Prime Minister delayed decisions on military deployments, because he 'wanted to ensure that the UN had a free rein to exploit all diplomatic efforts and to give weapons inspectors a reasonable period to do their work.'[44] The Diplomatic Editor of the *Daily Telegraph*, Anton La Guardia, wrote, 'The resumption of weapons inspections in Iraq puts in place another element of Britain's unspoken diplomatic strategy: the "dual containment" of Saddam Hussein and

America's hawks.' Some senior British officials were talking of a prolonged inspection period that put off the war indefinitely. 'Iraq is not a global threat. It's a regional threat,' said one senior Whitehall source. 'The policy of containment, if done properly, is the most desirable. If Iraq can be contained, the risks of war will outweigh the benefits.' While US hawks saw Resolution 1441 as a 'trigger' for war, British officials hoped it would be a 'safety catch' that would establish their preferred policy of containment.[45]

No wonder the US hawks learned to hate the British.

The pattern set during the February 2001 airstrikes on Iraq held throughout the year-long run-up to the war: public transatlantic solidarity; private US contempt for the British; private British reluctance and deep concern at the political costs of confrontation.

THE FATE OF IRAQ'S WEAPONS

What did happen to Iraq's weapons of mass destruction? A US Senate delegation to Iraq at the end of June 2003 came back with the suggestion that Iraq had had a weapons programme. Senator Carl Levin, a Democrat from Michigan, said, 'We were told that there was some evidence, which we should not reach any conclusion on, that there might have been a program that could lead to a relatively rapid constitution of a weapon.' Senator Jay Rockefeller, a Democrat from West Virginia, and the ranking Democrat on the Senate Intelligence Committee, suggested that Republicans were attempting to blur an important distinction between a programme and actual ready-to-go weapons.[46]

A key piece of evidence was the revelation in June 2003 that Iraqi intelligence agencies ran a network of secret cells that carried out chemical and biological research but produced no weapons. 'The laboratories were hidden in basements in houses around Baghdad with teams of just three or four people,' said a senior Iraqi intelligence officer, who procured supplies for the programme through an international network of front companies. 'But it was all just theory. The aim was to keep us up to date and ready so that if the sanctions were lifted or we needed to produce chemical or biological weapons again, we could start up immediately.' The officer, a general, insisted that US and British search teams would find no weapons. According to the general, the research programme was set up in 1996: 'We did small trials, experiments in basements or rooms. From the outside nobody would guess. But because of these cells we could start up production again very easily.' The existence of 'the forbidden programme' was confirmed by Dr Ala Saeed, who was head of quality control at the Al-Muthanna State Establishment, Iraq's main chemical weapons complex.[47]

This was consistent with the account given by the most important source of high-grade information about Iraq's weapons of mass destruction programmes ever obtained by the UN weapons inspectors: General Hussein Kamel, the former director of Iraq's Military Industrialization Corporation, was in charge of Iraq's missile programme and its chemical, nuclear and biological weapons programme for ten years until his defection to Jordan in August 1995. The general, Saddam Hussein's son-in-law, took crates of documents revealing past weapons programmes, and provided these to UNSCOM.

In an interview on 22 August 1995, Hussein Kamel told UN weapons inspectors, 'I ordered destruction of all chemical weapons. All weapons—biological, chemical, missile, nuclear—were destroyed.' He testified that after visits from inspectors the stocks of anthrax (which he described as the 'main focus' of the biological weapons programme) were completely destroyed. He said to the inspectors, 'You have [an] important role in Iraq with this. You should not underestimate yourself. You are very effective in Iraq.' All missiles were destroyed, but blueprints and moulds for production were retained. The transcript of this interview was leaked to *Newsweek* and then to Dr Glen Rangwala of Cambridge University at the end of February 2003.[48] The story was not taken up despite its significance for the central issue of the day.[49]

Dr Rangwala pointed out that US and British leaders (including President Bush, Prime Minister Blair, and Secretary of State Powell) all cited Hussein Kamel's revelations about the existence of Iraq's biological weapons programmes before 1991, but never mentioned the general's further revelations that these and other prohibited weapons had all been destroyed in 1991, and the programmes put in cold storage. At the time of his interview, Hussein Kamel was a defector, expecting to secure Western support in an attempt to overthrow and replace Saddam Hussein. He had no reason to support the regime he had just left behind, and his disclosures about the previous weapons programmes were deeply embarassing for Baghdad—as was his frank admission that documents and components for the weapons programmes had been secreted for the future resumption of weapons production.

AFTER MAJAR AL-KABIR

It seems entirely possible that no weapons of mass destruction will be found in Iraq, certainly none capable of being 'deployed' within 45 minutes as claimed in the British Government's September 2002 dossier. What then of the other major justification given for the war?

It is hazardous to speculate about the future of Iraq, but certain trends and patterns are clear even at the time of writing. The British and US Governments intend to recreate the former regime of Saddam Hussein in some form or other, and this is putting them on a collision course with the mobilized majority community. Referring to the experience of Liberation after the Second World War, it seems that the French precedent is no longer at all likely. In France, the Allies were forced to treat with General de Gaulle, but he did deliver for them, as his triumphant return home sealed the fate for the domestic, radical democratic, Resistance. At the time of writing, the Wolfowitz faction appears to have accepted that Ahmad Chalabi, leader of the Iraqi National Congress, will not play, if he was ever suitable for, and if he ever wished to play, the role of Charles de Gaulle, making his peace with the collaborators of the old regime.

The options therefore, in terms of relations with the popular movements, are either for the Italian model of peaceful subjugation of the popular movements, or the Greek precedent for unashamed colonial warfare against the anti-fascist Resistance. The key issues are likely to be demobilization and disarmament, the trigger issues for the Greek conflict. The deaths of six British soldiers (and an unknown number of Iraqis) in Majar al-Kabir on 24 June 2003 may presage further conflict over the issue of disarmament.

According to initial reports, British forces had signed an agreement not to conduct house-to-house weapons searches in Majar al-Kabir ('There is no necessity that the coalition and its different people be there [in the town]'[50]). In return, heavy machine-guns, rocket-propelled grenade launchers, grenades and weapons requiring more than one person to use them would all be handed over to the occupation forces. The British had given up hope of disarming the Iraqis of light weapons such as AK-47s. An official said, 'Most of the Iraqi tribes—especially in southern Iraq—think that weapons are part of their life and are something holy. If they try to take them away again there will be trouble.'[51]

This was not a case of 'Ba'athist remnants' fighting the invaders. The town of Majar al-Kabir was a Shia stronghold, in the hands of rebels, and the townsfolk actually demanded assurances from the British forces that Ba'athists and supporters of Saddam Hussein would be purged from any new administration.[52] The local guerrillas (who had been fighting Baghdad for years) captured the town on 7 April, well before US and British forces arrived. The militia, known as Hizbollah, though it has no links with the Lebanese group of that name, was actually ordered out of Majar al-Kabir by the US as soon as the guerrillas had taken control of the town. This loss of order led to devastating looting in the town, before the militia were allowed to return. A guerrilla commander interviewed by Patrick Cockburn remarked sadly, 'We were the only Iraqi city to liberate itself, and now this happens.'[53]

Despite the signing of the disarmament/no-search agreement on 23 June, British soldiers returned to the town to conduct an arms search the very next day. It was the town's fury over this breach of the agreement which appears to have created the clashes which escalated into the killing of the Royal Military Police officers (who had nothing to do with the searches). Muhammad Abdel Hassan, the police chief of the town, said the day after the killings, 'I am deeply sorry for their deaths. But I am afraid the British brought it upon themselves by their searches.'[54]

This whole pattern, of self-liberation, dispersal, attempted demobilization and forced disarmament, is very familiar from the aftermath of the Second World War. The next stages are also unfortunately predictable. Unless London and Washington can co-opt a substantial segment of the Shia religious establishment, Robert Fisk's prediction of a new front in the so-called 'war on terrorism' developing inside Iraq is likely to be fulfilled. If Tehran plays the role of Moscow, and its political allies in Iraq, such as the Supreme Council for the Islamic Revolution in Iraq, play the part of the Communist Parties in France, Greece and Italy after the Second World War, Washington may actually receive some assistance from Iran in the work of remaking Iraq to suit US, Saudi and Turkish interests in the region. However, covert or overt assistance from Tehran will not guarantee Iran protection from US propaganda; the 'Iranian terrorist threat' may yet become the justification for a low-intensity war against the peoples of Iraq. After all, Moscow's signal services to US and British occupation forces in Europe after the Second World War did nothing to halt the onset of the Cold War. Soviet co-operation in terminating anti-fascist purges, and in restoring right-wing, collaborationist establishments throughout much of the world did not prevent the portrayal of Western intervention in postwar Greece as a holy war against Communist subversion (when the Greek Communist Party was actually the last party of the Left to take up arms after 1945, and when its renewed guerrilla coalition was studiously ignored by Moscow's Cominform).

The initial post-war terrorism against the Greek Resistance was carried out by private gangs and official security forces composed of collaborators and British-sponsored Rightists. There is, at the time of writing, a question mark hanging over US and British intentions towards the security forces in Iraq, and their capacity for the kind of repression that would be needed to forcibly disarm the Shia militias, if it comes to that.

The day before the conflict in Majar al-Kabir, the occupation authorities announced a change of policy, placing more than 200,000 demobilized Iraqi troops, including members of regular Republican Guard units, on the coalition payroll, to receive monthly pay cheques of up to $150. 300,000 conscripts would be given a one-off severance payment. The four highest ranks, all members of the Special Republican Guard, and members of the Mukhabarat intelligence agency would all be excluded from the new scheme. The US authorities revealed that they intended to recruit and train a force of 12,000 troops within a year, building eventually towards a force of 40,000. Coverage of the new payment policy revealed that in the southern zone, British authorities in Basra had already avoided complying with de-Ba'athification by listing 8,000 out of 10,000 troops in the province as 'civil servants', and paying them accordingly.[55] Echoes of Britain's more lenient policy towards the fascists in Japan and Germany after the war.

REGIME UNCHANGED

What is clear and unambiguous is that Washington and London had no intention of forcing a real 'regime change' on Iraq, and, when the regime dissolved during the war of 2003, the US and UK attempted to rebuild that regime, with limited results. This was a policy with long roots. The two allies denied support to the highly successful revolts of 1991, and actually assisted Saddam Hussein's forces by permitting helicopter gunships to be used against the rebels. Brent Scowcroft, the US National Security Adviser at the time, made it clear later that he regretted the fact that the uprisings took place, because they made it impossible for the kind of military coup that the US would like to have seen to take place. Coming closer to the present, leaks throughout the year preceding the war of 2003 made crystal clear the preference in Washington and London for a military coup in Iraq rather than war. Ari 'one bullet' Fleischer and Donald 'exile in Belarus' Rumsfeld made it clear that the war was about one man and his entourage. President Bush, with his three-man ultimatum on the eve of war, and his cruise missile assassination attempt on the first night of war, underlined this message.

The much-publicized war plans and military deployments were leaked and announced in order to trigger a coup, by intimidating Iraqi military leaders. The media plan was also designed to trigger a coup, embedding Western reporters in the invasion force in order to relay to military commanders in Baghdad the relentless advance of the most powerful military machine in the world. The war plan itself was designed to trigger a coup, with a 'pause' at the gates of Baghdad to allow Saddam Hussein's 'henchmen' to replace him without the need for urban warfare.

The whole plan for postwar Iraq depended on there being a continuation of the fascist security forces. That was why the US was confident to invade with such light forces. As the *Guardian* newspaper reported at the end of June 2003, 'US and British commanders, in planning for postwar Iraq, made the mistaken assumption they would inherit an Iraqi army and police force which would maintain order.'[56] This was not an 'assumption'. This was a political decision to retain and use for their own purposes a police force integrated into a torture and terror state, and a military force with a semi-genocidal record against the Kurds, a record of unprovoked invasions, brutal occupations, chemical warfare against enemy soldiers and Iraqi citizens, a force which had violently suppressed the uprisings of 1991 which President Bush Sr had inspired with his call for action. This was not an accident or a pragmatic short-cut. This was a decision, taken at the highest levels, to retain the political and military institutions of Ba'athist fascism, which had tortured and massacred the peoples of Iraq for decades, and which had invaded two of Iraq's neighbours, triggering wars which killed hundreds of thousands of people. This was a decision to re-nazify Iraq.

Unfortunately, as we have seen, there is ample historical precedent for this policy, even in the case of Nazi Germany and fascist Japan. The 'de-nazification' programmes applied in Germany and Japan were shallow and ineffective, and reversed within a few years of the liberation of Auschwitz. In the British-occupied zone of Germany, SS officers were appointed police officers. As noted earlier, SS Lieutenant–Colonel Adolf Schult was chosen by the British to be the Chief of Police in Hanover. The British recruited former SS officers who had served in Poland and Russia, where the Nazi occupation forces had carried out some of the worst atrocities of the European war.[57] In Japan as in Germany, fascist intelligence officials were recruited to work for the West in the new war against Communism and 'subversion'.

What was wanted was 'stability'. Right-wing commentator David Frum, formerly a speechwriter for President George W. Bush, made some penetrating remark on the concept of 'stability' in the run-up to the war. Mr Frum excoriated the former US diplomat Wyche Fowler, the ambassador to Saudi Arabia appointed by President Clinton, who resigned his post in November 2002 and returned to the US to criticise the rush to war against Iraq. Mr Frum wrote: 'Fowler's is the authentic voices of the oil lobby, the people who ran America's Middle East policy more or less unchallenged until September 11: pro-Palestinian statehood, sceptical of Arab democracy, and concerned above all with the "stability" of the Middle East—meaning the preservation of the Saudi royal family.' Mr

Frum continued, 'Listen to the retired officials and distinguished public servants who have criticised President Bush's Iraq policy—the Brent Scowcrofts and the James Bakers, the Anthony Zinnis and the Laurence [sic] Eagleburgers—and you will hear that word "stability" over and over again. "Stability" means oil.'[58] This is a somewhat narrow interpretation, relevant to the Middle East in particular. (Incidentally, the characterization of prior US policy as pro-Palestinian demonstrates the depths of unreality and anti-Arab racism pervading Mr Bush's circle.)

What is very clear is that 'stability' has little to do with actual stability, peace, continuity, gradualism, and so on. So the pursuit of 'stability' in the aftermath of the Second World War required the preservation of the ruling (fascist) administrations in North Africa, Germany and Japan, whereas in France, northern Italy and Greece, 'stability' meant the overthrow of the ruling (anti-fascist) administrations. James Chace, journalist and member of the US foreign policy elite, once observed that it was necessary to 'destabilize a freely elected Marxist government in Chile' because 'we were determined to seek stability'. Noam Chomsky remarks dryly, 'Subversion to achieve stability is standard procedure, quite intelligible to those who have mastered PC rhetoric.'[59]

'Stability' is the reverse of 'terrorism'. President Bush said famously in the aftermath of 11 September, 'Either you are with us, or you are with the terrorists.'[60] 'Terrorism' means disobedience. 'Stability' means subservience.

The extent of the re-nazification of Iraq, even after Mr Bremer's supposed 'de-Ba'athification' order, was revealed at the end of June 2003 in the *Financial Times*. Charles Clover reported, 'Saddam's poachers become America's gamekeepers'.[61] On 9 May General Hussein Jassem al-Juboori, a former Republican Guard commander, was returning home when he was tipped off by a friend that US soldiers were surrounding his house. The general assumed they were there to arrest him. Instead they asked him to be governor of Salahadin province. At the time of writing, he governs the province from the capital, Tikrit, Saddam Hussein's home town. In that position, General al-Juboori has cancelled elections in Samarra ('They just couldn't agree among themselves, I had to step in.'), appointing a former Ba'ath Party official as mayor; employed former soldiers as police officers; and kept former Ba'athists on the payroll. With 90,000 high-ranking Ba'athists in his province alone, 'If I fired them all, we'd have 10,000 new revolutionaries. Instead they have become important contributors to the new system.' Asked about his policy, General al-Juboori said, 'We have a system now very much like they have in the United States. Our province is like an American state. In other words, I have all the power.'

The *FT* commented, 'Despite an order issued on May 16, banning the Ba'ath party, and another from May 22, dissolving the Iraqi military, US forces increasingly seem to be relying on selected strongmen like Mr Ijbara [another transliteration of Juboori] to run cities and provinces in the areas under their control . . . The increasing reliance on former regime figures to govern locally occurs as US troops come to terms with the fact that they cannot maintain security themselves.' In the southern city of Najaf, local elections were cancelled at the beginning of June, and the US appointed Abdul Min'im Amer Aboud mayor. This former colonel in the Iraqi artillery forces rode into Najaf on US special forces trucks in early April (perhaps alongside Mr al-Khoei).[62]

THE MEANING OF THE MASS GRAVES

Hussein Rabia, a local Shia Muslim, was shot and dumped in a mass grave outside Najaf in March 1991, as Saddam's military forces massacred Shias indiscriminately in reprisals against the US-inspired uprisings. The massacres took place under the gaze of US forces in southern Iraq, without interference from Washington. Mr Rabia survived.

Interviewed by *The Times* in early May 2003 near Najaf, in an area nominally under the control of US Marines, 'there was still fear on his face.' 'He said that there were many Baathists still walking freely in Iraq, who had to be stopped from ever returning to power. Above all, he wanted those responsible for the mass killings to be brought to court.'[63] This was to be a cry heard over and over again beside the mass graves in May 2003.

Mr Blair invoked the mass graves to justify his war, but the men who were part of the mass grave machine, who staffed the torture shops, who persecuted dissident play-wrights, were—in April and May 2003—restored to power by Mr Blair and by Mr Bush, and many of them continued to rule on 1 July 2003, despite a 'de-Ba'athification' order in mid-May.

The greatest obscenity of this war is that it was designed to retain 'Saddamism without Saddam', and it was followed by a serious and largely successful attempt to re-nazify Iraq—until checked somewhat by the mobilized rage of the Iraqi people.

Recall that despite Halabja, and despite the hanging of *Observer* journalist Farzad Bazoft on trumped-up charges of spying, diplomatic ties between Britain and Iraq were not broken, and £250 million trade credits granted to Iraq in November 1989 were honoured in full despite these enormities. Recall the penetrating words of a disillusioned Conservative MP on the day of Mr Bazoft's execution: 'I came to the House [of Commons] thinking politics was about ideas. Politics is about money. You decide about the money, and then make the ideas fit.'[64]

The clear intention of the US and British Governments is to enforce the old regime in Iraq, though with cosmetic modifications, and to enforce the old regime in the Middle East and throughout the world, the same regime that was imposed after the Second World War. This was not a war for 'regime change' at either level.

ENDURING VALUES

As noted earlier, there is in the West continuing reverence for the memory of the wartime anti-fascist Resistance (or at least the Western European wing of it). This universal respect is accompanied, however, by an equally universal ignorance of the ideals for which the Resistance fought, and the fate of those ideals, and of the Resistance movements generally, after the war. Basil Davidson, now known as a historian, once reflected on his experiences as a liaison officer with the partisans in Nazi-occupied Europe:

It all grew gradually clear even to political innocents like myself. In Greece and Jugoslavia, and to varying degree in all other occupied countries, large and serious resistance came and could only come under left-wing leadership and inspiration. Whole ruling classes had collapsed in defeat or moved into compromise with the nazis. With notable exceptions, the beaten generals and all their kind followed their governments and kings into exile, went into retirement, or took service with the nazi occupiers. . . the right-wing sold out and the centre simply vanished from the scene. . . Plenty of ordinary folk were ready to risk their lives, but only, as it soon transpired, if they were not risking them for king and conservatism. In these countries of bitter pre-war dictatorships, it further transpired, the self-sacrifice and vision required to begin an effective resistance, and then rally others to the same cause, were found only among radicals and revolutionaries.

All the evidence assembled later was going to confirm it: the politics of armed resistance had become the politics of a radical democracy. . . This was the politics they argued over around countless campfires or in shivering cold, and what they fought for in a multitude of engagements large and small, and what, more or less consistently, they very often died for.[65]

That current of radical democracy was one that flowed not only in Italy and France and Greece, but also in Vietnam and throughout South East Asia.

These were the ideals of the Action Party, which, as noted above, led about a quarter of the partisans in Northern Italy. Along with the Italian Socialists, the Action Party stressed industrial democracy, land reform, republicanism, and political decentralization.[66] These ideals were perhaps most clearly expressed by the will of the entire indigenous French Resistance, the *Conseil National de Résistance* (CNR) in the CNR Charter of 27 May 1943. The Christian Democrats, the Socialists, other independent social forces, and the Communist Party of France all agreed on a national reform agenda including 'the establishment of a true economic and social democracy, with the requisite eviction of the great economic and financial feudatories from the direction of the economy'. There was to be 'the return to the nation of the great monopolies, fruits of the labor of all, of energy resources, of the underground riches of the country, of the insurance companies and the major banks'. The Charter called for 'workers' participation in the running of the economy', and 'an independent trade-union movement with broad powers in the organization and management of the economic and social life of the country'.[67]

These are the kinds of ideals also, that, perhaps obscurely, move the 'anti-globalization movement', more accurately the 'global justice movement'. There is an intellectual and moral connection—a continuity of values—between the anti-fascist Resistance movements of the Second World War and the increasingly interlinked networks of resistance to corporate domination which are growing up today.

It may even be that these ideas resonate in some way with the aspirations of a significant element of the popular movements in Iraq. It may be that analogous values, though no doubt in an Islamic rather than a secular or Christian context, are held by a suppressed component of the anti-Western resistance in Iraq and elsewhere in the Middle East. If so, this is the real 'base' for common resistance, this is the ground from which a real war against terrorism can be fought, a war against US state terrorism, as well as a base for developing alternative forms of resistance which are effective and satisfying, and which can reduce the desperate motivation to adopt the means of terrorism.

The current of radical and nationalist democracy that burst forth in the wartime anti-fascist Resistance movements was dammed up by a postwar reaction sponsored and organized by Washington and London, and assisted by Moscow. There was an imperial reconstruction in which the wishes of the peoples concerned was entirely irrelevant, and the sacrifices of the Resistance counted for nothing. In witnessing the reconstruction of Iraq, and the reconstruction of the Middle East threatened by the Bush Administration, it will fall to the global peace and justice movements to develop the ideals of the wartime Resistance. It will fall to the popular movements in the West to develop new forms of solidarity with their struggling counterparts in the Middle East fighting against the rule of dictatorial systems, and against the restoration of collaborators and fascists.

John Reid, then the chair of the British Labour Party, tried to ague just before the war on Iraq that the impending invasion was entirely consistent with 'democratic socialism': 'It's long been a tenet of social democracy, of democratic socialism, to view with contempt fascism in all its forms.'[68] True, and an indicator of where the Labour Party is today, and where it was during the Second World War, when a Labour Minister could contemplate with equanimity the idea of a fascist coup against Mussolini that would lead to a more amenable form of dictatorship in Italy.

Where the Labour Party is today: engaged in the re-nazification of Saddam Hussein's Iraq, re-employing generals from the Republican Guards, re-hiring 'murdering bastard' police officers still using the old strong-arm tactics, and promoting the bureaucrats who kept the fascist machine well-oiled. Where the Labour Party is today: cancelling elections which could lead to the first signs of self-government for the people of Iraq, resisting their demands for democracy, and imposing strongmen of one kind or another throughout the country. Where the Labour Party is today: once again betraying the anti-fascist Resistance. The US–UK Atlantic Charter still lies unfulfilled, and betrayed by the continuing US–UK alliance against democracy and justice.

Unless the efforts to recover and develop the ideas of the anti-fascist Resistance are successful, there is another world that is possible, one summed up in the image of a resolute 14-year-old boy, standing unblinking by his family's bullet-riddled car, intoning, 'I hate Americans. I want revenge. I will wait, I will join a group, and, one day, I will kill Americans.'

Politics today begins and ends with 11 September. Each of us has the choice between justice and vengeance, and each of us bears responsibility for the consequences of our choice.

In early May 2003, the pedestal on which the world-famous statue of Saddam Hussein once stood bore a message for the US and British occupation forces, written in red letters: 'All Done, Go Home.'[69]

Postscript

WHAT WOULD YOU HAVE DONE?

If the concern was the proliferation of weapons of mass destruction, we should have developed and strengthened the Chemical Weapons Convention, the Biological Weapons Convention and the Nuclear Non-Proliferation Treaty, so that all countries in the world possessing or suspected of possessing weapons of mass destruction were subject to the same intrusive rules of inspection and monitoring to prevent the development and trading of weapons of mass destruction.

WHAT ABOUT THE THREAT FROM IRAQ?

There is no evidence that Iraq posed a significant threat either to its neighbours or to the West. Iraq's weapons programmes should have been dealt with by inspections, and by the institution of an internationally-supervised Ongoing Monitoring and Verification regime, something that the US is blocking at the time of writing, because Washington refuses to re-admit the inspectors to do the work required by Resolutions 687 and 1284.

THAT WOULDN'T HAVE GOT RID OF SADDAM.

Saddam Hussein is not gone: we have 'Saddamism without Saddam', as Ba'athist leaders are re-appointed. Washington and London had no intention of prosecuting regime change in Iraq. Even if they had had such an intention, this would have given them no right to invade Iraq to use violence for political ends—the definition of 'terrorism'.

Before the war, the best way to pursue real regime change would have been to lift the economic sanctions; empowering the Iraqi people and de-stabilizing the regime with a flood of unleashed expectations, while bringing enormous public health benefits.

Given that the war happened, afterwards the occupation forces should have recognized, encouraged and supported local democracy and the popular administrations which took over from the regime, and supported them in securing law and order. If police officers from the old regime had to be re-hired (which is questionable), they should have been employed and managed by elected neighbourhood and local authorities, who were best placed to know who was irredeemable.

The US and UK could have invited the UN to supply a transitional administration to support national elections and a constitutional convention, funded that programme, and withdrawn their forces as soon as UN peacekeepers began arriving in numbers. They should have committed themselves to clearing up all the dangerous debris of war, including depleted uranium, and paid compensation to the injured and bereaved.

NOTES

Web addresses are given where it is believed they will remain stable for some time. Articles in the *Washington Post* are all from the online version of the newspaper; page numbers are actually taken from there. Articles in the *Guardian* and *Observer* can be found online for free (at the time of writing), whether or not a URL is given in the note here. In general, it is often faster and easier to find a reference by typing a portion of quoted text into a search engine rather than trying to key in a long URL accurately. The references to debates in the House of Commons can be found by typing part of the quoted text and the name of the speaker into the advanced *Hansard* website search engine which can be found at <http://www.parliament.uk/hansard/hansard.cfm>.

Preliminary quotes
1 Richard Haass cited in in Andrew Cockburn and Patrick Cockburn, *Out of the Ashes: The Resurrection of Saddam Hussein* (New York, HarperCollins, 1999), p. 37.
2 Top US Senate official cited in *Time* magazine, 13 May 2002, p. 38.
3 Scott Ritter cited in *Daily Mirror*, 16 July 2002.

Echoing Voices
1 Catherine Green, 'My brother went to serve in Iraq and never came home. I wonder if Mr Blair lies awake at night thinking of his sacrifice as I do. I doubt it.' *Daily Mail*, 1 July 2003, p. 25.
2 'President Bush, Prime Minister Blair Hold Press Availability: Camp David, Maryland', 27 March 2003 <http://www.whitehouse.gov/news/releases/2003/03/iraq/20030327-3.html>. A journalist at the press conference apparently responded by shouting out, 'Because you two are both crazy.' Peter Stothard, 'When it is all over, we must go back and ask why this has happened,' *Times*, T2, 30 June 2003, p. 7.
3 David Hare, 'Betrayed', *Guardian*, G2, 23 June 2003, p. 4.
4 Letter, *Telegraph*, 30 December 2002, p. 19.
5 *Guardian*, 6 February 2003, p. 7.
6 Letter, *Independent*, 21 February 2003, p. 17.
7 Letter, *Guardian*, 24 February 2003, p. 21.
8 Letter, *Independent*, 25 February 2003, p. 19.
9 Letter, *Independent*, 25 February 2003, p. 19.
10 Letter, *Times*, 13 February 2003, p. 25.
11 *Newsweek*, 3 February 2003, p. 18.
12 Randeep Ramesh ed., *The War We Could Not Stop: The real story of the battle for Iraq* (London: Faber & Faber, 2003), p. 16.
13 *Mirror*, 21 January 2003, p. 5.
14 *Independent*, 27 March 2003, p. 4.
15 *Daily Telegraph*, 27 March 2003, p. 3.
16 *Independent*, 24 January 2003, p. 2. A totally different report of the same military PR event at which the Sergeant-Major spoke appears in the *Telegraph*, 24 January 2003, p. 21.
17 Vincent Graff, 'The danger man', *Independent*, *Review*, 23 June 2003, pp. 2–3.
18 Margaret Drabble, 'I loathe America and what it has done to the rest of the world', *Telegraph*, 8 May 2003, p. 22.
19
20 Hendrik Hertzberg, 'Blixkrieg', *New Yorker*, 10 February 2003, p. 34.
21 Brian Reade, 'He's holy illogical', *Daily Mirror*, 8 May 2003.
22 Nicholas Watt, 'Gulf reservist who thinks war is folly', *Guardian*, 28 February 2003 <http://www.guardian.co.uk/military/story/0,11816,904748,00.html>.
23 *Guardian*, 27 February 2003, p. 5.
24 Letter, *Times*, 11 January 2003, p. 25.
25 Andrew Tyrie, *Axis of Instability: America, Britain and the New World Order After Iraq* (London: Bow Group, March 2003), pp. 8–9. Available online from <http://www.bowgroup.org/pub/axisofinstabilitytext.pdf>.
26 *Daily Mirror*, 21 January 2003, p. 5.
27 'Iraq offer receives mixed reaction', BBC News Online, 18 September 2002 <http://news.bbc.co.uk/1/low/world/middle_east/2263027.stm>.
28 *Independent on Sunday*, 5 January 2003, p. 2; *Observer*, 5 January 2003, p. 2.
29 *Guardian*, 21 February 2003, p. 4
30 '"Decapitation strike" was aimed at Saddam', CNN Online, 20 March 2003 <http://edition.cnn.com/2003/WORLD/meast/03/20/sprj.irq.target.saddam/>.

Introduction

1 David Hare, 'Betrayed', *Guardian*, G2, 23 June 2003, p. 4.

2 *Independent*, 26 August 2002, p. 9.

3 *Guardian*, 31 August 2002, p. 5.

4 German Marshall Fund and Chicago Council on Foreign Relations, *A World Transformed: Foreign Policy Attitudes of the US Public After September 11* available from <http://www.worldviews.org/key_findings/us_911_report.htm#kf6>.

5 Martin Merzer, 'Poll: Majority oppose unilateral action against Iraq,' *Miami Herald*, 12 January 2003 <http://www.miami.com>.

6 *Financial Times*, 14 March 2003, p. 2.

7 *Times*, 30 August 2002, p. 1.

8 Julian Borger, 'Can the US go it alone against Saddam?,' *Guardian*, 31 August 2002, p. 5.

9 *Sunday Telegraph*, 16 March 2003, p. 6.

10 *Sunday Telegraph*, 16 March 2003, p. 18.

11 *Sunday Telegraph*, 16 March 2003, p. 18.

12 'Text of Donald Rumsfeld remarks', BBC News Online, 12 March 2003 <http://news.bbc.co.uk/2/hi/americas/2842943.stm>.

13 'Text of Donald Rumsfeld remarks'.

14 *Sunday Telegraph*, 16 March 2003, p. 18.

15 *Telegraph*, 14 March 2003, p. 16.

16 *Sunday Mirror*, 16 March 2003, p. 6.

17 *Sunday Telegraph*, 16 March 2003, p. 18.

18 Editorial, 'Stand-off at the Security Council,' *Financial Times*, 14 March 2003, p. 18.

19 *Sunday Times*, 23 February 2003, p. 14.

20 Giles Tremlett and Sophie Arie, 'Aznar faces 91% opposition to war', *Guardian*, 29 March 2003 <http://www.guardian.co.uk/international/story/0,3604,925118,00.html>.

21 Gary Younge, 'Europe poll sees US falling from favour,' *Guardian*, 19 March 2003 <http://www.guardian.co.uk/international/story/0,3604,917232,00.html>.

22 The letter itself did not actually support military action against Iraq, either in the immediate future, or even in principle. See <http://www.hungaryemb.org/Media&Communication/Statements/UnitedWeStand.htm>.

23 Ian Black, 'Inside Europe', *Guardian*, 31 March 2003 <http://www.guardian.co.uk/comment/story/0,3604,926069,00.html>.

24 *Telegraph*, 13 February 2003, p. 4.

25 Julian Borger, 'Bush fails to win over sceptical Europeans,' 5 December 2002 <http://www.guardian.co.uk/Iraq/Story/0,2763,854029,00.html>.

26 *Financial Times*, 10 January 2003, p. 10.

27 *Times*, 19 February 2003, p. 11.

28 'Iraq and an expensive exercise in democracy', *Financial Times*, 6 June 2003, p. 19.

29 'Iraq and an expensive exercise in democracy', *Financial Times*, 6 June 2003, p. 19.

30 President Johnson cited in Noam Chomsky, *Turning the Tide: US Intervention in Central America and the Struggle for Peace* (Boston: South End Press, 1985), p. 196. Professor Chomsky refers to Lawrence Wittner, *American Intervention in Greece* (Columbia: 1982), p. 303.

31 *Times*, 18 April 2003, p. 2.

32 *Hansard*, 18 March 2003, col. 773. Available online.

33 *Independent on Sunday*, 16 March 2003, p. 11.

34 *Sunday Telegraph*, 31 March 2002, p. 25.

35 Robert Worcester and Roger Mortimore, *Explaining Labour's Landslide* (London: Politico's Publishing, 1999).

36 Roy Hattersley, 'Socialism buried under a landslide,' *Independent*, 26 July 1999, Review, p. 5.

37 See pp. 102–3.

38 *Financial Times*, 22 February 2003, p. 6.

39 'Blair's mission impossible: the doomed effort to win a second UN resolution', *Financial Times*, 29 May 2003, p. 17.

Chapter I: Argument Over

1 Nick Cohen, 'The defeat of the left', *New Statesman*, 5 May 2003, p. 17.

2 Vernon Loeb, 'Rumsfeld Assails War Critics and Praises the Troops', *Washington Post*, 29 April 2003, p. A11 <http://www.washingtonpost.com/wp-dyn/articles/A51262-2003Apr28.html>.

3 This was the formula adopted, for example, in my own book *War Plan Iraq: Ten Reasons Against War on Iraq* (London and New York, Verso, 2002), p. 203.

4 *War Plan Iraq*, which was finished in mid-August 2002, argued precisely this point.

5 See Chapters XII and XIII.

6 *Guardian*, 8 March 2003, p. 4.

7 For an early example of this point being made, see Glen Rangwala, ' "Iraq briefing" now on-line', 6 April 2002 <http://www.casi.org.uk/discuss/2002/msg00515.html>.

8 *Times*, 11 January 2003, p. 25.

9 *The World This Weekend*, BBC Radio 4, 12 January 2003.

10 Tony Blair, foreword to the *Iraq's programme for Weapons of Mass Destruction—The assessment of the British Government*, 24 September 2002, quoted in *Times*, 25 April 2003, p. 17.

11 Secretary Colin L. Powell, 'Remarks to the United Nations Security Council', 5 February 2003 <http://www.state.gov/secretary/rm/2003/17300.htm>.

12 IAEA Director General Dr. Mohamed ElBaradei, 'The Status of Nuclear Inspections in Iraq: An Update', 7 March 2003 <http://www.iaea.org/worldatom/Press/Statements/2003/ebsp2003n006.shtml>.

13 *Sunday Times*, 16 March 2003, p. 2.

14 David Ensor, 'Fake Iraq documents "embarrassing" for US', CNN, 14 March 2003 <http://www.cnn.com/2003/US/03/14/sprj.irq.documents/>.

15 *Iraq's programme for Weapons of Mass Destruction—The assessment of the British Government* <http://www.number-10.gov.uk/output/page275.asp>.

16 State of the Union address, 28 January 2003 <http://www.whitehouse.gov/news/releases/2003/01/20030128-19.html>

17 Mark Huband and Mark Turner, 'Evidence about Iraqi uranium "not fake" ', *Financial Times*, 6 June 2003, p. 3.

18 *Iraq's programme for Weapons of Mass Destruction—The assessment of the British Government,* <http://www.number-10.gov.uk/output/Page277.asp>

19 Tim Trevan, *Saddam's Secrets: The Hunt for Iraq's Hidden Weapons* (London: HarperCollins, 1999), p. 414.

Chapter II: Regime Change

1 Randeep Ramesh, *The War We Could Not Stop: The real story of the battle for Iraq* (London: Faber & Faber, 2003), p. 18.

2 *Washington Post*, 28 January 2002, p. A01.

3 Randeep Ramesh, *The War We Could Not Stop: The real story of the battle for Iraq* (London: Faber & Faber, 2003), p. 19.

4 *Guardian*, 15 September 2001, p. 1.

5 Letter to President Clinton, 28 January 1998 <http://www.newamericancentury.org/iraqclintonletter.htm>.

6 *Financial Times*, 14 February 2002, p. 18.

7 Cited in Sarah Graham-Brown, *Sanctioning Saddam: The Politics of Intervention in Iraq* (London: I.B. Tauris, 1999), p. 20.

8 Security Council discussion, S/PV 2981, p. 116, cited in Sarah Graham-Brown, *Sanctioning Saddam*, p. 20.

9 *Guardian*, 1 May 1991, p 8.

10 Cited in Noam Chomsky, *World Orders, Old and New* (New York: Columbia University Press, 1994), p. 9.

11 'Iraq surveys show "humanitarian emergency"', 12 August 1999 <http://www.unicef.org/newsline/99pr29.htm>.

12 See my *War Plan Iraq*, pp. 55, 69 and 85–6 for more details; cited in Sarah Graham-Brown, *Sanctioning Saddam*, p. 65.

13 The evidence for the alleged Iraqi plot was comprehensively demolished by US investigative reporter Seymour Hersh in 'A Case Not Closed', *New Yorker*, 1 November 1993.

14 Dilip Hiro, *Neighbours Not Friends*, p. 163.

15 Sarah Graham-Brown, *Sanctioning Saddam*, p. 120.

16 Hans von Sponeck, 'It is an outrage that you repeat fabricated disinformation', *Guardian*, 4 January 2001 <http://www.guardian.co.uk/international/story/0,3604,417598,00.html>.

17 A pdf file of the Resolution can be downloaded from the list of Security Council Resolutions passed in 1991 at <http://www.un.org/Docs/scres/1991/scres91.htm>.

18 Dilip Hiro, *Neighbours Not Friends*, p. 159.

19 Richard Butler, *Saddam Defiant*, p. 226.

20 Paul Wolfowitz, 'Statement before the House National Security Committee', September 1998. <http://www.newamericancentury.org/iraqsep1898.htm>For connoisseurs of delicious irony, it should be noted that Mr Wolfowitz begins this statement by praising former UN weapons inspector Scott Ritter: 'It is an honor to appear as part of a hearing in which Scott Ritter testifies. Scott Ritter is a public servant of exceptional integrity and moral courage, one of those individuals who is not afraid to speak the truth.'

21 'How to attack Iraq', *Weekly Standard*, 16 November 1998 <http://www.newamericancentury.org/iraqmiddleeast2000-1997.htm>.

22 See Michael Eisenstadt, *The National Interest*, Winter 2001, for an interesting contribution to the debate.

23 Seymour Hersh, *New Yorker*, 24 December 2001, pp. 60, 59, 62.

24 This phrase was used in 2001 by the outgoing commander of US Central Command US Marine Corps General Anthony Zinni, cited in Seymour Hersh, *New Yorker*, 24 December 2001, p. 63.

25 'Pickering Hits Iraq's Handling of the Oil-for-Food Program', 3 August 2000 <http://usinfo.state.gov/topical/pol/arms/stories/00091807.htm>.

Chapter III: First Strike

1 David Frum, *The Right Man: An Inside Account of the Surprise Presidency of George W. Bush* (London: Weidenfeld & Nicolson, 2003), pp. 26, 27.

2 *Sunday Telegraph*, 18 February 2001, p. 5.

3 *Guardian*, 17 February 2001, p. 1.

4 Roger Cohen and Claudio Gatti, *In the Eye of the Storm: The Life of General H. Norman Schwarzkopf*, (London: Bloomsbury, 1991) p. 305.

5 Cohen and Gatti, *In the Eye of the Storm*, p. 306.

6 A search of the Project for the New American Century website, however, turns up only one mention of Mr Adelman's name—as a signatory to a 3 April 2002 letter to President Bush regarding Israel <http://www.newamericancentury.org/Bushletter-040302.htm>.

7 *Guardian,* 17 February 2001, p. 3.

8 *Observer*, 18 February 2001, p. 20.

9 'British-US strikes "followed escalation in Iraqi attacks" ', *Guardian*, 19 February 2001 <http://www.guardian.co.uk/Iraq/Story/0,2763,440175,00.html>.

10 *Washington Post*, 19 February 2001, p. A01.

11 'This man is dangerous', *Guardian* editorial, 19 February 2001 <http://www.guardian.co.uk/leaders/story/0,3604,439788,00.html>.

12 *Observer*, 18 February 2001, p. 20.

13 Ewen MacAskill and Richard Norton-Taylor, 'Britain seeks U-turn over Iraq bombing', *Guardian*, 8 January 2001 <http://www.guardian.co.uk/uk_news/story/0,3604,419199,00.html>.

14 Richard Norton-Taylor, 'Calmer tone on Iraq from MOD', *Guardian*, 25 January 2001 <http://www.guardian.co.uk/international/story/0,3604,427759,00.html>.

15 *Financial Times*, 21 February 2001, p. 3.

16 'Sanctions on Iraq "could go in six months" ', *Times*, 20 November 2000, p. 15.

17 'UK conciliatory over Iraq embargo', BBC News Online, 20 November 2000 <http://news.bbc.co.uk/hi/english/world/middle_east/newsid_1032000/1032423.stm>.

18 Richard Norton -Taylor, 'Bombing in Iraq an "undeclared war" ', *Guardian*, 11 November 2000 <http://www.guardian.co.uk/uk_news/story/0,3604,395890,00.html>.

19 *Daily Telegraph,* 17 February 2001, p. 21.

20 *Guardian*, 20 February 2001, p. 1.

21 'Powell Wants Iraq Sanction Changes', AP, 27 February, 2001.

22 'Bigger than Saddam', *Financial Times*, 18 February 2001.

23 *Economist*, 'Can sanctions be smarter?', 26 May 2001, and 'In search of an Iraq policy', 24 February 2001.

24 *Sunday Telegraph*, 18 February 2001, p. 5; *Sunday Times*, 18 February 2001, p. 15.

25 *Financial Times*, 17 February 2001, p. 6.

26 *Guardian,* 17 February 2001, p. 1; *Washington Post*, 19 February 2001, p. A08.

27 *Sunday Telegraph*, 18 February 2001, p. 5.

28 *Observer*, 18 February 2001, p. 21; *Sunday Telegraph*, 18 February 2001, p. 5.

29 *Observer*, 18 February 2001, p. 1.

30 *Sunday Telegraph*, 18 February 2001, p. 5.

31 *Daily Telegraph*, 17 February 2001, p. 21.

32 *Financial Times*, 21 February 2001, p. 3.

33 'Iraq: No UN Arms Inspectors Even if Sanctions Gone', Reuters, 26 February 2001.

34 *Independent on Sunday,* 18 February 2001, p. 25.

35 'Bigger than Saddam', *FT* website, 18 February 2001.

36 *Sunday Times*, 18 February 2001, p. 1.

Chapter IV: Sickly Inhibitions

1 Noam Chomsky, *Towards A New Cold War* (London: Sinclair Browne, 1982), pp. 188.

2 *New York Times*, 30 October 1985, cited in Noam Chomsky, *Necessary Illusions* (London: Pluto, 1989), p. 33.

3 Michael T. Klare, *Beyond the Vietnam Syndrome* (Washington DC: Institute for Policy Studies, 1982), p. 96.

4 See references in my *Chomsky's Politics* (London: Verso, 1995), p. 154.

5 David Frum, *The Right Man* (London: Weidenfeld & Nicolson, 2003), p. 136.

6 *USA TODAY*/CNN/Gallup Poll results, 28 November 2001, based on telephone interviews with 1,012 adults, conducted 26-27 November 2001 <http://www.usatoday.com/news/2001/11/28/poll-results.htm>.

7 Dorian Lynskey, 'Draft me!', *Guardian*, 22 January 2002, *G2*, pp. 12-13.

8 Duncan Campbell, 'The man who wants to tackle terrorism', *Guardian*, 9 July 2002, *G2*, p. 7.

9 *Guardian*, 17 February 2001, p. 3.

10 Letter to President Clinton, 28 January 1998 <http://www.newamericancentury.org/iraqclintonletter.htm>.

11 Bob Woodward, *Bush At War* (New York: Simon & Schuster, 2002), p. 49.

12 Woodward, *Bush At War*, p. 32.

13 Woodward, *Bush At War*, p. 32.

14 Woodward, *Bush At War*, pp. 25, 49.

15 Cited in Noam Chomsky, *9-11* (New York: Seven Stories Press, 2001), pp. 29 f. The date of the *NYT* article is difficult to determine from the context of the interview—it is either 18, 20 or 21 September 2001.

16 Please see <www.peacefultomorrows.org>. Some writings of the group are contained in my *War Plan Iraq*.

17 *Telegraph*, 20 September 2001, p. 2.

Chapter V: George Bush Lied

1 *Times*, 13 March 2003, p. 23.

2 *Newsweek*, 3 February 2003, p. 19.

3 State of the Union address, 29 January 2002 .<http://www.whitehouse.gov/news/releases/2002/01/20020129-11.html>.

4 See pp. 41, 77–8.

5 State of the Union address, 29 January 2002.

6 'President Delivers "State of the Union" ', 28 January 2003 <http://www.whitehouse.gov/news/releases/2003/01/20030128-19.html>.

7 Unlike the eight 'lead' attackers, who were all trained pilots, the other eleven did not leave messages for friends and family indicating they knew their lives were over. Regarding the other eleven hijackers,

> None of them had copies of the instructions for prayer and contemplation on the eve of the attacks and for "opening your chest to God" at the moment of immolation, which FBI agents discovered in the luggage of Mohamed Atta. It is understood the FBI has found evidence suggesting the 11 men expected to take part in 'conventional' hijackings—with the planes flown to distant airports, and the passengers and crew taken hostage while the hijackers presented demands. Items found among the 11 men's possessions suggest they had been preparing themselves for incarceration. One source said: 'It looks as if they expected they might be going to prison, not paradise.' The FBI analysis concludes the 11 may have believed the purpose of the hijackings was to free the perpetrators of previous extremist terrorist attacks on the United States, such as the first World Trade Centre bombing in 1993.

> David Rose, 'Attackers did not know they were to die', *Observer*, 14 October 2001 <http://www.observer.co.uk/international/story/0,6903,573685,00.html>. Intriguingly, in Osama bin Laden's video 'confession' of involvement in 11 September, the al Qaeda leader states that the 'brothers' he sent to take part in the attacks 'didn't know anything about the operation . . . we did not reveal the operation to them until . . . just before they boarded the planes', though they did knew it was 'a martyrdom operation'. *Newsweek*, 24 December 2001, p. 19.

8 Martin Merzer, 'Poll: Majority oppose unilateral action against Iraq', 12 January 2003 <http://www.miami.com/mld/miamiherald/4911975.htm>. Princeton Survey Research Associates questioned 1,204 Americans over 3-6 January 2003.

9 *Washington Post*, 1 May 2002, p. A09.

10 *Daily Telegraph*, 18 December 2001, p. 10. Another man *named* Mohammed Atta had visited the Czech Republic, but he was a different Mohammed Atta, and a man who *looked like* Mohammed Atta had met the Iraqi diplomat in question, but he was actually an Iraqi living in Germany. For more details, see *War Plan Iraq*, pp. 129–130.

11 *Daily Telegraph*, 20 September 2001, p. 10.

12 *Daily Telegraph*, 4 January 2002, p. 14.

13 *Independent*, 25 September 2001, p. 6.

14 It may be that in this case we will see a repeat of a Spanish fiasco. In March 2003, Spanish authorities released almost all of a group of 16 men accused of being al Qaeda militants after suspected chemical weapons material found at their homes turned out to be laundry soap. 'Two men are still being held, one for possession of forged identity documents and the other while police investigate equipment at his home.' The 16 men, mainly from Algeria, had been detained in the north-eastern region of Catalonia in January. *Times*, 22 March 2003, p. 25.

15 *Independent*, 4 February 2003, p. 12.

16 *Independent*, 4 February 2003, p. 12.

17 *Observer*, 2 February 2003, p. 17.

18 *Times*, 7 February 2003, p. 22.

19 *Guardian*, 6 February 2003, p. 1.

20 *Observer*, 2 February 2003, p. 17.

21 *Telegraph*, 4 February 2003, p. 13.

22 *Guardian*, 6 February 2003, p. 5.

23 *Observer*, 2 February 2003, p. 17.

24 *Observer*, 2 February 2003, p. 17.

25 *Telegraph*, 7 February 2003, p. 14.

26 I will follow the official US interpretation in treating this tape as coming from Osama bin Laden himself, though my own belief is that the al Qaeda leader died during or shortly after the US invasion of Afghanistan, and this tape recording is likely to have been made by a supporter. Ghislaine Alleaume, a French historian and Middle East expert, has suggested that Mr bin Laden had an amputated arm in a video broadcast on 27 December 2001. Subsequent messages purporting to be from the Saudi exile have included the name of the Prophet in Osama bin Laden's name, strengthening his apocalyptic aspect (the Mahdi, the final messenger will be recognised by the fact that he carries the name of Mohammed, according to the Koran). 'Bin Laden died from wounds suffered in Tora Bora air raid, says Arab expert', *Independent*, 10 May 2003, p. 13.

27 *Telegraph*, 13 February 2003, p. 16.

28 *Telegraph*, 13 February 2003, p. 16.

29 'Bin Laden tape: Text', BBC News Online, 12 February 2003 <http://news.bbc.co.uk/1/hi/world/middle_east/2751019.stm>. This is a full transcript by the BBC Monitoring Service.

30 'Bin Laden tape: Text', BBC News Online, 12 February 2003.

31 *Times*, 13 February 2003, p. 16.

32 'Bin Laden tape: Text', BBC News Online, 12 February 2003.

33 'Bin Laden tape: Text', BBC News Online, 12 February 2003.

34 'Bin Laden tape: Text', BBC News Online, 12 February 2003. Emphasis added.

35 *Telegraph*, 13 February 2003, p. 16.

36 James Risen, 'Terror Acts by Baghdad Have Waned, U.S. Aides Say', *New York Times*, 6 February 2002.

37 'US warned of substantial Iraqi resistance to military attack,' *Financial Times*, 1 August 2002, p. 7.

38 *Times*, 19 February 2003, p. 20.

39 'Al-Qaeda suspect "planning new attack" ', *Times*, 6 June 2003, p. 21.

40 *Telegraph*, 6 January 2003, p. 12.

41 Daniel Byman and Matthew Waxman, *The Dynamics of Coercion, American Foreign Policy and the Limits of Military Might* (Cambridge: Cambridge University Press, 2002) p. 209 n. 17. Just a month before the war on Iraq, the London *Times* received this letter from Professor Desmond G. Julian: 'Sir, Let us consider the worst (and probable) scenario. Saddam Hussein has links with al-Qaeda, he has chemical and biological weapons; he would like to share his weapons with al-Qaeda. If all this is true, Saddam Hussein will have already given these weapons to al–Qaeda. Is the war intended to close the stable door?' Letter, 13 February 2003, p. 25.

42 Gilmore Commission, 'First Annual Report to The President and The Congress of the Advisory Panel to Assess Domestic Response Capabilities for Terrorism Involving Weapons of Mass Destruction *I. Assessing The Threat*' (Washington DC: RAND Corporation, 15 December 1999) pp. 16-7. Available at <http://www.rand.org/nsrd/terrpanel/>.

43 Gilmore Commission, 'First Annual Report,' p. 18. The 'Fourth Annual Report' in December 2002 contains some weasel words designed to make the threat of transfer appear more realistic, but the analysis of the first report is not challenged.

44 Cited in John Sweeney, *Trading with the Enemy: Britain's Arming of Iraq* (London: Pan Books, 1993), p. 96.

45 Nathaniel Hurd and Glen Rangwala, 'U.S. Diplomatic and Commercial Relationships with Iraq, 1980–2 August 1990', 12 December 2001 <http://www.casi.org.uk/info/usdocs/usiraq80s90s.html>.

46 Cited in Sarah Graham-Brown, *Sanctioning Saddam: The Politics of Intervention in Iraq* (London: I.B. Tauris, 1999), p. 6. See Bruce W. Jentleson, *With Friends Like These: Reagan, Bush, and Saddam, 1982–1990*, (New York: W.W. Norton, 1994), p. 78.

47 'Tony Blair's speech to the Trades Union Congress in Blackpool', *Guardian* online, 10 September 2002 <http://politics.guardian.co.uk/speeches/story/0,11126,789688,00.html>.

48 Sweeney, *Trading with the Enemy*, pp. 92–94.

49 Sweeney, *Trading with the Enemy*, p. 83.

50 Con Coughlin, *Saddam: The Secret Life* (London: Pan Books, 2002), p. 245.

51 Andrew and Patrick Cockburn, *Out of the Ashes: The Resurrection of Saddam Hussein* (New York: HarperCollins, 1999), p. 83. This has since been updated and republished as *Saddam Hussein: An American Obsession* (London: Verso, 2002).

52 Cited in John Bulloch and Harvey Morris, *Saddam's War: The Origins of the Kuwait Conflict and the International Response* (London: Faber and Faber, 1991), p. 89.

53 *Independent*, 16 March 1990, cited in Sweeney, *Trading with the Enemy*, p. 171.

54 Press conference, 13 January 2003 <http://www.number-10.gov.uk/output/Page3005.asp>.

55 *Hansard*, 18 March 2003, col. 767.

Chapter VI: The First Ultimatum

1 *Guardian*, 27 February 2003, p. 23.

2 *Guardian*, 27 February 2003, p. 5.

3 *Financial Times*, 27 March 2003, p. 5.

4 *Financial Times*, 27 March 2003, p. 5.

5 *New Yorker*, 24 December 2001.

6 Randeep Ramesh, *The War We Could Not Stop: The real story of the battle for Iraq* (London: Faber & Faber, 2003), p. 19.

7 Thom Shanker and David Sanger, 'US Envisions Blueprint on Iraq Including Big Invasion Next Year', *New York Times*, 28 April 2002.

8 *Observer*, 11 July 2002, p. 2.

9 David Frum, *The Right Man: An Inside Account of the Surprise Presidency of George W. Bush* (London: Weidenfeld & Nicolson, 2003), pp. 222 f.

10 Suzanne Goldenberg and Julian Borger, 'How Cheney's revelation led towards the point of no return', *Guardian*, 17 January 2003 <http://www.guardian.co.uk/international/story/0,3604,876299,00.html>.

11 For more on the resistance from the military, please see *War Plan Iraq*, Chapter X, Reason 8, 'GI Joe Says No'.

12 *Observer*, 8 December 2002, p. 21.

13 *Time* magazine, 12 August 2002, p. 24.

14 *Guardian*, 24 January 2003, p. 1.

15 *Financial Times*, 28 October 2002 p. 9.

16 *Newsweek*, 19 May 2003, p. 16.

17 See *War Plan Iraq*, Chapter X, Reason 7, 'Ring of Anger: Iraq's Neighbours Fear Bush, Not Saddam'.

18 Bob Woodward, *Bush At War* (New York: Simon & Schuster, 2002), pp. 332 ff.

19 Woodward, *Bush At War*, p. 348.

20 'President's Remarks at the United Nations General Assembly', 12 September 2002 <http://www.whitehouse.gov/news/releases/2002/09/20020912-1.html>.

21 'President's Remarks at the United Nations General Assembly', 12 September 2002.

22 See *War Plan Iraq*, pp. 182–184.

Chapter VII: Disaster Strikes

1 'Iraq's letter to UN: Full text', 17 September 2002, BBC News Online <http://news.bbc.co.uk/1/hi/world/middle_east/2263455.stm>.

2 'Iraq's offer met with scepticism', *Guardian*, 17 September 2002 <http://politics.guardian.co.uk/foreignaffairs/story/0,11538,793788,00.html>.

3 'This is a tactical step by Iraq', *Guardian*, 17 September 2002 <http://www.guardian.co.uk/Iraq/Story/0,2763,793772,00.html>.

4 The text of the Resolution can be found at <http://www.un.org/Docs/scres/1991/scres91.htm>.

5 Cited in Dilip Hiro, *Neighbours, Not Friends* (London: Routledge, 2001), p. 76.

6 Scott Ritter, *Endgame: Solving The Iraq Problem Once and for All* (New York: Simon & Schuster, 1999), p. 156.

7 *Financial Times*, 12 November 1998 and 2 November 1998; *Economist*, 7 November 1998; *Independent*, 13 November 1998.

8 For more details on these incidents, please see *War Plan Iraq*, Chapter IV, 'Destroying UNSCOM'.

9 This is the relevant portion of transcript of the the special edition of the BBC programme *Newsnight* on 6 February 2003. The transcript is available from <http://news.bbc.co.uk/1/hi/programmes/newsnight/2732979.stm>.

TONY BLAIR: Well I can assure you I've said every time I'm asked about this, they have contained him up to a point and the fact is the sanctions regime was beginning to crumble, it's why it's subsequent in fact to that quote we had a whole series of negotiations about tightening the sanctions regime but the truth is the inspectors were put out of Iraq so—

JEREMY PAXMAN: They were not put out of Iraq, Prime Minister, that is just not true. The weapons inspectors left Iraq after being told by the American government that bombs will be dropped on the country.

TONY BLAIR: I'm sorry, that is simply not right. What happened is that the inspectors told us that they were unable to carry out their work, they couldn't do their work because they weren't being allowed access to the sites. They detailed that in the reports to the Security Council. On that basis, we said they should come out because they couldn't do their job properly.

JEREMY PAXMAN: That wasn't what you said, you said they were thrown out of Iraq—

TONY BLAIR: Well they were effectively because they couldn't do the work they were supposed to do.

JEREMY PAXMAN: No, effectively they were not thrown out of Iraq, they withdraw.

TONY BLAIR: No I sorry Jeremy, I'm not allowing you away with that, that is completely wrong. Let me just explain to you what happened.

JEREMY PAXMAN: You've just said the decision was taken by the inspectors to leave the country. They were therefore not thrown out.

TONY BLAIR: They were effectively thrown out for the reason that I will give you. Prior to them leaving Iraq they had come back to the Security Council, again and again, and said we are not being given access to sites. For example, things were being designated as presidential palaces, they weren't being allowed to go in there. As a result of that, they came back to the United Nations and said we can't carry out the work as inspectors; therefore we said you must leave because we will have to try and enforce this action a different way. So when you say the inspectors, when you imply the inspectors were in there doing their work, that is simply not the case.

JEREMY PAXMAN: I did not imply that, I merely stated the fact that they were not thrown out, they were withdrawn. And you concede they were withdrawn.

TONY BLAIR: They were withdrawn because they couldn't do their job.

This is an extraordinary account, implying an appeal back to the Security Council by UNSCOM, which never happened; a collective decision of the Security Council to withdraw the inspectors, which never happened; as well as a blanket refusal by Iraq to permit inspections of presidential palaces, which also never happened. The inspectors were 'effectively thrown out', that much is true, but the identity of the real agent responsible is utterly concealed.

10 See pp. 41, 77–8 for more information.

11 Dilip Hiro, *Neighbours, Not Friends*, p. 118. More information on these topics can be found in *War Plan Iraq*, Chapter IV.

12 *Sunday Times*, 15 November 1998, cited in Dilip Hiro, *Neighbours, Not Friends*, p. 158.

13 Christopher Dickey, 'Palace Intrigue', *Newsweek*, 14 October 2002, p. 20.

14 Annex to 'Letter dated 15 April 1998 from the Secretary-General addressed to the President of the Security Council', S/1998/326, 15 April 1998 <http://www.un.org/Depts/unscom/s98-326.htm>.

15 Scott Ritter, *Endgame*, pp. 144, 143. Again, there is more detail in *War Plan Iraq*.

16 See p. XXX.

17 'Iraq's letter to UN: Full text', 17 September 2002, BBC News Online <http://news.bbc.co.uk/1/hi/world/middle_east/2263455.stm>.

18 The offer to the UK was reported by Associated Press, 1 March 2002; and mentioned in *Independent*, 4 March 2002, p. 2; *Times*, 8 March 2002, p. 23. The offer to Congress was reported in the *Daily Mirror*, 6 August 2002, p. 2.

19 'UN weapons inspectors invited to Baghdad', BBC News Online, 2 August 2002, <http://news.bbc.co.uk/1/hi/programmes/breakfast/2167527.stm>.

20 Brian Whitaker, 'Serious offer or just an attempt to buy time?', *Guardian*, 3 August 2002 <http://www.guardian.co.uk/international/story/0,3604,768435,00.html>. An article by Dr Mudhafar Amin, head of the Iraqi Interest Section in London, about these offers is at <http://www.guardian.co.uk/comment/story/0,3604,770917,00.html>.

21 *Daily Mirror*, 6 August 2002, p. 2.

22 'Bush dismisses Iraq inspection offer', BBC News Online, 3 August 2002, <http://news.bbc.co.uk/1/hi/world/middle_east/2170275.stm>.

23 'Powell dismisses Iraq inspection offer', BBC News Online, 3 August 2002, <http://news.bbc.co.uk/1/hi/world/middle_east/2169719.stm>.

24 'Bush dismisses Iraq inspection offer', BBC News Online, 3 August 2002.

25 'List of Questions Submitted by the Iraqi Foreign Minister to UN Secretary-General On 7 March 2002', Iraqi News Agency <http://www.casi.org.uk/info/sabri020710.html>.

26 Dilip Hiro, *Iraq: A Report From The Inside* (London: Granta Books, 2003) p. 263.

27 *Washington Post*, 5 July 2002, p. A16.

28 'Excerpts: Saddam Hussein's letter', BBC News Online, 20 September 2002 <http://news.bbc.co.uk/1/hi/world/middle_east/2270520.stm>.

29 *Sunday Telegraph*, 22 September 2002, p. 29.

30 *Guardian*, 18 September 2002, p. 5.

31 Tim Trevan, *Saddam's Secrets: The Hunt for Iraq's Hidden Weapons* (London: HarperCollins, 1999), pp. 366, 411.

32 Trevan, *Saddam's Secrets*, p. 414.

33 *Iraq's programme for Weapons of Mass Destruction*, September 2002 <http://www.number-10.gov.uk/output/page277.asp>.

34 Newsnight interview, 6 February 2003. Please see n. 9 above.

35 Richard Butler, *Saddam Defiant*, p. 164. The 15 April report itself can be found at <http://www.un.org/Depts/unscom/unscmdoc.htm> (look for S/1998/326).

36 'A full report on the UNSCOM/IAEA inspections of Presidential sites in Iraq from 26 March to 4 April was sent by the United Nations Secretary General to Security Council members on 15 April.' Tony Blair, *Hansard*, Written Answers, 16

November 1998, col. 372. This answer can be found online using the Advanced Search facility at the Hansard site <http://www.parliament.uk/hansard/hansard.cfm>.

37 This exchange is unfortunately not available online, for some reason. Its existence can be verified using the Advanced Search facility at the Hansard site.

38 In the dossier's history of Iraqi non-co-operation with UNSCOM: 'In December 1997 Richard Butler reported to the UN Security Council that Iraq had created a new category of sites—"Presidential" and "sovereign"—from which it claimed that UNSCOM inspectors would henceforth be barred. The terms of the ceasefire in 1991 foresaw no such limitation.' This is taken from Tim Trevan, *Saddam's Secrets*, p. 364.

39 See page 177 and references.

40 For details of the various agreements, see Richard Butler, *Saddam Defiant: The Threat of Weapons of Mass Destruction and the Crisis of Global Security* (London: Phoenix, 2000), pp. 96 (Ekeus), 125 ff (Butler), 155 f (Annan).

41 The Resolution can be downloaded from <http://www.un.org/Docs/scres/1998/scres98.htm>.

42 See Richard Butler, *Saddam Defiant*, p. 155, or download the MOU from the UN website at <http://www.un.org/Docs/sc/letters/1998/sglet.htm> (look for S/1998/116).

43 *Hansard*, 24 February 1998, col. 174. You can find this page online by using the Advanced Search facility at <http://www.parliament.uk/hansard/hansard.cfm>. I am grateful to Dr Glen Rangwala for drawing this to my attention.

44 *Hansard*, 10 March 1998, col. 310. Once again, this page is available online.

45 *Hansard*, 3 November 1998, col. 709. This page is also available online.

46 'For now, for example, Mr Blix is assuming that special arrangements reached in the past between Iraq and the UN over access to presidential and other sensitive sites would be carried over. Although agreed in memoranda of understanding that are not part of UN resolutions, UN decision 1284 which created UNMOVIC stipulated that previous special arrangements would be adopted by the agency.' Roula Khalaf, *Financial Times*, 19 September 2002.

47 Roula Khalaf, *Financial Times*, 19 September 2002.

48 *Independent*, 21 September 2002, p. 11.

49 *Telegraph*, 21 September 2002, p. 20.

50 'Live webchat: Ask Jack Straw', Talking Point, BBC News Online, 3 October 2002 <http://news.bbc.co.uk/2/low/talking_point/forum/2285621.stm#1>

51 Brian Whitaker and David Teather, 'Weapons checks face tough hurdles', *Guardian*, 18 September 2002 <http://www.guardian.co.uk/international/story/0,3604,794008,00.html>.

52 Mark Oliver, 'UN split over Iraqi arms offer', *Guardian*, posted online 17 September 2002 <http://www.guardian.co.uk/Iraq/Story/0,2763,793694,00.html>.

53 Nicholas Watt and Nick Paton Walsh, 'UN resolution "open to change"', 30 September 2002 <http://www.guardian.co.uk/international/story/0,3604,801603,00.html>.

54 To be absolutely fair to the media, at the press conference in Vienna, Dr ElBaradei of the IAEA did indicate a difference between the idea of 'unrestricted, uninhibited and unconditional' access and the Special Group procedures for presidential sites, which required some form of advance notice: 'Under the existing mandate we have, we have now the assurances from the Iraqi side that we would have unrestricted, uninhibited, unconditional access to all sites in Iraq with the exception of the Presidential sites that are covered by the Memorandum of Understanding between the Security Council and the Government of Iraq.' However, this only indicated that there would not be 'unrestricted, uninhibited, unconditional' access to the presidential sites. Dr ElBaradei did not say, as the *Guardian* and other outlets reported, that the existing arrangements banned inspections of these sites. The transcript of this portion of the press conference can be found at <http://www.iaea.org/worldatom/Press/Focus/IaeaIraq/briefing.html>. There is also a video clip of this statement.

55 Ian Traynor and Julian Borger, 'US rejects Iraq inspections deal', *Guardian*, 2 October 2002 <http://www.guardian.co.uk/international/story/0,3604,802817,00.html>.

56 'Press Statement Agreed Between Hans Blix (UNMOVIC), Mohamed ElBaradei (IAEA) and Amir Al Sadi (Iraq)', IAEA, 1 October 2002 <http://www.iaea.or.at/worldatom/Press/P_release/2002/prn0215.shtml>.

57 'Press Briefing by Ari Fleischer,' 1 October 2002 <http://www.whitehouse.gov/news/releases/2002/10/20021001-4.html>.

Chapter VIII: Ambiguous Resolution

1 For reasons of space, this discussion omits elements that Washington tried and failed to introduce into the Resolution. For example, 'coercive inspections', with inspectors being accompanied by a multinational military arm strong enough to force immediate entry into any site at any time', a proposal described by a senior British Government official as 'an interesting idea, a perfectly valid approach'. *Financial Times*, 19 September 2002, p. 6.

2 The Resolution is available from the UNMOVIC site <http://www.un.org/Depts/unmovic/documents/1441.pdf>.

3 Blix, 'Notes for the briefing to the Security Council, 28 October 2002' <http://www.casi.org.uk/info/blix021028.pdf >.

4 *Guardian*, 27 November 2002, p. 20.

5 This argument was accepted by the High Court in dismissing CND's case. 'Law Report', *Times*, 27 December 2002, p. 35.

6 *Telegraph*, 19 December 2002, p. 14.

7 Vienna Convention on the Law of Treaties, 1969, available from the International Law Commission website <http://www.un.org/law/ilc/texts/treatfra.htm>.

8 Emphasis added. Resolution 687 can be downloaded from <http://www.un.org/Docs/scres/1991/scres91.htm>.

9 *Observer*, 8 December 2002, p. 21.

10 *Guardian*, 27 November 2002, p. 20.

11 *Guardian*, 27 November 2002, p. 20.

12 *Hansard*, 25 November 2002, cols. 52–3.

13 *Observer*, 8 December 2002, p. 21.

14 Article 60, Paragraph 2 of the 1969 Vienna Convention: 'A material breach of a multilateral treaty by one of the parties entitles: (a) the other parties by unanimous agreement to suspend the operation of the treaty in whole or in part or to terminate it either: (i) in the relations between themselves and the defaulting State, or (ii) as between all the parties;

(b) a party specially affected by the breach to invoke it as a ground for suspending the operation of the treaty in whole or in part in the relations between itself and the defaulting State;

(c) any party other than the defaulting State to invoke the breach as a ground for suspending the operation of the treaty in whole or in part with respect to itself if the treaty is of such a character that a material breach of its provisions by one party radically changes the position of every party with respect to the further performance of its obligations under the treaty.' <http://www.un.org/law/ilc/texts/treatfra.htm>

Clearly none of these qualifications applied to the United States either by itself, or with the United Kingdom, in relation to the disarmament provisions of Resolutions 687 and 1441.

15 You can find Dr Rangwala's arguments at <www.casi.org> using the search facility.

16 John D. Negroponte, U.S. Permanent Representative to the United Nations, 'Vote on the Iraq Resolution', 8 November 2002 <http://www.state.gov/p/io/rls/rm/2002/15018.htm>.

17 'Iraq/UNSCR 1441: Iraq—Joint statement by the People's Republic of China, France and the Russian Federation', New York, 8 November 2002, Embassy of France in the United States, 13 November 2002 <http://www.info-france-usa.org/news/statmnts/2002/iraq111302.asp>.

18 Michael J. Glennon, 'Why the Security Council Failed', *Foreign Affairs*, May/June 2003, p. 27.

19 The Legal Inquiry Steering Group held 'A Citizens' Legal Inquiry into the Legality of use of force against Iraq' on 11 October 2002 at Gray's Inn, London. The Inquiry was chaired by Professor Colin Warbrick, Professor of Law at Durham University. Rabinder Singh QC of Matrix Chambers argued the case for illegality, and Julian Knowles, also of Matrix, put the case for the UK Government. Professor Warbrick concluded that the UK's bombing raids into Iraq were in breach of international law, and that further armed force, in the absence of a clear UN Security Council mandate, would also be unlawful. CND mounted a legal challenge to the Government on 19 November 2002, culminating in a hearing before the High Court on 28 November 2002—which unfortunately was not allowed to come to trial, on the grounds that the courts would have to interpret UN Resolution 1441, not part of domestic law, and therefore outside the remit of the High Court. For more details, please see the website of Public Interest Lawyers <http://www.publicinterestlawyers.co.uk/iraq_war_legality_release.htm>.

20 Judgment available from 'The Iraq Hearing', BBC Radio 4 Online <www.bbc.co.uk/radio4/today/reports/international/iraq_hearing.shtml>.

Chapter IX: No Smoke, No Gun

1 Roland Watson, 'Bush says Saddam has 17 days left to decide his fate', *Times*, 21 November 2002 <http://www.timesonline.co.uk/article/0,,4281-488018,00.html>.

2 Philip Sherwell and David Wastell, 'Saddam "hiding the weapons in mosques" ', *Sunday Telegraph*, 17 November 2002, p. 35.

3 Toby Harnden, 'Blix verdict brings US to brink of war', *Telegraph*, 20 December 2002, p. 1.

4 'Even Britain, which has stood arm-in-arm with Washington on the issue, declined to utter the words [material breach],' David Usborne and Rupert Cornwell, 'MISSING, four tons of nerve gas, 8.5 tons of anthrax, and assorted nuclear bomb parts', *Independent*, 20 December 2002, p. 1.

5 'Prime Minister's Press Conference—25 November' <http://www.number-10.gov.uk/output/Page3004.asp>. As we saw in the last chapter, the Foreign Secretary made it clear that there had to be both a failure on the declaration and a pattern of non-cooperation before there could be a 'material breach'. Jack Straw, *Hansard*, 25 November 2002, col. 52.

6 Anton La Guardia, 'Inspectors told to get tough with Baghdad', *Telegraph*, 20 December 2002, p. 4.

7 Mohamed ElBaradei, 'The Status of Nuclear Inspections in Iraq: An Update', 7 March 2003 <http://www.iaea.org/worldatom/Press/Statements/2003/ebsp2003n006.shtml>.

8 'Remarks, Secretary of State Colin L. Powell To The United Nations Security Council February 5, 2003' < http://www.un.int/usa/03clp0205.htm>.

9 Paragraph 10: The Security Council 'Requests all Member States to give full support to UNMOVIC and the IAEA in the discharge of their mandates, including by providing any information related to prohibited programmes or other aspects

of their mandates, including on Iraqi attempts since 1998 to acquire prohibited items'. <http://usinfo.state.gov/topical/pol/terror/02110803.htm>.

10 'UN team flies in on three-week deadline', *Independent on Sunday*, 17 November 2002, p. 20.

11 Anton La Guardia, 'Inspectors told to get tough with Baghdad', *Telegraph*, 20 December 2002, p. 4.

12 Christopher Dickey, 'Palace Intrigue', *Newsweek*, 14 October 2002, p. 19.

13 William Rivers Pitt and Scott Ritter, *War on Iraq, What Team Bush Doesn't Want You To Know* (London, Profile Books, 2002), pp 38-39, 40. I am grateful to Gabriel Carlyle for drawing this to my attention.

14 Philip Sherwell and David Wastell, 'Saddam "hiding the weapons in mosques" ', *Sunday Telegraph*, 17 November 2002, p. 35.

15 *Iraq's Weapons of Mass Destruction—The Assessment of the British Government*, September 2002, Chapter 3 <http://www.official-documents.co.uk/document/reps/iraq/chap03.htm>.

16 'PM: "Saddam should take the peaceful route and disarm",' press conference, 13 January 2003 <http://www.number-10.gov.uk/output/Page3005.asp>.

17 'In a bind over Iraq', *Guardian*, 27 January 2003, p. 19.

18 *Telegraph*, 17 January 2003, pp. 8, 1.

19 *Telegraph*, 17 January 2003, p. 8.

20 *Times*, 11 January 2003, p. 25.

21 BBC Radio 4, *The World This Weekend*, 12 January 2003.

22 'Press Conference by the Executive Chairman of UNMOVIC, Dr. Hans Blix, and the Director General of the IAEA, Dr. Mohamed ElBaradei, in Baghdad, Iraq', 9 February 2003 <http://www.un.org/Depts/unmovic/> Recent Items.

23 *Financial Times*, 18 January 2003, p. 1.

24 *Telegraph*, 17 January 2003, p. 8; *Mirror*, 18 January 2003, p. 2.

25 *Guardian*, 17 January 2003, p. 5.

26 *Telegraph*, 18 January 2003, p. 2.

27 *Telegraph*, 18 January 2003, p. 1.

28 *Independent*, 18 January 2003, p.1; *Independent*, 20 January 2003, p. 2; *Mirror*, 20 January 2003, p. 2.

29 *Times*, 18 January 2003, p. 17.

30 Kamal Ahmed, Peter Beaumont, and Ed Vulliamy, 'Blair: war can start without UN arms find', *Observer*, 26 January 2003 <http://www.observer.co.uk/international/story/0,6903,882646,00.html>.

31 'In a bind over Iraq', *Guardian*, 27 January 2003, p. 19.

Chapter X: Colin Powell Lied

1 'Letter dated 15 December 1998 from the Executive Chairman of the Special Commission established by the Secretary–General pursuant to paragraph 9 (b) (i) of Security Council resolution 687 (1991) addressed to the Secretary–General', Annex II, to 'Letter dated 15 December 1998 from the Secretary–General addressed to the President of the Security Council', S/1998/1172, 15 December 1998 <http://www.un.org/Depts/unscom/s98-1172.htm>.

2 *Hansard*, 18 March 2003, col. 762. Please use the Search facility at <http://www.parliament.the-stationery-office.co.uk/pa/cm/cmhansrd.htm>.

3 Hans Blix, 'Notes for briefing the Security Council', 9 January 2003 <http://www.un.org/Depts/unmovic/recent%20items.html>.

4 Hans Blix, 'Briefing of the Security Council', 14 February 2003 <http://www.un.org/Depts/unmovic/recent%20items.html>.

5 UNMOVIC, *Unresolved Disarmament Issues: Iraq's Proscribed Weapons*, 6 March 2003. This is referred to inside UNMOVIC as the 'Cluster document' and is available from <http://www.un.org/Depts/unmovic/index>.

6 *Unresolved Disarmament Issues*, 6 March 2003, pp. 68, 72–73. These quotations are drawn from Glen Rangwala, *Claims and evaluations of Iraq's proscribed weapons*, 18 March 2003 <http://middleeastreference.org.uk/iraqweapons.html#index>.

7 See S/1999/94, 29 January 1999 <http://www.un.org/Depts/unscom/s99-94.htm>.

8 Glen Rangwala discusses the matter carefully in *Claims and evaluations of Iraq's proscribed weapons*, 18 March 2003 <http://middleeastreference.org.uk/iraqweapons.html#index>. Experts say that wet anthrax requires special treatment in order to survive for any length of time. From Dr Rangwala's account, no information seems to be available on whether Iraq was capable of carrying out these procedures. There is no evidence that Iraq was capable of drying anthrax, which would certainly have prolonged its infective life for years.

9 *Observer*, 17 March 2002, p. 15.

10 Letter to President Clinton on Iraq, January 26, 1998, <http://www.newamericancentury.org/iraqclintonletter.htm>. Note that this letter was written long before the demise of UNSCOM in December 1998.

11 *Observer*, 18 February 2001, p. 21.

12 *New Yorker*, 24 December 2001, p. 63.

13 *Washington Post*, 15 April 2002, p. A01.

14 *Time* magazine, 13 May 2002, p. 38.

15 *Telegraph*, 6 July 2002, p. 16.

16 'As a rule, the White House lets him loose in the media when it wants to bare its teeth, and the rest of the time it keeps him out of sight. Mr Cheney more or less conceded as much yesterday when he said: 'From time to time, they trot me out when it makes sense to do so. I'm sure as we get closer to the campaign, I'll be more visible.' *Guardian*, 8 May 2003, p. 14.

17 'Remarks by the Vice President to the Veterans of Foreign Wars 103rd National Convention', 26 August 2002 <http://www.whitehouse.gov/news/releases/2002/08/20020826.html>.

18 Bob Woodward, *Bush at War* (New York, Simon & Schuster, 2002), pp. 344-345.

19 *Independent*, 23 January 2003, p. 1.

20 *Telegraph*, 28 February 2003, p. 14.

21 *Guardian*, 6 May 2002.

22 'Blair's mission impossible: the doomed effort to win a second UN resolution', *Financial Times*, 29 May 2003, p. 17.

23 David Rennie, 'Powell boosts support in US', *Telegraph*, 10 February 2003, p. 4.

24 *Telegraph*, 6 February 2003, p. 1.

25 The relevant illustrations are available at the State Department website at <http://www.state.gov/r/pa/ei/pix/events/secretary/2003/17260.htm>. Slide 12 shows all three bunkers: the bunker with the 'security building' (illustrated in close-up in Slide 13) is identified by the lowest of the red rectangles. The two other bunkers (also shown in close-up in Slide 13) are the middle pair of red rectangles in Slide 12.

26 *Guardian*, 6 February 2003, p. 3.

27 *Financial Times*, 15 February 2003, p. 6.

28 *Financial Times*, 15 February 2003, p. 7.

29 *Guardian*, 6 February 2003, p. 3.

30 *Guardian*, 6 February 2003, p. 3.

31 *Guardian*, 6 February 2003, p. 3.

32 *Independent*, 6 February 2003, p. 3.

33 Secretary Colin L. Powell, 'Remarks to the United Nations Security Council', 5 February 2003 <http://www.state.gov/secretary/rm/2003/17300.htm>.

34 *Newsweek*, 17 February 2003, p. 20.

35 Peter Beaumont, Antony Barnett and Gaby Hinsliff, 'Iraqi mobile labs nothing to do with germ warfare, report finds,' *Observer*, 15 June 2003 <http://observer.guardian.co.uk/international/story/0,6903,977853,00.html>.

36 For example, *Telegraph*, 4 February 2003, p. 13.

37 *Times*, 6 February 2003, p. 14.

38 *Guardian*, 'Powell shoots to kill: But battle over Iraq is far from finished', 6 February 2003, p. 23.

39 *Guardian*, 6 February 2003, p. 3.

40 *Mirror*, 24 February 2003, p. 2.

41 *Guardian*, 6 February 2003, p. 1; *Telegraph*, 7 February 2003, p. 14.

42 *Guardian*, 6 February 2003, p. 2.

43 'Press Conference by the Executive Chairman of UNMOVIC, Dr. Hans Blix, and the Director General of the IAEA, Dr. Mohamed ElBaradei, in Baghdad, Iraq', 9 February 2003 in 'Recent Items' at <http://www.un.org/Depts/unmovic/>.

44 Secretary Colin L. Powell, 'Remarks to the United Nations Security Council', 5 February 2003 <http://www.state.gov/secretary/rm/2003/17300.htm>.

45 Ian Traynor, 'UK nuclear evidence a fake', *Guardian*, 8 March 2003 <http://www.guardian.co.uk/Iraq/Story/0,2763,910113,00.html>.

46 David Ensor, 'Fake Iraq documents "embarrassing" for U.S.', CNN, 15 March 2003 <http://edition.cnn.com/2003/US/03/14/sprj.irq.documents/>.

47 'State Department transcript of the interview with NBC's Meet the Press With Tim Russert', part of Thomas Eichler, 'Powell, Rice Argue For Regime Change in Iraq', US Mission to the EU, 9 March 2003 <http://www.useu.be/Categories/GlobalAffairs/Iraq/Mar0903PowellRiceIraq.html>.

48 See pp. 24–9.

49 *Telegraph*, 4 February 2003, p. 13.

50 See Glen Rangwala's *Claims and evaluations of Iraq's proscribed weapons* <http://middleeastreference.org.uk/iraqweaponsb.html#bexista>. The US and UK claimed that Iraq used its fermenters at al–Hakam, its known anthrax production site, at a greater capacity than it had declared, and therefore could have produced 20,000 litres of anthrax more than it declared to the inspectors. This assumes that the fermenters were run at maximum capacity during 1990. However, the Iraqi account was substantiated by the only documentation found relating to anthrax production—the 1990 annual report from al–Hakam, which UNSCOM considered reliable on other issues. UNMOVIC's working document, *Unresolved Disarmament Issues*, of 6 March 2003, found the al–Hakam report reliable and Dr Blix apparently accepted that the plant did not operate at full capacity during 1990. The British and US anthrax claims, politically so useful, actually stood on very shaky ground.

51 *Guardian*, 6 February 2003, p. 6.

52 *Guardian*, 6 February 2003, p. 6.

53 *Financial Times*, 6 February 2003, p. 17.

54 *Independent*, 6 February 2003, p. 16.

55 *Guardian*, 6 February 2003, p. 6.

56 Guardian, 6 February 2003, p. 1.

Chapter XI: Inspection Was An Option

1 See Paragraph 13 of UN Security Council Resolution 687 (3 April 1991) available from <http://www.un.org/Docs/scres/1991/scres91.htm>

2 Cited in Dilip Hiro, *Neighbours Not Friends* (London: Routledge, 2001), p. 155.

3 'Anticipating Inspections: UNMOVIC Readies Itself for Iraq', *Arms Control Today*, July/August 2000 <http://www.armscontrol.org/act/2000_07-08/blixjulaug.asp>.

4 Scott Ritter, 'The Case for Iraq's Qualitative Disarmament', *Arms Control Today*, June 2000 <http://www.armscontrol.org/act/2000_06/iraqjun.asp>.

5 Romesh Ratnesar and Andrew Purvis, 'To catch a cheat: Weapons inspectors expect Saddam to try to foil them. But now they have new tools of detection', *Time* magazine, 25 November 2002, p. 39.

6 Ratnesar and Purvis, 'To catch a cheat'.

7 Secretary Colin L. Powell, 'Remarks to the United Nations Security Council', 5 February 2003 <http://www.state.gov/secretary/rm/2003/17300.htm>.

8 'Briefing of the Security Council, 14 February 2003' in 'Recent Items' at <http://www.un.org/Depts/unmovic/>.

9 Ritter, 'The Case for Iraq's Qualitative Disarmament'.

10 *Times*, 7 February 2003, p. 19.

Chapter XII: Blitzing Dr Blix

1 *Guardian*, 22 January 2003, p. 1.

2 Richard Butler, *Saddam Defiant: The Threat of Weapons of Mass Destruction and the Crisis of Global Security* (Phoenix: London, 2000), p. 228.

3 *Daily Telegraph*, 20 November 1998, p.1.

4 Scott Ritter, *Endgame: Solving the Iraq Problem—Once and for All* (New York: Simon & Schuster, 1999), pp. 20–26.

5 For more on the inspection rules, see pp. 44–6. A detailed account of the 1998 crisis is in *War Plan Iraq*, pp. 49–53.

6 *Independent*, 17 December 1998, p. 4; *Times*, 22 December 1998, p. 1.

7 *Independent*, 23 December 1998, p. 7.

8 *Financial Times*, 17 December 1998, p. 8.

9 Butler, *Saddam Defiant*, p. 221.

10 Dilip Hiro, *Neighbours, Not Friends: Iraq and Iran after the Gulf Wars* (London: Routledge, 2001), p. 161.

11 Butler, *Saddam Defiant*, p. 224.

12 *Guardian*, 6 February 2003, p. 2.

13 This Resolution can also be obtained from the Documents section of the UNMOVIC site. On the consent issue, Dr Blix said, 'Clearly, we could not take anybody out of Iraq without his or her consent.' 'Notes for briefing the Security Council regarding inspections in Iraq and a preliminary assessment of Iraq's declaration under paragraph 3 of resolution 1441 (2002)', 19 December 2002, available from Recent Items at <http://www.un.org/Depts/unmovic>.

14 'Blix: "There is a very strong power behind us",' 27 November 2002, CNN <http://edition.cnn.com/2002/US/11/27/cnna.blix/>.

15 Hans Blix, 'Notes for Briefing the Security Council', 9 January 2003 available in 'Recent Items' at <www.un.org/Depts/unmovic/>.

16 Dr Blix, 'The Security Council, 27 January 2003: An Update On Inspection', available at 'Recent Items', UNMOVIC <www.un.org/Depts/unmovic/>.

17 Dr Blix, 'Briefing of the Security Council, 14 February 2003, available at 'Recent Items', UNMOVIC <www.un.org/Depts/unmovic/>.

18 *Guardian*, 10 January 2003, p. 1.

19 Dr Blix, 'Oral introduction of the 12th quarterly report of UNMOVIC', 7 March 2003, in 'Recent Items' at UNMOVIC <www.un.org/Depts/unmovic/>.

20 *Guardian*, 14 March 2003, p. 5.

21 *Guardian*, 6 February 2003, p. 5.

22 *Guardian*, 4 February 2003, p. 10.

23 *Telegraph*, 21 February 2003, p. 1.

24 *Financial Times*, 13 February 2003, p. 6.

25 *Guardian*, 21 February 2003, p. 4.

26 *Financial Times*, 21 February 2003, p. 5.

27 *Times*, 29 January 2003, p. 14.

28 *Daily Express*, 28 January 2003, p. 5.

29 *Daily Mail*, 28 January 2003, p. 5.

30 *Financial Times*, 28 January 2003, p. 9.

31 *Guardian*, 6 February 2003, p. 6.

32 *Financial Times*, 13 February 2003, p. 6.

33 *Telegraph*, 21 February 2003, p. 1.

34 *Guardian*, 25 February 2003, p. 5.

35 *Telegraph*, 26 February 2003, p. 12.

36 *Financial Times*, 13 February 2003, p. 6.

37 *Financial Times*, 24 February 2003, p. 6

38 *Telegraph*, 26 February 2003, p. 12; *Times*, 26 February 2003, p. 11.

39 *Sunday Telegraph*, 23 February 2003, p. 28.

40 Dr Blix, 'Oral introduction of the 12th quarterly report of UNMOVIC', 7 March 2003, in 'Recent Items' <http://www.un.org/Depts/unmovic/>.

41 Blix, 'Oral introduction of the 12th quarterly report of UNMOVIC'.

42 *Times*, 7 February 2003, p. 1.

43 Secretary Colin L. Powell, 'Remarks at the Center for Strategic and International Studies Washington, DC', 5 March 2003 <http://www.usembassy.org.uk/midest515.html>.

44 *Telegraph*, 8 March 2003, p. 1.

45 *Telegraph*, 6 February 2003, p. 1.

46 *Independent*, 23 January 2003, p. 1.

47 Ed Vulliamy and Peter Beaumont, 'Inspectors' mission faces long odds', *Observer*, 17 November 2002, p. 21.

48 Vulliamy and Beaumont, 'Inspectors' mission faces long odds'.

49 Secretary Colin L. Powell, 'Remarks at the Center for Strategic and International Studies Washington, DC', 5 March 2003 <http://www.usembassy.org.uk/midest515.html>.

50 *Guardian*, 6 February 2003, p. 6.

51 *Mirror*, 26 February 2003, p. 4.

52 *Telegraph*, 28 February 2003, p. 1.

53 *Times*, 23 January 2003, p. 2.

54 *Sunday Times*, 23 February 2003, p. 2.

55 *Telegraph*, 7 February 2003, p. 1.

56 'Press Conference by the Executive Chairman of UNMOVIC, Dr. Hans Blix, and the Director General of the IAEA, Dr. Mohamed ElBaradei, in Baghdad, Iraq', 9 February 2003. Available in 'Recent Items' at the UNMOVIC website.

57 *Telegraph*, 28 January 2003, p. 2.

58 *Financial Times*, 28 January 2003, p. 9.

59 *Financial Times*, 29 January 2003, p. 10.

60 *Guardian*, 29 January 2003, p. 4.

61 *Times*, 29 January 2003, p. 14.

62 *Times*, 29 January 2003, p. 14.

63 *Observer*, 16 February 2003, p. 18.

64 'Briefing of the Security Council, 14 February 2003, 'Recent Items', UNMOVIC <www.un.org/Depts/unmovic/>.

65 *Financial Times*, 15 February 2003, p. 6.

66 *Observer*, 16 February 2003, p. 17.

67 'Blair's mission impossible: the doomed effort to win a second UN resolution', *Financial Times*, 29 May 2003, p. 17.

68 Matthew d'Ancona, 'I agree with Blair on Iraq. And, boy, do I feel lonely', *Sunday Telegraph*, 12 January 2003, p. 21.

69 *Financial Times*, 28 January 2003, p. 9.

70 Dr Blix, 'Oral introduction of the 12th quarterly report of UNMOVIC', 7 March 2003. Available in 'Recent Items' at the UNMOVIC website.

71 *Time* magazine, 24 March 2004, p. 37.

72 Richard Norton-Taylor and Helena Smith, 'US offers immunity to Saddam: Rumsfeld and Powell back exile plan', *Guardian*, 20 January 2003

<http://www.guardian.co.uk/international/story/0,3604,878229,00.html>.

73 *Times*, 7 February 2003, p. 19.

74 *Guardian*, 4 February 2003, p. 10.

Chapter XIII: The Censored Document

1 'The Road to War', BBC2, transmitted 26 April 2003.

2 Patrick Wintour and Martin Kettle, 'Brought to the brink of defeat', *Guardian*, 26 April 2003, pp. 12–15.

3 'President Says Saddam Hussein Must Leave Iraq Within 48 Hours', Remarks by the President in Address to the Nation, The Cross Hall, 8:01 pm EST <http://www.whitehouse.gov/news/releases/2003/03/iraq/20030317–7.html>.

4 The Resolution is available from the Documents section of the UNMOVIC website: <www.un.org/Depts/unmovic/>.

5 Randeep Ramesh, *The War We Could Not Stop: The real story of the battle for Iraq* (London: Faber & Faber, 2003), p. 30.

6 Ewen Buchanan, telephone interview with author, 24 February 2003.

7 'Anticipating Inspections: UNMOVIC Readies Itself for Iraq', *Arms Control Today*, July/August 2000 <http://www.armscontrol.org/act/2000_07–08/blixjulaug.asp>.

8 *Financial Times*, 21 February 2003, p. 5.

9 *Guardian*, 25 February 2003, p. 5.

10 *Telegraph*, 22 February 2003, p. 14.

11 *Financial Times*, 22 February 2003, p. 6.

12 *Financial Times*, 24 February 2003, p. 1.

13 Colin L. Powell, 'Remarks at the Center for Strategic and International Studies', Washington, DC, 5 March 2003 <http://www.usembassy.org.uk/midest515.html>.

14 *Sunday Times*, 23 February 2003, p. 2.

15 *Times*, 25 February 2003, p. 1.

16 *Independent*, 8 March 2003, p. 2.

17 'Secretary Powell's Remarks at U.N. Security Council Meeting', 7 March 2003 <http://www.whitehouse.gov/news/releases/2003/03/iraq/20030307–10.html>.

18 *Telegraph*, 8 March 2003, p. 5.

19 *Telegraph*, 8 March 2003, p. 4; *Guardian*, 8 March 2003, p. 4.

20 'Military action more likely, says Straw,' *Guardian*, 15 March 2003 <http://www.guardian.co.uk/Iraq/Story/0,2763,914897,00.html>.

21 *Guardian*, 24 January 2003, p. 1.

22 *Newsweek*, 27 January 2003, p. 20.

23 *Newsweek*, 27 January 2003, p. 20.

24 *Independent*, 5 May 2003, Review, p. 3.

25 *Telegraph*, 9 January 2003, p. 1.

26 'Pentagon staff are also reluctant to see the diplomatic process drift on, having said that the optimal time to start military action in the Gulf would come some time between late November and early February.' James Harding and Carola Hoyos, 'Washington to force the pace on pressure against Iraq', *Financial Times*, 28 October 2002, p. 9; 'the clock is ticking for the military campaign; January and February, the preferred months for starting a war, are close.' Bronwen Maddox, 'Bush pursues victory on separate fronts', *Times*, 30 October 2002, p. 16.

27 *Sunday Times*, 23 February 2003, p. 13.

28 *Observer*, 2 February 2003, p. 15.

29 'While I lean towards March 24 as the more appropriate start date, place your money on it at your own risk.' Wesley Clark, 'Forces must be fully prepared', *Times*, 19 February 2003, p. 11.

30 *Independent on Sunday*, 23 February 2003, p. 11.

31 *Times*, 11 March 2003, p. 14.

32 'Anticipating Inspections: UNMOVIC Readies Itself for Iraq', *Arms Control Today*, July/August 2000 <http://www.armscontrol.org/act/2000_07–08/blixjulaug.asp>.

33 'New York—Press Encounter with the Secretary–General at the Security Council stakeout', 17 March 2003 <http://www.un.org/apps/news/infocusnewsiraq.asp?NewsID=433&sID=7>.

34 'Notes for briefing the Security Council on UNMOVIC's Readiness to Resume Operations', 22 April 2003. Available from 'Recent Items' <www.un.org/Depts/unmovic/>.

35 Kamal Ahmed and Ed Vulliamy, 'Blair sets out final terms to avoid war', *Observer*, 9 March 2003 <http://www.observer.co.uk/international/story/0,6903,910684,00.html>.

36 'Introduction of draft UNMOVIC Work Programme, Security Council', 19 March 2003. Available from 'Recent Items' <www.un.org/Depts/unmovic/>.

37 Gary Younge, 'Sad Blix says he wanted more time for inspections', *Guardian*, 20 March 2003 <http://www.guardian.co.uk/international/story/0,3604,917924,00.html>.

38 'Brief History of the Comprehensive Review', 30 January 1999, Monterey Institute of International Studies <http://cns.miis.edu/research/iraq/ucreport/history.htm>.

Chapter XIV: Authority And Power

1 Peter Hain, 'Progress on Iraq and the Middle East Peace Process', 11 September 2000. Available via the Search facility at from the Foreign Office website at <http://www.fco.gov.uk>.

2 'Statement in the Security Council by the British Ambassador to the United Nations, Sir Jeremy Greenstock', 17 December 1999. Available via the Search facility at from the Foreign Office website at <http://www.fco.gov.uk>.

3 The Resolution is available from <http://www.un.org/Depts/unscom>.

4 Richard Butler, *Saddam Defiant* (Phoenix: London, 2000), p. 226.

5 Cited in Dilip Hiro, *Neighbours Not Friends* (London: Routledge, 2001), p. 76; See *War Plan Iraq*, pp. 46–48.

6 *Guardian*, 7 February 2003, p. 4. This was an NBC News poll—but of only 400 people.

7 Richard Morin, 'Public US Backs U.N. Assent on Iraq: Poll Finds Americans Willing to Delay War to Gain Support', *Washington Post*, 25 February 2003. A total of 1,024 randomly selected adults were interviewed 19–23 February for the *Washington Post*-ABC national telephone survey. Margin of sampling error for the overall results was plus or minus 3 percentage points.

8 *Sunday Times*, 23 February 2003, p.13. The question in the *Sunday Times*/YouGov online poll, conducted over 20–21 February, was: 'Should Britain take part in a war against Iraq if there is a second resolution backing it?' Yes: 59; No: 30; Don't know: 11. The Yes vote was down from 72 per cent a month earlier.

9 *Telegraph*, 25 February 2003, p. 1.

10 letter, *Guardian*, 26 February 2003, p. 17.

11 'Bush: tomorrow is decision day for UN,' *Guardian*, 16 March 2003 <http://www.guardian.co.uk/international/story/0,3604,915442,00.html>.

12 'UNMOVIC supervised the destruction of two more Al Samoud 2 missiles, the computer software in a control vehicle to programme the missile, and missile parts, such as fuel tanks and warhead shells. Today's action brings to 70 the total number of Al Samoud 2 missiles destroyed since 1 March.' 'UNMOVIC IAEA Press Statement on Inspection Activities in Iraq', 16 March 2003. This can be found in the 'Baghdad Press Briefings' section of the UNMOVIC website <http://www.un.org./Depts/unmovic>.

13 *Independent*, 4 February 2003, p. 1.

14 This excerpt is taken from the Resolution as it is posted on the State Department website: <http://usinfo.state.gov/topical/pol/terror/02110803.htm>.

15 <www.bbc.co.uk/radio4/today/reports/international/iraq_hearing.shtml>.

16 The full text of the tests (with key adjectives and adverbs italicized):

> The United Kingdom would be ready to accept that Iraq has begun to demonstrate *full, unconditional, immediate* and *active* co-operation in accordance with its disarmament obligations under resolution 1441 (2002) if, by (date is subject to negotiation), Iraq has *satisfactorily* completed the following:
>
> **1.** Statement by President Saddam Hussein: President Saddam Hussein must make a public statement in Arabic, broadcast on television and radio in Iraq and in the government controlled media, that:
>
> Iraq has, in the past, sought to conceal its weapons of mass destruction and other proscribed activities, but has now taken a strategic decision not to produce or retain weapons of mass destruction or other proscribed items or related documentation and data;
>
> Iraq will *without delay* yield to Unmovic, the UN Monitoring, Verification and Inspection Commission, and IAEA, the International Atomic Energy Agency, for destruction *all* remaining prohibited weapons, proscribed items and related documentation and data; Iraq will *fully* co-operate with Unmovic and IAEA in *immediately* addressing and resolving *all* outstanding questions;
>
> It is the duty of *all* Iraqi Government personnel and citizens immediately: To cease *any* proscribed activity, To hand over *any* proscribed items or documentation and data about such items in their possession to Unmovic and IAEA, To volunteer information on previous and ongoing activities, and to provide to Unmovic and IAEA *all* co-operation, including by taking part in interviews outside Iraq; To disobey *any* orders received to the contrary;
>
> Failure to fulfil this duty would be considered a serious crime by the government. The government would, by (date is subject to negotiation) enact comprehensive legislation to ban all government personnel and citizens from supporting or engaging in proscribed activities, from retaining proscribed items, related documentation and data, and obliging all citizens to comply with all requests from Unmovic and IAEA.
>
> **2.** Interviews outside Iraq: At least 30 Iraqi scientists selected by Unmovic/IAEA must be made available for interview in a secure environment outside Iraq along with their families. They must co-operate *fully* with their interviewers.
>
> **3.** Surrender and explanations about anthrax: *All* remaining anthrax, anthrax production capability, associated growth media, and related weapons/dispersal mechanisms must be surrendered or *credible* evidence provided to account for their whereabouts; *Credible* evidence must also be provided that anthrax was not produced in 1991 and accounting for the anthrax Iraq claims was destroyed in 1991; *Credible* evidence must be produced concerning Iraq's efforts to dry BW (biological warfare) agents.

4. Destruction of missiles: Destruction must be completed of all Al Samoud 2 missiles and components, including all warheads, launchers, SA-2 missile engines [smuggled into Iraq], and equipment and components designed for the production and testing of the Al Samoud 2 missile.

5. Accounting for unmanned aerial vehicles and remotely piloted vehicles: *Credible* evidence must be provided on the purpose of all RPV/UAV programs, information on organisations involved, and the inventory of all items related to the programme (such as engines, GPS (Global Position Systems), guidance systems, air frames, etc.) including details of all tests made, of range capabilities, of payloads and of CBW (chemical and biological warfare) spray devices.

6. Surrender of and explanations about mobile chemical and biological production facilities: Mobile chemical and/or biological production facilities must be surrendered for destruction; A *complete* accounting must be provided for mobile chemical and/or biological facilities production programs. Details should also be provided of sites providing support for/servicing/hosting mobile facilities.

This text is taken from BBC News Online at <http://news.bbc.co.uk/1/hi/world/middle_east/2846021.stm>.

17 *Financial Times*, 13 March 2003, p. 2.

18 *Financial Times*, 13 March 2003, p. 20.

19 *Telegraph*, 21 February 2003, p. 16.

20 *Sunday Times*, 23 February 2003, p. 13.

21 *Telegraph*, 14 March 2003, p. 16.

22 *Time* magazine, 17 March 2003, p. 29.

23 Hansard, 18 March 2003, cols. 767, 765, 766.

24 'Interview given by Jacques Chirac, President of the Republic, to TF1 and France 2 television stations', 10 March 2003. An official transcript of much of the interview can be found at the French Embassy website <http://www.info-france-usa.org/news/statmnts/2003/chirac_irak031003.asp>.

25 'Interview given by Jacques Chirac, President of the Republic', 10 March 2003, emphasis added.

26 Kamal Ahmed, Gaby Hinsliff, Ed Vulliamy and Paul Webster, 'Final play in Blair's diplomatic gamble', *Observer*, 16 March 2003 <http://www.observer.co.uk/focus/story/0,6903,915126,00.html>.

27 'Blair's mission impossible: the doomed effort to win a second UN resolution', *Financial Times*, 29 May 2003, p. 17.

28 'Bush: tomorrow is decision day for UN,' *Guardian*, 16 March 2003 <http://www.guardian.co.uk/international/story/0,3604,915442,00.html>.

29 Text printed in *Independent*, 8 March 2003, p. 2.

30 'Blair's mission impossible: the doomed effort to win a second UN resolution', *Financial Times*, 29 May 2003, p. 17.

31 'Introduction of draft UNMOVIC Work Programme, Security Council 19 March 2003'. Available from 'Recent Items', at <http://www.un.org/Depts/unmovic>.

32 *Times*, 12 February 2003, p. 18.

33 *Independent*, 24 February 2003, p. 14.

34 Michael Prowse, 'Disrespect for the UN is not the way forward', *Financial Times*, 'Weekend FT', 5/6 April 2003, p. II.

35 *Observer*, 12 January 2003, p. 16.

36 Figures compiled from Anjali V. Patil, *The UN Veto in World Affairs 1946–1990* (London: Mansell, 1992).

Chapter XV: Regime Reloaded

1 'President Says Saddam Hussein Must Leave Iraq Within 48 Hours', 17 March 2003 <http://www.whitehouse.gov/news/releases/2003/03/20030317-7.html>.

2 'President Says Saddam Hussein Must Leave Iraq Within 48 Hours', 17 March 2003 <http://www.whitehouse.gov/news/releases/2003/03/20030317-7.html>.

3 Human Rights Watch, 'Genocide in Iraq: The Anfal Campaign Against the Kurds, A Middle East Watch Report' (New York: Human Rights Watch, July 1993) <http://www.hrw.org/reports/1993/iraqanfal/>. '[B]eneath the euphemisms, Iraq's crimes against the Kurds amount[ed] to genocide, the "intent to destroy, in whole or in part, a national, ethnical, racial or religious group, as such".'

4 'Press Briefing by Ari Fleischer', 18 March 2003 <http://www.whitehouse.gov/news/releases/2003/03/20030318-4.html>.

5 *Hansard*, 17 March 2003, cols. 710-1. This speech can be found using the search facility at the Hansard website <http://www.parliament.uk/hansard/hansard.cfm>.

6 *Telegraph*, 20 January 2003, p. 1.

7 *Sunday Times*, 29 December 2002, p. 18.

8 *Times*, 13 February 2003, pp. 16, 1.

9 *Guardian*, 20 January 2003, p. 1.

10 At the home page <http://news.bbc.co.uk/> please search for "After Saddam" (using the double quotation marks) and click on 'Who's Who in Post-Saddam Iraq' for the 'Baathist Comeback' section.

11 Luke Harding, 'Iraqi opposition slams plan for military governor,' *Observer*, 16 February 2003 <http://www.observer.co.uk/international/story/0,6903,896571,00.html>.

12 Kanan Makiya, 'Our hopes betrayed: How a US blueprint for post-Saddam government quashed the hopes of democratic Iraqis,' *Observer*, 16 February 2003.

13 Luke Harding, 'Iraqi opposition slams plan for military governor,' *Observer*, 16 February 2003 <http://www.observer.co.uk/international/story/0,6903,896571,00.html>.

14 *Guardian*, 27 February 2003, p. 6

15 *Financial Times*, 27 February 2003, p. 9.

16 Cesar G. Soriano, 'U.S. "mayor of Baghdad" steps down,' *USA Today*, 11 May 2003 <http://www.usatoday.com/news/world/iraq/2003-05-11-envoy-leaves-iraq_x.htm>.

17 *Telegraph*, 7 May 2003, p. 11.

18 *Observer*, 11 May 2003, p. 2.

19 'Saddam' Tape Tale: 'Victory Is Coming', CBS News.com, 7 May 2003 <http://www.cbsnews.com/stories/2003/05/08/iraq/main552875.shtml>.

20 Eric Slater, 'U.N. Officials Warn of a Humanitarian Crisis', *Los Angeles Times*, 4 May 2003.

21 Cesar G. Soriano, 'U.S. "mayor of Baghdad" steps down,' *USA Today*, 11 May 2003 <http://www.usatoday.com/news/world/iraq/2003-05-11-envoy-leaves-iraq_x.htm>.

22 *Sunday Times*, 4 May 2003, p. 25.

23 *Independent*, 5 May 2003, p. 10.

24 *Financial Times*, 5 May 2003, p. 1.

25 *Independent*, 5 May 2003, p. 10.

26 Tarik Kafala, 'US struggles to foster Iraqi leaders,' BBC News Online, 15 May 2003 < http://news.bbc.co.uk/1/hi/world/middle_east/3030569.stm>.

27 *Telegraph*, 18 April 2003, p. 13.

28 *Telegraph*, 18 April 2003, p. 13.

29 *Telegraph*, 16 May, p. 16.

30 Louis Meixler, Baghdad, 'Saddam would face trial in an Iraqi court', *Guardian*, 9 May 2003, p. 14.

31 *Independent*, 5 May 2003, p. 10.

32 Louis Meixler, Baghdad, 'Saddam would face trial in an Iraqi court', *Guardian*, 9 May 2003, p. 14

33 *Independent*, 5 May 2003, p. 10.

34 *Sunday Times*, 4 May 2003, p. 24.

35 *Financial Times*, 5 May 2003, p. 1.

36 Donald Macintyre, Baghdad, 'Baghdad still restless as Bush claims victory', *Independent on Sunday*, 4 May 2003, p. 16.

37 *Sunday Telegraph*, 4 May 2003, p. 17.

38 *Independent*, 5 May 2003, p. 10.

39 Michael Howard and Ewen MacAskill, 'Force fights a thankless battle to keep the peace in a lawless land', *Guardian*, 26 June 2003 <http://www.guardian.co.uk/international/story/0,3604,985176,00.html>.

40 *Telegraph*, 18 April 2003, p. 13.

41 *Sunday Telegraph*, 4 May 2003, p. 17.

42 *Mirror*, 2 April 2003, p. 8.

43 *Times*, 10 May 2003, p. 18.

44 *Telegraph*, 16 May, p. 16.

Chapter XVI: Hitler Won

1 *Times*, 28 February 2003, p. 22.

2 Charles Willoughby and John Chamberlain, *MacArthur, 1941–1951, Victory in the Pacific* (London: William Heinemann Ltd, 1956), p. 291.

3 See Gar Alperovitz, *The Decision To Use The Atomic Bomb and the Architecture of an American Myth* (London: Fontana Press, 1995).

4 Willoughby and Chamberlain, *MacArthur*, pp. 311-2.

5 Robert Harvey, *The Undefeated: The Rise, Fall, and Rise of Greater Japan* (London: Macmillan, 1994), p. 301.

6 Harvey, *The Undefeated*, p. 311.

7 Harvey, *The Undefeated*, p. 313.

8 John Welfield, *An Empire in Decline: Japan in the Postwar American Alliance System. A Study in the Interaction of Domestic Politics and Foreign Policy* (London: Athlone Press, 1988), pp. 66, 68.

9 Harvey, *The Undefeated*, p. 304.

10 The story is set out in Sheldon Harris, *Factories of Death: Japanese Biological Warfare, 1932–45* (London: Routledge, 1994).

11 Roger Buckley, *Occupation Diplomacy: Britain, the United States and Japan 1945–1952* (Cambridge: Cambridge University Press, 1982), p. 25.

12 Harry Emerson Wildes, *Typhoon in Tokyo: The Occupation and its Aftermath* (New York: Macmillan, 1954), p. 337.

13 Dennis Bark and David Gress, *From Shadow to Substance 1945–1963* (Oxford: Blackwell, 1993), p. 68.

14 Bark and Gress, *From Shadow to Substance*, pp. 78, 76, 79, 78.

15 Anthony Mann, *Comeback: Germany 1945–1952* (London: Macmillan, 1980), p. 65.

16 A.W. Harrison, cited in Buckley, *Occupation Diplomacy*, p. 117.

17 Tom Bower, *Blind Eye to Murder: Britain, America and the Purging of Nazi Germany—A Pledge Betrayed* (London: Andre Deutsch, 1981), pp. 186, 188.

18 Cited in Bower, *Blind Eye to Murder*, p. 188.

19 Bower, *Blind Eye to Murder*, pp. 183–6, 193, 318, 319, 331, 25.

20 Bark and Gress, *From Shadow to Substance*, p. 85.

21 Bower, *Blind Eye to Murder*, pp. 380–1.

22 William E. Griffith, 'Denazification Revisited,' in Michael Emarth ed., *America and the Shaping of German Society, 1945–55* (Oxford: Berg, 1993), p. 164.

23 Karl Deutsch and Lewis Edinger, *Germany Rejoins the Powers: Mass Opinion, Interest Groups and Elites in Contemporary German Politics* (Stanford: Stanford University Press, 1959), p. 59; Bower, *Blind Eye to Murder*, p. 156.

24 Deutsch and Edinger, *Germany Rejoins the Powers*, p. 39; Bower, *Blind Eye to Murder*, p. 156.

25 Deutsch and Edinger, *Germany Rejoins the Powers*, p. 38; cited in Bark and Gress, *From Shadow to Substance*, p. 80.

26 Noam Chomsky, *The Culture of Terrorism* (London: Pluto Press, 1988), p. 255.

27 Cited in Bower, *Blind Eye to Murder*, p. 173.

28 Noam Chomsky, *Turning the Tide* (London: Pluto Press, 1985), p. 197

29 See Chomsky, *Turning the Tide*, p. 198–201. For recent research into Argentina's part in this grisly story, see Uki Goni, *The Real Odessa: how Peron brought the Nazi war criminals to Argentina* (London: Granta Books, 2003).

30 Letter, 26 July 1983, cited in Noam Chomsky, *Turning the Tide*, pp. 199-200.

31 Chomsky, *Turning the Tide*, p. 200.

32 Unconditional surrender', *Telegraph*, 4 April 2003, p. 25.

33 Cited in Chomsky, *Turning the Tide*, p. 154.

Chapter XVII: Coup d'Etat

1 Cited in Noam Chomsky, *Powers & Prospects: Reflections on human nature and the social order* (Boston: South End Press, 1996), p. 68. See Edward Herman and Noam Chomsky, *Manufacturing Consent: The Political Economy of the Mass Media* (New York: Pantheon Books, 1988) and Chomsky, *Necessary Illusions: Thought Control in Democratic Societies* (London: Pluto Press, 1989).

2 Quotations from my summary of the Chomsky–Herman 'propaganda model' in *Chomsky's Politics* (London: Verso, 1995).

3 *Guardian*, 16 March 2002, p. 5.

4 *Newsweek*, 25 March 2002, p. 18.

5 *Sunday Telegraph*, 17 March 2002, p. 15.

6 *Time* magazine, 13 May 2002, p. 38.

7 *Time* magazine, 12 August 2002, p. 25.

8 Jason Burke, 'Surrender or die, Allies warn Saddam's soldiers', *Observer*, 17 November 2002, p. 20.

9 Jason Burke, 'Surrender or die, Allies warn Saddam's soldiers', *Observer*, 17 November 2002, p. 20.

10 *Guardian*, 6 January 2003, p. 14.

11 *Observer*, 2 February 2003, p. 6.

12 *Times*, 12 February 2003, p. 1.

13 *Newsweek*, 3 February 2003, p. 18.

14 *Times*, 14 March 2003, p. 22.

15 *Telegraph*, 21 February 2003, p. 17.

16 *Financial Times*, 12 February 2003, p. 8.

17 'Press Briefing by Ari Fleischer,' 1 October 2002 <http://www.whitehouse.gov/news/releases/2002/10/20021001-4.html>. Mr Fleischer was forced to apologise for breaching a US law forbidding the targeting of foreign heads of state: 'Let me put it this way: I had only one bullet, and I used it to shoot myself in the foot.' *Time* magazine, Europe edition, 14 October 2002 <http://www.time.com/time/europe/magazine/article/0,13005,901021014-361600,00.html>.

18 *Financial Times*, 12 February 2003, p. 8, emphasis added.

19 *Financial Times*, 19 March 2003, p. 3. The US was giving out rather mixed messages, though. While Mr Bush appealed to Iraq's military commanders and included only Mr Hussein's sons in his ultimatum, US officials had in the past referred to the 'senior leadership' that would have to leave Iraq. 'The White House yesterday also indicated that the list of officials who would have to leave Iraq was longer than the Iraqi President's immediate family.' Furthermore, there was no mention in Mr Bush's speech of an amnesty, either for the Hussein family, or for the regime insiders who might be tempted to remove the Iraqi leader. 'Clearly the message is that if the three are gone everything is up for grabs. But there is also the message that US troops would still be there and possibly that there would still be an occupation. This muddies the waters,' said Raad

al-Kadiri, a political analyst at The Petroleum Finance Company in Washington. The attempt to secure a coup may be the result of US inconstancy.

Doubts among insiders about the West's intentions had been 'reinforced by ideas of Saddam going into exile: people willing to see the west doing some sort of deal with Saddam', according to one Western official. Experts consulted by the *FT* in early February believed that the possibility of a last-minute deal between the UN and Mr Hussein meant that any move against him would wait until the war erupted. *Financial Times*, 12 February 2003, p. 8.

20 *Newsweek*, 27 January 2003, p. 23, emphasis added.

21 Ben Macintyre, Michael Evans and Roland Watson, 'How Bush gambled on an early strike to kill Saddam,' *Times*, 21 March 2003.

22 *Financial Times*, 22 March 2003, p. 2.

23 *Financial Times*, 22 March 2003, p. 2.

24 *Times*, 22 March 2003, p. 1.

25 *Sunday Times*, 16 March 2003, p. 9.

26 *Telegraph*, 15 March 2003, p. 10, emphases added.

27 *Times*, 22 March 2003, p. 1.

28 *Times*, 22 March 2003, p. 1.

29 *Times*, 22 March 2003, p. 1.

30 *Time* magazine, 31 March 2003, p. 33.

31 *Independent*, 22 March 2003, p. 7.

32 *Times*, 22 March 2003, p. 3.

33 *Newsweek*, 12 August 2002, p. 32.

34 Daniel Eisenberg, 'Can Anyone Govern This Place?', *Time* magazine, 26 May 2003, p. 43

35 Daniel Eisenberg, 'Can Anyone Govern This Place?', *Time* magazine, 26 May 2003, p. 43

36 *Times*, 25 February 2003, p. 14.

37 *Observer*, 2 February 2003, p. 1.

38 Jamie McIntyre, ' "Shock and awe" phase of Iraq war put on hold,' CNN Online, 21 March 2003 <www.cnn.com/2003/US/03/20/sprj.irq.pentagon/index.html>.

39 *Newsweek*, 31 March 2003, p. 47.

40 *Newsweek*, 31 March 2003, p. 48, emphasis added.

41 *Times*, 22 March 2003, p. 14.

42 *Times*, 22 March 2003, p. 14.

43 *Time* magazine, 24 March 2003, p. 37.

44 *Observer*, 2 February 2003, p. 1.

45 *Financial Times*, 19 March 2003, p. 4.

46 AP report at the end of Louis Meixler, Baghdad, 'Saddam would face trial in an Iraqi court', *Guardian*, 9 May 2003, p. 14.

47 *Guardian*, 5 May 2003, p. 15.

48 *New Yorker*, 24 December 2001, p. 63.

49 John Keegan, 'Where are all Iraq's soldiers hiding?', *Telegraph*, 4 April 2003, p. 6.

50 Terry McCarthy, 'What Ever Happened to The Republican Guard? A TIME investigation suggests most of the elite Iraqi forces survived the US bombardment,' *Time* magazine, 12 May 2003, p. 27.

51 *Time* magazine, 12 May 2003, pp. 26–27.

52 Michael Dobbs, 'For Wolfowitz, a Vision May Be Realized,' *Washington Post*, 7 April 2003, p. A17.

53 *Financial Times*, 12 February 2003, p. 8.

Chapter XVIII: Why Regime Stabilization?

1 *Financial Times*, 27 February 2003, p. 9.

2 *Guardian*, 27 February 2003, p. 6.

3 *Guardian*, 27 February 2003, p. 6.

4 *Guardian*, 27 February 2003, p. 6.

5 *Times*, 7 February 2003, p. 21.

6 *Times*, 7 February 2003, p. 21.

7 <http://www.hrw.org/wr2k1/mideast/saudi.html>.

8 Yitzhak Nakash, *The Shi'is of Iraq* (Princeton: Princeton University Press, 1994), p. 45.

9 Yitzhak Nakash, *The Shi'is of Iraq* (Princeton: Princeton University Press, 1994), pp. 6, 4, 6.

10 Yitzhak Nakash, *The Shi'is of Iraq* (Princeton: Princeton University Press, 1994), p. 273.

11 Yitzhak Nakash, *The Shi'is of Iraq* (Princeton: Princeton University Press, 1994), p. 28.

12 Human Rights Watch, *Weapons Transfers and Violations of the Laws Of War in Turkey* (November 1995) <http://www.hrw.org/reports/1995/Turkey.htm>.

13 Sarah Graham-Brown, *Sanctioning Saddam: The Politics of Intervention in Iraq* (London: I.B. Tauris, 1999), p. 227.

14 *Telegraph*, 27 February 2003, p. 17.

15 *Guardian*, 21 February 2003, p. 4.

16 *Telegraph*, 27 February 2003, p. 17.

17 *Independent*, 24 February 2003, p. 2.

18 *Financial Times*, 28 February 2003, p. 7.

19 *Financial Times*, 1 February 2002, Supplement, p. III.

20 *Guardian*, 15 March 2002, p. 17.

21 Cited in Noam Chomsky, *World Orders, Old and New* (London: Pluto Press, 1994), p. 9.

22 Cited in Andrew and Patrick Cockburn, *Out of the Ashes* (New York: HarperCollins, 1999), p. 37.

23 Official biography, State Department <http://www.state.gov/r/pa/ei/biog/5492.htm>.

Chapter XIX: Crushing The Resistance

1 Robert Fisk, 'So he thinks it's all over. . .', *Independent on Sunday*, 4 May 2003, p. 22.

2 Stephen Ambrose, *Rise to Globalism: American Foreign Policy Since 1938* (London: Penguin, 1986), p. 24. Britain's January 1941 'Notes on Policy and Practice in respect of Occupation of Italian East Africa' laid down the 'general rule': 'to utilise as far as possible all local administrative authorities.' Lord Rennet of Rodd, *British Military Administration of Occupied Territories in Africa During the Years 1941–1947* (London: HMSO, 1948), pp. 44 f, 51, 53, 103, 459, 460, 466.

3 Cited in Gabriel Kolko, *The Politics of War: The World and United States Foreign Policy, 1943–1945* (New York: Pantheon, 1990), p. 67.

4 Cited in James E. Miller, *The United States and Italy, 1940-1950: The Politics and Diplomacy of Stabilization* (Chapell Hill: University of North Carolina Press, 1986), p. 48.

5 Kolko, *The Politics of War*, p. 46.

6 Miller, *The United States and Italy*, p. 81.

7 Miller, *The United States and Italy*, pp. 94 f.

8 Miller, *The United States and Italy*, p. 140.

9 Miller, *The United States and Italy*, p. 141.

10 Kolko, *The Politics of War*, p. 55.

11 Kolko, *The Politics of War*, p. 63.

12 Miller, *The United States and Italy*, p. 156.

13 Miller, *The United States and Italy*, p. 156.

14 David Travis, 'Communism and resistance in Italy, 1943–8', in Tony Judt ed., *Resistance and Revolution in Mediterranean Europe 1939–1948* (London: Routledge, 1989) p. 102.

15 Hilary Footit and John Simmonds, *France 1943–1945* (Leicester: Leicester University Press, 1988), p. 164.

16 Footit and Simmonds, *France 1943–1945*, p. 169.

17 Footit and Simmonds, *France 1943–1945*, p. 170.

18 Jean Lacouture, *De Gaulle: The Ruler 1945 - 1970* (London: Harvill, 1991, translated by Alan Sheridan), p. 17; Maurice Larkin, *France since the Popular Front: Government and People 1936 - 1986* (Oxford: Clarendon Press, 1989), p. 116; Footit and Simmonds, *France 1943–1945*, pp. 158, 248.

19 Larkin, *France since the Popular Front*, pp. 124 f.

20 Footit and Simmonds, *France 1943–1945*, p. 245.

21 Footit and Simmonds, *France 1943–1945*, pp. 86 f.

22 Cited in Footit and Simmonds, *France 1943–1945*, p. 189.

23 Footit and Simmonds, *France 1943–1945*, p. 194.

24 Lacouture, *De Gaulle*, pp. 21–3; Footit and Simmonds, *France 1943–1945*, p. 229.

25 Cited in Lacouture, *De Gaulle*, p. 16.

26 Lynne Taylor, 'The *Parti Communiste Français* and the French resistance in the Second World War', in Tony Judt, ed., *Resistance and Revolution in Mediterranean Europe 1939–1948* (London: Routledge, 1989), p 75.

27 Haris Vlavianos, 'The Greek Communist Party: in search of a revolution', in Tony Judt ed., *Resistance and Revolution in Mediterranean Europe 1939–1948* (London: Routledge, 1989), p. 184.

28 Vlavianos, 'The Greek Communist Party', p. 184.

29 Vlavianos, 'The Greek Communist Party', p. 189.

30 Cited in Kolko, *The Politics of War*, p. 188.

31 Peter J. Stavrakis, *Moscow and Greek Communism, 1944-1949* (Ithaca: Cornell University Press, 1989), p. 38.

32 G.M. Alexander, *The Prelude to the Truman Doctrine: British Policy in Greece 1944-1947* (Oxford: Clarendon Press, 1982), p. 118.

33 Vlavianos, 'The Greek Communist Party', p. 197.

34 Peter Dunn, *The First Vietnam War* (London: C. Hurst & Company, 1985), p. 139.

35 Peter Dunn, *The First Vietnam War* (London: C. Hurst & Company, 1985), p. 173.

36 Peter Dunn, *The First Vietnam War* (London: C. Hurst & Company, 1985), p. 173.

37 Peter Dunn, *The First Vietnam War* (London: C. Hurst & Company, 1985), p. 231.

38 Cited in Peter Dunn, *The First Vietnam War* (London: C. Hurst & Company, 1985), p. 242.

39 Robert J. McMahon, *Colonialism and Cold War: The United States and the struggle for Indonesian Independence, 1945–49* (Ithaca: Cornell University Press, 1981), p. 85.

40 Mountbatten's personal diary, cited in Oey Hong Lee, *War and Diplomacy in Indonesia 1945-50* (James Cook University of Queensland, 1981), p. 82.

41 Edward Behr, *Anyone here been raped and speak English? A Foreign Correspondent's Life Behind the Lines* (London: New English Library, 1982), p. 28.

42 Behr, *Anyone here been raped and speak English?*, p. 34.

43 Churchill, 5 August 1943, cited in Basil Davidson, *Scenes from the anti-Nazi war* (New York: Monthly Review Press, 1980), p. 17; Roosevelt, 30 July 1943, cited in Kolko, *The Politics of War*, p. 45.

44 Cited in David Stafford, *Britain and European Resistance, 1940-1945: A Survey of the Special Operations Executive with Documents* (London: Macmillan, 1980), p. 191.

Chapter XX: Regime Revolutions

1 *Independent*, 5 May 2003, p. 10.

2 *Telegraph*, 18 April 2003, p. 13.

3 Andrew Marshall, 'British Hand Over First Iraqi Town to Civilian Rule,' Reuters, 15 May 2003.

4 Richard W. Carlson, 'Throwing Out the Baath Water: Saddam's henchmen gotta go,' *Weekly Standard*, 26 May 2003 <http://www.weeklystandard.com/Content/Public/Articles/000/000/002/688uufww.asp>.

5 Rory McCarthy, 'Power of protest forces out senior Ba'athist officials,' *Guardian*, 14 May 2003 <http://www.guardian.co.uk/Iraq/Story/0,2763,955461,00.html>.

6 *Times*, 17 May, p. 21.

7 Rory McCarthy, 'Power of protest forces out senior Ba'athist officials.'

8 *Independent*, 5 May 2003, p. 10.

9 *Times*, 17 May 2003, p. 21.

10 Hamza Hendawi, 'Shiites Reportedly Hunting Baathists,' Associated Press, 24 May 2003.

11 James Drummond and Nicolas Pelham, 'Shia clerics urge faithful to attack returning Ba'athists', *Financial Times*, 10/11 May 2003, p. 6.

12 Hamza Hendawi, 'Shiites Reportedly Hunting Baathists'.

13 Hamza Hendawi, 'Shiites Reportedly Hunting Baathists'.

14 Hamza Hendawi, 'Shiites Reportedly Hunting Baathists'.

15 'Arson attacks against homes of ex-Baath officials in southern Iraq,' Agence France Presse, 4 June 2003.

16 *Sunday Telegraph*, 18 May 2003, p. 28.

17 Guardian, 17 May 2003, p. 21.

18 *Guardian*, 17 May 2003, p. 15.

19 *Times*, 17 May 2003, p. 21.

20 *Telegraph*, 14 January 2003, p. 13.

21 *Financial Times*, 12 February 2003, p. 8.

22 *Time* magazine, 31 March 2003, pp. 36-7.

23 *Newsweek*, 31 March 2003, p. 45.

24 *Newsweek*, 31 March 2003, p. 48.

25 Kanan Makiya, 'Kanan Makiya's War Diary,' 26 March 2003, *The New Republic* Online <http://www.tnr.com/doc.mhtml?i=iraq&s=diary032603>.

26 *Independent*, 5 May 2003, p. 10.

Chapter XXI: Shia Power

1 'Uprising reported in Basra,' BBC News Online, 25 March 2003 <http://news.bbc.co.uk/1/hi/world/middle_east/2886235.stm>.

2 'Blair pledges support to "uprisings",' BBC News Online, 26 March 2003 <http://news.bbc.co.uk/1/hi/uk_politics/2886691.stm>.

3 'Basra: Why they are not cheering,' BBC News Online, 26 March 2003 <http://news.bbc.co.uk/1/hi/world/middle_east/2884769.stm>.

4 'Iraq war: Unanswered questions,' BBC News Online, 17 April 2003 <http://news.bbc.co.uk/1/hi/world/middle_east/2929411.stm#return>.

5 Keith Harrison, 'British "liberators" cheered in Basra,' BBC News Online, 9 April 2003 <http://news.bbc.co.uk/1/hi/uk/2932293.stm>.

6 *Guardian*, 2 April 2003, p. 5.

7 *Daily Telegraph*, 27 March 2003, p. 10.

8 *Daily Telegraph*, 27 March 2003, p. 24.

9 Yitzhak Nakash, *The Shi'is of Iraq* (Princeton: Princeton University Press, 1994), p. 276.

10 *Sunday Telegraph*, 12 August 2002, p. 28.

11 For details see my *War Plan Iraq* (London: Verso, 2002), Chapter VII, 'Regime Stabilization.'

12 Cited in Dilip Hiro, *Neighbours Not Friends: Iraq and Iran after the Gulf Wars* (London: Routledge, 2001), pp. 36–7.

13 *Financial Times*, 27 March 2003, p. 21.

14 *Financial Times*, 27 March 2003, p. 2.

15 *Financial Times*, 27 March 2003, p. 3.

16 Hilary Andersson, 'A war too big to comprehend,' BBC News Online, 5 April 2003 <http://news.bbc.co.uk/1/hi/world/from_our_own_correspondent/2920373.stm>.

17 'Basra protests against UK leader,' BBC News Online, 1 June 2003 <http://news.bbc.co.uk/1/hi/world/middle_east/2954096.stm>.

18 *Independent*, 26 April 2003, p. 16.

19 *Sunday Times*, 4 May 2003, pp. 24–25.

20 Anthony Shadid, 'Clerics Vie With U.S. For Power,' *Washington Post*, 7 June 2003, p. A01.

21 Shadid, 'Clerics Vie With U.S. For Power'.

22 Hamza Hendawi, 'Baghdad Clerics Want Strict Islamic Laws,' Associated Press, 2 June 2003.

23 James Drummond and Nicolas Pelham, 'Shia clerics urge faithful to attack returning Ba'athists', *Financial Times*, 10/11 May 2003, p. 6.

24 See p. 108–9.

25 *Financial Times*, 25 June 2003, p. 17.

26 *Financial Times*, 26/27 April 2003, p. 8.

27 *Independent*, 24 April 2003, p. 12.

28 *Guardian*, 5 May 2003, p. 15.

29 Ewen MacAskill, 'Baghdad waits in fear for rebuilding to start', *Guardian*, 9 May 2003, p. 15.

30 *Financial Times*, 25 June 2003, p. 17.

31 *Independent*, 24 April 2003, p. 12.

32 Hendawi, 'Baghdad Clerics Want Strict Islamic Laws,' Associated Press, 2 June 2003.

33 *Guardian*, 23 April 2003, p. 13.

34 Hendawi, 'Baghdad Clerics Want Strict Islamic Laws,' Associated Press, 2 June 2003.

35 *Times*, 24 April 2003, p. 15.

36 *Independent*, 24 April 2003, p. 12.

37 Yitzhak Nakash, 'All Iraqis Need a Stake in a Post–Hussein Nation,' *Los Angeles Times*, 8 December 2002.

38 Karen Armstrong, 'Faith and freedom: With a tradition of justice and secularism, there is no reason to fear Iraq's Shia resurgence,' *Guardian*, 8 May 2003, p. 23.

39 *Times*, 10 May 2003, p. 19.

40 *Financial Times*, 10/11 May 2003, p. 6.

41 'A new viceroy for Iraq', editorial, *Financial Times*, 13 May 2003, p. 22.

42 Karen Armstrong, 'Faith and freedom: With a tradition of justice and secularism, there is no reason to fear Iraq's Shia resurgence,' *Guardian*, 8 May 2003, p. 23.

43 Abdul Majid al-Khoei, Obituaries, *Times*, 11 April 2003 <http://www.timesonline.co.uk/article/0,,60-642239,00.html>.

44 Michael Wood, 'Abdul Majid al-Khoei: Wise and moderate Shia cleric murdered before he could contribute to the rebuilding of Iraq,' Guardian, 12 April 2003 <http://www.guardian.co.uk/Iraq/Story/0,2763,935242,00.html?=rss>.

45 <http://www.al-khoei.org/press_release.asp>.

46 Joshua Hammer, 'Murder at the Mosque Why was America's favorite Iraqi cleric killed? The inside story of a CIA connection, an Iranian mystery and a stash of dollars hidden in the holy man's robes,' *Newsweek*, 19 May 2003 <http://www.msnbc.com/news/912084.asp?cp1=1#BODY>.

47 Glenn Kessler and Dana Priest, 'U.S. Planners Surprised by Strength of Iraqi Shiites,' *Washington Post*, 23 April 2003, p. A01.

48 Kessler and Priest, 'U.S. Planners Surprised'.

49 *Guardian*, 5 May 2003, p. 15.

50 *Times*, 24 April 2003, p. 15.

51 Daniel Eisenberg, 'Can Anyone Govern This Place?', *Time* magazine, 26 May 2003, p. 43.

52 *Times*, 24 April 2003, p. 16.

53 *Times*, 24 April 2003, p. 16.

54 *Guardian*, 23 April 2003, p. 13.

55 *Independent*, 26 April 2003, p. 16.

56 Robert Fisk, 'So he thinks it's all over...,' *Independent on Sunday*, 4 May 2003, p. 22.

57 *Times*, 24 April 2003, p. 15.

58 Roula Khalaf, 'Freedom's reckoning', *FT magazine*, 26 April 2003, p. 23.

59 *Sunday Times*, 4 May 2003, p. 27.

60 Peter Beaumont, *Observer*, 4 May 2003, p. 23.

61 *Telegraph*, 24 April 2003, p. 14.

62 Hendawi, 'Baghdad Clerics Want Strict Islamic Laws,' Associated Press, 2 June 2003.

Chapter XXII: Sunni Rage

1 Charles Tripp, *A History of Iraq* (Cambridge: Cambridge University Press, 2000), p. 31.

2 Charles Tripp, *A History of Iraq*, p. 47.

3 *Guardian*, 6 May 2003, p. 16.

4 'Iraqis killed in Falluja protest,' BBC News Online, 29 April 2003 <http://news.bbc.co.uk/1/hi/world/middle_east/2984663.stm>.

5 'Iraqis killed in Falluja protest,' BBC News Online, 29 April 2003.

6 Phil Reeves, 'Iraqi rage grows after Fallujah massacre', *Independent on Sunday*, 4 May 2003, p. 17.

7 Phil Reeves, 'At least 10 killed by US soldiers firing on protesters outside school,' *Independent*, 30 April 2003, p. 2. The *Daily Telegraph* mentioned the bullet holes and marks, but neglected to mention that they were on another side of the school. Alan Philps, '13 Iraqis die as US troops fire into crowd,' *Telegraph*, 30 April 2003, p. 10.

8 Phil Reeves, 'Iraqi rage grows after Fallujah massacre', *Independent on Sunday*, 4 May 2003, p. 17.

9 Chris Hughes, 'We got close.. they started shooting,' *Mirror*, 30 April 2003, p. 11.

10 Phil Reeves, 'Iraqi rage grows after Fallujah massacre', *Independent on Sunday*, 4 May 2003, p. 17.

11 Phil Reeves, 'Iraqi rage grows after Fallujah massacre', *Independent on Sunday*, 4 May 2003, p. 17.

12 Jonathan Steele, 'To the US troops it was self-defence. To the Iraqis it was murder,' *Guardian*, 30 April 2003, p. 2.

13 Ed Vulliamy, *Observer*, 4 May 2003, p. 23.

14 Saul Hudson, 'Iraqis Warn US Killings Will Breed Terror Recruits,' Reuters, 1 May 2003.

15 Phil Reeves, 'At least 10 killed by US soldiers firing on protesters outside school,' *Independent*, 30 April 2003, p. 2.

16 Saul Hudson, 'Iraqis Warn US Killings Will Breed Terror Recruits,' Reuters, 1 May 2003.

17 'Protesters shot in Falluja,' BBC News Online, 30 April 2003 <http://news.bbc.co.uk/1/hi/world/middle_east/2988823.stm>.

18 Chris Hughes, 'With no warning the jeep's gun fired into the unarmed crowd.. seconds later two lay dead,' *Mirror*, 1 May 2003, p. 4.

19 *Sunday Times*, 4 May 2003, p. 24.

20 Saul Hudson, 'Iraqis Warn US Killings Will Breed Terror Recruits,' Reuters, 1 May 2003.

21 Daniel Williams, 'Fueling Pacification With Propane: In Fallujah, Army Seeks to Stem Unrest With Aid, Troop Reinforcements,' *Washington Post*, 4 June 2003, p. A14.

22 Daniel Williams, 'Fueling Pacification With Propane: In Fallujah, Army Seeks to Stem Unrest With Aid, Troop Reinforcements,' *Washington Post*, 4 June 2003, p. A14.

23 Ed Vulliamy, *Observer*, 4 May 2003, p. 23.

24 Daniel Williams, 'Fueling Pacification With Propane: In Fallujah, Army Seeks to Stem Unrest With Aid, Troop Reinforcements,' *Washington Post*, 4 June 2003, p. A14.

25 Jack Fairweather, 'Army sparks suspicion as it moves into Ba'ath party HQ,' *Telegraph*, 29 March 2003, p. 3.

26 *Sunday Times*, 4 May 2003, p. 24.

27 Phil Reeves, 'Iraqi rage grows after Fallujah massacre', *Independent on Sunday*, 4 May 2003, p. 17.

28 Daniel Williams, 'Fueling Pacification With Propane: In Fallujah, Army Seeks to Stem Unrest With Aid, Troop Reinforcements,' *Washington Post*, 4 June 2003, p. A14.

29 James Hilder, 'Charm offensive follows Fallujah crackdown,' *Times*, 16 June 2003, p. 15.

30 James Hilder, 'Charm offensive follows Fallujah crackdown,' *Times*, 16 June 2003, p. 15; Peter Foster (in Falluja), 'Demonstrators stone army vehicles as 10,000 protest in Basra,' *Telegraph*, 16 June 2003, p. 10 (reports that there have been 'repeated attacks on US soldiers', but fails to mention the April massacre); Rory McCarthy (in Falluja), 'Policing Iraqis tests US troops,' *Guardian*, 16 June 2003, p. 10 (no mention of the massacre); Charles Clover (in Baghdad), 'US army in big drive to curb Iraqi attacks,' *Financial Times*, 16 June 2003, p. 6 (mentions killings of US soldiers, and local opinion that revenge was the motive for attacks on US soldiers, but no mention of the April massacre); Patrick Cockburn (in Baquba), 'US troops ambushed amid drive to extinguish resistance,' *Independent*, 16 June 2003, p. 2 (does not mention Falluja at all, but notes deaths of US soldiers without mentioning the April Falluja massacre or any other civilian deaths caused by US forces).

Regime Unchanged

31 Hamza Hendawi, 'Iraq Sunnis Seethe Over Loss of Prestige,' Associated Press, 6 June 2003.

32 Hamza Hendawi, 'Iraq Sunnis Seethe Over Loss of Prestige,' Associated Press, 6 June 2003.

33 Phil Reeves, 'Iraqi rage grows after Fallujah massacre', *Independent on Sunday*, 4 May 2003, p. 17.

34 Hamza Hendawi, 'Iraq Sunnis Seethe Over Loss of Prestige,' Associated Press, 6 June 2003.

35 'Troops crack down on Saddam loyalists,' BBC News Online, 6 June 2003 <http://news.bbc.co.uk/go/pr/fr/-/1/hi/world/middle_east/2983486.stm>.

36 Rory McCarthy, 'US troops kill 97 Iraqis in new attacks,' *Guardian*, 14 June 2003, p. 2.

37 Hamza Hendawi, 'Iraq Sunnis Seethe Over Loss of Prestige,' Associated Press, 6 June 2003.

38 Patrick Cockburn, 'Battles rage across Saddam heartland where 70 Iraqis are killed by US forces,' *Independent*, 14 June 2003, p. 11.

39 James Hilder, 'US troops fall foul of honour and feuding,' *Times*, 12 June 2003, p. 16.

40 James Hilder, 'US troops fall foul of honour and feuding,' *Times*, 12 June 2003, p. 16.

41 Jack Fairweather, 'Triumph and tragedy cloud truth of conflict in the "Sunni Triangle",' , 14 June 2003, p. 19.

42 James Hilder, 'Charm offensive follows Fallujah crackdown,' *Times*, 16 June 2003, p. 15.

43 Charles Clover, 'Pro-Saddam fighters or feuding neighbours?', *Financial Times*, 12 June 2003, p. 13.

44 Richard Beeston, 'Ragged resistance draws US in for the long haul,' *Times*, 14 June 2003, p. 23.

45 Cockburn, 'Battles rage across Saddam heartland'.

46 Patrick Cockburn, 'Villagers enraged and baffled by American show of force,' *Independent on Sunday*, 15 June 2003, p. 19.

47 Rory McCarthy, 'Policing Iraqis tests US troops,' *Guardian*, 16 June 2003, p. 10.

48 Cited in *War Plan Iraq*, p. 201.

49 Catherine Philp, 'Mob fury as US soldiers shoot two protesters dead,' *Times*, 1 May 2003, p. 21.

Chapter XXIII: Capitalism's War

1 Cited in David Stafford, *Britain and European Resistance, 1940-1945: A Survey of the Special Operations Executive with Documents* (London: Macmillan, 1980), p. 191.

2 Cited in David Dilks, 'Introduction', in David Dilks, *Retreat from Power: Studies in Britain's Foreign Policy of the Twentieth Century*, Volume II: *After 1939* (London: Macmillan, 1981), p. 9.

3 Cited in David Dilks, 'Introduction'.

4 In Peter Catterall and C.J. Morris eds., *Britain and the threat to stability in Europe, 1918–1945* (London: Leicester University Press, 1993).

5 Noam Chomsky, *Turning the Tide: US Intervention in Central America and the Struggle for Peace* (Boston: South End Press, 1985), p. 47.

6 Reproduced in Walter LaFeber, ed., *The Origins of the Cold War, 1941-1947: A Historical Problem with Interpretations and Documents* (New York: John Wiley & Sons, 1971), p. 33.

7 Cited in LaFeber, ed., *The Origins of the Cold War*, p. 35.

8 Cited in John J. Sbrega, *Anglo-American Relations and Colonialism in East Asia, 1941-1945* (New York, Garland, 1983), pp. 17 f.

9 Joint Foreign Office and Colonial Office memorandum, August 1942, CO 825/35/4, no. 52.

10 *Stable Forces in a Strong Britain*, Statement on the Defence Estimates 1995 (London: HMSO, 1995) Cm 2800, p. 9.

11 Strategic Defence Review (London: HMSO, 1998), para. 19 <http://www.mod.uk/issues/sdr/priorities.htm>.

12 Wm Roger Louis, *The Origins of the Cold War, 1941-1947: A Historical Problem with Interpretations and Documents* (New York, Oxford University Press, 1978), p. 567.

13 US ambassador to China, General Patrick Hurley, cited in Christopher Thorne, *Allies of a Kind: The United States, Britain and the war against Japan, 1941-1945* (Oxford, Oxford University Press, 1978), p. 593.

14 The memoranda of the War and Peace Studies Project were revealed and analysed in L. Shoup and W. Minter, *Imperial Brain Trust* (New York: Monthly Review Press, 1977). This summary is drawn from Noam Chomsky, *Towards a New Cold War* (London: Sinclair Browne, 1982), pp. 95–7.

15 David P. Calleo and Benjamin M. Rowland, *America and the World Political Economy* (Bloomington: Indian University Press, 1973), cited in Noam Chomsky, *Towards a New Cold War* (London: Sinclair Browne, 1982), p. 408 n. 23.

16 Chomsky, *Towards a New Cold War*, p. 96.

17 Chomsky, *Towards a New Cold War*, p. 97.

18 Cited in Chomsky, *Towards a New Cold War*, p. 96.

19 Cited in Chomsky, *Towards a New Cold War*, p. 96.

20 Cited in Chomsky, *Towards a New Cold War*, p. 98.

21 Mark Curtis, *The Ambiguities of Power: British Foreign Policy Since 1945* (London: Zed Books, 1995), p. 93; Makins cited in David Dimbleby and David Reynolds, *An Ocean Apart: The Relationship Between Britain and America in the Twentieth Century* (New York: Random House, 1988), p. 212.

22 W. Scott Lucas, *Divided We Stand: Britain, the US and the Suez Crisis* (London: Hodder and Stoughton, 1996), pp. 292-3.

23 'Future Policy in the Persian Gulf,' 15 January 1958, FO 371/132 778, cited in Noam Chomsky, *Deterring Democracy* (London: Verso, 1991), p. 184.

24 Robert Komer cited in William Stivers, *America's Confrontation*, p. 93; Ronald Reagan cited in Christopher Paine, On the Beach: the Rapid Deployment Force and the nuclear arms race', in *The Deadly Connection: Nuclear War and US Interventionism* (Boston: American Friends Service Committee, 1983), p. 71.

25 John Kent, *British Imperial Strategy and the Origins of the Cold War*, (Leicester: Leicester University Press, 1993), p. 24.

26 CAB 66/51 WP (44) 304 7.6.44, cited in Kent, *British Imperial Strategy*, p. 26.

27 FO371/50912, memorandum by O. Sargent, 11 July 1945, cited in Kent, *British Imperial Strategy*, p. 56.

28 Chomsky, *Towards a New Cold War*, p. 100.

29 PPS 23, 24 February 1948, *FRUS 1948*, I (part 2), cited in Noam Chomsky, *Turning the Tide*, p. 48.

30 Noam Chomsky, *Turning the Tide*, p. 48.

31 Noam Chomsky, *Turning the Tide*, p. 49.

32 'Is Labour fit to govern?', editorial, *Daily Telegraph*, 11 March 2003.

Chapter XXIV: Regime Unchanged

1 Editorial, *Telegraph*, 15 February 2003, p. 27.

2 Sheryl Garratt, 'The Odd Trio', *Sunday Telegraph Magazine*, 22 June 2003, p. 15.

3 Artists Winning Without War petition <http://www.moveon.org/artistswinwithoutwar/>.

4 *Telegraph*, 27 February 2003, p. 16.

5 In Memoriam Online Network <http://www.inmemoriamonline.net/Profiles/Folders/B_Folder/Bennett_Oliver.html>.

6 *Telegraph*, 27 February 2003, p. 16.

7 'His mind won't be changed,' ITV News Online, 27 February 2003, cached by Google.

8 'Blair sits down with antiwar Britons,' CNN, 27 February 2003 <http://edition.cnn.com/2003/WORLD/europe/02/26/sprj.irq.blair.protesters/>

9 Armando Iannucci, *Telegraph*, 3 January 2003, 10 January; 'I'll be seeing you at the anti-war march on Saturday,' 13 February 2003. All three articles can be found online by searching for 'Iannucci' at <http://www.telegraph.co.uk>.

10 *Sunday Times*, 16 March 2003, p. 2.

11 For a few examples comparing the 'dodgy dossier' with Mr al-Marashi's work, please see Jonathan Rugman, 'Downing St dossier plagiarised,' Channel 4 News, 6 February 2003 <http://www.channel4.com/news/2003/02/week_1/06_dossier.html> or 'A piece of plagiarism?', BBC News Online <http://news.bbc.co.uk/1/hi/uk_politics/2736149.stm>.

12 Patrick Wintour, 'Straw rounds on Campbell', *Guardian*, 25 June 2003 <http://www.guardian.co.uk/guardianpolitics/story/0,3605,984351,00.html>.

13 'Why Blair needed the "dodgy dossier"', letter, *Independent*, 28 June 2003, p. 19.

14 *Sunday Times*, 10 March 2002, p. 2.

15 *Financial Times*, 20 April 2002, p. 2.

16 'The "sexed up" dossier broadcast', *Guardian*, 27 June 2003 <http://www.guardian.co.uk/guardianpolitics/story/0,3605,985980,00.html>.

17 'Journalist defends weapons claims', BBC News Online, 19 June 2003 <http://news.bbc.co.uk/1/hi/uk_politics/3003296.stm>.

18 Peter Beaumont, 'The BBC reported what we were all told—and it was right', *Observer*, 29 June 2003, p. 16.

19 'U.N. committee: No Iraq-al-Qaeda link', AP report in *USA Today*, 26 June 2003 <http://www.usatoday.com/news/world/iraq/2003-06-26-iraq-alqaeda_x.htm>.

20 *Telegraph*, 4 February 2003, p. 13.

21 *Guardian*, 6 February 2003, p. 1.

22 *Guardian*, 6 February 2003, p. 3.

23 *Financial Times*, 15 February 2003, p. 7.

24 Richard Wallace, 'Time wasters: Angry arms inspectors hit out at US spy chiefs', *Mirror*, 22 February 2003, p. 4.

25 Mohamed ElBaradei, 'The Status of Nuclear Inspections in Iraq: An Update', 7 March 2003 <http://www.iaea.org/worldatom/Press/Statements/2003/ebsp2003n006.shtml>. See also Chapter IX.

26 *Observer*, 17 March 2003, p. 15.

27 *Independent on Sunday*, 27 April 2003, p. 1..

28 Con Coughlin, 'Saddam has outwitted his enemies again,' *Sunday Telegraph*, 17 November 2002, p. 26.

29 'WMD emphasis was "bureaucratic",' BBC News Online, 29 May 2003 <http://news.bbc.co.uk/1/hi/world/middle_east/2945750.stm>.

30 Con Coughlin, 'Saddam has outwitted his enemies again,' *Sunday Telegraph*, 17 November 2002, p. 26.

31 *Hansard*, 18 March 2003, cols. 769–70.

32 *Hansard*, 18 March 2003, col. 767.

33 *Newsweek*, 24 March 2003, p. 31.

34 Nancy Gibbs, 'Double-Edged Sword', *Time* magazine, 30 December 2002–6 January 2003, p. 68.

35 Editorial, 'Why Britain should fight', *Daily Telegraph*, 27 January 2003, p. 21.

36 Kamal Ahmed and Ed Vulliamy, 'Blair sets out final terms to avoid war', *Observer*, 9 March 2003 <http://www.observer.co.uk/international/story/0,6903,910684,00.html>.

37 *Independent*, 6 April 2002, p. 6; *Guardian*, 10 April 2002, p. 8; *Guardian*, 16 March 2002, p. 1.

38 *Telegraph*, 7 February 2003, p. 12.

39 'PM: "Saddam should take the peaceful route and disarm",' 13 January 2003, <http://www.number-10.gov.uk/output/Page3005.asp>.

40 'Tony Blair on *Newsnight*—part one', 7 February 2003, *Guardian* online <http://politics.guardian.co.uk/foreignaffairs/story/0,11538,891112,00.html>.

41 *Hansard*, 18 March 2003, cols. 766–7.

42 Jonathan Freedland, 'Why voters still think he's a pretty straight kinda guy', *Guardian*, 19 February 2002 <http://politics.guardian.co.uk/polls/comment/0,11030,652498,00.html>.

43 *Telegraph*, 11 December 2002, p. 14; *Telegraph*, 14 December 2002, p. 1.

44 *Telegraph*, 11 December 2002, p. 14; *Telegraph*, 14 December 2002, p. 1.

45 *Telegraph*, 28 November 2002, p. 18.

46 Steve Turnham, 'Senate intel chairman suggests proof coming on Iraqi WMD: Distinction drawn between program and actual weapons,' CNN 3 July 2003 <http://edition.cnn.com/2003/ALLPOLITICS/07/03/sprj.nitop.senators.wmd/>.

47 Christina Lamb, 'Saddam's chemical labs "made no weapons",' *Sunday Times*, 8 June 2003.

48 John Barry, 'The Defector's Secrets', *Newsweek*, 3 March 2003; the interview transcrip and Glen Rangwala's comments appear at <http://traprockpeace.org/kamel.html>.

49 Media coverage is included at the Traprock Peace Centre website.

50 David Blair, 'Last stand at Majar al-Kabir', *Telegraph*, 26 June 2003, p. 1.

51 Patrick Cockburn, 'It began with some children throwing stones. It left a town turned into a battle zone and 10 people lying dead,' *Independent*, 26 June 2003, p. 3.

52 Daniel McGrory, 'Soldiers gunned down after fury over searches,' *Times*, 26 June 2003, p. 4.

53 Patrick Cockburn, 'It began with some children throwing stones. It left a town turned into a battle zone and 10 people lying dead,' *Independent*, 26 June 2003, p. 3.

54 Daniel McGrory, 'Soldiers gunned down after fury over searches,' *Times*, 26 June 2003, p. 4.

55 Peter Foster, 'Coalition pays Saddam's old soldiers up to £90 a month,' *Telegraph*, 24 June 2003, p. 12.

56 Michael Howard and Ewen Macaskill, 'Force fights a thankless battle to keep the peace in a lawless land', *Guardian*, 26 June 2003, p. 3.

57 Tom Bower, *Blind Eye to Murder: Britain, America and the Purging of Nazi Germany—A Pledge Betrayed* (London: Andre Deutsch, 1981), pp. 186, 188.

58 David Frum, 'Myth II: America wants war with Saddam because of oil', *Daily Telegraph*, 22 October 2002.

59 James Chace, *New York Times Magazine*, 22 May 1977, cited in Noam Chomsky, Year 501: The Conquest Continues (Boston: South End Press, 1993), p. 42.

60 President Bush, 'Address to a Joint Session of Congress and the American People,' 20 September 2001 <http://www.whitehouse.gov/news/releases/2001/09/20010920-8.html>.

61 *Financial Times*, 24 June 2003, p. 11.

62 *Financial Times*, 24 June 2003, p. 11.

63 *Times*, 6 May 2003, p. 15

64 *Independent*, 16 March 1990, cited in John Sweeney, *Trading with the Enemy: Britain's Arming of Iraq* (London: Pan Books, 1993), p. 171.

65 Basil Davidson, *Scenes from the anti-Nazi war* (New York: Monthly Review Press, 1980), pp. 93, 152–3, emphasis added.

66 Gabriel Kolko, *The Politics of War: The World and United States Foreign Policy, 1943–1945* (New York: Pantheon, 1990), p. 55.

67 Cited in Peter Novick, *The Resistance versus Vichy: The Purge of Collaborators in Liberated France* (London: Chatto & Windus, 1968), pp. 198–200.

68 Marie Woolf, 'MPs attack Reid for "socialist" Iraq policy', *Independent*, 28 February 2003, p. 4.

69 Ewen MacAskill, 'Baghdad waits in fear for rebuilding to start', *Guardian*, 9 May 2003, p. 15.

Index

1 'Britain's challenge to Blair: show us the evidence', *Independent*, 4 June 2003, p. 1

CONTRIBUTOR NOTES

Milan Rai

Milan Rai was awarded the Frank Cousins Peace Award (Research) by the Transport and General Workers Union in 1993. A founder member of the direct action anti-war group ARROW (see below) he has edited two ARROW pamphlets—*The Rabble Element: Police Interviews with Chris Cole and Milan Rai* (1991), and *ARROW Two Years On* (1993)—composed of interviews with ARROW members, some carried out by police officers. In 1998, with the support of ARROW, Milan Rai founded **voices in the wilderness uk**, the British branch of the US sanctions-breaking group (see below), and became one of two British citizens to be arrested for breaking the economic sanctions on Iraq by exporting medical supplies without an export licence. In July 2003, Milan Rai and some other members of ARROW formed a new anti-war organization named 'Justice Not Vengeance' (see below).

ARROW

This book is in large part an outgrowth of the work of ARROW (Active Resistance to the Roots of War), a London–based nonviolent direct action affinity group. Formed to oppose the Gulf War in September 1990, the group held an anti-sanctions/anti-war vigil outside the Foreign Office in Whitehall from 5.30pm to 7pm every Monday evening from July 1991 until the ending of economic sanctions in May 2003. From September 2001 to early 2003, ARROW gave away thousands of *ARROW Anti-War Briefings* free at mass demonstrations. As of July 2003, ARROW continues as a small affinity group, but the production and distribution of Anti-War Briefings, and the ARROW website, have been passed on to a group 'Justice Not Vengeance' (see below). ARROW c/o NVRN, 162 Holloway Rd, London N7 8DQ. Telephone 020 7607 2302.

Justice Not Vengeance

'Justice Not Vengeance' is a new British anti-war grouping initiated by ARROW founder members David Polden and Milan Rai to help empower and support local anti-war groups, and to supply campaigning materials including *JNV Anti-War Briefings*. JNV is committed to direct democracy in developing regional and national anti-war campaigning priorities, and horizontal communication of information, ideas and materials between groups. The basic principles of the proposed network are contained in the JNV 7 Points (an updated version of the 'ARROW 6 Points' for campaigning against war after 11 September), available from the JNV website <http://www.justicenotvengeance.org>. JNV, 29 Gensing Road, St Leonards-on-Sea, East Sussex, TN38 0HE. Telephone 0845 458 9571 (inside the UK) or 44 1424 428 792 (from outside the UK).

voices in the wilderness

voices in the wilderness was originally founded to oppose, and break, the economic sanctions on Iraq. Launched in 1996 by Kathy Kelly, Chuck Quilty and other long-time peace activists, **voices us** has become a major hub for anti-war activism. With participation from **voices in the wilderness uk**, founded in 1998 and co-ordinated by Gabriel Carlyle and Milan Rai (1998-2003), the campaign sent over 60 sanctions-breaking delegations to Iraq. Several of these delegations were 'interposition delegations' sent in response to the threat of imminent military action, building on the tradition of the Gulf Peace Team (as documented in *War and Peace in the Gulf: Testimonies of the Gulf Peace Team*, available from Voices US). In the aftermath of the 2003 Gulf War, **voices us** and **voices uk** have both broadened their anti-war campaigning, though with a special focus on Iraq.

voices in the wilderness, #634, 5315 N. Clark Ave, Chicago, IL 60640. Telephone 773 784 8065. <http://www.nonviolence.org/vitw>.

voices in the wilderness uk, 5 Caledonian Rd, London N1 9DX. Telephone 0845 458 2564. <http://www.voicesuk.org>.

INDEX

'I thought it was gangster capitalism,
nothing to do with morality at all.
Did Tony Blair mislead the country?
I suspect he did.'

John Peel, British radio presenter, 4 June 2003.[1]

Updates

Regular updates to this book will be posted on the anti-war website
<http://www.justicenotvengeance.org>

Readers are invited to contribute their own indexes via this website.